STATE OF THE UNION

POLITICS AND SOCIETY IN TWENTIETH-CENTURY AMERICA

Series Editors

William Chafe, Gary Gerstle, and Linda Gordon

A list of titles in this series appears at the back of the book

STATE
OF THE
UNION

A CENTURY OF AMERICAN LABOR

NELSON LICHTENSTEIN

PRINCETON UNIVERSITY PRESS
PRINCETON AND OXFORD

Published by Princeton University Press, 41 William Street,
Princeton, New Jersey 08540
In the United Kingdom: Princeton University Press, 3 Market Place, Woodstock,
Oxfordshire OX20 1SY

Library of Congress Cataloging-in-Publication Data
Lichtenstein, Nelson.
State of the Union : a century of American labor / Nelson Lichtenstein.
p. cm. — (Politics and society in twentieth-century America)
Includes bibliographical references and index.
ISBN 0-691-05768-0
1. Labor—United States—History—20th century. 2. Labor movement—United States—History—20th century. 3. Working class—United States—History—20th century. 4. Labor unions—United States—History—20th century. 5. Employee rights—United States—History—20th century. I. Title. II. Series.

HD8066 .L53 2001
331'.0973'0904—dc21 2001036863

British Library Cataloging-in-Publication Data is available

This book has been composed in Goudy

Printed on acid-free paper. ∞

www.pup.princeton.edu

Printed in the United States of America

10 9 8 7 6 5 4 3 2 1

For

the Labor Action Group

at

the University of Virginia

Contents

Preface and Acknowledgments

I MAY HAVE FIRST GOTTEN the idea for this book during a 1993–94 Fulbright fellowship in Finland that I shared with my spouse, Eileen Boris. Eileen and I held many academic and political interests in common, and in particular a concern for the rights of workers and the fate of the welfare state. But as Helsinki's days grew shorter and darker I found myself frequently waving good-bye to Eileen as she flew off to Stockholm, Berlin, or London to give one talk or another on the gendered, racial character of American class relations. Meanwhile, I explored some of the excellent local coffee shops. The Finns we knew, who had a direct internet connection into the heart of American academic culture, did not think my ideas about the history of U.S. trade unionism wrong; rather it was much worse, they felt them to be *boring*. Everyone had something to say about Malcolm X or Betty Friedan, but unionists like Walter Reuther, upon whose biography I was at work, simply generated a blank stare.

When we got back to the States, a new wind was blowing. John Sweeney's insurgency and his subsequent election to the leadership of the AFL-CIO indicated that some exciting developments might actually be taking place within the U.S. union movement. Early in 1996, the Century Foundation asked me to write a "background" paper for their new Task Force on the Future of Unions. This proved to be a liberating project because I had to start from scratch to explain why the labor movement was once thought to be so central to the health of American democracy, and why the unions had so rapidly fallen out of favor. The Task Force itself reached no useful consensus—unionism is a contentious subject after all—but I now felt the impulse to write for a broader political/policy audience.[1]

The 1996 Columbia University Teach-in with the Labor Movement spurred me on. Steve Fraser and I set the ball rolling for this notable event, and then looked on in fascination as unionists, academics, intellectuals, and assorted social activists shared the podium at Columbia and at two dozen other universities. We wanted to reinsert what Progressive-era reformers called "The Labor Question" into the center of American political culture, and we hoped such high-profile teach-ins would help reforge the bonds that had once linked the fortunes of organized labor to those of a larger democratic citizenship. Toward that end, these spirited conclaves may well have had some success. And this book continues the effort, even as I try to explain why solidarity and unionism no longer resonate with so large a slice of the American citizenry, and what can be done to again make the labor movement a vital force in a democratic polity.

I learned a good deal about the obstacles and possibilities inherent in this work during the years that I was on the faculty at the University of Virginia. I wrote most of this book in Charlottesville, where the Alderman Library proved most useful, and many colleagues interested and supportive. But during our campaign there to win an eight-dollar-an-hour "living wage" and to secure a real voice for all University of Virginia workers, I learned far more about the complex relationship that exists in contemporary American culture between notions of rights and those of solidarity. Our Labor Action Group, formed after a notably successful labor teach-in, found that ideas about trade unionism, workers' rights, and class were alien concepts, not only to many low-wage workers, but to some of our own key activists. Many assumed that unions and collective action were simply illegal in the state of Virginia. On the other hand, racial discrimination and its remedies—and to a lesser extent those involving gender inequality—constituted an entirely legitimate subject of inquiry, organization, and conflict at Mr. Jefferson's university.

Our task was to insert and raise the labor question into the consciousness and politics of the university. We wanted to enlarge the meaning of contemporary rights-consciousness and give to that struggle a collective, genuinely democratic meaning. We had our moments of weakness and of power, our successes and our failures. We won more money for the lowest-paid university employees, but any real democratization of the university remains as yet unrealized. Throughout, I found the students, faculty, and staff who comprised the core activists in the Labor Action Group among the most admirable and courageous individuals encountered in my lifetime. It is to them I dedicate this book.

Financial support for research and writing has come, in part or in whole, from the University of Virginia, the John Simon Guggenheim Foundation, the Rockefeller Foundation, the Twentiety-Century Fund (now the Century Foundation), and the Center for the Humanities at Oregon State University.

I have received helpful comments and encouragement from a large number of individuals. Ron Aronson and Sue Cobble were among the first to urge that I transform my Century Foundation essay into a full-length book. Thereafter, large portions of the manuscript were read and constructively commented upon by David Abraham, Jean-Claude Andre, Eileen Boris, David Brody, George Cotkin, William Forbath, Dana Frank, Dan Geary, Justin Hill, Meg Jacobs, Jennifer Klein, Sidney Milkis, Paula Rabinowitz, Larry Richards, Reuel Schiller, Judith Stein, Tom Sugrue, and Carl Bon Tempo.

Michael Kazin read the entire manuscript and offered important comments, as did Gary Gerstle, the series editor at Princeton. I am delighted to count them both good friends and good colleagues. Princeton University Press editor Brigitta Van Rheinberg prodded me along during the course of writing this book and then offered insightful comments that may well have made the final manuscript more readable and accessible to the general public. Marsha Kunin was an excellent copyeditor.

Finally, I have spent the last two years bouncing ideas and notions around with Eileen and our son, Daniel Lichtenstein-Boris. The former has helped explain to me the complexities inherent in the American social wage; the latter, who has just begun to dip his toe into the labor market, has never let me forget that there is a whole new generation out there that has never heard of Walter Reuther. Fortunately, this has not been much of an obstacle to their struggle against injustice and for a better world.

STATE
OF THE
UNION

Introduction

To understand the great contradiction that stands at the heart of American democracy today, stop by your local fast-food restaurant next time the craving moves you. At Burger King I enjoyed one of the combo specials. Then I picked up an employment application.

The first thing to note is right at the top. Under the heading "Equal Employment Opportunity Employer" is a bold and forthright assertion that: "Employer does not discriminate in employment because of race, color, sex, religion, national origin, age, disability, marital status, or liability for service in the armed forces of the United States."[1]

This statement is on the Burger King application for two reasons. First, it is the law of the land. In 1964, after demonstrations, marches, sit-ins, speeches, elections, and much lobbying, Congress passed the 1964 Civil Rights Act, which outlawed job discrimination on the basis of race, creed, religion, or sex. Thereafter, the Congress passed and presidents of both parties signed additional statutory legislation safeguarding equitable treatment regardless of age or disability. Laws were also enacted that were designed to generate rights to a healthy workplace, a financially secure pension, and time off to have a child or take care of a sick relative.

But there is a second reason why Burger King management has put the federal Equal Employment Opportunity Commission (EEOC) statement at the very top of the application. Americans consider workplace discrimination on the basis of race and religion and creed un-American. For nearly a third of a century we have had a national debate over the definition of such discrimination and the remedies that are useful and legal to eliminate it. But there is practically no debate about the need to stop it and compensate individuals for it, when discovered. The overwhelming majority of workers, employers, and politicians believe that the government has a right to insist that active discrimination not take place against anyone covered by Title VII of the 1964 Civil Rights Act or those many statutes that followed in its train. This seems so commonplace and commonsensible, that we forget the radical character of this law. If you own a restaurant or a factory or a motel or run a college, you can't make use of your property as you wish. The state mandates you to hire, fire, promote, and otherwise deal with your employees or clients according to a set of rules laid down in Washington and refined by the EEOC and the courts. If litigated, the courts will force an employer to pay real money in compensation and rehire or promote a worker if management is found to have transgressed this new kind of labor law.

The overwhelming legitimacy of such antidiscrimination law is attested to by the fact that workers file about 100,000 cases a year with the EEOC. There have been scores of books and hundreds of articles written attacking affirmative action, but few journalists, academics, or politicians question equal-employment law per se. Big business, and this includes the fast-food industry, is an advocate of "diversity" in hiring and promotion and it does not campaign for an elimination of the statutory employment rights enacted over the last third of a century. Indeed, it celebrates them, and when a large corporation like Texaco, Denny's, Shoney's, or Mitsubishi is found in noncompliance, millions of dollars are quickly spent to rectify the situation.[2]

Now let's return to our Burger King application. On the bottom of the flip side one will find a bit of language at the very end that requires some decoding. It says: "I understand and agree that if I should become employed by the Franchisee, I will have the right to terminate my employment at any time for any reason, or for no reason. I further agree that the Franchisee shall have the same right to terminate my employment. My employment at-will status cannot be modified unless such modification is set forth in writing in a document signed by both me and an officer or owner of the Franchisee."[3]

What's all this? Well, this boilerplate encapsulates the history of Anglo-American labor relations going back for more than a century.

Pre–New Deal labor law asserted that an employer is entitled to dismiss an employee "at will . . . for good cause, no cause or even for cause morally wrong, without thereby being guilty of legal wrong."[4] For a time, the Wagner Act and other New Deal labor laws seemed to offer a quite different model encouraging unions and collective bargaining, but the legal and moral eclipse of such an employment relationship is clearly embedded in the language of the Burger King application. In theory a worker can form a union and sign a "collective contract" at Burger King, but it is certain that management there will resist signing such an agreement with all the resources—the money, lawyers, personnel experts, and public relations—available to a multi-billion-dollar company in the United States. McDonald's, Wendy's, Taco Bell, along with Kmart, Wal-Mart, and Pizza Hut, do not recognize unions or sign collective-bargaining contracts. They would rather shut down the franchise than break precedent. They even shut down stores in Canada and Denmark, where the law is more liberal and the union movement stronger. They pay low wages and provide few benefits: as a consequence, the skill and education level is low, turnover extraordinarily high. Of course fast-food workers are not the only ones who face such managerial hostility. At the dawn of the twenty-first century, a full generation after the triumph of the civil rights movement, 90 percent of all private-sector workers in the United States are employed under at-will doctrines.

The problem facing American workers, the issue that puts a question mark on the democratic character of our polity, is summed up by the dichotomy sketched out here. In the last forty years a transformation in law, custom, and ideology has made a once radical demand for racial and gender equality into an elemental code of conduct. This is unquestionably one of the great steps forward in U.S. politics and workplace culture. But during that same era, the rights of workers, as workers, and especially as workers acting in an autonomous, collective fashion, have moved well into the shadows. The law, the managerial ethos, the opinion-forming pundits, indeed many workers themselves, have marginalized and ridiculed the idea that democratic norms should govern the workplace. Little in American culture, politics, or business encourages the institutionalization of a collective employee voice.

Managers who slash payrolls and break unions are subject to remarkably little public opprobrium, certainly not enough to modify their behavior very much. As one employment rights attorney put it with a certain irony, "It's a hell of a lot easier to get $100,000" for an individual client "than to get five cents an hour for blue collar workers." In 1997 the median jury award in employment bias and sexual harassment cases was $250,000, but payments to workers for violation of the other labor laws, the ones that protect workers against discrimination for trying to form a union or protest violations of the health, safety, and minimum wage laws were small, tardy, and paid, if at all, in the most grudging fashion.[5]

This book explains why the bifurcation sketched above has not always been so dramatic, and why the democratization of the work place, the solidarity of labor, and the social betterment of American workers once stood far closer to the center of the nation's political and moral consciousness. We start in the Progressive era when these issues were often bundled together as "the labor question." Even before the nation's most massive, sustained strike wave convulsed every industrial district in 1919, President Woodrow Wilson cabled Congress from Versailles:

> The question which stands at the front of all others amidst the present great awakening is the question of labor . . . how are the men and women who do the daily labor of the world to obtain progressive improvement in the conditions of their labor, to be made happier, and to be served better by the communities and the industries which their labor sustains and advances. . . . The object of all reform in this essential matter must be the genuine democratization of industry, based upon a full recognition of the right of those who work, in whatever rank, to participate in some organic way in every decision which directly affects their welfare.[6]

Wilson's understanding of the American labor question arose out of the dilemma generated by the emergence of industrial capitalism itself. How could the nation sustain a democratic citizenship in an era when the rise of both giant corporations and a laissez-faire orthodoxy in the labor market seemed to challenge so many of the values and institutions that Progressives thought essential to the maintenance of a democratic polity. The issue became acute in the era of the Bolshevik Revolution, when a radical, thoroughly antiliberal resolution to the conflict between capital and labor seemed on offer. From the Wilsonian perspective, of course, this revolutionary answer to the crisis of bourgeois legitimacy required a vigorous liberal response, briefly evident in the U.S. program of diplomatic and social reformism during World War I and its immediate aftermath.[7]

From the perspective of the labor movement itself, the Progressive-era labor question had two longstanding elements. By the turn of the twentieth century even the most ideologically adventuresome radicals had come to terms with the reality, and the necessity, of wage labor. If the values of a producer's republic still commanded near-universal respect, the task before Progressive-era laborites was to translate those virtues onto the modern industrial terrain. Thus unionists thought the price employers paid for their labor must still be infused with a political and moral value standing at odds to that of the free-market conservatives who calculated labor's reward as entirely dependent on the natural laws of supply and demand.

In the lexicon of their day, unionists and their progressive allies wanted "a living wage" sufficient to sustain a working-class family in dignity and comfort. The living wage idea was itself often shot through with patriarchal and racist assumptions, but it nevertheless generated a radical critique of the capitalist marketplace. The labor movement's critique of "wage slavery" therefore embodied not just a derogatory comparison between white and black labor, but the promise that good wages would generate the conditions necessary for industrial freedom itself.[8] As the eight-hour crusader Ira Steward put it in 1879, "when the working classes are denied everything but the barest necessities of life, they have no decent use for liberty." Twenty-three years later, the Anthracite Coal Commission, the protocorporatist model for a later generation of governmental commissions, boards, and institutions designed to ameliorate class conflict, declared that the maintenance of a "self-governing republic" itself required that "all American wage earners have a fundamental economic right to at least a living wage, or an American Standard of living." A new era of high-wage consumption bred not apolitical disinterest, but engaged citizenship and a potent working-class voice in the affairs of the day. John Mitchell, the mine union leader, called such a living, nonmarket wage the "second emancipation."[9]

But neither man nor woman lives by bread alone. With the rise of big business late in the nineteenth century, the dichotomy between the rights and privileges of citizenship and the power of concentrated capital became the very essence of the "labor question." During the crisis-plagued second industrial revolution—the epoch of economic instability, corporate mergers, and mass strikes—working-class radicals won a wide audience when they called for an extension into the realm of production and the sphere of the market the basic civil and political rights embedded in the Constitution and its post–Civil War amendments. The labor movement, Henry Demarest Lloyd told an 1893 labor assembly, has a definite, clearly defined mission. It seeks "to extend into industry the brotherhood already recognized in politics and religion, and to teach men as workers the love and equality which they profess as citizens and worshippers." Reformers called this idea "industrial democracy."[10]

This was not the same thing as socialism, which was predicated on the collective ownership of the means of production; nor was it simply an updated version of the nineteenth-century republican tradition, which celebrated the artisan craftsman of "manly bearing" and looked with some suspicion on those with lesser skill and independence. Rather, the advocates of industrial democracy saw the new system as the next stage in the evolution of American freedom. This Progressive-era impulse took the large industrial enterprise for granted as the basic building block of the new commonweal and looked for a solution to problems of authority, equality, motivation, and efficiency through its reorganization and democratization. To these reformers and unionists, industrial democracy certainly meant much more than mere collective bargaining, championed by the seemingly parochial craft unions of the era.[11]

Louis Brandeis made this clear in 1915 when he told a progressive audience crowding into Faneuil Hall that the task of the hour was the translation, under twentieth-century social and economic conditions, of those eighteenth-century "rights which our Constitution guarantees—the rights to life, liberty and the pursuit of happiness." All Americans, argued Brandeis, "must have a reasonable income" and regular employment: "they must have health and leisure," decent "working conditions," and "some system of social insurance." However, the "essentials of American citizenship" were not simply material. There could be no more "political democracy" in contemporary America, Brandeis told the U.S. Industrial Commission that same year, without an "industrial democracy," that gave workers an actual participation in the governance of the firms for which they worked.[12]

World War I and the social turmoil of its immediate aftermath briefly tripled the size of the union movement and generated a wave of institutional experimentation that included government arbitration, works councils, employer representation plans, producer cooperatives, and nationalization schemes for industry. William Leiserson, then an arbitrator in the men's clothing industry, thought all this was evidence for the growth of "constitutional government in American industries." William Forbath, a contemporary legal historian, has labeled this expansive Progressive-era impulse "democratic constitutionalism."[13] But whatever the nomenclature, all such reforms were buoyed by the Wilsonian rhetoric, as well as the war-era mobilization requirements, that sought to give a tangible reality to ideas of self-determination, democracy, and curbs on the power of industrial management. "Political Democracy is an illusion," asserted Frank Walsh, the progressive cochair of the National War Labor Board, "unless builded upon and guaranteed by a free and virile Industrial Democracy."[14]

Thus in an era when sauerkraut became "liberty cabbage," it was not difficult to put warfare-state patriotism at the service of militant unionism. Bridgeport machinists denounced Remington Arms as "The American Junkers" while the steelworkers of Birmingham called the Tennessee Coal and Iron Company the "Kaiser of Industrial America." Unionists in Akron distributed leaflets reading: "Wake Up! Machine Shop Workers, Wake Up! Uncle Sam proclaimed to the World that the freedom and democracy we are fighting for shall be practiced in the Industries of America." Likewise, cigar makers demanded "self-government in the workshop . . . part of the democracy for which our arms are fighting in France." Rhetoric attacking "Prussian management" had a particular appeal to the new generation of women workers, now heavily represented among semi-skilled factory operatives. Unlike traditional unionism—so often

Government production propaganda during World War I held out the promise of citizenship and industrial democracy for millions of immigrant workers. (Courtesy Joe McCartin)

identified with bitter strikes, craft pride, and male exclusiveness—the more expansive demand for "industrial democracy" legitimized a more inclusive, female-friendly sense of patriotic participation and equal citizenship.[15]

The experience of the Great War produced a generation of unionists, managers, and governmental experts who would later play decisive roles in erecting the New Deal version of industrial democracy. These eighteen months of hectic mobilization in 1917 and 1918 were a dress rehearsal for the wave of state building and social mobilization that would characterize Franklin Roosevelt's New Deal. Had World War I lasted longer, or the Wilson administration been more resolute, labor more unified, or big capital less antagonistic, a model of industrial democracy generated during this crisis might well have put in place a more permanent institutional legacy. But the monumental postwar strike wave—the largest in the history of the republic—collapsed in anger and repression. America's labor question remained unresolved, even exacerbated, because neither the labor movement nor the state, not to mention industrial management itself, generated the kind of relationships, in law, ideology, or practice, necessary to institutionalize mass unionism and sustain working-class living standards during the next decade.[16]

To many unionists, the quest for a living wage and the struggle for industrial democracy may well have defined just about the entire "labor question." But for most Progressive reformers, in the labor movement and out, this struggle was embedded within, and could hardly be distinguished from, a more pervasive "social question." As historian Alan Dawley once put it, "progressive reformers were 'social'-ists." Most grasped that society was an organic whole and most believed that government regulation of predatory private interests—or "capitalism" for those of a more systematic ideological outlook—was essential for the sake of a larger, more harmonious public interest. Poverty, inequality, sexual degradation, and industrial violence were linked social maladies, ameliorable, if not completely solvable through state action.[17]

Florence Kelley, the pioneering Chicago reformer whose European sojourn had schooled her in continental Marxism, sought to enlist a weak and reluctant regulatory state to advance the living standard for that portion of the working class—chiefly urban immigrant women and their offspring—who were neglected by the unions and subject to predatory exploitation in the labor market. As the brilliant strategist for the National Consumers League, Kelley was an indefatigable crusader against the twelve-hour day in the steel mills, child labor in textile mills, and starvation wages for women home workers. And she understood how a newly intrusive state could be deployed in this societywide class struggle. "The factory inspector enforces the law for the worker against the capitalist," she wrote in 1890. "The militiaman shoots down the worker by command of the capitalist. It is characteristic of the present status of the forces engaged on each side, that there are hundreds of thousands of militia and less than fifty factory inspectors in the United States today."[18]

Given the patriarchal assumptions of the Progressive years, reformers often found that a nascent "welfare state" could most easily be built if it were especially beneficial for mothers and children. This was certainly the perspective of many reformers, like those supporting the American Association for Labor Legislation or the movements for homework prohibition and mothers' pensions. They looked to Bismarck's Germany or to the Fabians of Great Britain for guidance and inspiration; and they won a signal, if temporary, victory in 1908 when the Supreme Court ruled, in *Muller vs. Oregon*, that state laws "protecting" women workers were constitutional because "a proper discharge of her maternal functions—having in view not merely her own health, but the well-being of the race—justify legislation to protect her from the greed as well as the passion of man."[19]

But such "maternalism" does not fully explain the evolution of American social provision during the first third of the twentieth century. A more inclusive and precise way of thinking about the meaning of Progressive reform and its impact on the labor movement is to see it as a multifaceted effort to raise the "social wage," that portion of the working class standard of living that did not derive from wages or from corporate beneficence. This social wage includes monetary entitlements such as pensions, unemployment insurance, and workman's compensation, but it also embodies a more far-ranging set of institutions: public education, city parks, mandated vacations, municipal services, health and safety regulations, minimum wage, child labor, and women's protective laws. In our own day, elements of such a social wage include government-funded health insurance, legal services for the poor, public housing, subsidized mass transit, and what was until 1996 a federal entitlement, Aid to Families with Dependent Children. As Gosta Esping Andersen defines it, the social wage "decommodifies" social protection, thus representing that "share of the nation's resources that is distributed according to social rather than market criteria."[20]

In the Progressive era and afterward, women have been the most active and farsighted of those reformers seeking to raise the American social wage. Accommodating themselves to a sense of women's innate gender "difference," late nineteenth-century women reformers saw the amelioration of urban poverty as but an expansion of "women's sphere," an exercise in "social housekeeping," while advocates of protective legislation invoked the special needs of women as "the mother of the race."[21] But in practice such maternalism was but a step removed from a systematic social democracy, that class-oriented reformism that seeks to make use of the state regulatory power to strengthen working-class institutions and living conditions. By 1912, perhaps the apex of Progressive reform, some thirty-eight states had passed child-labor laws and twenty-eight set maximum hours for women workers. Men benefited as well: workers' compensation laws were on the books in almost all states outside of the South, while in more than half of all jurisdictions laws were passed that limited the working hours of some categories of male workers.[22]

Unfortunately, the tawdriness of the American "social wage," in the Progressive era and afterward, has long been overdetermined. Well into the twentieth century the administrative state in the United States has been weak and fragmented; Southern congressmen wielded an effective national veto, while a remarkably powerful judiciary sympathetically accommodated the prerogatives of property and the laissez-faire ideology that sustained them. The courts declared many of the Progressive era laws invalid. In response, the labor movement adopted an extreme form of "voluntarism" that rejected efforts to raise the social wage, at least insofar as American-born, white, male workers were concerned.[23] The syndicalist left saw the state as an apparatus of repression, while official labor, which was just as antistatist, feared that any efforts to decommodify the wage relation would undermine the autonomy of the unions and sap the loyalty of their members. "Compulsory unemployment insurance," asserted AFL President William Green during the early months of the Great Depression, is "a union wrecking agency."[24] Meanwhile, this entire social discourse, whether that of reactionary judges, militant unionists, or social feminists, was saturated with a set of patriarchal assumptions and racial constructs that radically distorted efforts to think about the relationship between the labor question and the social wage in a fashion recognizable by reformers and unionists of a later day.

THIS BOOK IS ABOUT trade unions and their relationship to the meaning and resolution of the "labor question" outlined above. It takes at face value the definition of the question as put forward by the main body of Progressives, for they were the first generation of reformers to confront a capitalist economy whose ever-shifting technological reconfigurations cannot obscure its relentless capacity to reproduce inequalities of power and income. It tries to put the fate of the labor movement in this broader context so as to explore the extent to which institutional trade unionism has itself offered working-class Americans a road forward to higher wages, industrial democracy, and a generous social wage.

The narrative is a difficult one, and yet all the more interesting, because during the middle decades of the twentieth century the "labor question" seemed on its way, if not to resolution, then to a well-constrained manageability. In the two decades following 1933, American trade unions reached their twentieth-century apogee, whether measured by organizing success, economic power, or political influence. But these were also the years, as Steve Fraser has pointed out, when the potency of old labor question "receded like some faint echo from the distant political past." By the time of Franklin Roosevelt's death in 1945, organized labor was big and its power controversial. However, few in politics or social theory would then have argued that labor's status constituted the central dilemma of the social order, what Louis Brandeis had once called the "the paramount economic question in this country."[25]

The eclipse of the "labor question" seems well deserved when we glance at the social and legal history of the midcentury decades. The labor-law reforms of the New Deal era, the size and permanency of the unions, and the active interventions of the federal government regularized the conflict between capital and labor. These New Deal developments seemed to promise that the quest for an American "industrial democracy" had finally transmuted itself into a branch of social administration in which "collective bargaining," "industrial relations," and "personnel management" were carefully monitored by academic, administrative, and judicial experts. Strikes became routine and industrial violence infrequent (or at least well hidden).[26]

Meanwhile, working-class living standards doubled during the single generation following World War II (1947–73), and unemployment dropped to levels well below that of the first half of the century. Equally impressive, the social wage took a quantum leap upward, in both its quality and coverage of the employed population. As the unions became mass organizations linked to the Democratic Party, they cast off the antiquated voluntarism of the craft tradition and became partisans of wage and hour laws, Old Age Insurance, unemployment compensation, AFDC, publicly financed health insurance, and other components of the welfare state. Initially, African Americans had been excluded from much benefit coverage, but the civil rights revolution of the 1960s finally brought them within the New Deal fold. Meanwhile, most big corporations followed along with their own private version of the public welfare state, if only to avoid unionism, or just retain the productive loyalty of their workers.

But the "labor question" did not vanish, and it came roaring back at the end of the 20th century. Tepid productivity growth, decades of wage stagnation, job insecurity, stressful work, and a dramatic decline in union strength demonstrate that the issues that once confronted Woodrow Wilson and Louis Brandeis are with us still. During the long economic recovery that characterized the 1990s, the U.S. economy grew by almost 3 percent each year, but for most of that era the median income of American households suffered a continuous annual decline. Thus, by the turn of the millennium, real household income for young families (breadwinners under age thirty) stood at one-third less than their counterparts in 1973, even though their total working hours were longer and the educational level of the head of household higher than a generation before. In the first years of the new century median wages and family incomes were still below their 1989 level.[27]

Meanwhile, U.S. workers find that they hold a dubious world-class distinction: while working hours in all other large industrial countries are falling, Americans have now moved into first place—and surpassed the Japanese—in terms of the number of hours worked each year. During the last two decades the parents in a typical middle-class family increased their work time by about 10 percent. The pervasive midcentury expectation—that "labor-saving" technological innovations would generate leisured abundance—has evaporated in a world where productive, computerized Americans work two hundred hours per year more than the nearby Canadians, nearly four hundred above that of the industrious Germans.[28]

During the Progressive-era presidencies of Theodore Roosevelt and Woodrow Wilson, the growth of inequality between the new class of corporate rich and the mass of insecure wage earners seemed fraught with societal danger. When the *Titanic* sank in 1912 many saw the tragedy as a metaphor for the fate of a class-stratified capitalism. Indeed, the survival of so many upper-class passengers seemed a shameful indictment of the new inequality. Today, such class hierarchies have returned in an equally ugly fashion. Inequalities of wealth, income, and social security have returned to a pre–New Deal configuration. The U.S. income pyramid resembles that of Brazil more than it does that of Germany, Japan, or Italy. In 1965 the average chief executive made forty-four times the pay of a typical factory worker. At the turn of the millennium, that same CEO earned between three hundred and four hundred times the wages of a blue-collar operative or a clerical assigned to routine office work.[29]

Indeed, for many Americans hard, steady work has not generated a rising standard of living. The two largest private employers in the United States are Manpower, Inc., a temporary employment agency, and Wal-Mart, most of whose 750,000 "associates" have no choice but to work part-time at pay levels a dollar or two above minimum wage. Four out of five households take home a thinner slice of the economic pie than they did a quarter century before. Even in the booming 1990s, full-time, year-round work did not reduce poverty among the lowest-paid workers. In California's Silicon Valley, then world capitalism's innovative epicenter, real wages actually fell for the bottom third of all wage workers.[30]

This inequality is compounded by a remarkable assault on the social wage, that set of nonmonetary entitlements and institutions incrementally advanced by every generation of social reformers since Jane Addams and Florence Kelley fought for more parks, schools, and other social services in the Chicago slums. During the last quarter century, public education, unemployment benefits, employment-based health insurance, the "welfare" entitlement for dependent children, and Medicare have come into question and under attack. And even Social Security (Old Age Insurance), the crown jewel of New Deal era social provision, has become subject to a coordinated critique that almost surely will insert into this system an element of market-based "privatization." Although such social wage institutions have periodically faced fiscal shortfalls requiring their reorganization and reform, the dynamic eroding America's late-twentieth-century system of social provision has been far more ideological than budgetary. This is a function of the decline in the idea of social solidarity, of a virtuous public sphere, and of the will of the government to ameliorate the raw economic forces structuring the labor market.

Indeed, most governmental efforts to spark real wage growth and negotiate a consensual reform of the American workplace have come to a virtual impasse during the last few years, even when backed by influential corporate executives, top trade unionists, numerous elected officials, and the White House. During the first two years of the Clinton administration a remarkably ambitious set of reforms were put in play, but almost every initiative collapsed in the face of internal division and paralyzing opposition. Programs to stimulate school-to-work transitions, infrastructure construction, on-the-job training, and strategic industrial planning floundered during the early years of the administration even as it commanded Democratic majorities in both houses of Congress.

The failure of an elaborately crafted health-security initiative proved particularly devastating, for this program was one of the most ambitious and long-overdue pieces of social legislation put on the national agenda since the New Deal. Although the Clintons and their many advisers sought to orchestrate a grand compromise that would accommodate the divergent interests of just about every player in the health-care political economy, their effort collapsed in such a dramatic fashion that it threatened Social Security, undermined Aid to Families with Dependent Children, and put in jeopardy other venerable bulwarks of the American welfare state.[31] Shaken by these defeats, the Clinton administration soon de-emphasized the growth of wage inequality, the stagnation of living standards, and the need for a creative reform of the workplace, which had been important themes during much of the first term. Once again the labor question seemed to vanish from the social agenda.[32]

This eclipse has had many authors, but the key to them all is the unprecedented weakness of the American trade union movement. Its demise over the past quarter century is now a dismal and oft-told story, but the statistical record bears another brief review. At the onset of the twenty-first century, the 16 million organized workers represent 13.5 percent of the entire workforce; in the private sector, only 9 percent. This means that unions in the United States represent a lower proportion of all workers than in any other industrial democracy in the world. If 1953 is taken as the proportional apogee of U.S. trade unionism in the twentieth century, then organized labor is only one-third as strong today as it was forty years ago, only a quarter as strong in the private sector. In no industry does the trade union movement represent even half of all employees: even in the automobile industry, once the flagship of American labor, the parts sector is more than 80 percent non-union, while most of the German and Japanese transplants are also unorganized. Given such weakness, unionists have shelved the strike weapon. In 1999 there were only thirty-five strikes involving more than one thousand workers; twenty-five years before, there had been ten times as many.[33]

Not unexpectedly, the contemporary union movement has had a particularly difficult time reestablishing a sense of legitimacy and functionality within both the larger political economy and the micro-social world of workplace governance. Laborite economists such as Richard Freedman and Barry Bluestone, as well as most trade union leaders, have argued that unionism generates positive employment effects: lowering quit rates, raising job tenure, increasing productivity and skill levels. But this argument has won little assent in the corporate world, perhaps not unexpectedly at a time when many managers celebrate the "virtual corporation" and declare that a sense of contingent and temporary attachment to the firm represents the most technologically congruent, culturally sophisticated industrial relations policy. Management efforts to avoid or eliminate trade unionism hardly weakened as the Republican 1980s gave way to a new decade and a new administration. Long, bitter disputes at the *Detroit Free Press*, Caterpillar, Staley, Avondale Shipyards, Bridgestone-Firestone, Yale University, and the port of Charleston testified to management self-confidence and the weakness of the contemporary labor movement. Even the notable 1997 Teamster victory at United Parcel Service (UPS) did little to reverse the antiunion tide. Although tens of thousands of unionists and their supporters successfully mobilized much popular support against the nationwide corporation, the Teamster success at UPS generated no sea change in management thinking and relatively few organizing ripples in the economy's vast service sector.

Despite the new energy that has infused much of organized labor in the last half decade, the sad fact is that most union activism—at the bargaining table, the ballot box, and on the picket line—is designed to defend the status quo. Union efforts to preserve jobs and wage structures are the near universal subject of most major collective bargaining negotiations. Union contract settlements, even in an era of remarkably low inflation and unemployment, barely raise the living standards of those covered by their provisions; by the late 1990s the share of national income going to wages was at its lowest level in almost three decades. Meanwhile, company efforts to cut health-care costs and benefits generate more than two-thirds of all the strikes that do take place.[34]

This book is therefore predicated on the idea that a larger, more powerful, and more democratic trade-union movement is essential to any progressive resolution of the contemporary stalemate that structures social politics in the United States. As Progressive era labor partisans like Frank Walsh once asserted, the fate of American democracy is insolubly linked to the democratization of the world of work. Indeed, the political history of every industrial nation, from the early nineteenth century to the tail end of the twentieth, demonstrates the symbiosis between the growth of unions and the evolution of a democratic polity. A hundred years ago, reformers saw the unions as a counterweight to the overweening power of capital, while socialists saw them as the kernel of a new social order. In Euro-America both our fears and hopes have been tempered during the intervening decades: today, democratic theorists are apt to celebrate the pluralist democracy that arises out of a vibrant civil society, rather than the prospect of a collective commonwealth.

But even on this less imaginative terrain it is clear that the United States strays into dangerous territory when the republic allows for the virtual suppression of those institutions designed to represent directly the aspirations of the working population. Even in their shrunken state, trade unions are the most multiracial of all institutions and the most committed to the mobilization of those at the bottom of society. They remain the republic's largest set of voluntary organizations. Unlike church, synagogue, and mosque—or the National Rifle Association and the Sierra Club—the unions have a multifaceted character that gives them the potential to function as far more than either a religious institution or an interest group. Organized labor is unique and transcendent, for the unions combine features inherent to an expansive social movement, an ideological formation, a political lobby effort, and an institution designed to micromanage the labor market, both inside the workplace and out.[35]

These chapters review several decades of labor history, largely in the years after the onset of the Great Depression when the legal and political structures were first put in place for the emergence of the modern union movement. The book pays particular attention to those ideological and social issues that gave resonance within the larger polity to the union idea, or rather to those particular features of American trade unionism that most excited comment, hostility, and commitment. It is therefore not so much a narrative history as it is an examination of how trade unionism has waxed and waned in the nation's political and moral imagination, both among its devoted partisans and its intransigent foes.

Early chapters examine the sources of union growth during the 1930s and measure the extent to which New Deal–era unionism actually won shop democracy and a living wage, and not only for the most privileged in the working class. They explain why African American workers proved such steadfast industrial unionists and then analyse why midcentury collective bargaining was so inadequate to the needs of most women workers. The middle section of the book contains a somewhat revisionist reading of what has now come to be known as the era of the labor-management accord (1947–78), a discussion of the sometimes troubled relationship between the rights consciousness of the post-1960s era and the union idea, and an analysis of how and why so many postwar intellectuals and social theorists became disenchanted with the practice and promise of U.S. trade unionism. Two final chapters discuss, first, the disastrous, but not unexpected, "Reaganite" turn in corporate and governmental labor relations, and second, the more recent "Sweenyite" effort to revive the labor movement and rehabilitate the union idea itself.

Throughout, the book argues that the labor question has never been simply a function of the labor market, the character of production technology, the social composition of the workforce, or the state of business organization. These structures frame the issue and channel the discussion: they set limits on the character of struggle and debate. But the history and future of the nation's labor question remains primarily one of ideas, ideology, and social combat. At the turn of a new century, labor's greatest deficit is of the ideas necessary to again insert working America into the heart of our national consciousness.

CHAPTER 1

Reconstructing the 1930s

THE LABOR QUESTION STOOD close to the core of American politics and social imagination during the 1930s. This was not because the Great Depression made so many people poor and desperate, though it did, but because during the era of the New Deal an amelioration of the labor question seemed inexorably bound up with a structural solution to the crisis of American capitalism itself. Likewise, the impasse confronting republican citizenship, so well explicated by Progressive-era reformers, seemed soluble only if the democratic process, if the rights and liberties inherent in a genuinely republican polity, were given a social and industrial meaning that finally breached the walls erected by property and its managerial guardsmen. To this end the state-assisted growth and radical transformation of the trade union movement seemed essential.

Sixty years on, Americans have largely forgotten why the unions grew so explosively in the decade after 1933. Indeed, a programmatically convenient mythology has emerged to explain the appearance of mass unionism in the New Deal era. Embattled trade unionists at the dawn of the twenty-first century wistfully recall an era when the New Deal state seemed to stand solidly on their side, when the 1935 Wagner Act, then dubbed "Labor's Magna Carta," effectively protected organizing rights, and when industrial workers battled for union recognition with one voice and one fist. Such constructed memories inspire many a song and story, but they do little to aid our understanding of the union upsurge during the Great Depression.[1]

Social myopia is even greater on the other side of the class divide and among much of the larger public. There, a pernicious, politically pointed master narrative is peddled by nostalgic Reaganites, contemporary managers, and most journalistic heralds of the cyber revolution. They look with equanimity upon the contemporary demise of the union idea, imagining an unbridgeable divide separating our era from both the economic structures of the depression decade and the technology of the mass production regime that was thought to dominate the first half of the twentieth century. According to this mythic history, the trade union upsurge during the 1930s took place when unskilled, assembly-line workers revolted against a brutal set of arrogant bosses. Their movement and the unions that arose out of this upsurge have an honored place in American history. But since that time, blue-collar work has declined toward insignificance and managers have learned their lessons. Therefore, unions are today irrelevant because they no longer play a useful function, for either workers or capitalists, in our computer-driven, postindustrial, post-Fordist world.[2]

A closer look at what actually happened in the 1930s and 1940s demonstrates that the issues faced by unionists, policy makers, and corporate managers are hardly foreign to our own times. Trade unions are not merely a product of a given set of technological or managerial structures. Nor do they simply reflect the economic needs and social aspirations of a slice of the working population, no matter how pressing. Instead, mass unionism moved to the center of the political agenda during the 1930s because the state-assisted growth of these institutions seemed to offer solutions to two of the central problems confronting the early-twentieth-century political economy.

"Underconsumption" and Its Remedies

The first problem was "underconsumption," a concept that explains the very nature of the Great Depression itself. During the first three decades of the twentieth century, the United States had begun a painful and disruptive shift from an economy based on the great industries of the nineteenth century—steel, coal, textiles, railroads, lumber, meat packing, and shipping—to an electrically driven, gasoline-powered economy more directly dependent upon a high level of consumer demand. These new industries included automobiles above all, but also home appliances, entertainment, petroleum, chemicals, processed food, clothing, and mass merchandizing.

In the 1920s many of the older industries were "sick." Scores of railroads were in bankruptcy and millions of farmers had never recovered from the drastic fall in the price of tobacco, cotton, and wheat that followed the giddy expansion of World War I. For the quarter of all Americans who still lived on the land, economic hard times were a fact of life even before 1929. Likewise, in textiles and coal, overproduction and "cut-throat" competition made life miserable for hundreds of thousands of workers who saw their pay slashed by hard-pressed owners determined to squeeze every extra dollar out of the company cost structure. These idle factories and underproducing coal mines were a menace, not only to the worker's standard of living but to the health of American business. "Price cutting and aggressive competition for the same business at around or below cost is the general rule," observed an investment banker on the eve of the depression.[3] Wages were still "the main competitive battleground" in the production of cotton goods, wrote *Business Week* a few years later. "Price-cutting in textiles inevitably means wage-cutting. And when the latter becomes ruthless enough, the premium on good management, good machinery, good merchandizing is removed."[4]

The United States did have a booming set of consumer-oriented industries in the 1920s. The automobile had begun to revolutionize the spatial texture of American life. Likewise housing, commercial real estate, entertainment, merchandizing and electrical products were all enjoying an enormous boom, but "overproduction" had become a plague even here. In 1928 and 1929 sales lagged, inventories rose, factories cut their output, and unemployment rose. Even before Wall Street's crash in October 1929, many executives thought their markets saturated. For example, in 1923 new cars outsold used cars three to one, but by 1927 the ratio had been reversed. To solve the "used car evil" Chevrolet was paying dealers twenty-five dollars for each old car they destroyed.

But what was "overproduction" to the businessman was "underconsumption" to the worker's family and friends. Although the country's productive capacity had soared in the 1920s, the fruits of that abundance were distributed in a highly regressive fashion. In the decade that ended with the crash, output per worker in manufacturing leaped upward by a remarkable 43 percent, while wages barely held their own. Meanwhile, the incomes of the very rich—the top 1 percent of the population—rose from 12 to 19 percent of that generated by the entire nation. And wealth itself—in stocks, bonds and real estate—was concentrated among these high flyers to a degree never seen before or since. Workers and farmers were buying all those used cars in 1929 because they couldn't afford new ones.[5]

This growing inequality was reinforced by the concentration of productive capacity and financial power among but a relative handful of enormously big corporations. By 1929 the two hundred largest U.S. corporations controlled half of all corporate assets. These institutions were no longer merely "private enterprises" but had become quasi-public institutions whose ability to establish prices and direct investment held enormous consequences for millions of Americans. In 1927 Henry Ford touched off a brief, nationwide recession when he abruptly shut down his billion-dollar company, stopped supplier plant purchasing, and laid off 100,000 workers, all in order to retool his assembly lines from Model T to Model A production.[6]

During the first two years of the depression the country's largest manufacturing firms tried and failed to sustain wages, prices, and production. Many large corporations cut hours, spread the work, and sought to avoid another round of competitive pricing. By reducing hours and reassigning jobs, the Westinghouse Electric Corporation retained almost all employees with over ten years' seniority at its huge East Pittsburgh plant; and U.S. Steel did not cut wages until 1931. But these large firms were exceptional. Most farms, construction companies, retail outlets, and midsize manufacturers could not afford to retain excess workers, even part-time. Such employers wanted prices to stabilize and wages to rise, but only for their competitors. Even during the boom of the late 1920s industry efforts to voluntarily stabilize wages and prices had been undercut by the entrepreneurial "chiselers" who sabotaged such schemes in textiles, coal production, building construction, and the garment trades.[7]

Thus the downward spiral of the Great Depression continued. Between 1929 and 1933 the gross national product (GNP), the sum of all the goods and services produced in the country, fell 29 percent. Construction was down 78 percent, manufacturing 54 percent, and investment a staggering 98 percent. In the summer of 1932, the steel industry operated at only 12 percent of its capacity. Fewer miles of railroad track were built in 1932 than in any year since the Civil War.[8] At the depression nadir, many people began to think that American capitalism had failed. In Dearborn, Michigan, a 1932 march of three thousand unemployed Ford workers, who appealed to America's most famous industrialist for jobs, heating coal, and rent money, came under a hail of police tear gas and gunfire, killing four and wounding sixty. As department store magnate Edward Filene later put it, "the machinery of production choked with its own product, unemployment spread like pestilence, and the world starved in the midst of plenty."[9]

The corporate heroes of the 1920s were in disgrace, while the free market generated little more than wave after wave of social misery. The state would have to restructure, and continuously regulate, a faltering American capitalism. Adolf Berle and Gardner Means, two academics later active in the Roosevelt Administration, codified this emerging consensus in their 1932 classic, *The Modern Corporation and Private Property*. Big businesses, argued Berle and Means, were controlled by a self-serving strata of managers who had effectively insulated their authority from both shareholder ownership and consumer pressure. Corporate officials "administered" prices, oppressed their workers, and ignored shareholder interests. Thus if the power they wielded was somehow illegitimate, then workers, consumers, and government regulators might well intervene to restructure the wage-price relation and make corporate decision-making far more democratically accountable.[10]

A broad upward shift in working-class purchasing power was essential. This prescription made the economic and political interest of a new union movement, the only prospective institution then capable of policing an upward revision of industrywide wage standards, largely synonymous with that of the nation as a whole. This proto-Keynesian idea was embedded within the legislation establishing the

National Recovery Administration (NRA), which was to be Franklin Roosevelt's principal initiative designed to restore prosperity during the first two years of the New Deal. The NRA repudiated laissez-faire economics and, in its place, sought to codify American capitalism by promulgating scores of industry "codes" that would put a floor under wages and prices, and a ceiling on hours and effort. "No business which depends for existence on paying less than living wages to its workers has any right to continue in this country," asserted FDR when he signed the National Industrial Recovery Act (NIRA). "The aim of this whole effort," the president explained, "is to restore our rich domestic market by raising its vast consuming capacity."[11]

Labor's voice was essential to such industry self-regulation, because only the trade unions possessed an intimate, internal knowledge of business conditions. Only they could "enforce" government-mandated minimum-wage standards and maximum-hour regulation. As retailer Edward Filene noted wryly at the NIRA hearings of 1933, "Our labor unions have a better understanding of what is good for business today than our chambers of commerce have."[12] Thus Section 7a of the NRA proved an important and controversial part of each industry code. It required that "employees shall have the right to organize and bargain collectively through representatives of their own choosing . . . free from the interference, restraint, or coercion of employers."[13] Such a revolution in the nation's labor law, argued Robert Wagner, the New York senator who championed the depression-era union movement, was to ensure that "[t]he fruits of industry must be distributed more bounteously among the masses of wage-earners who create the bulk of consumer demand.[14]

Consumption, Security, and "The American Standard"

An important strand in the language of the working-class movement in the 1930s was thus "consumerist," but there was nothing conservative or deradicalizing about such "bourgeois" aspirations. A century before, when the "producing classes" bulwarked a virtuous republic, the designation "consumer" seemed not far removed from that of the dysfunctional "parasite." But the New Deal worked an imaginative revolution: now mass consumption stood shoulder to shoulder with mass production as a foundational component both of a humane capitalism and a reinvigorated democracy. The New Deal and the new labor movement took the nascent consumer culture of the twentieth century and made of it a political project.[15] An "American" standard of living was becoming a right of citizenship, and if the achievement of that new entitlement required a radical transformation of the American political economy, so be it. Roosevelt's secretary of labor, Frances Perkins, put it this way in 1933: "If . . . the wages of mill workers in the South should be raised to the point where workers could buy shoes, that would be a social revolution.[16]

The New Deal and the new labor movement enfolded this new political economy within a powerful set of moral dichotomies. For a considerable proportion of the working class, the unemployment and poverty of the early depression years was nothing new. The fear, insecurity, and shame of those years had been the common, lifelong condition of perhaps half, and certainly a third, of the American people. But now such distress, or the prospect of falling into such an abyss, became a potent element within the entire political culture. The New Deal served to politicize such private nightmares, giving to them a visibility and legitimacy unknown since the heyday of urban Progressivism. Gerald Markowitz and David Rosner entitled their book of workers' letters about life on the job, "Slaves of the Depression," because of the powerlessness and humiliation generated by chronic want and unpredictable employment. These letters did not reflect an honorable poverty: rather the bad times bred deference, subordination, bondage, in short, the negation of republican citizenship.[17] "For years and years," wrote John Peele, a textile union leader in South Carolina, "those who toil in industry have dreamed of Democracy, [but] for those who produce the wealth there has been Industrial Slavery." To Peele, enactment of the NIRA in 1933 put labor "upon the threshold of industrial freedom."[18]

This was journalist Leona Hickok's startling discovery when she toured the nation for relief administrator Harry Hopkins in 1933 and 1934. With the depression generating unemployment and insecurity even among those with solid white-collar credentials, the "old poor" within and just below the employed working class once again became a highly visible, highly political stratum. The Communists and Socialists, with their unemployed marches and anti-eviction demonstrations, had helped mobilize this discontent and turn working-class eyes to the state for a solution to local problems, both on the job and in the community. These "radical boosters of the state," as Lizabeth Cohen has termed them, prepared the way for the expansive sense of entitlement workers came to feel when they looked to the New Deal for a solution to their problems. A state relief administrator reported to Hickok that among poor clients, the attitude was "changing from one that used to be a modest request for help temporarily," to one "demanding their share of what the government has to give." Far from generating a sense of passive dependency, New Deal relief programs, and especially those involving work and wages, generated an active sense of citizenship.[19] As Cohen has put it "the New Deal's impact should be measured less by the lasting accomplishments of its reforms and more by the attitudinal changes it produced in a generation of working class Americans who now looked to Washington to deliver the American dream."[20]

But what was the character of that dream? Here Roosevelt played a powerful role as a master rhetorician who demonized the old order as one of fear, inertia, and illegitimate power. "The only thing we have to fear is fear itself," he famously announced in his first inaugural; and in his equally skillful "Four Freedoms" speech of early 1941, he prepared Americans for wartime sacrifice by putting the New Deal's social democratic aspirations, to assure "freedom from fear" and "freedom from want," on an equally exalted level with the classically liberal freedoms of religion and speech.[21]

Against fear and humiliation the New Deal and the new unions counterpoised "security." This was an idea—if not a condition—that achieved near hegemony during the 1930s and 1940s. "What do they want, these millions of newly organized workers?" asked labor journalist Mary Heaton Vorse. "Security first of all. They want the right to work."[22] FDR echoed and advanced this sentiment. Putting forth his administration's program in 1934, the president asserted, "Among our objectives I place the security of men, women, and children of the Nation first."[23] FDR returned to this theme again and again, during World War II when the specter of a postwar slump seemed all too

Migrant Mother, Nipomo, California. Dorothea Lange's 1936 Farm Security Administration photograph is the most arresting visual icon of the Great Depression. Poverty, fear, and insecurity are drawn from the face and posture of an unknown 32-year-old pea picker. (Credit: FSA/OWI Collection, Library of Congress)

MORE SECURITY FOR
THE AMERICAN FAMILY
WHEN AN INSURED WORKER DIES, LEAVING DEPENDENT CHILDREN AND A WIDOW, BOTH MOTHER AND CHILDREN RECEIVE MONTHLY BENEFITS UNTIL THE LATTER REACH 18.
FOR INFORMATION WRITE OR CALL AT THE NEAREST FIELD OFFICE OF THE
SOCIAL SECURITY BOARD

By 1939 the New Deal had made family security a watchword for its social programs. (Credit: Franklin D. Roosevelt Presidential Library)

real, the president insisted on the need for a "Second Bill of Rights" to provide citizens with the right to a job, medical care, education, housing, and a decent income. "The one supreme objective for the future," he declared, "can be summed up in one word: Security, and that means not only physical security which provides safety for attacks by aggressors. It means also economic security, social security, moral security."[24]

So universal was security consciousness that even opponents of the New Deal sought to champion this aspiration. At the 1939 New York World's Fair, the Equitable Insurance Company sponsored a "Garden of Security." Nine years later the militantly conservative National Association of Manufacturers (NAM) admitted that "The employee's urge for security is stronger than ever, and every company has a responsibility to make maximum provision . . . to cushion employees against the economic hazards."[25]

Industrial Democracy

But if the New Deal state and the newly vigorous trade unions had only been successful as wage-fixing institutions designed to solve the problem of "underconsumption," their appeal would have been diminished considerably, not only among policy-making elites, but even more so among the mass of American workers. Hence the second great rationale for the state-assisted birth of mass unionism during the Great Depression: industrial democracy. A huge proportion of all those who became unionists during the 1930s and 1940s were African Americans, Mexican Americans, or from European immigrant families. For them the New Deal and the new unionism represented not just a higher standard of living, but a doorway that opened onto the democratic promise of American life. Security constituted not just freedom from material want, but a social, psychological fortress from which to challenge illegitimate power, both on the job and off.

By the onset of the depression decade, most reformers and radicals thought that a great contradiction lay at the heart of American capitalism. Outside the walls of the private enterprise, American political culture celebrated a Jeffersonian world of free speech, democratic participation, and masterless autonomy. But within the corporate world, and the nearby industrial municipalities, autocracy, obedience, and social deference were the order of the day, bolstered by a century of legal precedent and business practice. When confronting their employer, American workers had no statutory right to free speech, assembly, or petition. In the reactionary era right after the First World War, thousands of unionists were fired, blacklisted, and literally forced out of town. The judiciary stubbornly adhered to an imaginary world of "free labor" in which individual workers freely and equitably negotiated their pay and perks with those who hired them at the great corporations that now bestrode the land.[26] Pro-union workers called Aliquippa, Pennsylvania, "Little Siberia," because of the czarlike rule of the Jones and Laughlin Steel Company. J&L president Tom Girdler was a paternalist who paid good wages and boasted that his door was always open. But "we couldn't call our souls our own," reported a fearful steelworker, "We couldn't think unionism.[27]

No contradiction in American life, save that of African American slavery and its Jim Crow offspring, so violated the nation's democratic norms. With the rise of the continental corporation at the end of the nineteenth century, this dichotomy became the very essence of the labor question. President Roosevelt himself was acutely aware of this dilemma; indeed, his reconceptualization of American liberalism was predicated on the belief that the greatest threat to the republican form of government now came from concentrated capital far more than from an overweening state. Thus did FDR famously attack the "money changers" and "economic royalists" when he accepted his party's renomination in June 1936. "Philadelphia is a good city in which to write American history," he began, evoking a Jeffersonian-Madisonian theory of republican citizenship. "Necessitous men are not free men," he asserted, and then argued that in the twentieth-century world, economic inequality made political equality meaningless. Before the New Deal, he charged, "(a) small group had concentrated into their own hands an almost complete control over other people's property, other people's money, other people's labor—other people's lives. For too many of us life was no longer free; liberty was no longer real; men could no longer follow the pursuit of happiness."[28] Such rhetoric opened the door not only to a season of liberal statecraft, but to the most expansive ambitions of the union movement. As John L. Lewis declaimed in a national radio address just a week later, "Let him who will, be he economic tyrant or sordid mercenary, put his strength against this mighty upsurge of human sentiment now being crystallized in the hearts of thirty millions of workers who clamor for the establishment of industrial democracy and for participation in its tangible fruits."[29]

The "industrial democracy" of John L. Lewis, no less than that of Franklin Roosevelt, was therefore predicated upon a thoroughly republican sense of democratic governance. Advocates of "industrial democracy" saw the new system as but the next stage in the evolution of American freedom. The task of modern government, asserted FDR himself, was "to assist the development of an economic declaration of rights, an economic constitutional order."[30] It encompassed collective bargaining, of course, but it evoked a far more ambitious social agenda. On the shop floor, industrial democrats envisioned an "industrial jurisprudence," a constitutionalization of factory governance, and the growth of a two-party system that put unions and managers on an equal footing. An "American standard of living" for employed workers would be bulwarked by an entitled social "security" enfolding the rest of the population. "Industrial tyranny," asserted Senator Robert Wagner, was "incompatible with a republican form of government.[31] The responsibilities and expectations of American citizenship—due process, free speech, the right of assembly and petition—would now find their place in factory, mill, and office. A civil society would be constructed within the very womb of the privately held enterprise.

If the content of such rights and norms was thoroughly bourgeois, their achievement required something close to revolutionary action, or so it seemed during the summer and fall of 1934. Factory militancy in the 1930s was inspired far less by the Bolshevik aspirations of 1917 than by the virtuous republican values of 1776, but in either case, much turmoil was to follow. In Toledo, Minneapolis, San Francisco, and Kohler, Wisconsin, pitched battles in the streets put a set of fledgling unions at odds with the police, the national guard, and employer-sponsored militia. Farm laborers and cannery workers fought against tremendous odds in the California fields and packing houses. And in the nation's largest single strike, 350,000 textile workers walked out in a massive uprising that shut down mills from Maine to Alabama. These walkouts often took on the flavor of a general political strike, and these upheavals were often led by radicals: Communists on the San Francisco docks and in the California fields; Trotskyists among the Minneapolis truckers; independent leftists in Toledo; and Christian populists all along the Piedmont textile belt. There were thousands of arrests, hundreds of injuries, and dozens of dead, including six killed by vigilantes in Honea Path, South Carolina. Workers faced a crushing defeat in the Piedmont mills, the California fields, and in the company town of Kohler, even as militant new unions emerged in San Francisco and Minneapolis. But whatever the outcome, the upheaval of 1934 put a resolution of the labor question at the very center of American politics.[32]

These upheavals came at a transitional moment in American political culture. Since the days of Jefferson and de Tocqueville, American leaders of politics and enterprise have celebrated a society that is formally democratic and individualist. Much political rhetoric, in the nineteenth century and afterward, has devalued the idea of self-organization along either class or interest-group lines. The most convenient attack, certainly by those in power, has been to subvert the legitimacy of insurgent claims by asserting that conflict and instability are a product of internal corruption, outside agitation, or alien ideologies. In the United States, therefore, even more than in Europe or Latin America, those who defend the industrial and social status quo have deployed a racially tinged nationalism in their own class interest. Late in the nineteenth century, employers and politicians blamed radical immigrants and unpatriotic socialists for the strikes of that era. During and after World War I, "100 percent Americanism" became synonymous with the antisocialist, anti-immigrant efforts of vigilante groups like the American Legion or the KKK to smash the labor movement and the left. Union organizers and radical agitators manhandled by such groups, or by the police themselves, were often forced to kneel and kiss the American flag as a sign of their loyalty to the nation and its institutions.[33]

But liberals, labor, and the left successfully captured the flag during the 1930s. Franklin Roosevelt proved a master manipulator of the symbols of national pride and identity. His fireside chats, which so often announced an expansive New Deal program, drew listeners into the Oval Office, where the president told them of his absolute confidence in the ability of the American people to pull themselves out of the depression. The early New Deal employed marching bands, parades, and the ubiquitous Blue Eagle symbol to heighten the feelings of national unity and national mobilization. And so too did the union movement, whose leaders cloaked themselves in the expansive, culturally pluralist patriotism that the New Deal sought to propagate. "Unionism is the spirit of Americanism," asserted a union newspaper that appealed to immigrant workers long excluded from a full sense of citizenship.[34]

An emblematic moment came on the day in 1933 when Secretary of Labor Frances Perkins visited the unorganized steel workers of Homestead, Pennsylvania, to hear their grievances and explain to them New Deal labor policy. In a town tightly controlled by the United States Steel Corporation, the burgess (mayor) abruptly cut short a Perkins speech in the city hall when union militants—he called them "undesirable Reds"—sought to make their voices heard. Ushered onto the street amid a crowd of angry steelworkers, Perkins and her party were temporarily bewildered. Where would she continue her talk and answer the many questions anxious steelworkers put to her? The city park? "You can't do that," shouted the red-faced mayor, "there is an ordinance against holding meetings in a public park."[35]

But the secretary of labor would not be stymied, and when she saw an American flag flying above the local post office building she quickly led the working-class throng inside. There, in the lobby of this federal institution, under a flag representing the power of a self-confident, reformist government, Perkins resumed her speech detailing for a largely immigrant audience their new rights under the law. She later wrote, "We ended the meeting with hand-shaking and expressions of rejoicing that the New Deal wasn't afraid of the steel trust."[36]

All of America's great reform movements, from the crusade against slavery onward, have defined themselves as champions of a moral and patriotic nationalism, which they counterpoised to the parochial and selfish elites who stood athwart their vision of a virtuous society. Success is well advanced when a Lincoln, a Roosevelt, or a Johnson links his statecraft to the growing power of an insurgent social movement. Indeed, such legitimization is an essential element in the movement's capacity to transform dissent and protest into majoritarian sentiment. Thus, the depression-era labor movement deployed huge American flags in all its struggles, even those led by avowed leftists. The national banner symbolized the power of a newly assertive federal government and the kind of ethnically diverse Americanism the new unionism and the New Deal sought to build. Waving the Stars and Stripes, American unionists announced that they too were part of a patriotic tradition that was expansive enough to enfold a new industrial democracy.

The Wagner Act

As it was codified into the New Deal labor law, industrial democracy had a twofold character. As we have seen, it promised to generate the industrial citizenship demanded by so many workers and reformers. But industrial democracy was also a procedure for dispute resolution, for generating consensual order and long-term stability within an industrial realm wracked by violence and conflict for nearly a century. For some managers, and for a growing set of influential industrial relations experts, the labor question consisted less of an absence of democracy in the workplace than of the inefficiency of a work-force that was too often absent, alienated, or in revolt. In this context, the New Deal effort to encourage collective bargaining represented a psychologically sophisticated technique for the social integration of employees and their enterprise. Industrial democracy would engender that most precious commodity of the workaday world: informed and willing consent. This was the way in which arbitrator William Leiserson, himself an East European immigrant, saw collective bargaining, as but the latest, Whiggish, stage in the unfolding of the democratic idea. Leiserson, who would later play a key role in the development of New Deal labor law, argued that the "joint meetings of employers and union representatives, like the parliament of England, are at the same time constitutional conventions and stature making legislatures.[37]

And to Harvard's Sumner Slichter, then the dean of American labor economists, collective bargaining routinized and channeled social conflict by "introducing civil rights into industry, that is, of requiring that management be conducted by rule rather than by arbitrary decision." But even Slichter saw this new "industrial jurisprudence" as representing far more than the employee "voice" that contemporary industrial relations experts see as a key to enhanced productivity. New Deal reformers made that argument as well, but to their generation, collective bargaining represented even more: a normative social order establishing a new constitutionalism within American factories and mills. As the arbitrator and law school dean Wayne Morse put it somewhat later, "The progress of civilization cannot be stemmed. We must advance from the application of the law of the jungle to the use of the law of reason. Facts must be substituted for accusations; labor disputes must be approached upon the basis of calm deliberation and an intelligent consideration and understanding of the economic and social problems involved.[38]

Such was the hope invested in the Wagner Act, passed by the U.S. Congress in June 1935 and promptly signed by President Roosevelt early the next month. Unlike Section 7a of the National Industrial Recovery Act, which had proven itself toothless even before the Supreme Court declared the NIRA unconstitutional, Senator Robert Wagner's statute was a carefully drafted "Magna Carta" for the labor movement. The law was a radical legislative initiative because it was designed to put in place a permanent set of institutions situated within the very womb of private enterprise, which offered workers a voice, and sometimes a club, with which to resolve their grievances and organize themselves for economic struggle. It guaranteed workers the right to select their own union by majority vote, and to strike, boycott, and picket. And it enumerated a list of "unfair labor practices" by employers, including the maintenance of company-dominated unions, the blacklisting of union activists, intimidation and firing of workers who sought to join an independent organization, and the employment of industrial spies. To determine the will of the workers, the new law established a National Labor Relations Board, which heard employee complaints, determined union jurisdictions, and conducted on-site elections. Whenever a majority of a company's workers voted for a union to represent them, management had a legal obligation to negotiate with that union alone over wages, hours, and working conditions.

It is particularly important to note that the framers of the Wagner Act were determined to stamp out "company unionism," that is, employee organizations that were set up or dominated by management. To do so the new labor law banned any kind of management participation in or encouragement to a union, and it proscribed proportional representation, which would have allowed more than one union to represent workers in a given trade or company. In contrast to the situation in France, Great Britain, or Sweden, the U.S. government, acting through the National Labor Relations Board, would "certify" only one worker organization as the exclusive voice of the workers in a particular unit, which Senator Wagner and like-minded advocates expected to be companywide in character.

This New Deal determination to absolutely proscribe any kind of employer involvement in the new unionism bears directly on proposals made during recent years to make the labor law more amenable to various sorts of management-driven employee involvement schemes and other "team" production efforts. Under such company-funded arrangements, selected workers, foremen, and managers would meet on a periodic basis, thereby avoiding any "adversarial" relationship between employees and their immediate bosses. Today, such ideas are hailed, especially in conservative political circles, as productivity-enhancing heirs to the industrial democracy idea itself. But union pioneers in steel, auto, and electrical products, as well as the authors of the Wagner Act, had plenty of experience with company efforts to divide, manipulate, and "speed up" their employees. Wagner and his colleagues saw such management-dominated company unions as nothing more than a corporate effort to thwart and corrupt the authentic voice of a firm's employees. In moments of industrial turmoil—during World War I and in the first two years of the New Deal—industrialists had sponsored such schemes in order to co-opt the union impulse. They did provide an element of "voice," and in a

The Wagner Act brought the democratic process into the heart of corporate America. Here workers vote in a National Labor Relations Board election at the Ford Motor Company in May 1941. (Credit: Archives of Labor History and Urban Affairs, Wayne State University)

1934 effort to maintain industry cooperation with the recovery effort, President Roosevelt appointed a series of labor boards that practically endorsed them.[39]

All union leaders, as well as the principal framers of the Wagner Act, successfully argued for an absolute ban on these company-sponsored unions, because they contended that such institutions would merely perpetuate managerial power and exacerbate social divisions within the workforce. Wagner Act proponents accepted as reality the class divisions that structured the society and its workplaces. They knew that an ersatz industrial democracy could never provide a sound basis for the kind of vibrant shop representation and collective bargaining necessary to propagate the union idea and alter management behavior.[40]

The Labor Movement and Its Divisions

But a law is not a social movement. Seemingly progressive labor laws stand useless and unenforced on the statute books of many nations. To give the Wagner Act real social and political meaning, the United States required a working-class mobilization of explosive power and institutional strength. It was a social movement that would have to arise despite the indifference, in some cases amounting to hostility, of labor's erstwhile allies in Washington. During the summer of 1935, when Franklin Roosevelt signed the new labor law, the obstacles to the creation of such a vibrant union movement seemed overwhelming. The Supreme Court, which had deployed a narrow, nineteenth-century interpretation of the Constitution's commerce clause to invalidate the NRA, seemed likely to declare the even more sweeping provisions of the Wagner Act unconstitutional as well. Large corporate employers were so certain that the Wagner Act was unenforceable that they ignored the new statute and fought union organizing efforts. Indeed, companies like General Motors, DuPont, and Republic Steel did more than simply help fund a legal challenge to the Wagner Act: they hired scores of labor spies, fired union activists, stocked up on guns and tear gas, and financed a campaign in the press and on radio against the New Deal union idea.

Meanwhile, the leadership of the American Federation of Labor (AFL) seemed both unwilling and unable to wage the necessary fight. The AFL, whose leaders were largely steeped in a tradition of craft unionism, had no comprehensive strategy for organizing the semiskilled production workers who composed the majority of workers in the great mass-production industries. The AFL adhered to a longstanding philosophy of "exclusive jurisdiction" within its own ranks, which meant that the various craft unions—the carpenters, machinists, electricians, and so forth—would seek to organize but a thin slice of the workforce in each factory, mill, or construction work site. There is nothing inherently dysfunctional about craft organization, either in the 1930s or today. By seeking to monopolize a well-defined, occupational labor market, craft unions can set the technical, educational, and ethical standards for any given job. Apprenticeship programs help keep unions at the cutting edge of technological change, and in Germany and other European countries, they have long provided an effective school-to-work transition.

Indeed, such union schemas, enforced by the closed shop and the hiring hall, often gave unionism a "professional" feel that opened the door to white- and gray-collar workers, including draftsmen, journalists, engineers, teachers, architects, actors, and sales personnel. Two of the most successful, innovative, and high-prestige unions launched during the Great Depression were essentially craft organizations of this sort: the American Newspaper Guild (ANG) and the Screen Actors Guild (SAG). Both used the term "guild," rather than trade union, in deference to the middle-class sensibilities of some of their potential members. They were founded and led by "stars": the salty, sophisticated columnist Heywood Broun symbolized the combative spirit of the ANG for many years, while in Hollywood the SAG cache was ensured by the presence of Eddie Cantor, Charles Chaplin, Joan Crawford, Jane Wyman, Robert Montgomery, James Cagney, and Ronald Reagan in its leadership. Publishers and studio chiefs were outraged that their "talent" had organized against them: both unions were denounced as subversive. And indeed they were, because the recruitment to the union banner of such attractive figures subverted the hierarchical, celebrity culture promoted by so many press barons and studio moguls.[41]

But craft unions of this sort were quite the exception. In the 1930s, AFL unionism was tainted by a patriarchal, racist odor that kept it at odds with so many of the new immigrants and the nation's African American population. AFL leaders mistrusted workers not of Northern European ancestry, and they were often contemptuous of radicals or those workers without a proper "trade." The great rivalry that would soon divide the union movement in the United States was based not only on a celebrated dispute over the craft versus the industrial form of organization, but more fundamentally on the disdain with which so many in the AFL hierarchy greeted the immigrants and unskilled Southerners who comprised the bulk of the workers in steel, packinghouse, automobile, and other mass production industries. Much of the AFL was rooted in the Protestant lower-middle class and the old labor aristocracy of Northern European descent. These men and women had a substantial stake in the old order, be it the comfortable politics of a Midwestern town or the chance to climb a few steps higher within the workplace hierarchy. Through the Masons, the Knights of Columbus, the Protestant churches, through kinship and friendship, they had forged a hundred and one social and cultural links with those more solidly bourgeois. Teamsters' president Daniel Tobin gave voice to such sentiment when he derided "the rubbish that have lately come into other organizations. We do not want the men if they are going to strike tomorrow." And the leaders of the Cleveland Metal Trades Council, composed of highly skilled Northern Europeans for the most part, spurned efforts to organize assembly line workers in their city. "You can't organize the hunkies out there," the secretary of the Council declared in response to a request for assistance from workers in the White Motor plant. Likewise at the Richmond, California, Ford plant, AFL local officials turned their backs because they did not think the auto workers there were "intelligent enough to be organized at that time."[42]

Thus there were "culture wars" in the 1930s, too. Union growth, militancy, and power in that era was based on a working class that was no more homogeneous than that of our own time. Nearly all of the recent social histories of this era emphasize the fierce ethnoreligious fissures that confronted union organizers and energized the political conflicts splintering so many unions. The New Deal made shop-floor citizens of Eastern European Catholics, African Americans, French Canadians, and migratory Appalachians whose relationship to the old German, Irish, and Northern Protestant elite had been one of deference and subordination. Moreover the new unions, with their leaven of radical Jews and anticlerical Catholics, with their rationalizing, modernizing, and cosmopolitan outlook, threatened the lifetime of social capital and ethnic privilege built up by those whose outlooks were more parochial and insular. No wonder that the 1930s saw a recrudescence of right-wing agitation and red baiting wherever the union impulse disrupted the old order. Thus the terrorist Black Legion flourished in Pontiac and Flint, and the KKK at Packard and at auto assembly plants in Indiana, Missouri, and Texas. Company-sponsored vigilante groups had little difficulty winning recruits in either California agribusiness or the industrial towns of upstate New York and New England.[43]

Skilled workers were often in the vanguard of industrial unionism during the 1930s (Credit: George Meany Memorial Archives)

If this troubled history serves to demolish the convenient but mythic imagery of labor solidarity in the 1930s, it may have much contemporary usefulness. Although the cultural and racial fissures break along different lines today, union organizers confront a working class that is just as heterogeneous as that of seventy years before. The difference then between an Anglo-Gaelic tool-and-die maker at Ford's giant River Rouge complex outside Detroit and a first generation Hungarian assembler in Cleveland was just about the same in terms of training and outlook as that between an immigrant Chinese programmer in Seattle and a native-born data-entry home worker in Omaha. In the 1930s, as at the turn of the twenty-first century, unionism in the needle trades has required the harmonization of a bewildering array of immigrant ethnic particularisms.

Likewise, the entrenched racial and occupational hierarchies in construction, health care, and municipal service require as much attention today as in the past. The unionization process does not demand homogeneity in either skill, ethnicity, or language. Nor does the growth of a more uniform consumer culture have much of an impact on the union consciousness of working-class Americans. Instead, trade unionism requires a compelling set of ideas and institutions, both self-made and governmental, to give labor's cause power and legitimacy. It is a political project whose success enables the unions to transcend the ethnic and economic divisions always present in the working population. "Class consciousness," wrote E. P. Thompson, is "made," not "given."[44]

Leadership

Such was the task confronting the unionists who looked to the leadership of United Mine Workers (UMW) president John L. Lewis and Sidney Hillman of the Amalgamated Clothing Workers (ACW). Lewis and Hillman were industrial unionists who thought the organization of all workers, regardless of skill or tradition, the most effective basis for the growth of labor's power in the mass production industries. But even more important, they broke with the rest of the AFL because they thought that passage of the Wagner Act, the insurgent mood within the working class, and the increasingly antibusiness tenor of the White House meant that there would never be a better time to unionize industrial workers and push the New Deal toward the kind of social democratic politics and policies they favored. If unions led by men such as themselves could seize this opportunity, then organized labor would multiply its membership, economic power, and political clout. If not, a huge opportunity would be lost, or else others would assume the task of rebuilding the labor movement—either the Communists or Socialists on the left, or the followers of such authoritarian demagogues as the anti-Semitic radio priest, Father Charles Coughlin, on the right.

By the fall of 1935 Lewis, Hillman, and a few like-minded colleagues concluded that any mass organizing effort would have to take place under the banner of a new Committee for Industrial Organization outside the old AFL framework. Although this split in labor's ranks did not become permanent until 1937, it was neatly symbolized at the AFL's October 1935 convention in Atlantic City. When William Hutcheson, the stand-pat president of the Carpenters' Brotherhood, tried to silence an advocate of industrial unionism by citing a parliamentary rule, Lewis shouted, "This thing of raising points of order all the time on minor delegates is rather small potatoes." Hutcheson rose to the bait, calling Lewis a "bastard." Lewis jumped to his feet, observed a reporter. "Quick as a cat, he leaped over a row of chairs toward Hutcheson, jabbed out his right fist, and sent the carpenters' president sprawling." Hutcheson left the floor with blood on his face, while "Lewis casually adjusted his tie and collar, relit his cigar, and sauntered slowly through the crowded aisles."[45]

Lewis was no radical. In the United Mine Workers, the burly, sonorous-voiced union leader had a well-deserved reputation as an autocrat who voted Republican in most elections. Nevertheless, he was determined to organize the labor movement by industry, not by craft. "Great combinations of capital have assembled to themselves tremendous power and influence," he warned. "If you go in there with your craft unions they [the employers] will mow you down like the Italian machine guns will mow down Ethiopians in the war now going on in that country."[46] Equally important, industrial unionism was essential to the defense of American democracy and republican virtue. "The Kings of Money and Lords of Finance" threatened a "Tory Revolution," thundered Lewis. Only a strong labor movement, now enduring its own "Valley Forge" could hope to restore a "self-governing republic."[47]

The amazing success of the CIO campaign during the next two years rested on its ability to tap the energy of thousands of grassroots activists while at the same time providing the national coordination and leadership that enabled the new unions to confront such multistate corporations as U.S. Steel, General Motors, and Firestone Tire and Rubber. Because of their exceptional ability as mass organizers, Lewis hired scores of communists and socialists and backed their efforts with big money from the treasury of his United Mine Workers. When reporters probed his decision to hire so many Communists, Lewis replied, "Who gets the bird, the hunter or the dog."[48] As it turned out, the dog got quite a few birds: the leftists with whom Lewis cooperated were energetic, young, and confident they were marching with the tide of history. Union radicals like the auto worker Walter Reuther, the longshore leader Harry Bridges, and Mike Quill of the Transport Workers would soon emerge as labor's new men of power.

Such radicals were and are essential to the organization of a trade union movement, in the United States even more so than in countries with an established socialist tradition. Indeed, if it were left to those whose aspirations were shaped merely by the trade union idea, most labor drives would have died at birth. This is because the founding of a trade union is a personally risky business whose costs and dangers are disproportionately born by those who take the early initiative. Even with the Wagner Act on the books, union spark plugs still gambled with their jobs, and sometimes their lives. Most workers therefore remained passive, not because they endorsed the industrial status quo, but because defeat might well threaten what little security they had managed to achieve. Their fear proved management's greatest ally, then and now. Only those individuals with an intense political or religious vision, only those radicals who saw the organizing project as part of a collective enterprise, and only those who understood the unions as a lever with which to build a new society could hope to calculate that the hardships they endured might reap such a magnificent political and social reward.

In a sense therefore, the union activists and organizers of the 1930s were always "outside agitators," because they did start their journey outside the mainstream of working-class opinion. Thus workers who had first been radicalized by the old Industrial Workers of the World (IWW) or by the new Communist Party stepped forward as union pioneers. And equally overrepresented among the rank-and-file founders of the CIO were those immigrants and their offspring whose social imaginations had once been fired by Irish nationalism, German socialism, Caribbean-American Garveyism, and the revolutionary movements in Mexico, the Czarist Empire, and the Philippines. But when and if these early radicals built a successful union and recruited to its ranks the bulk of the workforce, then this union vanguard became a distinct political minority, thus giving rise to the conservative charges of a later day that radicals, and especially the Communists, had "infiltrated" the very unions in which they had played so decisive a founding role.[49]

But radicals could not build the new union movement alone. The CIO organizing drive was also linked to the transformative spirit of the New Deal at flood tide. John L. Lewis wanted "a President who would hold the light for us while we went out and organized," so the industrial union movement broke new ground by linking its fortunes with the reelection of Franklin Roosevelt. Lewis himself provided the national Democratic Party with an unprecedented half-million-dollar contribution from the UMW treasury, but in this election as in so many others during the New Deal era, money was the least of the contributions labor offered the Democrats. Throughout the urban North the new unions recentered the party's electoral base, providing thousands of reliable precinct workers during each campaign season, and shifting to the Democratic column millions of new voters energized by the promise of industrial citizenship. In turn the CIO held the friendly neutrality of the federal government during the most crucial phase of its organizing work.[50]

Roosevelt's 1936 campaign rhetoric verged on the anticapitalist. He denounced the "economic royalists" who sought to "impose a new industrial dictatorship." He charged that the forces of "organized money are unanimous in their hate for me, and I welcome their hatred." And he asserted that during his first administration "the forces of selfishness and of lust for power met their match." When Roosevelt and Lewis appeared together at a mass open-air meeting in the Pennsylvania anthracite region, the president offered a ringing endorsement of the miners' union, the CIO, and collective bargaining. Such rhetoric paid off. As one millworker in the South noted, Roosevelt "is the first man in the White House to understand that my boss is a son of a bitch."[51] Stressing the New Deal's social welfare and union rights legislation and identifying himself with the aspirations of wage earners and small property owners, FDR garnered 60 percent of the total popular vote and carried every state but Vermont and Maine. Unlike the latter-day landslides of Dwight Eisenhower and Ronald Reagan, Roosevelt's election-day success in 1936 was one of party as well as personality. The Republicans lost twelve more seats in the House of Representatives, giving the Democrats three-quarters of the total. In the Senate, seven new Democrats were elected, giving the president's party nearly eight of every ten seats in that body. And Democratic gubernatorial candidates also won in Michigan, Ohio, Pennsylvania, and New York, where important battles for union organization were sure to be fought.[52]

Though the Roosevelt vote included traditionally Democratic strongholds in the Mountain West and the Deep South, urban working people composed the core of the new Democratic electorate. Overwhelming support came from the newly enfranchised children of turn-of-the-century Southern and Eastern European immigrants and from the native-born millions, black and white, who left the land for the cities during the 1920s. For them a vote for Roosevelt and the New Deal was practically a rite of citizenship. Thus when the president's campaign motorcade passed through Michigan's industrial cities, virtually every assembly line came to a halt as workers crowded to the windows, even though the fledgling United Automobile Workers (UAW) had but a handful of members in the state.[53] In 1920 the Republicans had captured the twelve largest cities with a plurality of more than 1.5 million votes, but in 1936 Roosevelt and the Democrats swamped their opponents in these now solidly Democratic bastions by a margin of more than 3.5 million. In some Midwestern industrial cities the Polish and Italian Democratic vote was over 90 percent. These new urban, "ethnic," working-class voters would remain the backbone of the nation's Democratic majority for the next third of a century.[54]

A set of "Little New Deals" transformed the company-town politics of scores of industrial cities in New England, Pennsylvania, and the Midwest. Eric Leif Davin has called this the triumph of a "blue collar democracy," and indeed it was. In the arc of once feudal Pennsylvania steel towns, voting rights, civil liberties, and local police power finally fell into working-class hands. "For the first time in the history of Monongahela Valley, people were . . . no longer cowed by the pressure of the mill superintendent"—observed labor partisan George Powers—"there was a new freedom over the land." In Homestead, where Madam Perkins had once had such trouble finding a speaker's platform, FDR carried the electorate by a five-to-one margin, after which a labor slate swept every office in the town. In Aliquippa, steelworkers marched behind election signs that proclaimed, "America is yours, Organize and claim it!"[55]

CIO! CIO! CIO!

"You voted New Deal at the polls and defeated the Auto Barons," union organizers told Michigan workers late in 1936. "Now get a New Deal in the shop."[56] Buoyed by Roosevelt's smashing reelection, CIO efforts to organize the basic industries of America came to a climax in what is undoubtedly the most significant work stoppage in twentieth-century American history, the dramatic "sit-down" strike at the General Motors Corporation (GM) in the winter of 1937. Throughout the middle decades of the twentieth century, General Motors was the largest and most profitable corporation in the United States, and one of the most sophisticated. It was not a sluggish giant, but a nimble, technically proficient organization. *Fortune* magazine then called GM "the world's most influential industrial unit in forming the life patterns of the machine age." With 110 manufacturing and assembly plants scattered across the nation, with a quarter million employees and half a million stockholders, General Motors was "the perfect exemplar of how and why American business is Big." GM managers were increasingly hostile to both the New Deal and the new unions. CIO political objectives, reported President Alfred Sloan to his stockholders, were an "important step toward an economic and political dictatorship." In the mid-1930s the company spent more money than any other in the nation on labor spies.[57]

Autoworkers sought to counter this enormous power with an industrial, companywide trade union that could defend their health and dignity on the shop floor, their job security during layoffs, and their standard of living. The grievances of these relatively well-paid workers did not so much involve wages, as they did arbitrary supervision, economic insecurity, and the dehumanizing "speed-up" characteristic of Taylorized mass production in the twentieth century. The foremen "treated us like a bunch of coolies," a Chevrolet employee in Flint later remembered. "'Get it out. If you cannot get it out, there are people outside who will get it out.' That was their whole theme." But because of the industry's seasonal production cycle, employees worked long, hard hours during the winter and spring, only to be unemployed for up to three months when the factories were retooled later that same year.

Foremen and other managers had the unfettered right to discipline, fire, lay off, and rehire at their own discretion. The corporation had successfully resisted union and NRA efforts to make "seniority" (the length of time a worker had been employed) govern an employee's promotion and recall rights. Management argued that it needed the "flexibility" to hire, fire, and promote in order to keep operations efficient, but the experience of thousands of workers was quite a different one: they saw such managerial prerogatives as a weapon with which to penalize unionists and reward the "red apples." Such is the mid-20th-century origin of many contemporary union "work rules" that are said to stifle efficiency and bloat the payroll. But from the worker's point of view, the demand for seniority, for well-defined job classifications, and other such working standards arose out of the chronic battle with factory supervisors, who sought not a workplace rule of law, but the maintenance of a capricious autocracy.

The General Motors strike had its epicenter in Flint, Michigan, the corporation's key production center and, by 1936, a huge company town. The mayor, police chief, and three city commissioners as well as Flint's newspaper, radio station, and school officials all were or had been on the GM payroll. General Motors' Chevrolet, Buick, Fisher Body, and AC Spark Plug plants employed four of every five workers in the city. Overwhelmingly white and male, most of these workers had migrated to Flint from Appalachia or the rural Midwest. For the fledgling United Auto Workers, the burden of conducting the actual struggle with General Motors rested on the same relatively small group of committed activists who would be essential to the union-building process in other industries. They were an energetic group of young ideological radicals who ran the day-to-day affairs of the strike, a few hundred sit-downers in each plant, and a handful of veteran unionists of national reputation posted to Flint during all or part of the conflict.

The success of the UAW had a dual basis. First, the sit-down tactic itself—the physical occupation of more than a score of GM factories—effectively stopped production. The tactic was not new, but the UAW deployed it on an aggressive scale in order to maximize the leverage of a militant minority and avoid conflicts with the police and strikebreakers. During the course of the six-week factory occupation, Flint sit-downers held frequent meetings, conducted classes in labor history, put on plays, prepared their meals, and scrupulously avoided damage to company property or products. They drew upon nearly a decade of labor-left political and social activism to construct a counterhegemonic union culture with which to challenge GM's corporate worldview. The UAW radicals demanded abolition of the speed-up, an end to "red-apple" favoritism, a shorter work week, and "a minimum rate of pay commensurate with an American standard of living." The Supreme Court would shortly declare the sit-down tactic a violation of corporate property rights, but the wave of factory occupations in 1937 nevertheless reflected the legitimacy achieved by another kind of popular social right: the proprietary claim of so many workers toward their jobs and their livelihoods.

Second, labor's Democratic Party allies kept Michigan's powerful militia forces temporarily at bay. Because the sit-down strike tactic was of questionable legality, the Flint police sought to oust the strikers on more than one violent occasion. But the transformation of the 1936 election into something of a referendum on the industrial status quo led key political figures, including Frank Murphy, the newly elected Democratic governor of Michigan, and President Roosevelt himself, to think twice. Neither Murphy nor FDR deployed the national guard or the army to evict the strikers and restore "public order" in the accustomed, promanagement, fashion. Thus the contest in Flint and other industrial cities would be fought out in the factories and streets and neighborhoods where union activists held the greatest advantage. Here, and in several other similar industrial conflicts of the late 1930s, the unionists were often organized into paramilitary formations, "flying squadrons," of which the Women's Emergency Brigade, led by the twenty-three-year-old Socialist firebrand, Genora Johnson, was one of the most effective and celebrated.[58]

General Motors finally reached a settlement with the UAW-CIO on February 11, 1937. The signed contract was but four pages long, but it proved a remarkable victory, not only for the employees of America's largest corporation, but for millions of other workers. GM recognized the union as the sole voice of its employees and agreed to negotiate with UAW leaders on a multiplant basis. This meant that union activists had for the first time the right to speak up, recruit other workers, and complain to management without fear of retribution. "Even if we got not one damn thing out of it other than that," declared a GM employee in St. Louis, "we at least had a right to open our mouths without fear." Indeed, an enormous sense of self-confidence, democratic participation, even liberation swept through working-class ranks. "Everybody wants to talk. Leaders are popping up everywhere," reported a Michigan organizer. Huge crowds thronged the Flint streets: it was a celebration that Roy Reuther, a key auto union militant, would later liken to "some description of a country experiencing independence."[59]

Across industrial America the GM settlement transformed the expectations of workers and managers alike. In Flint and elsewhere, most workers had not actively supported the initial strikes, picket lines, and demonstrations. But the rest were not necessarily pro-company, or even neutral in the conflict. They were fearful bystanders whose union consciousness would crystallize only after the CIO had stripped management of its capacity to penalize their union loyalty. Thus, in almost every industrial district, workers poured into the new unions: many workers were initially organized into citywide units that cut across corporate boundaries and union affiliations. They shouted "CIO, CIO, CIO!"[60]

A fever of organization gripped working-class communities in a huge arc that spread from New England through New York, Pennsylvania, and the Midwest. Nearly 5 million took part in some kind of industrial action that year, and almost 3 million joined a union. In

Detroit a rolling wave of sit-down strikes seized dozens of factories. "Somebody would call the office," recalled a CIO organizer, "and say, 'Look, we are sitting down. Send us over some food.'" In the motor city, workers occupied every Chrysler Corporation facility, twenty-five auto-parts plants, four downtown hotels, nine lumberyards, ten meatpacking plants, a dozen industrial laundries, three department stores, and scores of restaurants, shoe stores, and clothing outlets. When the police evicted female strikers from a cigar company and a few stores along lower Woodward Avenue, the labor movement shut down many factories and put 150,000 workers in front of city hall.[61]

Such raw power made the kind of headlines that influenced even the nation's most conservative elites. There were no sit-down strikes at U.S. Steel, but president Myron Taylor read GM's capitulation at Flint as a sign that "complete industrial organization was inevitable" To avoid a violent conflict with its own workers, Taylor, who presided over the second-biggest manufacturing company in the world, the corporation that had smashed the nationwide steel strike in 1919, agreed in March 1937 to raise wages and recognize the CIO's Steel Workers' Organizing Committee as sole bargaining agent for its employees. Scores of other corporations followed suit, and in April the Supreme Court, whose conservative judges also read the headlines, surprised almost everyone by endorsing the constitutionality of the Wagner Act.[62]

The industrial drama of early 1937 again demonstrates the extent to which the growth of trade unionism in the United States is an exceedingly episodic phenomenon. Great moments of plebeian enthusiasm, as in the eight-hour agitation of the 1880s, the syndicalist impulse of the World War I era, the union-building years that followed the Upheaval of 1934, and the rise of a public employee labor movement in the 1960s, come but once each generation. Between 1933 and 1937 American unions recruited about 5 million new members, at least half coming during just a handful of months in 1937. This amazing growth was a product of a virtuous ideological and institutional dynamic in which an idea—industrial democracy—came to stand as a solution to the nation's social and economic ills. But industrial unionism's moment of unrivaled triumph proved exceedingly brief. Within weeks of the CIO's great victories at General Motors and U.S. Steel, the radical challenge posed by mass unionism generated a furious opposition: from corporate adversaries, Southern Bourbons, craft unionists, and many elements of the New Deal coalition itself. The labor movement would continue to expand its ranks for more than a dozen years. During World War II another four million members were added, but the unions would never again enjoy a political environment as favorable as that which transformed American work life during the years between 1934 and 1937.

Chapter 2

Citizenship at Work

As THE GREAT DEPRESSION turned into World War II, many Americans thought the nation well on the way toward a resolution of its chronic labor question. The American trade-union movement was clearly a power in the land. By 1941 the unions represented some 9 million workers; by 1945 they had organized another 6 million. The great mass production industries: steel, auto, electrical products, meatpacking, and rubber were well organized, and so too were many of the crucial transport and infrastructure occupations: railroads, trucking, shipping, municipal transit, commercial construction, and electric power generation. News of strikes, negotiations, organizing drives, and labor legislation filled the headlines. Such public controversy demonstrated that labor's claims commanded attention, even respect, for the character and potency of trade unionism were now central issues at the ballot box, in the legislative chamber, and in the deliberations of the highest court.

Labor was big, the New Dealers were in office. But real questions remained: To what extent did the new unionism and the New Deal actually generate the industrial democracy, the social security, and the standards of living so long sought by early twentieth-century reformers, unionists, and radicals? To what extent had workers become full citizens at work? To answer these questions we have to take a closer look at the bargaining system and the new social citizenship that emerged late in the 1930s. We must measure its reach and impact, within the factory and office, outside its blue-collar core, and among white women, African Americans, and all those for whom the new unionism had a quite variegated and even contradictory character.

Labor's greatest impact came at the site of production, through a democratic reform of the way in which workers and mangers came to share governance of the American workplace. We remember, and oftentimes celebrate, the system of industrial unionism hammered into place by the CIO because of the dramatic transformations it generated at such world famous companies as Chrysler, General Electric, Goodyear, Armour, and Bethlehem Steel. As the culture and power of a rights-conscious citizenship inserted itself into the very fabric of shop society, a model of industrial democracy emerged that was powerfully subversive of the old industrial order. Even employers saw it as the wave of the future, which is why executives at such intransigent anti-union firms as DuPont, Kodak, IBM, Weirton Steel, and Thompson Products (now TRW) erected their own parallel system of workplace governance. These mimicked many of the collective bargaining arrangements, including grievance procedures, seniority lines, and systems of wage determination, generated in the industrial union sector. But this version of industrial democracy was not hegemonic, even within unionized industry, for it immediately encountered resistance from a quite different model promoted by the craft unions of the American Federation of Labor. These venerable institutions adapted the craft union idea to the new legal and political environment generated by the New Deal and the warfare state that so quickly followed. By 1940 the AFL was larger than the CIO: by the time these two rival federations merged fifteen years later, the AFL was actually twice as big.

The Fruits of Industrial Unionism

Industrial unionism in the mass production sectors of the economy proved the testing ground for the New Deal answer to the twentieth-century labor question. What would an accounting look like during the heyday of this new unionism in the two decades following the CIO breakthrough in 1937? First, unionism did successfully spread throughout most Northern and Western firms in the manufacturing, mining, and transport sectors of the economy. Unionization rates in auto, steel, rubber, meatpacking, electrical products, trucking, coal mining, glassware, newspaper printing, aircraft, shipbuilding, clothing manufacture, and municipal transport were well over 80 percent in the decade after World War II.[1] This was by no means a sure thing in 1937 when the "Roosevelt Recession" later that year brought the CIO organizing drive to an abrupt halt. Corporations like Ford, International Harvester, Douglas Aircraft, and the "Little Steel" producers repulsed the new unionism, sometimes in bloody confrontations with company thugs and local police. Ten unionists were murdered—most shot in the back—on Memorial Day 1937, as they fled from a police fusillade outside the Republic Steel plant in South Chicago.[2]

But the post-1940 employment boom sparked by the government's ultra-Keynesian mobilization program gave the labor movement a second chance, while the necessity for a strike-free production effort required that the Roosevelt administration would ensure union growth during the years after Pearl Harbor. With unemployment at its lowest level in the twentieth century, no wartime worker feared the loss of a paycheck if he or she signed with the union. In the electrical industry an organizer recalled: "We'd circulate membership cards in front of the management. . . . I remember a two-year period, 1942–43, where we went through some sixty-six or sixty-eight plants, organized them, and held elections. We lost one!"[3] Because the government's new War Labor Board saw the advance of an institutionally secure trade unionism as essential to the success of the war effort, managers were forced to sign new contracts adjudicated by that powerful wartime agency. Thus when another depression failed to materialize after 1945, mass unionism had achieved a certain stability, and despite an increasingly difficult legal and political environment, labor still won more NLRB elections than it lost. By 1953 more than one in three nonfarmworkers were members of a trade union.[4]

Real wages doubled in the United States between 1940 and 1967. By the 1950s "underconsumption" seemed far less of a problem, and among many social commentators, it was common to assert, as *Fortune* magazine did in 1951, that the "worker is to a remarkable extent a middle class member of a middle class society."[5] Given the wage stagnation that has characterized the last decades of the twentieth century, this growth in midcentury living standards seems positively heroic. During the 1940s life expectancy advanced three years for whites and five years for blacks, largely because more people were getting three square meals a day.[6] Economists debate the extent to which the unions themselves were responsible for this achievement because these were also years of enormous productivity growth and Keynesian fiscal stimulus. But clearly the unions had a lot to do with it because they helped determine the extent to which the working class would win its share of that growth dividend. They bargained hard for wage increases in almost every contract, and in the 1950s most of the key unions in the pace-setting industries secured automatic cost-of-living adjustments that protected real wages from inflationary erosion. Significantly, those same contracts prevented an actual income decline for employed workers during the postwar era's frequent recessions, a notable break with the pattern of 1921 and 1930–32, and in our own time, when real wages dropped during the downturns of 1980–82 and 1990–91.

A remarkable, generation-long equalization of wages within the working class accompanied this larger income growth. In the years leading up to the Great Depression, industrial capitalism had generated a radically divergent set of pay structures. Southern wages in textiles, lumber, meatpacking, and coal mining lagged well behind those in the North. Factories in small towns paid less than those in large metropolitan areas, even when owned by the same firm. Within each workplace, skilled work commanded a huge pay premium over that of common labor, sometimes 300 percent. And a bewildering array of job assignments, classifications, pay incentives, and favoritisms ensured the growth of inequality within the work force. U.S. Steel maintained more than 26,000 different rates, some purposely designed to fragment and divide the workforce. "A man at the blast furnace does the same work another fellow does at the open hearth, but gets a few cents an hour less," reported a steel union official in 1942. "Now frankly it's not a question of starving. . . . It's just not right. A man does not see any sense in it and gets pretty mad. Who wouldn't?"[7]

These pay inequalities mirrored ethnic, racial, and gender divisions in the working population, sometimes because unequal pay was offered for equal work, but more frequently because of an endemic segregation within the production hierarchy. Thus African Americans were almost always consigned to the dirty and difficult tasks: in the North foundry work, the hog kill, kitchen labor, janitorial duties, and the paint shop; in the South hand tobacco stemming, rough lumber work, and dollar-a-day agricultural labor. The work of white women was just as segregated and devalued as that of African Americans. During the early depression years, employers gave to the customary sex discrimination of that era an even harder edge: banks, school boards, and some federal agencies simply fired women when they got married. Working women were rarely advanced to supervision, usually assigned to routine tasks, and frequently paid less money for work identical to that of white men.[8]

Industrial unionism began to shrink these wage differentials within the working class. It was a matter both of ideology and of organizational survival. Uniform, companywide wage standards were essential in order to reinforce a sense of solidarity within the workforce and deprive managers of an incentive to shift work to low-paid regions, factories, or departments. Otherwise, workers were just "organizing themselves out of a job."[9] This was a never-ending task, but by the end of World War II, a new economic principle had been established. Multiplant, unionized firms like General Motors and U.S. Steel now conceded that local labor market conditions no longer guided management when it came to establishing either the plant level wage structure or individual rates on specific jobs. In turn these companies "subcontracted" many of their most difficult wage rationalization problems to the unions, which now presided over the sensitive task of defining the precise meaning of equal pay for equal work all across the industrial archipelago. A North-South pay gap remained in many industries, but it declined dramatically in the 1940s. The United Mine Workers eliminated it entirely in coal, and with the assistance of the War Labor Board it shrank in textiles, meatpacking, trucking, and shipbuilding. Finally, and perhaps most significantly, the CIO unions pushed up the wages of the lowest-paid workers by negotiating pay increases, not in percentage terms, but in straight cents per hour. This gradually flattened out the wage pyramid in most factories and mills. By

1960 relative wage differentials within the auto industry had declined by 60 percent, a pattern replicated throughout unionized industry.[10]

This shift toward a uniform, nationwide wage pattern represented one of the industrial union movement's most significant steps toward a progressive transformation of the American class structure. Factories within the same firm, and companies within the same industry, would cease to compete for lower wages, and within those factories and occupations, wage differentials would decline, compressing and restructuring the blue-collar social structure. Unionized factory workers could move out of the tenements even as the impoverished company towns began to vanish. Given the ethnic, gender, and racial character of so many industrial jobs, the incremental equalization of working-class incomes provided the economic bedrock upon which the unions and their liberal allies championed racial equality and cultural pluralism at midcentury. Discrimination remained ugly and overt in many union and management practices, but the actual wage differentials between the work of men and women, and whites and blacks, even at their carefully segregated jobs, declined during the heyday of mass industrial unionism.[11]

Shop Democracy

But neither man, nor woman, lives by bread alone. Above all, industrial democracy stood for industrial justice, which meant that the unions had to fight the pervasive insecurity and arbitrary discipline that so many workers thought the essence of factory autocracy under the old regime. In the 1930s and 1940s modern personnel management was coming into its own, but no matter how well structured the corporate hierarchy—or how explicit the employment rules promulgated by top management—supervisors, foremen, and straw bosses all had the capacity to make life miserable for those under them. "Before organization came into the plant," reported a 1941 UAW handbook for its shop stewards, "foremen were little tin gods in their own departments. They were accustomed to having orders accepted with no questions asked. They expected workers to enter into servile competition for their favors."[12]

The establishment of a strong shop steward system was the most important way in which the new industrial unions sought to transform the foreman's empire. Union activists demanded a steward for every foreman and a committeeman for every department. In its stewards' handbook, "How to Win for the Union," the UAW declared its vigorous system of shop stewards and committeemen a "weapon of democracy" that would overthrow the foreman's "small time dictatorship" and install a "democratic system of shop government." To the steward, it announced: "Your relationship with the foreman should be that of equals seeking a solution to a common problem. But don't forget: the stronger the organization behind you, the more powerful your argument."[13]

In such a context, "collective bargaining" embodied a wide range of tactics and practices that defined the relationship between workers and their employers. At the shop-floor level, day-to-day conflict over production standards and workplace discipline permeated the structure of work and authority in most factories and mills. The early union contracts were sketchy and ambiguous, and their meaning was worked out in battles large and small. Few workers accepted the distinction between contract negotiation and contract administration; thus shop-floor assemblies, slowdowns, and stoppages proliferated during the first decade of the new industrial unions. Among workers, militancy and organization were dialectically dependent, building confidence and hope in a new and powerful synthesis. Direct shop-floor activity legitimized the union's presence for thousands of previously hesitant workers, and such job actions established a pattern of union influence and authority unrecognized in the early, sketchily written contracts.

Such a system of shop democracy flourished during the CIO's early years. At Studebaker it became standard practice for shop stewards to meet every morning to plan their approach to the day's work. Exercising effective control over the company's piece-rate pay system, they thought of the foremen as "just clerks." In the farm equipment industry, stewards held a veto over the work norms set by supervision, and at Armour's main Chicago plant, packinghouse union stewards developed a tactic they called "whistle bargaining." Each steward wore a whistle around his or her neck. Whenever a supervisor declined to discuss a grievance, the steward gave a blast on the whistle and the department halted work. When the issue was resolved, the steward whistled twice and production started once again.[14]

These militant unionists were not anarchists, nor did they pull "wildcat" strikes in a capricious or heavy-handed fashion. Rather they saw their activism and advocacy as but an argumentative defense of the work rights they expected the existing contract to embody. As the UAW advised, "Lawyers have been able to use a Constitution written over 150 years ago to cover the complex issues of modern life. A bright steward should be able to do just about as well with his contract."[15] Their efforts were frequently thwarted, but the task was of unequaled import: the construction, from the bottom up, of a system of industrial justice, custom, and entitlement.

No issue was more important than a defense of the seniority system. Today, the seniority idea is often derided as tantamount to the protection of incompetence, deadwood, and corruption. Managers want flexibility and vigor in their workforce, and in the corporate downsizings of recent years, those out the door have more often than not been the fifty-somethings with plenty of tenure behind a desk or counter. But the seniority idea cannot be dismissed quite so lightly. Its ethical basis lies in the respect and veneration all societies owe those of experience, age, and continuous tenure. Seniority was, and is, a key facet in the moral economy of American work life. Long before the New Deal, most companies paid lip service to the seniority idea, even as they enraged workers when they periodically broke it.[16]

Few American workers were so radical as to think that their union should actually run the factories. But a large majority were convinced that their tenure gave them a kind of "property right" in the job at which they labored and a first call upon any better one that opened up. In a worker's life cycle, the codification of a workplace seniority right embodied a substantial element of that "security" for which FDR and other depression-era liberals spoke so fervently. By eliminating deference and favoritism, the seniority list generated a new realm of freedom and dignity. Thus, as a moral and political imperative, the importance of job seniority can hardly be overemphasized. When General Motors and the CIO signed their very first contract in March 1937, seniority provisions took up fully 35 percent of the six-page text.[17]

Midcentury executives hated such work rules and the system of shop steward power sustaining them because this new code of shop-floor rights seemed to threaten both the flexibility managers thought necessary to run an efficient workplace and their understanding of the deference they expected workers to pay their immediate supervisors. As an ideology of management practice and factory organization, Taylorism enjoyed its greatest impact during the half century that began in 1920. Its authoritarian, hierarchical influence was enhanced by the demands of the U.S. war effort, when so many executives analogized their mass production effort to that of a military combat structure in which officers (executives) commanded the sergeants (foremen), who told the rank and file what to do. Union activism, especially that animated by shop-steward power, seemed a dire threat to this order. When industrial relations expert Neil Chamberlain surveyed six mass-production industries right after World War II, managers told him they were painfully aware that this kind of union activism had eroded their shop authority. "We recognize that in some of our shops the union committeemen exercise greater authority than the foreman," acknowledged a rubber company executive. And in the auto industry, Chamberlain was informed, "If any manager in this industry tells you he has control of his plant, he is a damn liar."[18]

This situation was inherently unstable, even before the conservative turn in American politics after World War II put union militancy and shop activism under a cloud. Whatever its inherent legitimacy among rank-and-file workers, the shop traditions that periodically shut down the line or disrupted production subverted the very idea of a collective-bargaining agreement. Managers denounced such activism as illegimate "wildcat" stoppages that violated the contract and robbed collective bargaining of its usefulness. They complained that unless union leaders guaranteed labor peace during the life of an agreement, their incentive to bargain would disappear. And most union officials, from John L. Lewis and Sidney Hillman right down to the most radical local union leader, had to recognize the logic of this imperative, which is one reason that a tradition of shop syndicalism never quite achieved the kind of legitimacy in the post-1940 era that it had won during the era of the Industrial Workers of the World a generation before.[19]

However, industrial unionists and their policy-making allies thought they had found a solution to their dilemma—in grievance arbitration. Here was the essence of the new industrial democracy, a jurisprudence that moved grievances up through the factory hierarchy, from foreman to plant manager to top personnel executive. Unionists and managers argued away at each step, offering evidence and witnesses in lawyerlike fashion. Finally, an impartial arbitrator, often a law or economics professor, made the final adjudication. This system had been born in the chaotic garment trades, where the arbitrators were all-around "fixers," and then was adopted wholesale by the labor and management in the mass production industries, especially after the War Labor Board insisted that such a system was essential if the unions were to honor the no-strike pledge they offered the nation right after Pearl Harbor. For the life of each contract, it promised industrial peace, productive order, and a measure of shop-floor justice. A wartime arbitrator hailed it as the substitution of "civilized collective bargaining for jungle warfare."[20]

For many years unionists considered this system a great victory because it deprived managers of yet more of their unilateral power within the enterprise. Workers could not be discharged without "just cause"; instead a system of "progressive discipline" ensured that most workers had a second or third or fourth chance. Arbitrators often tilted toward the union when it came to the systematic classification of jobs, the institution of equal pay for equal work, and the balance between "merit" and seniority when it came to in-plant promotions. Company executives complained about the inflexibility of the system, but the UAW's Walter Reuther summed up the laborite worldview when he told a wartime government panel: "We know that unless you have rules to govern the relationship of people, both Labor and Management, on the lower levels in the Agreement, unless these rules are explicit, you will revert back to where they pick this guy, not because he has potential, but because he lets the foreman run over him."[21]

The AFL Worldview

The rise of an industrial union model dominates our historical imagination when we recall the New Deal–era effort to engender a new

To constitutionalize the shop floor regime, workers had to take their grievances out of the mills. Here a Pennsylvania steel worker explains a dispute to an official of his union. (Credit: FSA/OWI Collection, Library of Congress)

industrial democracy at the workplace. But the CIO model was never entirely dominant, for the kind of unionism identified with the American Federation of Labor also enjoyed a renaissance that bears some scrutiny. Top AFL leaders were shocked by the dramatic emergence of the CIO in 1937, and for more than a decade, they waged organizational and political warfare against it. To understand their anger and their tactics, one must understand their worldview. Trade unionists like Samuel Gompers and his successor, William Green, AFL president after 1924, believed that the "House of Labor" must be autonomous and independent, the sole spokesman for all labor, whether organized or not. Because of its half-century experience with reactionary judges, hostile governors, and indifferent presidents, the AFL was far more skeptical of government power than the CIO, whose leaders were among the most enthusiastic boosters of the New Deal state and the Roosevelt cult. From this AFL perspective, unionism's greatest legislative triumph during the depression years was not the Wagner Act, but the 1932 Norris-LaGuardia law, which put an end to the injunctions and sweeping judicial orders that had crippled so many strikes and boycotts.[22]

The AFL hated the early NLRB, the activist, newly powerful government agency that tended to marginalize craft-union claims in favor of CIO-style bargaining units as most appropriate to the spirit of the industrial democracy idea. "We will mobilize our political and economic strength in an uncompromising fight until the Board is driven from power," declared AFL president Green in 1938, "The Board is a travesty on justice."[23] So bitter was this fight that the AFL joined with some of the new unionism's most steadfast enemies—GOP congressmen, lawyers for the National Association of Manufactures, and racist, labor-baiting legislators from the South—to thwart the NLRB and revise the Wagner Act. Such an unholy alliance soon made its impact felt. By 1941 Roosevelt had appointed men to the NLRB who respected craft-union traditions, and Congress began to pass laws targeted at the strikes and political activities of the industrial unions (they were usually vetoed by the president). State officials and legislatures became increasingly hostile to CIO-style industrial unionism, and the courts accommodated craft prerogatives while narrowing the capacity of the industrial unions to organize against intransigent employers.

It's easy enough to condemn this AFL strategy as self-serving, shortsighted, or worse. Politically, the AFL courted disaster, for the leaders of the craft federation split the union movement at just the moment when conservative forces were remobilizing against labor and the New Deal. By denouncing the Wagner Act as "unbalanced" and the NLRB as "left-wing" or "biased," the AFL opened the door to a decade of conservative assault that culminated in passage of the Taft-Hartley Act, denounced by both AFL and CIO as a "slave labor law."[24] But there was a certain logic to this AFL madness, which might well hold some insight for the dilemmas faced by American unionists two generations on.

The AFL objected in particular to the NLRB's statist presumptions. That agency's power to determine the appropriate size and makeup of a union's bargaining unit and then conduct an election to determine the will of the workers in that unit seemed to undermine an older, more autonomous tradition of trade unionism. For more than half a century the AFL had jealously guarded its right to organize the world of work as it saw fit. Thus each union claimed "exclusive jurisdiction" over its trade or industry, which in practice meant that the AFL was often more interested in "organizing" the employer than the workers. "We didn't want the workers," remembered AFL-CIO president George Meany, who got his union start in a Bronx plumber's local. "We merely wanted the work. So far as the people that were on the work were concerned . . . they could drop dead."[25] Thus secret-ballot, majority-rule determinations of the will of the employees at a particular work site were unnecessary, even dysfunctional. As these anti-statists saw it, a dedicated cadre of committed unionists fought for all the workers in their trade: by their presence and their power they achieved the legitimacy that won employer recognition and worker allegiance, regardless of the outcome of any formal vote or referendum. Many AFL leaders therefore saw the emergence after 1939 of a frequent, bitterly contested set of NLRB-supervised jurisdictional contests as an affront to the dignity and purpose of their organization. These government-run elections were a product, first, of the intense AFL-CIO rivalry, and then, of a set of NLRB rulings that for a time devalued craft-union claims and made the state's certification election just about the only way a union could achieve recognition from an employer.[26]

The Craft Alternative

Despite the AFL's growing alienation from the main currents of New Deal labor reform, the unions that remained within the Federation flourished after 1937. The AFL reaped many benefits from the upsurge of worker militancy and industrial unionization. Once insular AFL leaders such as Teamsters' president Dan Tobin and Carpenters' president William Hutcheson saw the CIO successfully campaigning within what they considered their jurisdictions, they began organizing the same workers they had previously scorned. The Machinists, the Boilermakers, and the International Brotherhood of Electrical Workers actually transformed many of their affiliated locals into industrial unions so as to compete directly with the CIO. And in meatpacking, food processing, shipbuilding, and the retail trades, the AFL more or less transformed itself into an industrial union competitor to the CIO. The success of the AFL was greatly aided by the not-so-covert appeal it often made to many anti-union employers. On the whole, AFL unions failed to advance the shop-steward system pushed by the early CIO, they were often overtly racist, and they proclaimed themselves champions of an aggressive brand of anti-Communism. Employers were therefore often happy to negotiate with AFL unions and sign "sweetheart" contracts in order to avoid "Lewis's Reds."[27]

The Teamsters union was one of the most important of the AFL success stories. Before the depression, their ranks had been limited to truck drivers hauling goods within a few of the nation's big cities. But after radicals in Minneapolis demonstrated that organizing warehousemen and other goods handlers could strengthen the union, Teamster locals throughout the nation began recruiting workers whom even the CIO ignored: men—and they were almost always men in the late 1930s—whose episodic and unskilled labor on the loading docks and in the warehouses put them at the very bottom of the white working class. The Teamsters also began signing up long-distance, intercity drivers. Within five years, the union had grown to 440,000 members and raised wages substantially in the motor transport industry. Teamster success was not a product of mobster "muscle," although young organizers like Jimmy Hoffa and William Brennen in Detroit were not afraid to wage violent strike battles against employers or rival unions. Instead, innovative organizing tactics, tailored to the new consumer-goods distribution industry, proved the key to rapid union growth. Along the Pacific Coast and throughout the Upper Midwest, the Teamsters deployed the "hot cargo" boycott with particular efficacy. By blockading shipments from non-union firms, the Teamsters were able to cripple hostile employers even before they had begun to sign up the truckers. Then Teamster organizers used this market leverage to "leapfrog" into hostile territory, telling both workers and their bosses that adherence to a regionwide trucking contract would generate stability through uniform rates and wages. In this fashion the Teamsters unionized the trucking barns of Omaha, Kansas City, Memphis, and Los Angeles, queen city of the open shop. By 1960 the Teamsters, with two millions members, were the nation's largest union.[28]

But the craft unionism that stood at the ideological center of the old AFL also enjoyed a new burst of health because this model of worker representation defended a set of work rights in a fashion often superior to that of the CIO itself. Craft unionism, which dominated the printing trades, the construction industry, precision manufacturing, and the new airline industry was predicated upon the union's capacity to monopolize the labor market in a specific skill or trade. Craft unionists were therefore fiercely committed to the defense of the general "employment" security of their members, rather than the "job" security of particular workers at specific work sites. They insisted upon a "closed shop" which meant that workers must join the union before they secured employment in their trade or occupation. The union's key regulatory institution was the hiring hall that the craft local—if it proved strong enough—forced employers to use when they sought a work crew for a particular task. From the hiring hall, the union assigned the work, rotated and rationed the available jobs, and evaluated the skill of the workers. Indeed, the craft unions frequently enrolled first-line supervisors, whose relationship to the rest of the work crew was less that of an industrial "driver" than that of an experienced coordinator of the work. This meant that craft unionists were uninterested in a defense of the elaborate seniority systems that so engaged the industrial unions; nor did they put much stake in grievance arbitration, because if workers lost their jobs, they merely cycled back through the hiring call and soon found other positions of similiar skill and remuneration. Thus did Matt Smith, who spoke for skilled tool-and-die workers in the auto industry, denounce what he called the CIO's "all pervading seniority racket."

> Now a worker's economic life is controlled by his position on the job expectancy list of some company. . . . No worker in his right mind now travels from one city or state to another looking for work. . . . This vicious system has resulted in workers being as securely tied to a certain employer as the old serfs were fastened to a specific landowner. Workers do not bother about getting more experience. The tree of knowledge is neglected—the only important thing is to get firmly established in the upper branches of the seniority tree."[29]

Waitresses and longshoremen were two unlikely groups of workers who made effective use of a craft, or to use the phrase of historian Dorothy Sue Cobble, of the "occupational" model of trade unionism.

Waitresses defined themselves as female food servers; for them, any work that hinted of food preparation, pantry duties, or cleaning was proscribed by the union bylaws and the collective bargaining agreement. Culinary employers relied on the hiring halls maintained by the Hotel Employees and Restaurant Employees International Union in cities like San Francisco, Chicago, and Butte for a steady supply of "good and reliable" full-time workers. Women workers found this hiring arrangement particularly useful because it gave them, rather than the employer, control over when and how much they worked. As long as they maintained their union standing, waitresses could quit a job and "lay off" to take care of the child-rearing or other domestic duties that fell to their lot. On the job, the union wage scale set the minimum pay, but in many contracts "first-class help" could earn much more.[30]

Longshoremen were among the classic proletarians of the first half of the twentieth century: unskilled casual laborers hired each morning at the dockside "shape-up" for a few hard hours of work with sling and hook. After the "Uprising of '34," the International Longshoremen's and Warehousemen's Union (ILWU), which would soon affiliate with the CIO, abolished the shape-up all along the West Coast and substituted a union-run hiring hall that decasualized the work and gave to these once-despised "wharf-rats" high wages, political clout, and unprecedented control over their cargo-handling work. They called themselves the "Lords of the Dock," so that by the 1950s membership in the ILWU was a ticket to some of the most sought-after blue-collar jobs in Long Beach, Honolulu, Oakland, San Francisco, Portland, Seattle, and Vancouver.[31]

Occupational unionism thus had a certain radical, democratic potential, but the disrepute into which this form of unionism fell at midcentury was hardly misplaced, certainly not among those who looked to the New Deal—era labor movement as a wellspring of social transformation. The big craft unions of that era—the carpenters, the plumbers, the railroad brotherhoods—were politically conservative, racially and sexually exclusive, and ill equipped to manage technological change. As we shall see, CIO-style industrial unions shared many of these same problems, but the very structure of the craft-union setup exacerbated these tendencies. Their obsessive determination to monopolize the labor market usually meant that African Americans and women were excluded from membership; indeed in many instances, union eligibility was limited to a particular ethnic group or even to the offspring of current members. In Brooklyn the longshoremen were almost invariably Italian, on the Chelsea piers they were Irish, and from Baltimore southward predominantly African American. Northern Europeans dominated the electrical trades in most big cities, while Germans, Bohemians, and Anglo-Gaelic immigrants for a time maintained a union of skilled metal craftsmen even within the heart of the mass-production auto industry. On the railroads racial and ethnic hierarchies were endemic to the structure of work. Blacks were excluded from the top positions of conductor and engineer, and only in the South could they work, for a time, in the second-level jobs of locomotive firemen and brakemen. Indeed, in the 1920s and 1930s white firemen waged a bloody, two-decade-long war to eliminate African Americans from their brotherhood.[32]

Such racial and ethnic exclusiveness made the craft unions an ally of the old order: gangsters actually ran some locals, nepotistic families presided in many others. Thus in Baltimore, Memphis, San Francisco, New York, Detroit, and other unionized cities, craft unions supported municipal and state politicians who stood against the New Deal and the liberal-labor coalition that sought to perpetuate its program. The Detroit Federation of Labor supported racist, reactionary mayoral candidates against the liberals championed by the UAW; in New York the powerful, corrupt International Longshoremen's Association backed Tammany Hall, not the New Dealish coalition presided over by Fiorello La Guardia.[33] In postwar Chicago, the powerful construction trades became part of the patronage machine whose most famous chief was Richard Daley; and in Memphis, the craft-dominated labor council denounced as an "outside agitator" Martin Luther King when he led marches in support of municipal sanitation workers in the days just before his assassination in 1968. Today, California's powerful union of penitentiary guards has established itself as one of that state's most determined advocates of a huge prison system and the draconian laws necessary to keep its inmate population growing.[34]

Compounding these problems was the incapacity of many craft

unions to adapt to technological change. This was not endemic to their structure, because skilled workers can often leapfrog from an obsolete technology to one at the forefront of production efficiency. The Teamsters moved from horses to trucks, the locomotive engineers from coal to diesels, and the carpenters from wood to many of its substitutes. But because of their obsession with the control of a certain technological niche, craft unions are vulnerable to employer deployment of a new work process or technique that disrupts, or eliminates outright, their labor monopoly. This happened in longshoring, where cargo containerization replaced the stevedore gang after 1960; in plumbing construction, where plastic pipe de-skilled the installation job; and it enabled managers in the newspaper business to slash the power and pay of the printing trades, whose legendary control of the press room evaporated with the computerization of the industry. Deployment of new technologies can also eliminate the jobs of workers organized on an industrial basis, but because workers are primarily attached to a company, and not a trade, those with high seniority have won some protection from the transformation in the technics of production. In contrast, craft unionists who have defended an outmoded or redundant organization of work might temporarily win a battle, but they almost always lost the war, both ideological and occupational. The word "featherbedding" gained widespread currency in 1943, when the railroad unions sought to keep firemen employed on locomotives that no longer ran on wood or coal. Unions often claimed that such overstaffing ensured a safer work environment, but whatever the merits of the case, featherbedding and other sorts of "dummy" work violated popular notions of efficiency and fairness, to the detriment of the entire trade union idea.[35]

Breaching the Color Line

"The problem of the twentieth century," wrote W. E. B. DuBois at the dawn of that century, "is the problem of the color line." The line divided the working class and its institutions as thoroughly and brutally as it did every other aspect of American life. Indeed, people of color in the United States have, until the last few decades, been almost entirely a working-class population. Thus, if the labor question were to have any sort of resolution during the twentieth century, then the extent to which the unions and their erstwhile allies in government redrew the color line would determine the validity of the solutions put forward.

The abolition of state-sponsored racism is commonly thought a product of the civil rights movement of the 1950s and 1960s. But the trajectory of that movement is more accurately traced if we understand that its modern origins lay in the reform of labor relations that began during the New Deal era itself. As we have seen, the craft unions were almost without exception racial and ethnic exclusionists. Their effort to control the local labor market reinforced and codified the prejudices and preferences of both workers and employers. In the decades before midcentury this craft union apartheid proved so successful and so monolithic that it seemed almost invisible. In most of the more skilled building-construction crafts, in transport occupations like the locomotive engineers and over-the-road truck driving, in craft unions requiring a long apprenticeship, racial issues were nearly nonexistent because racial exclusion was so customary and so complete.

Not so with the mass-production industries or the unions that arose to reorder labor relations within the nation's factories, shipyards, and mills. During the heyday of the CIO, a demographic revolution had begun to transform the nation's African American population, and to a lesser extent its Hispanic, Filipino, and Puerto Rican people, transforming them from rural, agricultural laborers into some of the most proletarian, urban elements of the working population. By 1940 nearly half of all African Americans were city dwellers, and during World War II, another 10 percent of the Southern black population moved to the urban North.

This great migration was enormously significant because of the strategic edge it gave to this overwhelmingly working-class population. African Americans were moving to the North at a moment when the voting population of the nation's largest cities constituted the backbone of the Rooseveltian coalition. African Americans switched their historic allegiance from the GOP to the Democrats during the 1934 and 1936 elections; by 1948 Northern Democrats had become routinely solicitous of their votes.[36] Moreover, in a pattern quite different from that of the nineteenth century—or the late twentieth—African American men who migrated out of the rural South were drawn to jobs that often lay at the very heart of industrial America. The work was dirty, dangerous, and poorly paid, but it was vital, essential to the production process itself: by 1940 thousands of blacks could be found on the killing floor in the packinghouses of Chicago, in the giant production foundry at River Rouge, as blast-furnace and coke-oven "helpers" in Pittsburgh and Gary, and belowdecks on many an oceangoing steamer.

If these industries were to be organized, and if the union strike weapon was to have any potency, then the loyalty of African Americans and other racial minorities had to be won. This task could not be taken for granted, because white working-class racism and craft-union exclusion had made African Americans skeptical bystanders when it came to the fate of the U.S. labor movement. African Americans had often served as strikebreakers during the great strikes of 1919, and as late as 1934, they were noticeably unenthusiastic about the New Deal reform of labor relations. In tobacco processing and other labor-intensive Southern work, NRA minimum-wage standards encouraged mechanization and the elimination of African American workers. Some blacks labeled it the "Negro Removal Act." Meanwhile, in Baltimore, New York, Chicago, and other large cities, African Americans launched "Don't Buy Where You Can't Work" campaigns, insisting that white-owned stores in black communities hire black clerks and sales people. In the early 1930s these protests had a Garveyite (black nationalist), and sometimes an anti-Semitic flavor, culminating in the Harlem riot of 1935. Not unexpectedly, many black organizations, like the Urban League and the NAACP, remained standoffish as the union movement revived, and many African American workers still looked to paternalistic employers, like Henry Ford or even the Pullman Company, as their economic saviors.[37]

Herrenvolk Democracy

If all this were not enough, white working-class racism saturated American political culture during the midcentury decades. This was the era in which the "whiteness" of so many immigrant Americans took on a sharper, more well-defined edge. Fraternal organizations of the foreign born, which had once reaffirmed the cultural and political heritage of many second-generation ethnics, lost thousands of members in the 1930s and 1940s. As a consequence, American Catholics—Polish and Italian as well as Irish—abandoned much of what remained of their defensive ghetto mentality. Indeed, the recomposition of an ethnically heterogeneous, episodically employed proletariat into the self-confident, increasingly homogeneous "white" working class of the postwar era was a product of New Deal liberalism itself. The sense of social entitlement generated by the New Deal and the new unions, immediately followed by an entire male generation's participation in the still-segregated military, provided the institutional and ideological basis for a new Americanization movement that subordinated older ethnic identities within a transcendent sense of whiteness.[38]

In many factories and mills white workers came to see their committeemen and union seniority system as protectors of a new sort of property right to the job. If security was a watchword of the New Deal and the new unionism, it now came into conflict with the new rights consciousness generated by African Americans seeking an entrée into the mainstream of blue-collar industrial life. In steel mills, shipyards, and auto plants, the emergence of trade unionism froze in place many of the segregated, hierarchical job structures originally generated by pre-union managerial practice and a racially stratified labor market. In the negotiation of a new set of seniority rights and job progressions, many white workers favored the kind of "departmental" seniority system that ratified a discriminatory system of preference and segregation, even over those black workers with longer plantwide seniority. In the steel industry, for example, black workers who started in the hot, noisy blast furnaces won job security after a few years, but only if they remained in that segregated occupation. Most union leaders had neither the will nor the power to recast such Jim Crow hiring and promotion practices. If government officials or racial liberals sought to abridge this system, they courted violent racial conflict, as during World War II, when a spectacular wave of "hate" strikes shut down scores of factories and shipyards.[39]

Racial apartheid proved the norm outside the factories as well.

The new unionism did little to end the social and residential segregation pervasive in working-class America. Although union meetings were integrated—and often the very first biracial event workers of either race had attended—activities that even hinted at "social equality" remained a flash point. "If you ask them to your dances, they'll come and they won't just dance with each other," the white president of a SWOC women's auxiliary complained, "but some of them will try to dance with white people. . . . There's something about colored men that just makes you afraid."[40] Workers lived in segregated housing, went to segregated schools, and attended segregated churches. In the world of Chicago's packinghouse workers, reports historian Roger Horowitz, "a social and cultural apartheid" separated Poles and Lithuanians from their black coworkers. Railroad yards, warehouses, and a hostile Irish neighborhood lay between the Slavic Back of the Yards and the all-black South Side neighborhood a mile to the east. "We only saw the colored when we were at work or coming home," recalled Polish packinghouse worker Gertie Kamarczyk, "we just kept to ourselves and they did too."[41]

Although Northern white workers remained staunch New Deal Democrats, they fiercely defended residential apartheid through the 1940s and 1950s. As Thomas Sugrue, Kenneth Durr, and John McGreevy have shown in such graphic detail, this white defensive militancy became the submerged rock upon which so much postwar labor-liberalism would splinter. During World War II and afterward the effort of blacks to move into white working-class neighborhoods met with well-organized, often violent opposition. In Detroit during the two decades after 1945, there were at least two hundred instances in which white homeowners violently resisted residential integration. White workers saw their racially exclusive neighborhood as but another New Deal entitlement, ratified well into the postwar era by restrictive mortgage covenants and FHA lending regulations that practically mandated a segregated suburbia. Such racial polarization on the home front had its political reflection as well. In Baltimore, Detroit, Chicago, Boston, and other centers of labor strength, municipal politics had a hard racial edge well before George Wallace, Richard Nixon, and other national politicians deployed the "white backlash" of the 1960s and 1970s to win working-class votes. In Detroit, where one might have expected the UAW to play a decisive role in local politics, union leaders faced defeat after defeat in the mayoralty contests of the 1940s, when white rank and filers spurned those labor-liberals who favored public housing, neighborhood integration, and a fair employment law.[42]

"Negro and White: Unite and Fight"

Such were the difficulties, but the union movement that emerged in these years nevertheless proved a powerful weapon deployed by people of color in their fight for dignity and citizenship at midcentury. To this battleground, the CIO brought both new ideas and new forms of struggle. Ideology was less significant than practice, but rhetoric was nevertheless important in a country where, even on the Left, a color line had been accommodated for more than three generations. For example, in pre–World War I California, trade-union militancy had been synonymous with the most thoroughgoing set of anti-Asian polemics; and in the East and South many lodges of the once-socialist International Association of Machinists excluded African Americans from membership well into the twentieth century. Socialists like Jack London, not to mention AFL stalwarts like Samuel Gompers, argued that Asians, African Americans, and other nonwhite people represented a sort of vast, worldwide lumpen proletariat, unschooled in the ethics of solidarity, eager to serve capital, and thus subversive of white wages and living standards.[43]

At the leadership level, blatant racism of this sort became rare in the years after 1935. Officials of the CIO, like Philip Murray, who presided over the drive in steel, forthrightly promised that "there shall be no discrimination under any circumstances, regardless of creed, color, or nationalities." ILWU president Harry Bridges gave an anti-fascist inflection to racial liberalism in 1945 when he asserted his union's "unequivocal" commitment to "equality for all." To do otherwise "would be to pick up the banner of fascism where Hitler dropped it."[44] And at union meetings throughout the CIO, officers and members addressed each other as "brother" or "sister" regardless of race.

But a kernel of the old racialism echoed on, even within formal union ideology. Until the end of the 1930s, progressive labor leadership had taken its inspiration from the socialist tradition. Eugene Debs, William Haywood, and Norman Thomas had put the difficulties confronting black workers and white firmly within a class framework, perhaps too firmly. Non-Communist CIO progressives saw the "Negro question" as but a function of a larger class inequity. Walter Reuther, whose labor radicalism had been shaped by the Debsian politics of his father, thought "racial tensions and hostility toward minorities . . . a product of irrational emotions and impulses . . . bred and grown strong in an economic environment of scarcity." Only in a new world of economic abundance can "the Negro hope to end his tragic search for justice." Likewise, Philip Murray warned that the "need for a full employment program must be satisfied *before* we can answer the question of what will happen" to the Negro in the post–World War II economy. Thus African American liberation would be a product of labor's victory, not a precondition for that advance.[45]

This perspective ran parallel to the main body of New Deal thought on the race question. Rooseveltian liberals, foremost among them FDR himself, were infamously timid when it came to making a direct assault on Southern racial norms. To his NAACP critics, the president argued that the New Deal's economic reforms were held hostage by Southern congressional Bourbons, who threatened to exercise a powerful veto if his administration conflated an assault on Dixie's racial hierarchy with the rest of the administration's labor- and social-reform program. Like their CIO cousins, New Deal liberals initially believed that the economic transformation of the South would itself undermine Jim Crow conditions. Thus FDR's 1938 "Report on the Economic Conditions in the South," written by some of the most pro-labor of the Southerners in his administration, avoided almost all mention of racial issues.[46]

This rather deterministic solution to the "Negro question" was replaced within just a few years by a far more forceful perspective whose politics were summed up in the Communist slogan of the 1930s: "Negro and White: Unite and Fight." Communist advocacy of this slogan is ironic because, during the early 1930s, Communists thought of African Americans in the United States as a "national" minority, akin to that of the Latvians or Ukrainians in the old Russian Empire, for whom "self-determination" stood at the top of the political agenda. With the coming of the Popular Front later in the 1930s this ultraradicalism would moderate, but it left an extraordinarily important legacy—to the Left, to the labor movement, and to the pluralist content of American progressive politics.[47]

For all their crude Stalinist instrumentalism, the Communists set the ideological standard by which American labor-liberalism would come to measure racial progress. Formal equality between African Americans and whites would not be limited to the work site or to the union membership roster. It must prevail at every level of existence: in the courts and at the ballot box, certainly, but also in the realm of social life: the neighborhoods, schools, summer camps, dance halls, and marriage beds. This was a startling breakthrough, quite different from antebellum abolitionists or the generation of Progressives who had founded the NAACP a quarter century before. To the black community the Communists advertised their new racial militancy when in 1931 they launched a nationwide campaign to defend nine African American youths accused of raping two white women on a train near Scottsboro, Alabama. Although the *Chicago Defender* had distanced itself from much of the Communist Party (CP) agenda, the paper's African American editor nevertheless marveled at "the zealousness with which [the CP] guards the rights of the Race."[48] Outside the white South, the bugaboo of "social equality" lost most of its punch as the depression years waned. Within the unions, even those led by Communists, racial practices diverged substantially from racial ideology, but after 1940 no labor leader could appear as anything but a racial liberal if he or she aspired to national influence.[49]

But the slogan "Negro and White: Unite and Fight" cannot be taken at face value. It requires a further bit of deconstruction. The operative word here is "fight," not "unite," because our post-1954 understanding of "integration" was hardly on the agenda even of left-wing labor in the 1930s and 1940s. Given the racism that saturated so much of American society, including the far reaches of the labor movement, "unity" might well imply the subordination of black aspirations to that of white. As C. L. R. James put it, "'Black and White,

Unite and Fight" is unimpeachable in principle. . . . But it is often misleading and sometimes even offensive in the face of the infinitely varied, tumultuous, passionate, and often murderous reality of race relations in the United States."[50]

Therefore racial militancy in the labor movement had a historically specific quality during the heyday of the CIO. Crucial to this impulse was an understanding that African Americans needed their own leaders, stewards, campaigns, even their own unions, within the labor movement, so as to ensure that their "national" interests had a hearing. Racial militants did not so much advocate "integration" per se—the word was absent from the labor movement during the 1940s—but sought instead nondiscrimination, fair employment, political enfranchisement, higher pay, and equal pay. African Americans and their allies in the union movement fought for power, income, and racial dignity; integration and desegregation might well be products of this struggle, but they were secondary to the main objective. As we shall see in chapter 5, by the time integration emerged as a key element on the labor-liberal agenda, it represented an actual devaluation of this laborite perspective.[51]

By the end of World War II a half million black workers had joined unions affiliated with the CIO. A Rosenwald Fund study concluded, not without misgivings, that "the characteristic movements among Negroes are now for the first time becoming proletarian," while a *Crisis* reporter found the CIO a "lamp of democracy" throughout the old Confederate states. "The South has not known such a force since the historic Union Leagues in the great days of the Reconstruction era."[52] The 1941 strike at the Ford Motor Company proved the high-profile event that symbolized the inauguration of a generation-long alliance between black workers and the new industrial unions. When the UAW struck the great Rouge production complex in Dearborn, where African Americans constituted nearly 20 percent of the sixty thousand who labored there, the rejection of Ford paternalism by this strategic minority assured both a union victory that spring and the subsequent labor alignment of virtually all elements of Detroit's black community. Within the Rouge the unionization process, particularly radical in its reorganization of shop-floor social relations, helped generate a talented, heavily politicized cohort

By 1941 African-Americans had inaugurated a new era of civil rights activism. (Credit: FSA/OWI Collection, Library of Congress)

of activists whose presence was soon felt at every level of the UAW, within the NAACP and the Urban League, and in the polarized world of Detroit politics.[53]

In the vanguard of such racial progressivism were a set of black-led unions that emerged as a powerful voice that spoke for all African American workers. Under the superb leadership of A. Philip Randolph, the Brotherhood of Sleeping Car Porters took advantage of the prolabor mood in the 1930s to win from the Pullman Company union recognition, higher wages, job security, and a cut in hours for the 35,000 African American and Filipino porters and maids who comprised the union's rank and file. Pullman porters lived in every major railroad town, so their jobs and paychecks were now protected by a union with a signed contract. Thus Randolph led an army of sturdy citizen-workers who soon made their weight felt on the civil rights frontier. In 1941 the Brotherhood proved the backbone for Randolph's March on Washington Movement, which successfully sought a Roosevelt Administration guarantee of "fair employment practices" in the new defense industries.[54]

And just a few years later other black-led unionists demonstrated their political potency as well. African Americans had taken the leadership of an important set of local unions at Swift and Armour in Chicago, in key Detroit foundries, at Reynolds Tobacco in Winston-Salem, and the cotton compress mills of Memphis. The white-led hate strikes of World War II were countered by African American demonstrations, strikes, and political mobilizations in those very same factories. As working-class African Americans flooded in, the Detroit chapter of the NAACP became the largest in the nation, 24,000 strong. As St. Clair Drake and Horace Cayton pointed out in 1945, the rise of the CIO generated new opportunities for black empowerment. Negroes did not "dismantle their *racial* organizations," because "they believe that their bargaining power *within* the labor movement will be strengthened if they stick together."[55] The energy and activism that emerged out of these new sites of black empowerment generated a cohort of post–World War II civil rights activists. The Brotherhood's most famous rank and filer was E. D. Nixon, the Montgomery NAACP leader who recruited Martin Luther King, Jr. to the leadership of that city's historic bus boycott. Likewise, Emmett

Till's 1955 Mississippi lynching became an international cause célèbre, not because of its brutality or uniqueness, but because the black teenager's Chicago relatives had the political and financial support of the Second City's enfranchised black community and its union-based civil rights movement.

Shop-Floor Citizenship

In both North and South black America was resolutely pro-union: African Americans signed their dues cards early, voted union when the NLRB conducted a ballot, and stayed out on strike even when their white brothers and sisters began to cross the picket lines. In the South this union consciousness proved an actual embarrassment to those CIO leaders who feared that white workers would reject any union seen as an essentially black, "nigger-loving" organization. Not unexpectedly, the proportion of all unionists who were African American increased steadily during the postwar era: by 1960 African Americans were more likely to be union members than any other ethnic or racial group.[56]

And such pro-union sentiment extended to the entire African American population. In 1958, for example, conservatives expected to win a sizable chunk of the black vote in their effort to enact anti-union, "right-to-work" statutes in several Northern states. African Americans were well aware that many craft unions were notoriously exclusionary. Moreover, in the 1950s blacks still gave up to 30 percent of their vote to Republican candidates. But the right-wing effort to win over the minority vote proved an utter failure. In Ohio and California, African Americans, in unions or not, voted against "right-to-work" by more than 90 percent, which was a more decisive margin than that of even white trade unionists.[57]

How do we explain this remarkable degree of union consciousness? White working-class racism saturated American political culture, so it is therefore all the more remarkable that the union movement still remained the most favorable midcentury terrain upon which racial liberalism could flourish and African Americans advance their interests. The paradox is resolved, or at least understood, when we realize that both for the new immigrants and for people of color, the new unionism brought a semblance of citizenship rights to the shop floor. The New Deal and the new unions put in place a set of legal structures, bureaucratic procedures, and social expectations that "enfranchised" millions of African Americans years before the demise of the poll tax, the white primary, and the segregated school. Despite all the racism and segregation that can be found in the midcentury workplace, CIO-style unionism—with its signed contracts, seniority rights, clearly defined wage scales, shop stewards, and grievance procedures—generated a kind of industrial citizenship that stood against the paternalism, deferential subordination, and violence of the old order.

To African Americans, as well as other "un-Americans" long subject to the capricious exercise of an ethnically coded set of discriminations, the very bureaucratization of labor relations inherent in mass unionization had an impact that was liberating in the world of daily work life. Unionism forced the company to pay "the job not the man," asserted a black Birmingham steel worker. Likewise, packinghouse worker William Raspberry well understood the security generated by this form of shop-floor constitutionalism. "CIO came along and said, well, if you get on a job, from the day you're hired, your seniority starts. And whoever comes behind you, gets behind you. Color has nothing to do with it."[58]

CIO organizer and publicist Lucy Randolph Mason, who visited Memphis just after black workers had organized there, offered yet another description of how a sense of organized empowerment replaced the old factory paternalism. A newly elected black union officer told her that "his boss came by his workplace and said, 'Are you feeling good?' and I said 'yes.' Then he said 'How did you like that three cents an hour raise I gave you last week?' I said, 'The committee will talk to you about that.'" Such curt assertiveness would have been unthinkable, cause for firing or worse, before the union. But with a CIO presence on the shop floor, taking such an aggressive, well-defined position against the employer became reasonable behavior, part of a newly legitimate interpersonal relationship. We have moved here from deference and custom to order, democracy, and a new citizenship.[59]

Moreover, the kind of uniform wage raises generated by the New Deal and the trade unions disproportionately benefited African American workers. During the depression, black America had moved en masse to FDR and the New Deal because even the imperfect deployment of national standards for relief, industrywide wages, and other social provision had a dramatically beneficial impact on African Americans. "The really important thing about WPA is that it is a guarantee of a living wage," explained *Amsterdam News* reporter Carl Lewis after FDR's smashing Harlem victory in 1936. "It means Negroes don't have to work for anything people want to give them. This helps lift the standards of all Negroes, even those not on WPA."[60] Indeed, WPA and other government assistance programs enrolled the black poor well out of proportion to their numbers in the population, often to the acute embarrassment of New Deal officials. In Cleveland, Chicago, and rural Georgia alike, almost half of all WPA workers were African American in 1938. Likewise, union contracts that raised and rationalized the wage standard, which reduced or eliminated racial, regional, and occupational pay inequities, boosted black pay more than white. The 1940s proved a spectacular decade for African American income growth (it rose from 40 to 60 percent that of white), because full employment, union power, and wartime mobilization policy all worked to raise and nationalize industrial and agricultural pay standards. This was a phenomenon well understood by most African Americans, and even more so by the increasingly anti-union, anti–New Deal defenders of the New South's racial order.[61]

Although blacks and whites would not bowl together, eat together, or vote for the same municipal candidates, such racism had its limits, for a shared dependence on wage labor forced on the races cooperation, even "solidarity." Many local unions gave political recognition to Mexicans and African Americans where these minorities comprised a significant proportion of the workforce. They adopted the old United Mine Worker formula, where a black was put on the executive board or made a vice president. As a Kansas City packinghouse worker reminded his white brothers and sisters in 1944, African American labor was indispensable to their own success. The union would have failed, "if it hadn't been for the Negro joining with you. . . . We are not asking for favors. We will take what is coming to us."[62] Such recognition and representation might well degenerate into a purely ceremonial, Tammany Hall ritual, but in places like Memphis, Birmingham, Newport News, Houston, Jacksonville, Kansas City, and Atlanta the very presence of such interracial union leadership represented a radical challenge to the old order.

The Fair Employment Practices Commission

When it came to state policy, Franklin Roosevelt's 1941 executive order establishing a Fair Employment Practices Commission (FEPC) proved the most graphic fruit of this African American quest for industrial citizenship. For the first time since Reconstruction, the federal government had put racial discrimination itself on the national policy agenda. Like the National Recovery Administration, the National Labor Relations Board, and the Works Progress Administration, the FEPC was one of the New Deal's great mobilizing bureaucracies. With a committed interracial staff and an expansive mandate, it legitimatized black protest, asserting a new social right to fairness on the job and at the hiring gate. As Gunnar Myrdal put it in *An American Dilemma*, FDR's executive order and the FEPC "represent the most definite break in the tradition of federal unconcernedness about racial discrimination on the nonfarm labor market. . . . They represent something of a promise for the future."[63] Unlike the NLRB, the FEPC worked with and through individuals, taking the complaints of specific workers, investigating their grievances, and issuing directive orders. Now, said the Urban League's Lester Granger, "[e]mployment is a civil right." And like the Freedman's Bureau of 1866, which wanted to put land into the hands of newly enfranchised blacks, the FEPC endorsed an industrial version of the new social citizenship. FDR himself ratified this advanced definition of New Deal liberalism in his 1944 State of the Union address in which he outlined "a second bill of rights under which a new basis of security and prosperity can be established for all—regardless of station, race, or creed."[64]

The FEPC mandate was broad, targeting discrimination not only against African Americans, but against Jews, Hispanics, and other minorities, although gender per se was not recognized as an actionable category. Its energetic interracial staff probed employment discrimination by employers, unions, and government agencies. As an administrative entity, the FEPC was pitifully weak, far more so than the NLRB or the Department of Labor, which was responsible for enforcing the Fair Labor Standards Act. The FEPC could do nothing to modify segregation in the armed forces; and in the South, federal nondiscrimination policy was little more than a legal fiction. In the Galveston shipyards, for example, African Americans worked at skilled jobs for the pay of unskilled helpers. When the FEPC filed three cases against the shipyard and one against a Boilermakers' Union local, other federal agencies declined to cooperate, so FEPC intervention proved ineffectual. On the other hand, the federal government often acted forcefully in the North. In Philadelphia, which was second only to Detroit as a center of war production, the FEPC and the War Manpower Commission ordered the city's transit system to promote eight African Americans to positions as streetcar drivers. When the system's white employees responded with a protest strike, closing down Philadelphia's entire transit system, the U.S. government sent in eight thousand soldiers to break the strike and enforce FEPC orders.[65]

The FEPC experience was important because the controversies that swirled about it prefigured the race and rights discourse that reemerged during the tumultuous season after Congress passed the 1964 Civil Rights Act. The wartime FEPC, and the Northern, state-fair employment commissions that emerged in the next decade, began to put in place many of the legal strategies and administrative techniques that proponents of "affirmative action" would follow three decades later. FEPC approached discrimination on a case-by-case basis, under a model of arbitration derived from CIO grievance procedures and WLB industrial adjudication. A parajudicial system of arbitrators would hear individual grievances and, if necessary, require employers to take corrective measures. But just as in the 1970s, these fair-employment commissions found that discriminatory intent was often difficult to prove against a particular employer who took advantage of a racially distorted labor market. Employment statistics by race and gender would have to be assembled, therefore, and the definition of what constituted a proper job "qualification" was soon subject to much debate and litigation.[66]

Despite the opposition it faced from Northern business and Southern oligarchs, as well as its own statutory weakness, the FEPC helped advance the new sense of militant industrial citizenship. "I am for this thing call Rights," a disgruntled African American women wrote to the FEPC. Soon a wave of direct, forceful action by black workers and their allies turned such rights-talk into action. African American employees at Chrysler's Dodge division walked out three times during 1941 to protest racial discrimination by both union and management. In 1943 three thousand black foundry men quit work over issues of job discrimination at the River Rouge complex. Shortly thereafter, an integrated crowd of ten thousand, carrying banners that proclaimed "Jim Crow Must Go" and "Bullets and Bombs Are Colorblind," marched to Detroit's Cadillac Square, where union and NAACP leaders joined together to declare that "full and equal participation of all citizens is fair, just, and necessary for victory and an enduring peace." There were at least twenty-two strikes by black workers during the next two years protesting employment discrimination in defense industries. For more than two decades this same labor-NAACP coalition constituted the backbone of the lobby effort that pushed Congress to enact a "permanent FEPC." Given the resistance of the white South and the suspicions of Northern capital, it would take something close to a social revolution in the 1960s to finally transform FEPC into Title VII of the 1964 civil rights act.[67]

A new sense of citizenship made itself manifest even during the race riots that scarred Mobile, Detroit, Los Angeles, and St. Louis during the summer of 1943. African American workers were not simply victims of white violence and prejudice. What is remarkable and "modern" about race relations after 1940 is the extent to which the black community stood its ground, found allies, and fought back. The "hate" strikes did not intimidate black industrial workers who used federal agencies, union grievance procedures, and NAACP protests to win their new job rights. And the wartime race riots resembled the insurgencies of the 1960s far more than they did the pogromlike white outbursts of the years before 1919. Like the riots of the World War I era, much violence arose when white crowds invaded black neighborhoods, but in 1943, African Americans also took to the streets in deadly confrontation with the police and white vigilantes.[68]

New Deal Masculinity

In sharp contrast to the rise of a new rights consciousness among African Americans, neither the new unionism nor the New Deal made much of an ideological assault upon the rigidly gendered structure of work and welfare during the midcentury decades. Feminism had an exceedingly low profile during the laborite mobilizations of the 1930s and 1940s. Indeed, for the first time since the rise of abolitionism, a major current of American reform failed to put women's rights high on its agenda. For most New Deal policy makers, working-class radicals, and social service administrators, the restoration of male dignity and livelihood stood at the center of concern. "Why not issue an order that all married women whose husbands are employed be dropped from payrolls?" advised a typical letter-writer to an NRA official. Hostility to jobs for married women, on the government payroll or not, was remarkably popular. In the 1930s George Gallup reported he had never seen people "so solidly unified in opposition as on any subject imaginable including sin and hay fever."[69] Not surprisingly, therefore, New Deal work relief initiatives systematically devalued women's work, both in the home and on the job. The Civilian Conservation Corps accepted no women, and of the millions of unemployed who participated in other New Deal work programs, less than 10 percent were women. The New Deal built roads and dams: teaching, child care, and public heath received a lower priority.[70]

Organized labor's poster and billboard iconography invariably portrayed the working-class movement as a powerful white male with muscles, even when the workers such imagery represented were women and dark-skinned. Official CIO pronouncements demanded "equal pay for equal work," but the sign carried by one male picket proved more eloquent and revealing: "Restore Our Manhood," it implored. "We Receive Girls' Wages."[71] The unions recruited almost 1 million women in the 1930s and added 2 million more in the next decade. Women unionists were found largely in the garment and

The proletarian New Deal was largely for men. (Credit: Works Project Administration Poster Collection, Library of Congress)

electrical products trades, in clerical and sales work, canning and tobacco processing. But even in industries where most workers were women, male union activists did not welcome female leadership. Thus those women who played leading roles in the labor movement were remarkably atypical: divorcees, widows, political radicals, or members of intensely union-conscious households. Meanwhile most working women were still young, unmarried, and living at home with their parents.

But the sexism of male unionists was not the only problem. African American men found that the shop-floor constitutionalism instituted by the new unions provided a favorable terrain upon which to advance their collective power and secure new political rights. However, this same focus on union contractualism put women workers at a distinct disadvantage, at least compared to the situation during the formative months and years of the labor movement, when a plebeian, communal impulse gave women a far larger and more legitimate function in the social struggle. In these early union-building episodes, women often played an essential role in linking the labor movement's shop activism to the larger community. Women workers were a key part in the labor upsurge when an organic element of that movement included rent strikes, soup kitchens, and neighborhood political mobilizations. A 1936 news story in Akron reported, "Shoulder to shoulder with their men, the wives, daughters, and sisters of strikers marched through the business district to strike headquarters in a great victory parade." But such dramatic linkages were far less important than the more subtle fashion in which women made the union impulse present throughout the neighborhoods and communities. Labor-based tenant organizations, soup kitchens, food cooperatives, recreation halls, singing societies, and education programs drew women workers as well as the wives and daughters of male unionists into a dense, supportive social network that thickened the ties of solidarity inside and outside the factory. Most unions organized women's auxiliaries, whose very existence testified to a sense of family solidarity.[72]

But once NLRB policy, union leadership, and popular consciousness came to define the contractual relationship at the work site as the essence of a successful union, the place for women's participation in the movement narrowed. Meetings were held less frequently, and at night, the women's auxiliaries declined or were replaced by women's departments inside the union bureaucracy, while the food cooperatives and drama workshops seemed increasingly superfluous. To the extent that organized labor ceased to manifest the flavor of a social movement, the role of women was increasingly defined as "auxiliary" to the work of these organizations. Except for the most left-wing of the unions, women's issues remained marginal to laborite ideology until the second wave of feminism arrived late in the 1960s.[73]

This did not mean that mass unionism could not have a large impact on the extent to which social citizenship was redefined in gender terms. During the 1930s many women had been excluded

Despite much union sexism, women played a vital role in building the CIO when the labor movement was still a community mobilization. (Credit: International Woodworkers of America, Ph 34, Special Collections & University Archives, University of Oregon)

from whole categories of employment on the basis of either their gender or their marital status. Banks, school boards, and some federal agencies simply fired women when they got married. Private employers excluded women from a majority of all industrial jobs and from most white-collar supervisory positions. And many trade unions, including those in the CIO, endorsed these discriminatory practices.

Indeed, unions themselves sought to ban women from many occupations, including typesetting, bus driving, and assembly-line work, on the grounds that employers would otherwise substitute cheap female labor in the place of more highly compensated men. As late as 1941 unionists at the Kelsey-Hayes Wheel Corporation conducted a successful, authorized strike demanding "the removal of all girl employees from machine work," after which the UAW adopted a formal resolution opposing "any attempt to train women to take the place of men on skilled jobs until such time as the unemployed men have been put back to work."[74]

Equal Pay for Equal Work

Institutional sexism of this sort was unsustainable during the war, when women workers took advantage of the labor shortage to fill hundreds of job categories once considered entirely "male." The number of employed women rose from 11 million to nearly 20 million. In electrical manufacturing, half of all workers were women by 1944. African American women, who had been largely confined to agricultural labor and domestic work before the war, made a dramatic and, in some instances, a bitterly resisted entry into higher-paying and more dignified factory, clerical, and sales work.

In response, the union movement reversed course and became the staunchest supporter of "equal pay for equal work." The men who led the unions feared that their managerial adversaries would use a tide of cheap women workers to erode male wage standards, if not during the war itself, then in the years afterward when unemployment might once again become a threat. Higher, equal wages for women would help forestall this assault by reducing capital's incentive to substitute female workers for male. The War Labor Board did mandate such equal pay for equal work in a landmark General Motors case of 1942. But like mainstream labor, its motivation was neither feminist nor even rights-conscious. Unlike concurrent rulings that denounced racial work classifications and pay inequities in language of the most soaring character, the wartime board justified wage equality for women in terms of efficient "manpower" utilization. Such a rationale was reinforced during the war by government propaganda that sounded a patriotic, but hardly a feminist, trumpet. "Instead of cutting the lines of a dress, this women cuts the pattern of aircraft parts," announced *Glamour Girls of '43*, a government newsreel. "Instead of baking a cake, this women is 'cooking' (her) gears."[75] This technosocial perspective became near hegemonic during the Cold War era when it was advocated even by antilabor Republicans seeking an efficient deployment of all available "manpower." "Whenever we refuse to put into operation this concept of equal pay for equal work," argued Arthur Flemming, President Eisenhower's secretary of health, education, and welfare, "we are just refusing to face the manpower aspects of our defense mobilization program in an intelligent and realistic manner."[76]

Such equal pay policies were not much of a victory for women, either in theory or practice. When they were actually implemented they did little to equalize male and female wages because the midcentury idea of "equal pay for equal work" did nothing to ameliorate the paternalism practiced by so many employers and unions toward their women workers. Nor did equal pay policies breach the walls that divided almost all jobs into those labeled for women or for men. During World War II federal agencies managed the great tide of young female workers by sex-segregating office work at the same time as they deployed much of the managerial paternalism inherent in the then faddish "human relations" theories that derived from the personnel work of Elton Mayo. In many white-collar workplaces, gender stereotypes were now embedded within the new science of personnel management.[77]

Meanwhile, as an even larger army of women entered the wartime factories, most employers maintained a de facto set of sex discriminations by dividing the work into jobs labeled "light" or "heavy," which simply moved, but did not eliminate, the gendered wage frontier. The United Electrical Workers (UE), whose workforce was nearly half female, aggressively petitioned the wartime mobilization agencies not only to eliminate the pay gap between men and women doing the same work, but also between those doing comparable work in sex-segregated jobs. The UE actually won its case in 1945, but with the end of the war, Westinghouse and General Electric refused to comply; indeed, they made the continuation of a female wage differential part of the management agenda during a set of bitter postwar strikes. For the next three decades comparable worth issues were off the public policy agenda, which is the main reason that employers mounted such flaccid opposition to the Equal Pay Act when Congress finally passed it in 1963.[78]

But the biggest obstacle to women's industrial citizenship did not actually arise from the pay discrimination they experienced or the job ghettos into which they fell in office or factory. Most women were burdened by a "double day" whose impact could be felt at every stage of their life cycle and their work "career." Given the set of patriarchal expectations and responsibilities borne by women during these mid-century decades, formal equality at the work site generated an inequitable, disparate impact on their overall pay, pensions, and career prospects. The work careers of women were far more episodic than those of men, and women tended to labor in low-wage, non-union industries such as textiles, laundries, retail trade and other service industries. Labor-liberals had long recognized this social inequity, which is why the trade unions, along with social feminists like Eleanor Roosevelt and Frances Perkins, had steadfastly opposed congressional enactment of an Equal Rights Amendment (ERA)—pushed forward by Alice Paul's National Women's Party—during the entire era from the 1920s until the rebirth of modern feminism in the late 1960s. The ERA mandated formal equality for women, but in doing so would eliminate much of the "protective" labor legislation passed on behalf of women workers during the Progressive era. Such protective legislation had often been based on a patriarchal definition of a woman's moral and physical capacity, but it nevertheless rested on an accurate understanding that for most working women, simple civil equality masked de facto discrimination and exploitation at the workplace. Thus the Republican Party and many employer groups endorsed the ERA during the 1940s and 1950s, just as organized labor, Northern Democrats, and almost all union women denounced it.[79]

Social feminists hoped that protective legislation for women workers would inevitably spread to all workers: their strategy found partial vindication in the 1938 Fair Labor Standards Act, which finally abol-

These unionized arc welders at North American Aviation in Inglewood, California would have a hard time holding on to their jobs after the end of World War II (Credit: Franklin D. Roosevelt Presidential Library)

ished most child labor, put a floor under factory wages, and rolled in the forty-hour workweek. Since women occupied many of the lowest and most vulnerable posts in the world of work, many expected that female workers would be disproportionately aided by a higher minimum wage, by the regulation of working time, and by other workplace protections and income supports.[80]

Unfortunately, the racial and gender assumptions of New Deal–era legislators, unionists, and policy makers made certain that the new social wage standards would help least those who needed them the most. As Alice Kessler Harris demonstrates in a careful exploration of New Deal–era social citizenship, implicit ideas about the extent to which a wage earner was a legitimate, independent "worker" shaped the differential access of all citizens to the new social benefits offered in the 1930s and the decades that followed. The inequitable character of the social wage that emerged from the legislative chamber was a product not just of the power wielded by Southern Bourbons and patriarchal unionists, for few New Deal architects of federal social policy could escape a set of invisible assumptions that privileged white male breadwinners and marginalized all those whose attachment to full-time work was insecure and whose work lives were spent in the fields, the kitchens, or in other occupations usually held by white women and African Americans of both genders.[81]

Thus unemployment insurance, which was funded as part of the 1935 Social Security Act, excluded 55 percent of all African American workers and 80 percent of all women workers, including more than 87 percent of wage-earning African American women. Likewise, the Fair Labor Standards Act covered only 14 percent of working women, compared to 39 percent of adult working men, when it was first enacted. Indeed, the depression-era minimum wage was so low that under its provisions no worker could earn the average weekly industrial wage in any state, even if he or she worked a forty-hour week. And when it came to Old Age Assistance (what we commonly call Social Security), New Deal policy makers had made such an ideological investment in a family characterized by female dependence on a male breadwinner that the payroll taxes paid by women bought far less insurance protection than those paid by men. It would take more than thirty years for Congress and the courts to rectify the imbalance.[82]

Beyond this system of federally financed social provision, the character of a community's child-care facilities, schools, housing, transport, and health provision determined for women, far more than for men, the degree to which they could take advantage of even the formal employment rights they might enjoy in the most well-unionized workplace. In the UAW as well as the Packinghouse Workers, women workers were not subject to overt, contractual discrimination. They had much the same pay and pension rights as men, but a union commitment to equal treatment on the job was not enough to level the field upon which women participated in the labor force. Given the responsibilities that so many wives and daughters were expected to meet when it came to pregnancy, child care, and family nurturance, their employment stability was invariably less than that of men. Thus women workers ended up with less seniority, lower pay, and poorer pensions than their male counterparts. Women's labor-force participation rates rose steadily after World War II, but the contractual formalism of even the most progressive unions made certain that women workers would remain second-class citizens.[83]

If a firm-centered system of collective bargaining could not resolve the female labor question, neither could it offer a satisfactory solution to the work life difficulties faced by other workers, whatever their gender, race, ethnicity, skill, or age. The quality of work site citizenship depended on the larger economic and political structures within which it was embedded. At the end of World War II virtually all union leaders recognized that any effort to provide security and dignity for their members required that they look well beyond the factory, mill, or office building where they held, or hoped to win, a union contract. The status of American labor could hardly be divorced from the larger questions posed by the postwar transformation of culture, politics, and community.

CHAPTER 3

A Labor-Management Accord?

DID A "LABOR-MANAGEMENT ACCORD" resolve the labor question in the prosperous years after the end of World War II? Many historians, policy makers, and labor partisans have argued that such a beneficent social compact governed industrial relations for nearly a third of a century, from 1947 until sometime in the late 1970s. Writing early in the 1980s economists Samuel Bowles, David Gordon, and Thomas Weisskopf were among the first scholars to retrospectively identify such a "tacit agreement between corporate capitalists and the organized labor movement." A. H. Raskin, the veteran labor reporter for the *New York Times*, simultaneously recorded the end of the post–World War II era: a "live-and-let-live relationship rather than endless confrontations." Then in the 1990s AFL-CIO president John Sweeney called for the restoration of the "unwritten social compact" between capital and labor. Sweeney, the son of a struggling New York bus driver, declared himself a "product of the social compact that lifted America out of the Great Depression and lifted working Americans into the middle class. . . . For employers back then, decent wages and benefits and high standards of corporate responsibility were seen as good business and good for business." Robert Reich, President Clinton's first secretary of labor, spent much of his tenure jawboning corporations to live up to their side of this presumptive accord.[1]

But the very idea of such a harmonious accord is a suspect reinterpretation of the postwar industrial era. Phrases like "social compact," "social contract," and "labor-capital accord" were first deployed in the early 1980s by liberals and laborites anxious to condemn wage cuts, denounce corporate union busting, and define what they seemed to be losing in Reagan's America. The terminology of social peace and cooperation used to describe industrial life in the pre-Reagan era was actually absent from the language of either labor or management during the 1950s and 1960s.

During the first two decades after World War II few unionists could have been found to declare their relationship with corporate America particularly agreeable or stable. Most would have thought the very idea of a "social compact" between themselves and their corporate adversaries a clever piece of management propaganda. In 1948, when C. Wright Mills published *The New Men of Power*, he found that 55 percent of labor leaders in the AFL and 69 percent of those in the CIO "feel that the threat of fascism in America is serious or is likely to become so in the near future." And in 1951 when *Fortune* magazine declared contemporary union workers "middle-class member[s] of a middle-class society," most trade-union officials scoffed at the claim.[2]

The 1940s and 1950s were years of historically high strike levels and of corporate-sponsored ideological warfare. Real wages doubled in the twenty years after 1947, but strikes were also ten times more prevalent than in the years after 1980. Moreover, if a certain industrial relations stability did come to characterize labor relations in core industries like auto and steel, it hardly characterized those growing sectors of the economy where wages were low, output labor intensive, and management militantly anti-union. And even in industries that were the very model of big-time collective bargaining, shop-floor conflict proved endemic and widespread. As Jack Metzgar reminds us in his moving account of steel unionism in the 1950s, the largest strike in American history took place in 1959 over issues not unlike those that motivated the Homestead combatants of 1892.[3]

Indeed, if such an accord could be said to exist during these years, it was less a mutually satisfactory concordat than a dictate imposed upon an all-too-reluctant labor movement in an era of its political retreat and internal division. At best it was a limited and unstable truce, largely confined to a well-defined set of regions and industries. It was a product of defeat, not victory.[4]

Politicized Bargaining

That defeat has a name, a legal construct, an institutional expression: it is "collective bargaining." Such a judgment will surely surprise many who have come to see, or been taught, that such periodic bargains—between the management of a single firm and its unionized workers—were the core function of organized labor in the post–Wagner Act era. In its heyday, collective bargaining seemed a metaphor for pluralist democracy itself. What better mechanism could allow for the periodic recalibration of the economic and social share that each sector, class, and interest demanded in a complex, industrial society?[5]

But in the crucial fifteen years that stretched from 1933 to 1948, collective bargaining of this sort hardly described the system whereby labor and capital struggled for influence, income, and power. Instead, a highly politicized system of interclass conflict and accommodation put not just wages and working conditions in play across the negotiating table, but the fate of the New Deal impulse itself. Elections, legislative battles, strikes, organizing campaigns, and labor negotiations were seamlessly interwoven.

Against the wishes of almost all private employers, the state played a decisive role in the outcome of the bargaining that took place between the parties in every crisis that put the relationship between workers and capitalists in the headlines during the years that followed.[6] As Sidney Hillman, the founder of the CIO's Political Action Committee (CIO-PAC) put it in 1943, American workers "can no longer work out even their most immediate day to day problems through negotiations with their employers and the terms of their collective agreements. Their wages, hours, and working conditions have become increasingly dependent upon policies adopted by Congress and the National Administration."[7]

American unions certainly had the power and capacity to conduct such politicized bargaining. By 1945 the trade unions stood near their twentieth-century apogee. About 30 percent of all American workers were organized, a density greater than at any time before, and at a level that for the first time approached that of Northern Europe. Unions seemed on the verge of recruiting millions of new workers in the service trades, in white-collar occupations like banking and insurance, across great stretches of the South and Southwest, and even among the lower ranks of management.[8] "Your success has been one of the most surprising products of American politics in several generations," Interior Secretary Harold Ickes told a cheering CIO convention just after Roosevelt's 1944 reelection. "You are on your way and you must let no one stop you or even slow up your march." Three years later the sober-minded Harvard economist Sumner Slichter, still counted U.S. trade unions "the most powerful economic organizations which the country has ever seen."[9]

This new power was by its very nature political, for the New Deal had thoroughly politicized all relations between the union movement, the business community, and the state. Capitalism seemed unstable and individual capitalists parochial, so the system needed guidance from the state, whatever the immediate interests of individual entrepreneurs and managers.[10] The war intensified this trend, advancing the nation toward the kind of labor-backed corporatism that would characterize social policy in northern Europe and Scandinavia. In this system highly organized social "blocs" struck periodic economic bargains through a process of political, societywide negotiation. Corporatism of this sort placed capital-labor relations within a highly centralized governmental context, where representatives of the contending "peak" organizations bargained politically for their respective constituencies.[11] From the early New Deal years forward, such corporatist arrangements, involving the Business Advisory Council, the National Association of Manufacturers, the AFL, and the CIO, as well as key government policy makers, had become increasingly formalized. As late as November 1945 President Truman convened such a tripartite conclave to set postwar wage policy and determine the power and prerogatives of unions and management in the postwar era.[12]

The premier examples of such corporatist institutions in 1940s America were the War Labor Board (WLB) and its wartime companion, the Office of Price Administration (OPA), administrative regimes that began to reorder wage and price relations within and between industries. The War Labor Board, for example, helped unions add 5 million new workers in just three short years. Moreover, this tripartite agency socialized much of the trade-union movement's prewar agenda, thus mandating seniority and grievance systems, vacation pay, night-shift supplements, sick leave, and paid mealtimes as standard working-class "entitlements."[13]

The Office of Price Administration was another one of the late New Deal's great mobilizing bureaucracies that helped build a powerful administrative state. Like the NLRB and the Fair Employment Practices Commission, OPA's effectiveness depended upon the organized activism of huge numbers of once voiceless individuals. In 1945 OPA employed nearly 75,000 and enlisted the voluntary participation of another 300,000, mainly urban housewives, who checked the prices and quality of the consumer goods regulated by the government. OPA chief Chester Bowles, a spirited New Deal liberal, called the volunteer price checkers "as American as baseball." Many merchants denounced them as a "kitchen Gestapo," but the polls found that more than 80 percent of all citizens backed OPA price-control regulations. In response, the National Association of Manufacturers poured as much money into anti-OPA propaganda as it would later spend on agitation for the legislation that became the Taft-Hartley Act. NAM called OPA an agency leading to "regimented chaos," an oxymoronic phrase that nevertheless captured business fears of a powerful state whose regulatory purposes are vitalized by an activist, organized citizenry.[14]

Politicized bargaining, both within the Washington corridors of power and without, opened the door to a social-democratic America. At the end of World War II most trade unionists, especially those in the new industrial-union wing, saw collective bargaining as but one element of a far broader labor-left agenda that they thought essential to the success of their social ambitions. During World War II, the unions had been largely frustrated in their efforts to win a large voice in the work of the War Production Board and other government councils that controlled investment and manpower policy, but such ambitions were given a freer rein in the years just after 1945. Although the end of the war was certain to limit the scope of WLB and OPA authority, most liberal and labor spokesmen still saw their programmatic reconstitution as the kernel of a postwar "incomes" policy that would rationalize the labor market, set profit and price guidelines, and redistribute income into worker and consumer hands.[15]

Inspired by reformist Catholic social doctrine, many CIO leaders also agitated for both a guaranteed annual wage and a set of industry councils designed to inject a governmental and a union voice into the highest levels of corporate decision making. The Steelworkers wanted the industry to build more plants, and the United Automobile Workers tried to protect the market share of independent producers like Hudson, Packard, and Kaiser. Meanwhile virtually all labor liberals put a tax-funded rise in the nation's social safety net near the top of their political agenda. This was largely embodied in the Murray-Wagner-Dingle bill, which foresaw a near European level of social-welfare spending for health care and unemployment benefits as well as old-age pensions under Social Security.[16]

Politicized bargaining of this sort demanded of the trade unions an organic amalgamation of strike action, organizing activity, and political mobilization. Consequently, 1946 yielded two decisive examples of such political unionism. Under Walter Reuther's leadership the UAW struck General Motors for 113 days in the fall and winter of 1945–46. Reuther called for a 30 percent increase in wages without a rise in the cost of cars. GM denounced his demand as un-American and socialist, but in reality Reuther was seeking to put some backbone into the Truman administration's efforts to sustain price controls and working-class living standards during the crucial demobilization era. To forestall the widely expected postwar slump, left-Keynesians like Reuther were not interested in a new round of government spending, the fiscal prescription favored by liberals a generation afterward. Instead, the UAW program, "Purchasing Power for Prosperity," saw the progressive redistribution of income as the key lever by which unions and the government might sustain aggregate demand. Or, as Reuther put it early in 1946, "The fight of the General Motors workers is a fight to save truly-free enterprise from death at the hands of its self-appointed champions."[17]

That same year witnessed the CIO's celebrated effort to organize the South. Operation Dixie had two goals. First, organizers sought to unionize Southern textiles, eliminate the North-South wage differential, and thereby forestall the massive flight of jobs and capital out of New England. Second, and even more pressing, the CIO saw the unionization of the South as the central element in an assault upon the industrial oligarchy of that region, whose rule, both at home and in Washington, rested upon the disenfranchisement of the Southern working class, both black and white. Verily, the link between CIO-style unionism and the mobilization of an increasingly self-confident black movement had become apparent to the political leadership of the white South, whose militant opposition to even the most attenuated New Deal reforms can be dated from the birth of this interracial alliance in the late 1930s. The unions therefore sought to break the power of the Bourbons by striking at their heartland, the bastions of racial discrimination and low-wage labor in the newly proletarianized regions of the Deep South. During the war, both labor federations had made substantial inroads in that region, organizing more than 800,000 new workers. In Winston-Salem, for example, wartime organization of the heavily black Reynolds Tobacco Company overnight transformed that city's NAACP chapter into the largest and most vital in the seaboard South, which in turn opened local politics to black participation for the first time since the Populist era.[18]

Beginning in 1946, Operation Dixie sought to replay these local breakthroughs on an even larger scale, in the process mobilizing an interracial electorate that could realign the very shape of Southern politics. "When Georgia is organized," predicted one CIO official, "you will find our old friend Gene Talmadge trying to break into the doors of the CIO conventions and tell our people that he has always been misunderstood."[19]

Finally, the union movement sought to make its political weight felt in an independent and aggressive fashion. The United States had no labor party, but both the AFL and the CIO built political machines that gave labor a distinctive, well-defined political profile at both the national and local levels. The unions invented the political action committee in the 1940s: during the 1944 election the CIO-PAC proved the backbone of the Roosevelt reelection effort in the urban, industrial North. Labor wanted to "realign" the Democratic Party by purging the Dixiecrats; and the CIO toyed with the idea of building a new, labor-based party. Heavily unionized states like New York, Pennsylvania, Ohio, Michigan, Illinois, and California were demographic powerhouses at midcentury, while the anti-union "sunbelt" remained marginal in presidential politics. Unionism boosted turnout and Democratic Party loyalty for fully a third of the electorate, so partisan politics in the early postwar era had something of a social-democratic flavor. The Democratic Party remained a fractious coalition, but in the North and on the West Coast, the interests of organized labor, both symbolic and real, could not be ignored. From 1948 until 1964 every Democratic candidate for president launched his campaign with a Labor Day rally in Detroit's Cadillac Square.[20]

But the larger ambitions of the union movement were defeated in the immediate postwar years. To understand this defeat we must look not only at the labor politics of the 1940s, but at the two great forces in American life whose hostility to union power made the prospects for even a narrowly construed labor-management accord problematic at best. First, in no other industrial nation was corporate management so hostile to the power, or even the existence of trade unionism itself. And second, the white governing class in the American South, which had been supportive of many early New Deal initiatives, turned on the unions with an unprecedented ferocity when the racial implications of mass unionism became apparent.

American Exceptionalism, Management Style

Since the early years of this century, scholars and journalists have devoted much ink to explaining why the American working class is "exceptional" when compared with the ostensibly more radical and class-conscious workers of Europe and Latin America. But the most "exceptional" element in the American system of labor-capital relations is the hostility managers have shown toward both the regulatory state and virtually all systems of worker representation. Thus, business support for the National Recovery Administration's system of state-supervised cartelization collapsed by 1935, even before the Supreme Court declared such a regulatory scheme unconstitutional. And despite much wishful historiography, no well-organized "corporate liberal" cohort of enlightened businessmen supported either the Wagner Act or the Social Security Act, the two linchpins of New Deal social reform.[21]

As early as 1948, C. Wright Mills divided conservative business sentiment along an axis that counterpoised an anti-union, entrepreneurial set of "practical conservatives" from their "sophisticated" brethren in industries characterized by an oligopolistic market structure. Since then historians and political economists have refined Mills's typology. In the late 1960s scholars identified a set of New Deal–era "corporate liberal" businessmen who advocated unionism as a stabilizing feature of the industrial landscape. Still later some historians emphasized the importance of the business "realists," who, during the 1940s, came to accept a well-constrained collective-bargaining regime. Meanwhile, many scholars have counterpoised both the corporate liberals and the realists to the entrepreneurial reactionaries of the South and West who categorically rejected collective bargaining.[22]

But this typology overstates by far the extent to which business ideology and practice has diverged from an anti-statist, anti-union norm. Business hostility to trade unionism and to the state structures that supported it had three historic, "exceptional" sources in the United States. The first arose out of a profound ideological commitment to what most businessmen saw as their inherent managerial prerogatives. The second reflected the relatively decentralized, hypercompetitive structure of many key industries, and the third arose out of the economic and ideological transformations generated by fifteen years of depression and war.

The tradition of American management was one of self-confidence and autonomy. In sharp contrast to their counterparts in Britain or Germany, American businessmen had presided over economic institutions that were of both continental scope and vast revenue long before the rise of a powerful state or the emergence of overt class politics. In every other capitalist nation, a strong bureaucratic state either preceded or emerged simultaneously with the appearance of the multidivisional firm, but this pattern was inverted in the United States. Although the government famously aided railroad development in the nineteenth century, such assistance and regulation proved the exception rather than the rule when it came to the great industries of the second industrial revolution: chemicals, autos, rubber, food processing, chain stores, and movies. Thus, throughout the classic era of U.S. industrialization, from the Civil War into the

1920s, the most critical decisions about the direction of American economic development were in private hands.[23]

This legacy made businesses hugely jealous of their prerogatives when they confronted both the new unionism and the New Deal. Indeed, American executives first began to use the term "free enterprise" to describe the American capitalist system in the 1930s. Such nomenclature reflected an effort, however crudely put, to distinguish U.S. conditions from those in Europe, where the state, the gentry, and the unions constrained entrepreneurial activity and regulated the labor market. Moreover, such a definition of U.S. capitalism highlights the desperate sense of autonomy America's captains of industry sought to rescue from both the New Deal and the new unions. To them this dual threat represented a Europeanized collectivism, because even the limited constraints imposed by America's mixed social-welfare regime seemed radical indeed. This was "creeping socialism," also a term first coined by business-oriented conservatives in the New Deal era. As Alfred Sloan of General Motors analogized at the end of World War II: "It took fourteen years to rid this country of prohibition. It is going to take a good while to rid the country of the New Deal, but sooner or later the ax falls and we get a change."[24]

In addition, American business never enjoyed a successful system of self-regularization or cartelization, often characteristic of Europe and the Far East. The American market was of continental magnitude and regional variation. Despite much talk of giant trusts and industrial oligarchy, the U.S. system was a "disorganizational synthesis," a revealing phrase coined by historian Colin Gordon. Ironically, the relative conservatism of the American labor movement, especially that derived from the AFL tradition of "voluntarism," celebrated firm-centered bargaining and eschewed independent political action, thus exacerbating this competitive disorder. American employers never came to see a system of collective bargaining as a "lesser-evil" when compared to continental socialism or British Labour politics. Indeed, American capitalists saw even the most narrowly focused brand of unionism as highly detrimental to their "prerogatives" because the shop-centered thrust of such unionism ensured that labor costs were unlikely to be distributed evenly among competitors. In France, Germany, Sweden, and Great Britain, industrial cartels and associations arose naturally out of the insularity and class cohesion of their leading industrialists. But in the United States, the regional competitiveness endemic to the industrial archipelago gave ambitious entrepreneurs the opportunity to undercut trustification and managerial cooperation. Thus, in the United States, the very disorganization of the capitalists put a premium on keeping labor costs flexible, production techniques plastic, and unions weak.[25]

Finally, a generation of depression and war had forced Americans to confront the transition of economic power from local interests and regional corporate networks to public agencies and federal officeholders with a far different constituency. New Deal statism and union egalitarianism were tied to White House fixers and university planners whose interests lay with the urban machines, ethnic minorities, organized labor, and northern blacks. Jews, Catholics, and professors now had their hand in making decisions, once the exclusive provenance of Protestant businessmen and state officials of a similar heritage.[26]

Roosevelt's Court-packing plan of 1937 represented the decisive moment in the crystallization of an aggressive brand of anti-union, anti–New Deal sentiment. For more than half a century the Supreme Court had been the conservative defender of property against government regulation from above and labor upheaval from below. When FDR offered the nation his plan to expand, and thereby pack the Court with New Dealers, he opened the door to a world of antigovernment invective. Indeed, FDR's Court-packing plan may be taken as the occasion at which modern conservatism achieves both a mass base and its ideological coherence. Until 1937 small producers, farmers, middle-class shop owners, as well as workers and consumers, saw the large, national business corporation as their enemy and nemesis. They hated the railroads, banks, mining companies, chain stores, and agricultural equipment makers. The government loomed far smaller in their social imagination, and when it did, it symbolized the agricultural extension service, internal improvements, and the maintenance of social order.[27]

But Roosevelt's Court-packing plan, proffered in the very midst of the sit-down strikes, worked a symbolic revolution, for it seemed to embody all that was threatening in the social and political upheavals of the New Deal. There was the assault on property, the overreach of executive power, the subversion of a hallowed institution of American government, and the New Deal alliance with a radical social movement that threatened the status and power of the old middle class.[28]

More trouble was to follow. Almost a third of a million small business firms folded during World War II, more than 10 percent of all those existing at the end of the 1930s. Manufacturing companies with fewer than one hundred workers saw their proportion of total output drop from more than a quarter to less than a fifth. The loss of autonomy particularly threatened small-town bankers, merchants, manufacturers, and others in the "old" middle class. For these citizens and others, an intrusive federal government symbolized the daily threat to individual and traditional values.[29] Big business on the other hand, emerged from the war with enormous sophistication and self-confidence. Unlike their counterparts in continental Europe, or even the British Isles, who had been tarred with the brush of collaboration or appeasement, American business leaders found the wartime experience one of both commercial success and political advance. They felt in little need of the kind of state-sponsored labor-management collaboration that helped legitimize a mixed capitalist economy in Germany, France, and Italy in the immediate postwar era.[30]

Given these ideological propensities and structural imperatives, we can understand the horror with which the vast bulk of American business confronted the New Deal and its allies within the suddenly powerful industrial unions. Conservatives repudiated the corporatist vision as either Stalinism, servitude, or both. They now gave to the defense of an older conception of liberty and property a self-confident morality and political élan it had lacked for a generation. Thus did Eugene E. Wilson of the United Aircraft Corporation warn that unless the postwar power of a laborite New Deal was stanched, "Christian freedom will give way to atheistic slavery, cooperation to compulsion, hope to fear, equality of opportunity to privilege, and the dead hand of bureaucracy will close the throttle on progress."[31] Likewise, General Motors considered the stakes of transcendent consequence during the UAW's postwar strike: "America is at the crossroads! It must preserve the freedom of each unit of American business to determine its own destiny. . . . The UAW-CIO is reaching for power. . . . It leads surely toward the day when union bosses . . . will seek to tell us what we can make, when we can make it, where we can make it, and how much we can charge."[32]

Such sentiments were not simply those of "brass hat" industrialists, but resonated widely among the literate public. Trade union leaders were routinely denominated as "union bosses" and "labor skates" because their power was a fundamentally illegitimate transgression upon the decentralized producer republic that still retained a powerful imaginative grasp on the minds of so many entrepreneurs and professionals whose social roots lay with the Protestant bourgeoisie. *The Saturday Evening Post*, which put Norman Rockwell's anachronistic celebrations of small-town America on the cover, published essays that routinely turned union leaders into "bosses," "czars," "barons," "dictators," and "lords," while relegating the rank and file to the status of "serfs," and "slaves."[33] And F. A. Hayek's *The Road to Serfdom*, which the University of Chicago first published as an academic tome in 1944, was selling hundreds of thousands of copies each year by the end of the decade.[34]

The Unreconstructed South

Decisively reinforcing the anti-union potency of this corporate–small producer bloc were the industrial and agricultural oligarchs of the white South. During the New Deal era, Southern politics and political economy were governed not only by the endemic racial hierarchies of the region, but by the fundamentally undemocratic character of its politics. Most Southern states were not organized according to "republican" principles. The overrepresentation of rural regions, both in state legislatures and the federal Congress, was positively gothic. In these regions the courthouse gang and a thin stratum of property-owning farmers monopolized politics, untroubled by either an opposition party, press, or faction. The poll tax, the white primary, and the vigilance of the county registrar limited the franchise to levels characteristic of Europe early in the nineteenth century. Blacks were excluded from the vote, but so too was a huge proportion of the white working class. In Virginia, Mississippi, South Carolina, and Arkansas, voter turnout (as a proportion of all adults) stood at 20 percent or less.[35]

Southern white elites, whose partisans comprised more than a third of the Democratic legislators in Congress, were determined to preserve this system. Unlike the Republicans, Southern Democrats did not object to the expansion of New Deal power, per se, nor to federal infrastructure spending or the regulation of the market. Indeed, the South, and Southern agriculture in particular, proved a staunch ally and beneficiary of New Deal state building. The Tennessee Valley Authority transformed life in four Southern states while Dixie business benefited enormously from the military spending that flooded the region during the Second World War and the Cold War decades that followed.

But Southern white elites fought desperately, cleverly, and successfully against those nationalizing impulses that sought to democratize the region and align its labor relations and racial norms with those of the North and West. No set of politicians was more sophisticated in understanding the extent to which the New Deal's legitimization of the union movement and its orientation toward a rationalized, national labor market subverted the power of the old oligarchy and threatened the region's low-wage advantage.[36]

Southern politicians deployed a threefold line of defense, a threefold veto over New Deal efforts to bring class relations in the South into conformity with a Northern model. First, the South's powerful delegation in Congress simply excluded much of the region's people and industry from the scope of New Deal social legislation. Neither the Wagner Act nor Social Security covered agricultural labor or domestic service, which then employed more than half of all African Americans. Likewise, Southern legislators crafted the minimum wage, first set in the 1938 Fair Labor Standards Act, so that it had no impact on pay scales in textiles, tobacco processing, lumber, and other characteristic Southern industries. Not unexpectedly, these same congressmen took their first postwar opportunity to filibuster the Fair Employment Practices Commission to death when it came up for renewal in early 1946.[37]

Second, the South defended its peculiar institutions behind a system of decentralized administration. Virtually all of the New Deal's "social wage" legislation—including unemployment insurance, aid to families with dependent children, work relief and housing assistance—was administered by state and local officials in accordance with social and economic norms largely determined by ruling elites. Thus welfare and unemployment payments in the Deep South were sometimes but a tenth those in New England and New York. Political scientist Michael Brown has aptly called this system "truncated universalism." By way of contrast, the Wagner Act was national in scope and standard, which accounts for much of the ferocious resistance it met in the South.[38]

The Southern elite defended its power with one final entrenchment: they simply nullified much New Deal social legislation, especially the labor law, when it empowered opponents of their regime. Even during World War II when the National Labor Relations Board and the War Labor Board were cloaked in patriotic robes, textile firms, tobacco processors, and independent oil producers were endemic violators of the labor law. Indeed, Southern textile interests pioneered most of the legal and economic techniques that effectively abrogated the Wagner Act, including illegal firings, plant shutdown, litigious delay, and managerial intimidation of workers before an NLRB election. By the late 1950s Texas, Georgia, and the Carolinas led the nation in outright union-busting.[39]

Under such conditions it is not surprising that Operation Dixie was a thorough failure. The CIO had put up a million dollars, recruited some two hundred organizers, and opened scores of offices throughout the South. Not to be outflanked, the AFL almost immediately opened its own rival campaign to bring authentic "American" unionism to the region. But the resistance from the political and industrial leadership of the white South proved overwhelming, and the proportion of union nonfarm labor in the South declined from just above 20 percent in 1945 to half that twenty years later. Meanwhile, white supremacists made the CIO-PAC a whipping boy in each election season, leading to the defeat of such pro-union racial moderates as Claude Pepper and Frank Graham in 1950. By then the Southern congressional delegation was even more monolithically reactionary than it had been five years before.[40]

The failure of Operation Dixie ensured that the political weight of an essentially undemocratic Southern polity would continue to inject a distorting, "Prussian" element into American statecraft. Even as union densities rose to European levels in the late 1940s, an alliance of Republicans and Dixiecrats in Congress vetoed union–Democratic Party efforts to bolster the American welfare state or defend the Wagner-era labor relations regime. And because of the vital role the South still played in national Democratic Party politics, even those liberals elected from solidly pro-labor constituencies were drawn into compromise and coalition with the right. The CIO bargained with the Democratic Party "much as it would with an employer," admitted union political operative Jack Kroll in the early 1950s.[41]

To have organized the South in the late 1940s would have required a massive, socially disruptive interracial campaign reminiscent of the CIO at its most militant moment in the late 1930s—indeed, a campaign not dissimilar from that which the modern civil rights movement would wage in the 1960s. Moreover, it would have required the kind of federal backing, both legal and ideological, offered by the Wagner Act in the 1930s and the Supreme Court's *Brown* decision twenty years later. But such a campaign never jelled in 1946 and 1947. Red-baiting and race-baiting had long been staples of Southern anti-unionism, but instead of directly confronting these attacks, labor leaders, CIO as well as AFL, sought to deflect Southern xenophobia by excluding Communists and other radicals from participation in Operation Dixie. Thus the human resources from the Communist-led trade unions and Popular Front institutions like the Southern Conference for Human Welfare and the Highlander Folk School were shunted aside. The legacy of this exclusion would reemerge during the 1960s when organized labor in the South stood mute or hostile in the midst of that era's civil rights revolution.

The white South's economic strength in 1946 also proved a large obstacle to union efforts to win a broad following in the region. The New Deal's massive intervention in the agricultural economy of the South subsidized farm mechanization and tilted the balance of power in rural areas still further to the political and social interests of large landowners. In the long run New Deal agricultural policies would proletarianize millions of rural blacks and set the stage for the civil rights movement, but in the late 1940s such displacement merely generated a labor surplus that intensified racial competition at the bottom of the labor market.[42] Moreover, direct federal pressure upon the white South would remain quite timid in the postwar years, notwithstanding the celebrated bolt of the Dixiecrats at the 1948 Democratic convention. Reluctant to fragment the Democratic coalition, President Truman tried long and hard to accommodate both civil rights liberals and Southern white supremacists. "The strategy," an assistant later explained, "was to start with a bold measure and then temporize to pick up the right-wing forces."[43]

If we therefore combine an American managerial caste whose ethos defended its prerogatives with unprecedented vigor, together with a low-wage region largely impervious to New Deal social regulation, we have the ingredients for a most dramatic era of capital mobility, perhaps more so than in the history of any industrialized state. As Tom Sugrue, Jefferson Cowie, and Bruce Schulman have demonstrated, capital flight from the unionized North began almost immediately after World War II. Deindustrialization was not a product of 1960s-era ghetto riots or the heightened international competition of the 1970s. It began when companies like General Electric, RCA, Thompson Products, Swift, Armour, Alexander Smith, Ford, and J. P. Stevens sought to solve their "labor problem" by simply replacing one workforce with another.[44] Under such conditions, any idea that a labor-management accord might have a multigenerational life was wishful thinking.

Taft-Hartley

The 1947 Taft-Hartley law prefigured and codified much of labor's postwar retreat. Union failure to win some leverage over corporate pricing policy in 1946, combined with the collapse of price controls later that summer, represented a defeat for the kind of politicized economic bargaining that was so distasteful to American businessmen. When an inflationary spiral during the summer and fall of 1946 seemed to discredit the interventionist, Rooseveltian state, 10 million working-class voters remained at home in the midterm elections.

The result was a Republican sweep in the fall and the election of a new Congress that put the containment of union power and the reprivatization of collective bargaining at the top of its agenda.[45]

Backed by a coalition of business conservatives, Southern Bourbons, and anti-labor ideologues, the new Republican Congress quickly passed the Taft-Hartley Act over President Harry Truman's veto. Passage of the Taft-Hartley Act proved a milestone, not only for the actual legal restrictions the new law imposed on the trade unions but as a symbol of the shifting relationship between the unions, the state, and the corporations at the dawn of the postwar era. It made certain that for the unions, the "accord" of the next three decades would generate a set of depoliticized unions and an increasingly insular collective-bargaining regime. And the Taft-Hartley legacy assured that an accord established even on such perverse principles was doomed to instability and erosion.

Taft-Hartley's most overtly ideological, best-remembered consequence was the purge of the Communists from official union posts. The law required that all trade unionists sign an affidavit asserting they were not Communists, by organizational affiliation or belief. This section of the law generated enormous bitterness among trade unionists of all political colorations. It exacerbated an ideological war within the CIO and emasculated the political influence of hundreds of Communist-oriented union leaders, even as leftists and civil libertarians waged a successful, decade-long legal battle to overturn the prohibition.[46]

The clause was obnoxious to contemporary unionists because it inscribed in the law a class distinction and a stigma that even the most anti-Communist trade-union officials found repugnant. Only trade unionists had to sign such an affidavit, not employers. Thus denunciations of the clause came not only from the Left but from such veteran anti-Communists as John L. Lewis, who labeled Taft-Hartley "the first ugly, savage thrust of Fascism in America."[47]

Given such laborite hostility and the subsequent damage the anti-Communist clause wreaked on the unions, one might have expected much advocacy, from the ranks of employers and congressional conservatives, for the insertion of this clause into the Taft-Hartley Law. But the issue figured hardly at all, either in the rhetoric of those businessmen who championed Taft-Hartley or in the testimony offered at the exhaustive congressional hearings on the bill in February and March 1947. Such silence speaks volumes, for these were the very months in which the White House established a federal loyalty review board, in which the House Committee on Un-American Activities stepped up its inquisitorial work, and in which the president enunciated the Truman Doctrine, which may well be taken as the moment that the U.S. government declared an ideological Cold War against the Soviets.[48]

Two reasons account for this curious silence. First, the enormous legal and ideological warfare touched off by the clause was a function, not so much of the Right persecuting the Left—which was true enough—but of a civil war within the ranks of labor and its liberal allies that long antedated Taft-Hartley. Long before Joseph McCarthy appeared on the national scene in 1950, questions about the legitimacy of the Communists within the Left and in ranks of labor had fractured the progressive wing of the New Deal coalition. Anti-Communist radicals like Sidney Lens and ex-socialists like Walter Reuther and Reinhold Neibuhr denounced the Communists as "counterfeit revolutionaries," because so much of their politics, even when pro-union and anticapitalist, was really a function of their ideological allegiance to Soviet power. The UAW, the UMW, the International Ladies' Garment Workers' Union as well as the American Civil Liberties Union and other institutions of labor-liberalism had already put anti-Communist provisions in their constitutions. Taft-Hartley added a new front in this battle, but it was not essential to the prosecution of this particular civil war.[49]

More important, business leaders believed that when it came to bargaining issues or shop-floor militancy, the distinction between Communists and their more conventional trade-union counterparts was rather slim. "Nothing is more dangerous than to assume that those who today attack 'Communists' within their union, and who are in consequence unthinkingly labeled 'right-wingers,' are *ipso facto* believers in private enterprise or in our form of government," warned Stuart Ball, counsel for Montgomery Ward, late in 1946. "It is not necessary to pin the label of 'Marxist' upon a labor leader to prove that what he believes is incompatible with our basic political and economic beliefs."[50] In textiles, retail trade, shoemaking, and tobacco, business played the anti-Communist card to keep its workplaces union free. But the real issue was always unionism, not Communism.[51]

Unionists understood this dynamic, but by 1947 the fate of the labor movement had become completely interwoven with the state structures necessary to sustain it. Although both the AFL and the CIO initially favored a boycott of Taft-Hartley, such a nullification would also deprive them of access to the NLRB, to bargaining unit election procedures, and to what protections the labor law still afforded them against anti-union employers. The Communists, who were influential in unions representing about a million workers, were therefore sacrificed to the Cold War's growing requirement for political orthodoxy, both at home and abroad.[52]

But this amputation had an even larger price, for Taft-Hartley did more than eliminate an unpopular political faction. American Communists gave their allegiance to a brutal dictatorship, but they were not simply creatures of that foreign power, no matter how many telegrams and how many rubles flowed from Moscow to their Union Square headquarters. Instead, the tragedy of their demise lay in the organic leadership U.S. Communists gave to so much that characterized midcentury social liberalism: opposition to the Cold War, trade-union militancy, protofeminism, and above all, the movement for the liberation of African Americans. This trade-union left represented an anchor for many of these movements. Whether by self-destruction or political purge, the elimination of the Communists from so much of American political life diminished the role to which issues of class and union power would play in the emergence of the Civil Rights Movement and the New Left little more than a decade later.[53]

Taft-Hartley thus did much to depoliticize the unions by curbing interunion solidarity and ghettoizing the power of the labor movement. The new law codified the union-hostile status quo in the cotton South and the entrepreneurial Southwest, especially after most states in those regions took advantage of Section 14b to ban the union shop and enact "right-to-work" statutes. Such laws had a twofold purpose: they kept the unions financially and organizationally fragile, but even more important, they represented an ideological onslaught of the first order, because now the "rights" of anti-union workers were given the same moral weight as those loyal to the union idea. Likewise, another Taft-Hartley revision of the Wagner-era labor law gave to employers the right to "free speech" during NLRB elections. Given the employment power wielded by management, such anti-union speech was normally indistinguishable from intimidation. But once again the real issue was not the technical definition of "speech," but the devaluation of the idea of worker-self organization independent of managerial influence.[54]

Labor's Sociological Frontier

The Taft-Hartley law substantially redefined labor's sociological and organizational frontier. Its ban on the secondary boycotts made it illegal for unionized workers in one firm to boycott the products of another in support of their strike or organizing drive. The strong could not come to the aid of the weak, which in practice proscribed the organizing techniques so effectively deployed by the transport and longshoring unions to extend unionism into retail trade, food processing, and warehouse work. To understand the potency of this lost weapon, one might recall the political, as well as the economic, effectiveness of the boycott against non-union grapes deployed by Caesar Chavez, whose farmworker constituency lay outside the labor law during the 1960s. And the same might be said for the enormously effective mobilization mounted against those American corporations whose trade and investments sustained the apartheid regime in South Africa during the 1970s and 1980s. In both cases the legal no-man's-land governing their boycotts, strikes, and campaigns provided fertile terrain for the growth of cross-class, cross-union social movements.

Taft-Hartley's debilitating exclusion of foremen and supervisors from labor-law coverage proved the single most powerful weapon crafted by labor's opponents under the new statute. The unionization of supervisory employees represented one of the most important sociopolitical phenomena of the late New Deal era. With the rise of mass production and bureaucratic rationality, first-line supervisors had become both a linchpin in the production process and an anomalous "man in the middle" buffeted from below and above by militant workers and the managerial quest for efficiency and control. The Foreman's Association of America (FAA) claimed neutrality in the "ceaseless struggle between ownership and wage labor," but it functioned like a trade union and allied itself with the CIO.[55] Indeed, in a 1945 ruling that involved Packard foremen, the NLRB used the same criterion advanced by the FAA itself in distinguishing first line supervisors from top management: they were employees under the Wagner Act because they did not set policy. By 1946 the FAA and other such organizations had organized thousands of supervisors throughout the industrial Midwest.[56]

To America's top managers, foreman unionization spelled industrial anarchy, which was the language they used to describe union control of the shop-floor work environment. "We must rely upon the foremen to try and keep down those emotional surges of the men in the plants and urge them to rely on the grievance procedure," argued a Ford Motor Company spokesman. "If we do not have the foreman to do that, who is going to do it?" Seniority rights, grievance procedures, and union representation by foremen were subversive because if lower-level supervisors felt less threatened by orders from above, then the immense social and psychological pressures generated from below would surely turn them into unreliable agents of corporate power. Hence the managerial recourse to the military analogy. "Picture if you can the confusion of an army in the field," asserted a Detroit machine-shop executive, "if the non-commissioned officers were forced to listen to the commands of the men in their ranks as well as those of their superior officers."[57]

Foreman organization, however, did not just threaten to weaken management authority at the point of production. It also eroded the vitality of corporate ideology in society at large by shattering the unitary facade of management and opening the door to a much larger definition of what constituted a self-conscious working-class identity. "The Foreman Abdicates" ran a *Fortune* headline in 1945, but the larger issue was whether or not the lower middle class—clerical workers, salesmen, store managers, bank tellers, engineers, and draftsmen—would also abandon their identification with the corporate order. "Where will unionization end?" asked GM's Wilson, "With the vice presidents?"[58] The *Legislative History* of the Taft-Hartley Act put it this way: "Supervisors are management people. . . . It seems wrong, and it is wrong, to subject people of this kind, who have demonstrated their initiative, their ambition, and their ability to get ahead, to the leveling process of seniority, uniformity and standardization."[59] The deunionization of the foremen and their forced-draft conscription back into the managerial realm was therefore essential to the reghettoization of the union movement and the victory of management all along the white-collar frontier.

The magnitude of labor's defeat on the issue of supervisory unionism has become clearer with each passing year. The unionization of finance, engineering, insurance, banking, and other private-sector service industries proved virtually impossible with the ban on supervisory unionism. The ranks of these white-collar and service-sector workers would swell over the next few decades. Indeed, the proportional size of the managerial-professional workforce doubled in the half century since the end of World War II, and by the 1990s the Census Bureau defined more workers as managerial, professional, and technical than blue-collar. Few were actually true executives or independent professionals, but the evolving labor law for the most part failed to take the new sociology of work into account. Or rather, it gave a perverse, Orwellian reading to the nation's occupational transformation, so that huge numbers of middle-wage, nonsupervisory workers, including game wardens, registered nurses, fast-food restaurant "managers," purchasing agents, dentists, medical interns, paralegals, engineers, newspaper editors, and college professors at private schools have been denied protection either by the NLRB or by the wage-and-hour provisions of the Fair Labor Standards Act. FLSA regulations put the wage floor for workers deemed executive, administrative, or professional employees at little more than the minimum wage.[60]

Whatever the other cultural or social obstacles to their empowerment, the legal straitjacket imposed by Taft-Hartley ensured that the unions reborn in the New Deal would now be consigned to a roughly static geographic and demographic terrain, an archipelago that skipped from one blue-collar community to another in the Northeast, the Midwest, and on the Pacific Coast. Top executives quickly real-

After 1947 the Taft-Hartley law made organizing more difficult, especially in the South where textile industry managers forced the unions onto the defensive. (Credit: George Meany Memorial Library)

ized that the legal vulnerability of their first-line supervisors and technical professionals had transformed this growing employee strata into an anti-union weapon of the first order. Managers successfully demanded supervisory-professional "loyalty" against the union threat. Thus the very conditions that once made first-line supervisors vulnerable to rank-and-file influence—their daily contact, rapport, and sociological affinity—gave managers and anti-union consultants the incentive to conscript this stratum as the shock troops who are thrown into the anti-union battle at the first hint of an organizing campaign.[61]

In the 1950s, the NLRB often protected supervisors who refused to report to top management the union activities of their subordinates, but the erosion of the standard by which the courts judged employer interference in the free exercise of employee rights has also stripped supervisors of this protection. When labor's organizing activities threaten a union-free company today, standard operating procedure requires that management call a meeting of all first-line supervisors in order to threaten or fire those who resist implementation of the anti-union strategy. As one labor organizer noted, once managers "make it a point to frighten the supervisors," the supervisors "turn around and frighten the employees."[62]

Firm-Centered Bargaining

Taft-Hartley may not have been the "slave-labor" law denounced by CIO and AFL alike, but if it destroyed few unions outright, it did nonetheless impose a set of constraints that encouraged trade-union parochialism and penalized any serious attempt to project a classwide political-economic strategy. To the corporations this was a major, long-sought victory that made certain union strength would be limited to the oligopolistically structured industries of the industrial heartland. Thus, even the most liberal of the CIO unions found practical and necessary a narrowly focused, defensive brand of private-sector collective bargaining. This was made even more manifest in the wake of President Truman's reelection in 1948. Although his victory came in a contest that saw the most class-polarized vote in the twentieth century, almost all of his legislative efforts to advance a postwar New Deal—national health insurance, repeal of Taft-Hartley, federal aid to education, a new FEPC, and a farm subsidy program that would have cemented the Democratic alliance between small farmers, urban workers, and organized consumers—were rejected by the dominant conservative coalition in Congress.[63]

The stage was therefore set for the union-management "accord" that framed industrial relations during the next three decades. At first the unions proved reluctant partners. In 1948 General Motors first offered the UAW "cost of living/annual improvement factor" clauses, which would guarantee auto workers protection against inflation, and a real annual increase in their standard of living. The union accepted—a "blue plate special," Walter Reuther called it—but without any illusion that such a bargain represented a fulfillment of its larger postwar program. The UAW still fought for an overall shift in the sociopolitical balance of power. As Reuther put it, "General Motors workers cannot be bribed with the wooden nickels of inflation into withdrawing from the fight against the greedy industrialists and subservient politicians who caused and condoned the price rises which are now undermining the living standards of millions." The union therefore characterized its 1948 contract, the first with a Cost of Living Adjustment (COLA) clause, as but a "holding action" that would temporarily protect the income of GM workers in the "context of today's economic and political reaction."[64]

However, such ideological opposition was soon put aside. In the political stalemate that followed Truman's reelection, it became clear that no social-democratic breakthrough was in the offing, toward either corporatist wage bargaining or an expansion of the welfare state. Meanwhile the Cold War onset of what even administration officials described as a "permanent war economy" made certain that inflationary pressures were deeply embedded within the postwar boom. It was in such a context that the UAW and General Motors negotiated a new collective bargaining agreement that decisively reprivatized the wage and welfare bargain in America's most important industry. The five-year UAW-GM contract of May 1950 guaranteed pensions, health insurance, the union shop, and a 20 percent increase in the standard of living of those auto workers who labored under its provisions.[65]

Unionists like UAW president Reuther were now fulsome in their praise, while *Fortune* magazine dubbed the agreement "The Treaty of Detroit." "GM may have paid a billion for peace but it got a bargain," wrote *Fortune*'s Daniel Bell, himself once a comrade of Reuther's in the Socialist Party. It was the first major industry contract "that unmistakably accepts the existing distribution of income between wages and profits as 'normal' if not 'fair.' . . . It is the first major union contract that explicitly accepts objective economic facts—cost of living and productivity—as determining wages, thus throwing overboard all theories of wages as determined by political power and of profits as 'surplus value.'"[66] By the early 1960s, the COLA principle had been incorporated into more than 50 percent of all major union contracts. And in the inflationary 1960s and 1970s it spread even further: to Social Security and military pensions, and to wage determination in some units of the government and the non-union private sector.[67]

But no matter how good the wages, the firm-centered character of this bargaining system generated the kind of workplace parochialism that soon gave capital a decisive advantage. In the 1950s, even more than in previous decades, industrial relations theory was premised upon a "pluralist" understanding of power in the workplace. Once a union had been installed, workers and managers bargained on a "level playing field," while a system of grievance arbitration mimicked the judicial function in civil society. But this theory misperceived reality, and as a consequence it was deeply, fatally flawed.[68]

Under such a system, capital had the upper hand, if not in any given set of negotiations or arbitrations, then systematically and over time. Managers held the initiative when it came to the introduction of new technology, the redeployment of capital, and the pattern of corporate growth or decline. Although workers might stop production for a week or a month, management always had the option to do so permanently, by shifting capital to a new facility, state, or nation. And because workers had to create a crisis, to halt service or production, to make their voice heard, capital seemed the champion of social peace in the court of public opinion and in the corridors of power. Thus working-class militancy, if confined to any given work site, had a self-limiting character, because it generated both higher production costs and overt industrial disharmony, which management sought to flee. This was not always apparent during the 1940s and 1950s when unemployment was low and production capacity in high demand, but it became disastrously clear after the recession of 1957–58 when the great deindustrialization of urban America began in earnest.[69]

Moreover, midcentury industrial pluralism proved exceedingly unsympathetic to self-activity from below. The system of quasi-autonomous shop stewards took the first hit, because their influence depended not simply on efficient grievance handling, but on their capacity to actually mobilize rank-and-file workers for direct conflict with lower-level supervisors. Arbitrators, government officials, and many top union leaders denounced such activism as "self-help," "unauthorized," and "wildcat" activities. Yale law professor Harry Shulman, America's most respected midcentury arbitrator, offered a Weberian defense of this system when he penalized Ford shop stewards for shutting down production at the giant River Rouge works late in World War II. "An industrial plant is not a debating society," lectured Shulman. "Its object is production. When a controversy arises, production cannot wait for exhaustion of the grievance procedure. . . . authority is vested in Supervision. It must be vested there because the responsibility for production is also vested there; and responsibility must be accompanied by authority."[70]

This denigration of shop activism did not cease with the end of the World War II–era production imperatives. The corporations and the courts were determined to snuff out the "self-help" tradition, and most trade-union leaders followed along, not so much because they were "sellouts," but because the bargaining structures that evolved after the war privileged across-the-board wage-and-benefit awards and devalued the localistic, individualized grievance issues that constituted the rationale for steward power and the daily routine of grievance arbitration. By the mid-1950s Chrysler steward B. J. Widick complained, "[O]ur contracts are becoming such legalistic documents as to be unworkable in terms of real, genuine labor relations; and we are getting this whole new body of law which is just fantastic. . . . In the old days, he [the steward] was the Union, he was the Contract. . . . Now he is a Philadelphia lawyer. It's embarrassing."[71] The embarrassment—for shop activists—deepened later that decade when the Supreme Court ruled, in its *Lincoln Mills* decision and a set of cases brought by the United Steelworkers, that arbitration awards were enforceable in the courts, and by injunction if necessary.[72] "The entire labor movement is like a giant bar association of non-licensed attorneys," observed labor lawyer Tom Geoghegan a third of a century later. "Arbitration is what people mean, essentially, when they talk about 'our modern system of industrial self-government.' They mean mini-lawsuits, millions of them, jam-packed in big backlogs, going back for years."[73]

The Private Welfare State

This depolitical privatization of what had been the union movement's larger sociopolitical agenda also extended to the negotiation of a set of what were once called "fringe benefits": pensions, medical provision, vacations, and supplemental unemployment insurance. But fringe benefits are hardly fringe issues. They constituted an effort to generate, in the collective-bargaining process, a job-dependent version of the more universal welfare states then being constructed out of the social rubble that had been pre-war Europe. But this union effort to generate a privatized welfare-state equivalent to those built by social-democratic governments in Europe proved a strategic error of the first order, whose legacy plagues us yet.

The 1940s were an era of welfare experimentation and planning. The trade unions hoped that as in Britain the social solidarity generated by the wartime experience would give rise to a universal system of health insurance and higher social-security benefits. The government had already begun to provide pregnancy and infant care services for millions of military wives. The 1944 Servicemen's Readjustment Act (GI Bill) generated a new educational entitlement, and the Wagner-Murray-Dingell bill of that same era forecast a comprehensive postwar system of health insurance funded and administered through Social Security.[74]

The stakes were high because the level, scope, and political meaning of the entire social wage was on the postwar table. If social provision was funded by the tax system and administered by the state, then benefits were more likely to be universal, equitable, and cheap. The New Deal would win a new lease on life. And unions could concentrate on their core function where they were most effective: the representation of worker interest at the point of production.

Employers opposed a higher social wage for the very same reasons unions found it attractive. The corporations would bear a large proportion of the taxes needed to pay for it. But even more important was the extent to which a generous welfare state drove a wedge between workers and their employer. Employees would have less loyalty to the company, could switch jobs more easily, and were certain of an essential income-in-kind even if they were ill, unemployed, or on strike. Managers needed to rewin the loyalty of their employees by providing some of the social security that the New Deal and the new unions so effectively celebrated. Big insurance companies found in this newly important workingclass value a vast market, but to tap it, asserted one insurance publication, they had to start "keeping up with the social planners."[75]

Thus the stage was set for the explosion of firm-centered "fringe-benefit" bargaining that began after 1950. The revival of postwar conservatism had blocked any expansion of the welfare state, so the unions made the strategic decision to turn to the collective-bargaining table to win pensions, health insurance, and other nonwage benefits from big companies. Their task was facilitated by a change in the tax law that enabled companies to write off such expenses as business deductions, as well as judicial decisions that declared fringe-benefit issues within the scope of mandatory collective bargaining.[76]

Most union officials remained proponents of a more universal welfare state, but in practice they came to celebrate the incremental advance of this privatized system. And for about a quarter century it seemed to work. At its apogee in the mid 1970s, company-paid pensions covered 49 percent of the private-sector workforce. Private health insurance reached two-thirds of all workers under sixty-five, most of which came through an employer. Blue-collar workers in the big unionized firms enjoyed wages far superior to those of Europe and social-welfare benefits at least as good as those in West Germany, Sweden, and Great Britain.[77]

As long as the unions were strong and social liberalism a powerful governmental impulse, unionized industry set the pattern. Indeed this was called "pattern bargaining," or what one historian described as the "soft corporatism" of the 1950s and 1960s. Critical wage and benefit bargains negotiated by the big unions set the norm for the less favorably situated workers, thus generating a kind of social welfare settlement in the United States that was characteristic of the more formally corporatist industry-labor relationships in Northern Europe. To avoid CIO-style unionization, managers at DuPont, Thompson Products, Weirton Steel, and other firms in the core industrial sector helped set up "independent" unions and then carefully tracked the wage and benefit pattern established in automobiles and steelmaking. Meanwhile, IBM, Kodak, Polaroid, and other technologically innovative firms, many near-monopolies linked to the defense sector, were so well insulated from market pressures that they could offer blue-collar production workers the kind of lifetime employment stability and pension benefits normally reserved for white-collar technicians and professionals. A kind of quasi corporatism even structured bargaining relationships in highly competitive industries like trucking, coal, construction, and the airlines, where New Deal efforts at regulatory cartelization had persisted and where the unions themselves had played a decisive role in organizing the employer associations with which they bargained.[78]

But even before this system fractured in the 1980s, it was a misanthropic creature. Firm-centered, job-dependent welfare benefits may have opened a booming market for the insurance companies and represented a politically sophisticated corporate personnel policy, but it was an exceedingly poor substitute for the universal welfare state once sought by the postwar union movement. Because of its work-related character, the privatized welfare state perpetuated inequality and inefficiency. It was patriarchal and racially coded because most white women and minorities worked in either non-union or low-paying jobs where the "pattern" established at the economy's core was but faintly reproduced. It could never become universal because not all adults are in the labor force; moreover, it assumed a level of enterprise stability that no set of managers in a technologically innovative society could guarantee. And when it came to health insurance, the firm-specific, fee-for-service model generated by the corporations, the American Medical Association, and the big insurance companies opened the door to both double-digit medical-care inflation and inequitable insurance coverage. The new welfare capitalism that emerged out of the postwar labor-management accord generated islands of security, with high waters all around.[79]

A Brief Accord

This system collapsed in stages, with the final, cataclysmic implosion arriving sometime in the early 1980s. The anti-Communist purge fragmented bargaining unity in the electrical industry, which gave firms like General Electric and Westinghouse the freedom to set up scores of non-union plants and reestablish regional wage differentials. Likewise, the 1951 collapse of textile unionism at the big Dan River

Mills in Danville, Virginia, signaled Southern manufacturers that they could safely ignore the wage standards set by unionized mills in New England. Then during the recession of 1957–58, the most severe since before World War II, scores of unionized supplier plants closed their doors or fled the urban North for low-wage havens south of the Mason-Dixon line.[80]

As for the collapse of pattern bargaining in the 1980s, a considerable debate now rages as to the origins and meaning of its downfall. The conventional wisdom holds that the American accord could exist only insofar as the United States remained an insular, continental market; once the globalization of trade internationalized the supply of labor, even the strongest unions found it impossible to defend their capacity to "take wages out of competition." The slow decline in the levels of union density that set in after 1953 therefore reflected not so much a waning of union strength in the core industrial sectors but rather the understandable incapacity of the unions to break out of their blue-collar-job ghetto. The complacency of some unionists, notably AFL-CIO president George Meany, who famously remarked that "it doesn't make any difference" if the unionized sector of the workforce continued to shrink, was justified insofar as uniform wage patterns were maintained in the remaining well-organized industries. Thus, the really precipitous decline in union power and membership came only in the late 1970s when firms once thought to be natural oligopolies, like those making steel, cars, and construction equipment, suddenly found themselves competing across a new international market with companies whose unit labor costs stood at one-half or less that of their own.[81]

The internationalization of the labor market in the 1970s did drive a stake through the heart of the soft corporatism that characterized the postwar accord, but this system was already suffering from multiple wounds and maladies. For all its apparent solidity, pattern bargaining in the United States had a remarkably anemic life. It never spread much beyond the oligopolistically structured core industries, and even there it required a strong union that could equalize labor costs in order to make the pattern hold. Where unions were weak, as in electrical products and textiles, or where domestic competition was fierce, as in automotive parts and food processing, wage and benefit guidelines established in Detroit, Pittsburgh, or Chicago were reproduced only imperfectly. In 1947, for instance, retail clerks earned about two-thirds as much as auto workers, but after the big inflationary surge of the late 1960s and early 1970s they took home but one-third as much. Even in the unionized auto parts industry, only about one-quarter of all companies, employing 40 percent of the workforce, followed the Big Three pattern during the 1950s. When inflation became a chronic problem after 1965, wage inequality within the blue-collar manufacturing sector increased dramatically.[82]

Nor did the corporatized welfare state encompass more than a highly segmented fraction of the American working class. White male workers in stable firms were its chief beneficiaries. Women, whose work careers were often episodic, were far less likely to build up the continuous employment time necessary for a pension or a long vacation. Likewise, African American and Latino men found that the firm-centered benefit system worked against them because their disproportionately high level of employment in low-wage, marginal firms often deprived them of full access to the social benefits and regular wages characteristic of the core economy.

Because so much of the postwar social struggle has taken place at the level of the firm rather than within a broader political arena, the American industrial-relations system has reinforced the economy's tendency to construct such segmented and unequal benefit and compensation schemes. This multitiered system of social provision has served to erode solidarity within the working class and has made it difficult to counter claims that welfare spending and the push for social equity are harmful to economic growth. The classic resentment felt by many blue-collar workers toward those on state-supported welfare has at least one root in the system of double taxation that the organized working class has borne in the postwar era. Union workers pay to support two welfare systems: their own, funded by an increasingly burdensome "tax" on their total pay periodically renegotiated in the collective-bargaining contract, and that of the government, paid for by a tax structure that grew more regressive as the postwar years advanced. In turn, organized labor has come to be perceived (and all too often perceives itself) as a special-interest group, whereby its advocacy of welfare-state measures that would raise the social wage for all workers has taken on an increasingly perfunctory quality.[83]

Big-time collective bargaining gave an illusion that the negotiating table was level. Here the UAW's Walter Reuther and Ford's John Bugas shake on the 1949 contract, which established company-funded pension benefits. (Credit: Wide World Photos)

Ironically, the relatively decentralized, firm-centered character of the postwar system has generated not flexibility but dysfunctional rigidities within both the office and shop-floor work regime and within the world of union governance. In a system of radically unequal wages and private social provision, parochial job-control strategies have much appeal to unionized workers. Detailed work rules, rigid seniority structures, and hard bargaining over new technology represented a rational union response, given the inability of the postwar labor movement either to make wages and working conditions more equitable or to offer a broader political response to layoffs and job dislocation caused by technological change.

One solution to this industrial-relations problem has been a European-style "works council" arrangement in which shop stewards from various unions compose a bargaining council that negotiates with management on a continuous basis. Because such works councils are not part of the union structure itself—they don't bargain over wages, for example—a certain degree of mutual problem solving with lower-level management is possible. But the works-council model had no chance in midcentury America. Managers saw shop-steward power as a nightmare, subversive of their "prerogatives," and the independent organization of lower level supervision—a real possibility in the mid-1940s—as tantamount to production anarchy. Meanwhile the unions knew that unless they nailed down a set of contractual work rules and monopolized the voice of all those they claimed to represent, American managers would not hesitate to weaken or subvert the union itself.[84] Thus, in 1959, in one of the longest strikes of the postwar era, the United Steelworkers shut down every firm in basic steel, in defense of contract clause 2B, which mandated that technological innovations that threatened to reduce staffing in the mills could not take place without prior union approval. Union-management stalemate on this issue would prove devastating to the health of an industry soon to face a wave of imported steel from highly efficient foreign furnaces constructed after the end of World War II.[85]

Corporatism in the Sixties?

During the 1960s the cohort of old New Dealers who actually staffed the domestic side of the New Frontier made one last effort to politicize the bargaining regime, reverse the slow decline of labor's weight in American politics, and put in place a labor-management concordat. They failed, but the gambit itself offers an instructive lesson from which to evaluate the potential for a corporatist solution to the labor problem at the very height of the Cold War.

President Kennedy sought to wage the Cold War with vigor, sustaining U.S. diplomatic and military supremacy. He thought defense of the dollar as the world's reserve currency essential to the projection of American power. Given the fixed exchange rates of that era, inflation had to be kept under strict control in order to manage the nation's increasingly difficult balance-of-payments problem. Kennedy therefore sought to repoliticize wage negotiations in the core industries in order to reach a settlement within a set of guideposts that linked noninflationary wage growth with the aggregate annual productivity increase. The key player in this effort was Arthur Goldberg, a longtime strategist and lawyer for the United Steelworkers; now secretary of labor in the new administration, Goldberg set up a high-profile Labor-Management Advisory Committee, a corporatist institution that Goldberg hoped might evoke the collaborationist spirit and successful statecraft of World War II. Part of its job was to negotiate an "incomes" policy to ensure that the new wage guideposts fixed by the Council of Economic Advisers—eventually set at 3.2 percent—were respected by both labor and capital.[86]

Many of the issues that would later bedevil the U.S. economy and its system of industrial relations were now put on the administration's labor-relations agenda: the threat of international competition, the effort to "manage" new technologies, and the relative distribution of national income between labor and capital. Despite some internal grumbling, trade-union leaders were quite willing to accommodate themselves to the Kennedy/Goldberg incomes policy if it was part of a more general, corporatist settlement that expanded employment, raised incomes, and forestalled a new round of managerial assaults upon the unions. Labor supported an "incomes" policy that institutionalized the status quo: the unions had been shaken by the recent managerial offensive, and they wanted to preserve the existing distribution of income between labor and capital. This would keep U.S. industry competitive in the emerging world market and give the labor-liberal coalition some leverage over managerial pricing and investment decisions.[87]

Much of the early 1960s debate over "automation" also took place within the context of whether management or labor should bear the costs or reap the benefits of the rapid technological change that was characteristic of manufacturing and transport services in this era. There were two union approaches to this issue. Many craft unionists—including those in the railroad brotherhoods, the printing trades, and construction—fought a rearguard battle in which specific job-destroying technologies were proscribed outright until union resistance became so costly, and unpopular, that a favorable monetary deal could be struck. In exchange for either a large lump-sum payment or an ironclad seniority guarantee for existing workers, the union opened the floodgates to the kind of technological innovation that utterly transformed work and unionism in the industry. The nation's politically insulated collective bargaining regime blocked a societywide approach to the dilemma of technological change, so such a deal was attractive to even the most radical of unionists. Thus in

1960 the erstwhile Communist Harry Bridges negotiated a "Mechanization and Modernization" agreement that accelerated the "containerization" of all West Coast longshoring work. Registered ILWU stevedores took home a bundle, and the union retained control of the newly mechanized work, but the ILWU shriveled as longshoring practically vanished from the West Coast occupational landscape.[88]

This strategy was often accompanied by an effort to reduce the workweek and curb excessive overtime in order to spread the existing work. Led by AFL-CIO president George Meany, an ex-plumber from the Bronx, the labor federation officially endorsed the thirty-five-hour workweek in 1962. Meany and his building-trades allies retained much of their pre–New Deal worldview: they were not Keynesians but saw competition for a limited set of jobs as a fundamental constraint faced by the labor movement.[89]

By contrast the social-democratic, mass-production wing of the union movement emphasized job creation, not job rationing. They saw the "automation" issues as best resolved through a program of Keynesian stimulation and labor-market reforms, not unlike those famously in place in Sweden. Goldberg wanted to strengthen and federalize state employment departments, so as to end discrimination—not only racial bias, but inequitable treatment that arose out of regional and occupational blockages as well. He wanted a more fluid, national market in labor so that patterns set in the high-wage core of the economy would spread more easily to the contingent labor force. Goldberg and other labor-liberals schooled in the employment politics of the depression and World War II understood that racial discrimination deepened black poverty, but that the poor performance of the economy, especially as it impacted blue-collar workers, remained the chief problem. They saw job creation, not a more equitable rationing of the existing employment opportunities, as the key to racial progress.[90]

Labor-liberals also rejected the shorter workweek because they stood by the belief that Americans in general and blue-collar workers in particular were still in real need of more of the world's basic material goods. (This was a viewpoint shared by Kennedy, as well, who saw proposals for a thirty-five hour workweek as virtual sabotage in the Cold War context.) Within the house of labor the ex-socialist

Walter Reuther was the most vociferous opponent of the shorter workweek. In a celebrated exchange of the early 1950s, he made graphically evident his Keynesian, macroeconomic understanding of the problem. When the auto-union leader toured one of Ford's newly automated engine plants, an executive taunted him with the remark, "You know, Walter, not one of these machines pays union dues." To which Reuther shot back, "And not one of them buys new Ford cars, either."[91]

With Goldberg's backing and Kennedy's interest, the Reutherite wing of the union movement pushed to introduce elements of a Swedish-style system into U.S. labor relations. American social democrats wanted a "technological clearinghouse" to keep track of trends in automation, and, in order to limit the inflationary pressures that generated so many industrial disputes, labor sought a "permanent price hearings agency" to counter the "administered prices" so easily set within the oligopolistic sector of the economy. Most important, American liberals wanted to reimpose social and political controls on capital mobility, to forestall deindustrialization in the urban North, while directing new investment toward the "depressed areas" that Senator Paul Douglas and writer Michael Harrington had once again made part of the affluent society's social imagination. These new initiatives were not simply government spending programs. Rather, the labor-liberals of that era sought to incrementally recast the sociopolitical environment so as to sustain a revitalized labor-management accord.[92]

Not unexpectedly, the most powerful corporations wanted no part of a new corporatist arrangement. Whatever the consensus reached inside Goldberg's Labor-Management Advisory Committee, it never extended to the most critical management players. This became dramatically clear in April 1962, when Goldberg's effort to broker a rock-bottom wage-price concordat in the steel industry collapsed in an explosive confrontation between U.S. Steel and the Kennedy White House. Facing low-wage imports and Kennedy administration pressure, the United Steelworkers of America agreed to a contract that just about froze labor costs. But U.S. Steel CEO Roger Blough would not reciprocate. In what JFK considered an absolute double cross, U.S. Steel raised tonnage prices, followed by the rest of the industry. Kennedy's fury soon leaked to the press: "My father always told me that all businessmen were sons of bitches, but I never believed it until now." The Goldberg-Kennedy effort to orchestrate even the softest sort of tripartite corporatism was dead.[93]

By mobilizing the prestige and power of the federal government, including the Defense Department's procurement leverage, President Kennedy did force U.S. Steel and the rest of the industry to rescind its price hike. But this was a Pyrrhic victory. The collapse of the stock market one month later was taken by most in the administration as a warning that any additional confrontation, or any formal effort to create a labor-management accord, would carry a disastrous economic cost and generate a huge political backlash.[94]

The Unquiet Decades

Industrial peace was not a virtue of the postwar collective-bargaining regime. Although journalists and academics often commented on the routine character of industrial relations in the 1950s, their measuring rod was taken from the extraordinarily tumultuous, and seemingly unpredictable, decade that followed the 1934–37 upheaval. Equally important, many of the most influential commentators, then and later, have either been disappointed leftists who disparaged the consumerist struggles of the postwar working class, or those social scientists who found consensual functionalism wherever industrial conflict seemed to rear its disruptive head. So the strikes of that era have disappeared from our social imagination, which is one reason the idea of a labor-management accord has proven so convenient.

But American unions proved remarkably combative. From the late 1940s through the early 1970s, strike levels in the United States stood higher than at any time, before or since. During the 1950s, organized labor averaged 352 big work stoppages a year. That dropped to something like 285 a year throughout the next two decades, before plummeting to 83 in the 1980s and even less during the century's last decade. The number of workers involved in stoppages followed a similar trajectory. In the steel industry alone there were national strikes in 1946, 1949, 1952, 1956, and 1959. The UAW shut down at least one of the big three automakers at almost every contract renewal between 1948 and 1973. And there were also well-organized work stoppages among workers not normally thought of as particularly union conscious: grocery clerks, taxi drivers, deliverymen, oil refinery workers, and in the 1960s, schoolteachers, hospital staff, and post office employees.[95]

Now that such "routine," annual stoppages have practically vanished from our socioeconomic life, we can understand their organic relationship to the "accord" of those years. Industrywide or companywide strikes were unknown in those nations, such as Germany, Sweden, and Great Britain, where a corporatist social compact really did exist early in the postwar era. In the United States, on the other hand, the necessity for such work stoppages demonstrated the extent to which both capital and labor felt aggrieved by the postwar labor-relations settlement. There was a continual testing of the boundaries, a repeated probe for weaknesses in the adversary's organizational armor. But these strikes did play a most vital function: they policed management policy, making certain that the standards won in the union sector would flow to millions of non-union workers, both white and blue. Thus white-collar workers were virtually immune from layoff in the 1950s and 1960s: during recessionary times most *Fortune* 500 companies kept their white-collar staff on the payroll even as layoffs cut deeply into the ranks of unionized blue-collar workers. IBM put even its production workers on salary in 1959 as a union-avoidance strategy. Many non-union firms happily plagiarized the wage, benefit, and grievance standards organized labor had won in its periodic strikes and contract renegotiations. Sears, Kodak, DuPont, as well as virtually all firms in banking and insurance, kept the pay of their employees a half step ahead of workers doing similar work in unionized firms.[96] Finally, the very recurrence of these midcentury strikes reinforced a sense of union consciousness among millions of working Americans. Except in the South, management found picket lines hard to break during the first three decades after the end of World War II. Since wage inequalities were muted, replacement workers—still called "scabs"—were not easy to find, and when they were, managers knew that their deployment in a strike would generate years of social strife.[97]

A militant set of entrepreneurial, family-owned firms were the shock troops in capital's battle to undermine union power and trans-industry labor standards. Although big business had the market power to pass on to consumers the burden of higher wages, smaller firms, usually in more competitive markets, felt heavily penalized when unions demanded industrywide wage bargains. They had neither the pricing leverage nor the high productivity to absorb the high wages paid by industry leaders like Ford Motor, American Airlines, the big-city construction firms, or well-unionized grocery chains like Safeway and Giant.[98]

Industrial warfare was therefore continuous on the small-producer, non-union frontier: at Kohler, Lone Star Steel, Thompson Products, Allen-Bradley, Cone Mills, Sears Robeck, and in California agriculture. Along with key corporations in the Southern textile industry, these smaller, often family-owned firms provided the financial and organizational support for the National Right-to-Work Committee, founded in 1955; and they generated much of the impulse that put "right-to-work" referenda on the ballot in California, Ohio, and other industrial states during the 1958 elections.[99]

During the Taft-Hartley debates, conservative Republicans had tried and failed to ban industrywide bargaining, or as its detractors liked to call it, "monopoly unionism." Without the destruction of this institution, NAM's Ira Mosher had then argued, "practical operating problems are neglected and social philosophies and ideologies are emphasized. . . . In short there is a marked tendency in such circumstances to emphasize the 'class struggle' and to argue and fight for political ends."[100]

A decade of exposure to industrywide bargaining had done little to moderate such views. American conservatives feared and denounced the kind of corporatist settlement that might emerge from transcompany bargaining, if only because small and midsized entrepreneurial firms were sure to feel a regulatory squeeze under any such arrangement. Attorney Donald Richberg, who moved from union stalwart to staunch reaction during the 1930s and 1940s, now declared that industrywide bargaining inevitably led to "big government . . . a Socialist labor government."[101] But such a specter was not the only problem with "monopoly unionism." Inflation was mild in the 1950s, certainly compared to what had come right after World War II—and what would come two decades later—but this incremental rise in the cost of living nevertheless had a right-wing bite during an era in which most of the working population remained without COLA protection. Indeed, inflationary pressures came to seem but an index of irresponsible labor power. Thus in 1956 the National Association of Manufacturers was able to denounce the "purchasing power fallacy" because "the wage-price spiral gets no one anywhere." Likewise, Ohio's Timken Roller Bearing Company, a prototypical family firm close to the Taft wing of the GOP, bought magazine ads that warned, "As STEEL goes . . . so goes inflation!" Not unexpectedly, Timken proved a pillar of the Ohio "right-to-work" campaign in 1958.[102]

Given such atmospherics, the nation's big industrial firms took their first real opportunity—the recession of 1957–58—to launch an aggressive effort to renegotiate the balance of power within the industrial relations realm. U.S. Steel, at the epicenter of this counteroffensive, was determined to reduce labor costs, boost profits, and modernize its mills. CEO Roger Blough denounced as "phantom profits" the inflation-swollen earnings of his firm. To rewin control of the balance sheet, U.S. Steel management sought to breach the set of contractual work rules that the United Steelworkers had fought for in the 1930s and that virtually every worker considered the chief fruit of the shop-floor constitutionalism for which the union stood. As we shall see in chapter 4, this counterattack was given heavy ideological reinforcement by the sensational McClellan Committee hearings of 1957 and 1958, whose exposé of Teamster criminality struck a serious blow to the legitimacy of the entire trade-union movement. The 116-day steel strike of 1959 proved the most spectacularly visible consequence of this corporate offensive. Counting hours of work lost, it was the largest single industrial conflict in the nation's history.[103]

The anti-union right finally found its champion in Republican senator Barry Goldwater, who got his political start in Phoenix by successfully mobilizing his fellow retailers on behalf of Arizona's 1948 "right-to-work" law. By the end of the 1950s he was declaring industrywide bargaining "an evil to be eliminated," and Walter Reuther "a more dangerous menace than the Sputnik or anything Soviet Russia might do in America."[104] By the time Goldwater ran for president in 1964, liberals were wont to question his sanity. But if Goldwater's views on nuclear warfare were cause for alarm, his understanding of the trajectory that would be followed by U.S. industrial relations proved remarkably prescient. Presided over by Goldwater's most successful ideological heir, industrywide bargaining collapsed early in the 1980s, and with it what remained of the nation's exceedingly tenuous "labor-management accord."

CHAPTER 4

Erosion of the Union Idea

DURING THE 1950S AND 1960S the reputation of American unions and of the entire New Deal bargaining system began a precipitous decline. Even as unions reached their twentieth-century apogee, as economic institutions and as mass membership organizations, the old labor question practically vanished from popular political discourse. The quest for an industrial democracy at the work site came to an abrupt end in all but the most radical circles. At the very moment in which a rights-conscious revolution began to transform American political culture, the model of collective action, of democratic empowerment embodied in the Wagner Act, was reaching something close to an ideological dead end.

This was a project, not so much of the political right, which still polemicized against "monopoly unionism," but of radical intellectuals and centrist liberals, whose critique of postwar trade unionism proved far more demoralizing and, in the long run, more politically and jurisprudentially consequential. In the United States intellectuals, jurists, journalists, academics, and politicians came to see the unions as little more than a self-aggrandizing interest group, no longer a lever for progressive change. This critique would have a vast influence in the academy, among social movement activists during the 1960s and 1970s, and throughout the judiciary, where a discourse of "rights" soon came to have a powerfully corrosive impact on the legitimacy and integrity of the union idea.

Big Labor

Although the erosion of the union idea was largely an ideological and cultural phenomenon, it was surely advanced by a highly visible transformation of the trade unions themselves. The unions were now "Big Labor": in the 1950s and 1960s it seemed to many former allies that caution, bureaucracy, and self-interest had replaced the visionary quest for solidarity and social transformation that had been a hallmark of the depression decade. Collective bargaining had become a self-contained system, and the unions, so it was thought, had "matured," even become part of the "establishment."[1] This indictment rested upon much social myth, but an institutional reality was there as well. Compared to Europe, to Canada, and to much of the depression-era world of American labor, individual trade unions were now internal oligarchies, administratively top-heavy with technicians and officials, and increasingly parochial in their bargaining strategy and political outlook. This was a product of much history and politics: the birth of the new unions under a New Deal wing, the forced-draft quest for production and social peace during World War II, and the anti-Communist purge that chilled the union movement's more adventuresome spirits.

But even more important, the stolid quality of postwar U.S. unionism reflected the institutional constraints and legal structures under which the unions were forced to function. Ironically, it was the very decentralization and fragmentation of the postwar bargaining system, the hostility of management, and the relative weakness and vulnerability of the labor movement that generated a huge stratum of full-time officials, put a premium on authoritarian leadership, devalued independent politics, and opened the door to a whole set of corruptions that became an integral part of the postwar union mythos.

The firm-centered system of U.S. bargaining generated a positively baroque industrial-relations regime. By the 1980s when labor claimed only about 16 percent of the wage and salary workers as members, there were nevertheless 175,000 collective-bargaining agreements in force. American workers were represented by 70,000 local unions, roughly 275 state and regional organizations, and 174 national

Democracy or Oligarchy? Local officers conduct an International Woodworkers of America meeting during the 1950s. (Credit: IWA, Ph 34, Special Collections & University Archives, University of Oregon)

unions, of which only 108 were affiliated with the AFL-CIO. By way of contrast West Germany, with a far higher union density and more centralized set of bargaining structures had only 19 unions, 17 of which were members of the powerful union federation, Deutsche Gewerkshaftbund (DGB).[2] Of course, unionism was not only more decentralized in the United States than in Europe, but the individual sub-units were burdened with a set of servicing functions unknown in countries where either a labor party or a stronger welfare state assumed those responsibilities. Many unions in the United States—and quite often these were local unions representing but a few hundred members—were responsible for the negotiation and administration, not just of wage schedules and seniority systems, but of pension benefits, health insurance, and various kinds of supplemental unemployment aid. In addition, unions at the local, regional, and national levels directly lobbied state and national officeholders, endorsed candidates, and raised money and troops for their campaigns.

All this activity sustained the largest and best-paid stratum of full-time salaried officers in the labor-movement world. "International" unions (because of their Canadian membership) directly employed several hundred staffers, while virtually every local of more than a few hundred workers supported a paid official. Functionary worker ratios in the United States were something like one in three hundred at the end of the 1950s, while the European average was about one full-time officeholder per two thousand unionists. The U.S. had sixty thousand full-time union officers in 1960, compared to just four thousand in Great Britian.[3] Not unexpectedly, these top-heavy, well-paid bureaucracies proved highly resistant to rotation in office, quite as much as in the UAW, whose leadership advertised its adherence to democratic procedure in an extravagant fashion, as in the Teamsters or the building trades, where little pretense was made of such democratic norms. Indeed, the outright corruption of unions like the Teamsters, the National Maritime Union, the Laborers, East Coast Longshoremen, and Confectionary Workers was a product of the near irresistible temptations faced by an entrenched stratum of union officials when given the opportunity to administer health, welfare, and pension funds that mounted into the billions.[4]

The burdensome and decentralized union-servicing function meant that, whatever the politics or personalities of those who led individual unions, the time, money, and effort that went into organizing and internal education fell away sharply. Radicals had always been the best organizers, but where they had not been purged, they were now subtly derided as missionaries or idealists, and paid accordingly. "In established unions the accent has shifted principally to administrative work," complained a 1961 report from the Center for the Study of Democratic Institutions. "Organization tends to be segregated into a specialized activity" of low prestige and political reward. Not unexpectedly, the proportion of union resources devoted to this task declined steadily from the 1940s onward.[5]

When it came to postwar union pathologies, the big International Brotherhood of Teamsters (IBT) was usually Exhibit A. The Teamsters grew rapidly in the postwar era because the trucking industry and its satellites, including warehousing, food processing, and supermarkets, ballooned in size and significance. By 1970 the IBT was the nation's largest union, with more than 2 million members. Teamster locals were often quite militant during these years, spurred on by the battles necessary to expand the frontier of service-sector unionism and the jurisdictional disputes that often accompanied such organizing efforts. Meanwhile, rank-and-file Teamsters, especially in the core warehouse and over-the-road transport sectors, were remarkably self-confident and aggressive, in part because the extreme fragmentation of the industry—there were almost 65,000 trucking companies hauling freight in 1971—meant that few firms could long withstand a strike or a slowdown.[6]

But Teamster "success" was structured so as to conform, in only a slightly exaggerated fashion, to the peculiar dynamics of the postwar industrial-relations system. Reflecting the fragmented character of their employer counterparts, and, after 1947, a labor law that stifled even the crudest forms of interunion solidarity, the Teamster union itself was composed of an often fractious set of feudal baronies that coincided with the regional scope of each local labor market. Although top union leaders like Dave Beck and Jimmy Hoffa were often labeled "boss" or "czar," their operational control of union bargaining structures—outside of their own regional fortresses—was tenuous at best. Hoffa was actually the union's most aggressive centralizer, but his efforts proved largely futile, and in the end quite dangerous. Top Teamster officials did play fast and loose with the union's big pension funds, but the real locus of bargaining power and political influence remained on the local and IBT conference levels.[7] These nepotistic barons saw themselves as salesmen of labor, often competitive entrepreneurs who certainly had no sympathy for the industrywide bargaining still opposed by so many employers. Indeed, such Teamster officials were just the kind of business unionists that the sponsors of the Taft-Hartley Act sought to encourage: insular, nonideological, and hostile to the brand of social unionism that required working-class solidarity. As the labor economist Walter Galenson put it in 1962, Beck and Hoffa "made no bones about the fact that they were in business—the business of selling labor—and if alongside their main wares they were engaged in selling other goods which yielded personal profits, what harm to the members?"[8]

By way of contrast, the United Auto Workers was characterized by far less internal strife and far less corruption, not because Walter Reuther was a more idealistic figure than Jimmy Hoffa, although he was, nor because auto workers were more honest and peace loving than truckers, but because UAW bargaining structures were more unified and hierarchical, which was itself a function of a more oligopolistic industry structure and of the key, early NLRB and WLB rulings that centralized industry bargaining arrangements. This did not make for internal union democracy, but it did put in place a bureaucratic, rather than a feudal, governing regime. When the UAW negotiated its celebrated five-year contract with General Motors in 1950, Walter Reuther and his unified leadership team expected that in return for GM's unprecedented wage and benefit package, they could guarantee a strike-free era of social peace in more than a hundred GM plants. "This kind of collective bargaining," concluded economist Frederick Harbison, "calls for intelligent trading rather than table pounding . . . for internal union discipline rather than grass roots rank and file activity."[9]

In politics as well as collective bargaining, the relative weakness and fragmentation of the unions sharply limited their societywide influence. In the quarter century that followed the end of World War II a solid majority of all unionists remained faithful Democrats, certainly when voting for president or their Capitol Hill representative. When the sociologist Arthur Kornhauser surveyed the political attitudes of Detroit autoworkers in 1952 he found that they "are not going 'middle class,'" a view sustained by the incisive reportage of journalist Samuel Lubell, who found that "this same kind of class voting can be seen in every American city."[10] Indeed, the unionization of more than one-third of all workers outside the South had given to party politics a social-democratic dimension; thus in 1954 and 1958, not to mention the landslide of 1964, liberal-labor forces made substantial legislative headway.

What had changed between the 1930s and the 1950s was not some abstract measure of political consciousness, but the range of opportunities for political expression and social action that confronted workers and their organizations. Labor's electoral mobilizations never bore the fruit expected of them, for the liberal wing of the Democratic Party could not bring to bear its full weight, either within its own party or in the national legislature. Although unions in meatpacking, steel, automobiles, and electoral products sought to link their bargaining posture to a larger social-democratic project, the concentration of their membership and economic clout in a Northeastern/Midwestern industrial heartland limited their political leverage, not only on the national level, but even within relatively industrialized states like Indiana, Missouri, and Nebraska where the labor movement faced a strong rural/small producer opposition. The Teamsters and the construction trades often allied themselves with conservative municipal machines, some Republican in party affiliation; and in the South the vacuum created by the absence of a union presence in textiles, food processing, and light manufacturing meant that the national Democratic Party would long contain a militant Southern wing hostile to unionism or to a significant rise in the social wage. "He who would understand politics in the large may ponder the status of labor," wrote political scientist V. O. Key in 1953, the year in which labor's membership stood at its proportional apogee, "a numerically great force in a society adhering to the doctrine of the rule of numbers, yet without proportionate durable political power as a class."[11]

The merger of the AFL and the CIO in 1955 ratified these changes in the labor movement. With the CIO's expulsion of the Communist-dominated unions, few substantial political differences remained between the two federations. The AFL, dominated by the construction trades and other business unionists, was almost twice the size of the CIO. It was therefore fitting that the chief of the new AFL-CIO would not be the CIO's energetic president, Walter Reuther, but the AFL's organizationally cautious George Meany, who would later boast that he had never walked a picket line or led a strike. "We do not seek to recast American society in any particular doctrinaire or ideological image," Meany asserted. "We seek an ever rising standard of living."[12]

Under Meany, the AFL-CIO remained a staunch advocate of New Deal–style social reform, but its strategy and culture were completely at odds with the industrial union upsurge of the 1930s. Except during the biannual election season, the AFL-CIO discouraged marches and demonstrations, including those against unemployment in the late 1950s and in support of civil rights during the early 1960s. Winter executive board meetings were invariably held at a Florida resort hotel. And the merged labor movement stopped singing. Folk songs and labor songs had a vaguely leftist, rank-and-file flavor, so when Henry Fleisher, an old CIO staffer, proposed a new AFL-CIO songbook right after the merger, he was met with incredulity by Virginia Tehas, George Meany's longtime secretary. "What are you trying to do, make fools of us? . . . They don't sing at union meetings." Fleisher told her union singing built morale on the picket line, but Tehas replied, "Well, I've never heard of anything so ridiculous in my life." A new union songbook was eventually published, but with "The Star-Spangled Banner" up front, well before "Solidarity Forever" and the Joe Hill ballads.[13]

Pluralism: Industrial and Otherwise

Although U.S. unions and their bargaining arrangements were always subject to a certain criticism, and not only from the corporations, one of the most remarkable features of the early postwar landscape is the extent to which mainstream intellectuals, legal experts, and labor economists celebrated what we can now so clearly see as the gross deformities inherent in this laborite world. At midcentury most American liberals thought the doctrine of "industrial pluralism" constituted the twentieth century solution to the labor question. From the Progressive era forward, policy-making intellectuals like John R. Commons, William Leiserson, Harry Millis, and Edwin Witte, saw the unfolding of a state-sponsored collective-bargaining regime as the sure path to social peace, class equilibrium, and industrial democracy. "I concede to my radical friends," Commons wrote in 1934, "that my trade-union philosophy always made me a conservative. It is not revolutions and strikes we want, but collective bargaining on something like an organized equilibrium of equality."[14]

Such views won even greater power and prestige during the 1940s and 1950s. The phrase "industrial democracy" practically vanished from the vocabulary of political life and union discourse. Likewise, "the labor question" no longer seemed much of a question at all. It was subsumed within the social technics that had become the language of collective bargaining and labor law. As we shall see, however, the very legitimacy achieved by American trade unionism in the immediate postwar era contained a self-destructive contradiction. As union corruption and complacency came under attack, and as the rights revolution saturated American politics and culture after 1963, the very same set of political and social ideas that had once sustained trade unionism now devaluated and marginalized these same institutions in the last third of the twentieth century.

In the previous chapter, we saw how the collective-bargaining idea stood counterpoised to the politicized bargaining and tripartite corporatism for which Progressive-era reformers and New Deal unionists had fought. By the early 1950s, "collective bargaining," a firm-centered set of bargaining arrangements "free" of overt politicization, was all that remained of the old idea of an industrial democracy. But now liberal intellectuals, journalists, and not a few unionists took this political-organizational retreat and recast it as a triumphal solution to the labor question, in the process turning the idea of industrial pluralism into something very close to a celebration of the status quo. Indeed, in the Cold War context, "free collective bargaining" was precisely that, which is why the AFL-CIO, the State Department, and the Voice of America hailed its depoliticized virtues around the globe.

"Collective bargaining is the great social invention that has institutionalized industrial conflict," wrote the labor economist Robert Dublin in 1954. "In much the same way that the electoral process and majority rule have institutionalized political conflict in a democracy, collective bargaining has created a stable means for resolving industrial conflict." And to drive the ideological point home, academic colleague Arthur Ross offered an elbow to those whose politics had once been more expansive. "One of the great virtues of collective bargaining . . . is that it permits the formulation of limited issues which are amenable to resolution and blurs over large differences of principle. . . . This, of course, is revolting to those who will settle for nothing less than 'basic solutions.'"[15]

Such sentiments fit nicely with the leadership style of a George

Meany, a Jimmy Hoffa, or even a Walter Reuther, but they clearly misjudged the far more ominous industrial dynamic at work in postwar America. Why then did so many American academics and intellectuals engage in such wishful social thinking? Why did industrial pluralism become so ideologically well rooted, despite the manifest illusions that lay within the wood?

For those who presumed to analyze midcentury industrial life, the history of contemporary capitalism was a nightmare from which they were trying to escape. American liberals, and not a few radicals, were in full flight from the class politics of the European socialist tradition and the ambitious social engineering that had been part of both Progressive era reform and New Deal state building. All the most influential intellectuals and academics of this era had been adults in the 1930s or early 1940s, and a considerable number had stood on the left, including Seymour Martin Lipset, Daniel Bell, Reinhold Neibuhr, John Kenneth Galbraith, Will Herberg, Clark Kerr, Robert Dahl, and James Burnham. But these were the "twice born," to use the phrase of Daniel Bell, men and women who had rejected the socialism of their youth for a more sober and limited creed.[16] To them feckless majorities in a mass, industrialized society generated a runaway democracy that might well subvert liberal values and democratic processes. The political ambitions so fearfully projected by the fascist and Stalinist regimes of Europe made a decentralized, nonideological, interest-group theory of politics on this side of the Atlantic seem desperately attractive, even more so when "populist" demagogues, from Huey Long to Joseph McCarthy, subverted civil liberties and democratic comity. Classes, capitalists, and collective struggle might yet exist, but these social theorists sought and found an Americanized version that repudiated the ideological polarization of prewar Europe. To the influential sociologist Seymour Martin Lipset, the American class struggle would always be "a fight without ideologies, without red flags, without May Day parades."[17]

Two wishful presuppositions underlay this optimistic conservatism. Postwar students of industrial society were not procapitalist ideologues. Many remained critics of the corporation and disdainful of business leadership. But that was just the problem: they devalued capitalism as a system of power, and in its place saw profits and production within a bureaucratically structured matrix. Thus Peter Drucker, the Austrian émigré who became the nation's most important management theorist since Frederick Taylor, considered the modern U.S. corporation the paradigmatic institution of the contemporary world, "the representative social actuality." But if Drucker was a herald of corporate America, he was equally determined to divorce such views from any taint of the old free enterprise, laissez-faire. To Drucker and to a generation of societal savants who would follow, the corporation was essentially a political, planning mechanism, a Weberian rationalization of industrial society. The "rights of capital" had been replaced by the "responsibilities of management." Thus in his pioneering study of General Motors, published just after World War II, Drucker eschewed the usual categories of business analysis—profits, prices, labor costs, and the like—and emphasized "the traditional questions of politics and political analysis" as applied to the internal life of the large corporation.[18]

Unlike Drucker, Arthur Schlesinger, Jr. was a liberal democrat. When he published *The Vital Center* in 1949, Schlesinger declared himself a part of the "Non-Communist Left." He was a militant New Dealer who thought the pivot of American history turned upon the conflict between the business community, often in alliance with a not-so-democratic state, and the plebeian movements and their intellectual allies, who sought to rebalance the social scales. "Class conflict" wrote Schlesinger in *The Vital Center* "is essential if freedom is to be preserved, because it is the only barrier against class domination."[19]

But Schlesinger shared with Drucker a conviction that neither class nor economics stood at the fulcrum of social choice. Like so many others who had witnessed the rise of Stalinism and fascism and experienced the power of the warfare state, he was transfixed by the specter of an organizational revolution that transcended property relations and business interests. This was the "wishful thinking" recently identified by historian Howard Brick. It entrapped many postwar liberals, giving them hope for a kind of "silent revolution" that promised the effective suppression of the market and the subordination of economic affairs to social regulation.[20] "Britain has already submitted itself to social democracy," wrote Schlesinger in *The Vital*

Center, and "the United States will very like advance in that direction through a series of New Deals and the advance will be accelerated if the country fails to keep out of a depression." But Schlesinger expected no dramatic conflict, because in a post–New Deal America the differences among classes "are much less impassable than the differences between capitalist democracy and authoritarianism; and sometimes in the heat of battle the warring classes tend to forget their family relationship."[21]

A second variety of postwar wishful thinking sought to transform and devalue the meaning of work itself. In a burst of optimistic prognostication, public intellectuals like Norbert Wiener, William Foote White, David Reisman, Herbert Marcuse, and Clark Kerr argued that first, a new world of postwar consumption would replace work and production as the social and moral focus of life, and that second, the decline in the hours of work and the growth in leisure-time activities would further marginalize the work experience. In their classic studies of midcentury blue-collar life, sociologists Eli Chinoy and Robert Dublin found that factory workers just wanted to get out of the factory, not make life there better. "If this finding holds generally," wrote Dublin, "the role and significance of work in American society has departed from its presumed historical position." Indeed, whatever the valuation of traditional work, the days of the factory were numbered. Just as tractors, reapers, and other forms of mechanization had slashed the farm population, so too would automation generate such an increase in factory productivity that blue-collar work would practically vanish. And as for the growing world of the salaried, white-collar employees emplaced within the bureaucratic corporation or other large entity, both David Reisman and C. Wright Mills affirmed their alienation and psychological disengagement, a judgment available in the influential white-collar novels of that era, including Saul Bellow's *Adventures of Augie March* and Sloan Wilson's *The Man in the Grey Flannel Suite*.[22]

All this made the appeal of pluralist theory and political culture well-nigh irresistible. If capitalism had begun to morph into a more politically malleable system, if classes did not really clash in the United States, and if the experience of work was becoming increasingly marginal to the bulk of the population, then a theory of society that put interest-group parochialism at its center might well flourish. Thus did American intellectuals begin a two-decade-long love affair with what Amherst College political scientist Earl Latham called "the group basis of politics." To Columbia's David Truman "this pluralistic structure is a central fact of the distribution of power in the society. . . . Within and among these groups, or rather their leading elements, a large fraction of the strengths and weaknesses of the American system is to be found."[23] Stable, nonideological conflict was the natural product of the peaceful clash of interest groups. Government does not plan, or even lead, but as Latham argued, it "referees the group struggle, ratifies the victories of the successful coalitions, and records the terms of the surrenders, compromises, and conquests in the form of statutes."[24]

"In a pressure group society, labor has a legitimate political role," wrote Daniel Bell, in 1952 the labor editor of *Fortune* magazine. From this influential post he offered the kind of analytical cynicism that made labor relations palatable to a skeptical business readership. Bell thus labeled modern trade unionism, "the capitalism of the proletariat." Within the labor movement Bell foresaw an inevitable conflict in which the unions as a market-shaping interest group won out against organized labor considered as an "ideological conception."[25] Likewise, Reinhold Neibuhr, who had denounced Henry Ford from a Detroit pulpit in the 1920s, summed up much conventional wisdom at the end of the 1950s. "Collective bargaining has come to be regarded as almost as basic as the right to vote," he told the labor-liberals who read the staunchly anti-Communist *New Leader*. "[T]he equilibrium of power achieved between management and labor . . . is one of the instruments used by a highly technical society, with ever larger aggregates of power, to achieve that tolerable justice which has rendered Western Civilization immune to the Communist virus."[26]

If political pluralism and its industrial variant, collective bargaining, were to function with effectiveness, then the interest groups involved required the kind of internal discipline necessary to sustain a coherent leadership and a de facto oligarchy. Robert Dahl actually defined twentieth century democracy as a "polyarchy," in which real pluralism flourishes, but only as competing elites bargain, compromise, and govern. When it came to labor and management, therefore, the old dream of an industrial democracy, animated by a mass of alert citizen-workers, seemed suddenly antique. Just as management represented an enlightened bureaucracy, so too did the unions best advance the interests of their members when they were led by officers of expertise and long tenure. "As long as things go well, the average union member doesn't want self government and is annoyed and resentful when an attempt is made to force its responsibilities on him," wrote the former Communist Will Herberg, in a 1943 formulation of this perspective. Fifteen years later Clark Kerr saw no reason to alter that judgment. "Union memberships are traditionally apathetic except in some crisis, and very little can be done about it. Compulsory strike votes proved a farce in World War II, and most bargaining issues cannot properly be put to membership vote."[27]

Kerr, then president of the University of California, considered himself a "liberal pluralist" who sought to guard the rights of the individual in the union and in other private associations. But like so many industrial pluralists, he thought self-discipline an overriding necessity. "Some loss of freedom," he wrote in 1958, "is inevitable in an effective industrial system. It will occur, more or less, whether the system is run by the employers alone, by the state alone, or even by the unions alone. Industrial society requires many rules and reasonable conformity to these rules."[28] Seymour Martin Lipset, also a star of Berkeley's social science faculty, gave to Kerr's Weberian observations a categorical élan. The oligarichical governance of American trade unions was a good thing because too much democracy led to internal division, ideological politics, and weakness in the face of the corporate enemy. "Unions, like all other large-scale organizations are constrained to develop bureaucratic structures," wrote Lipset in his 1960 masterwork, *Political Man: The Social Basis of Politics*. To Lipset, therefore, "[i]nstitutionalized democracy within private governments is not a necessary condition for democracy in the larger society." Such private oligarchies provide "a secure base for factionalism and real vested interests at the same time that they limit individual freedom within the organization and allow a degree of autonomy of action for both the leaders and the organization."[29]

This perspective was hardly confined to the academy. The wildcat strikes that proliferated during World War II and Korea made managers more appreciative of a "responsible" union leadership. Thus the Taft-Hartley Act made the international union legally responsible for actions by subordinate locals and minor officials. And when Dwight D. Eisenhower spoke at the AFL's 1952 convention, the GOP presidential nominee asserted that "unions have a secure place in our industrial life. . . . healthy collective bargaining requires responsible unions and responsible employers. Weak unions cannot be responsible."[30]

Six years later, Arthur Goldberg, the influential counsel for the Steelworkers, made the same point, albeit with some left-wing flavoring. Justifying the high-handed methods used by USW officials to defeat their internal union opponents, Goldberg argued that trade unions should not be held to the same standard as other democratically organized voluntary organizations. The unions were in a state of continual warfare with a set of corporate adversaries who took every opportunity to use divisions in the workforce to subvert them. "Even where the existence and status of a union is unquestioned—as, for example, in the basic steel industry—it is unlike political government in that it cannot legislate by itself on the matters of primary concern to it—wages, hours and working conditions. . . . If there is analogy to political government, the analogy is to a political government [during] a revolution, and which is periodically at war."[31]

During the 1950s the labor law sustained this pluralist perspective. "It is a mistake for the Government to enact regulations for the internal government of unions," opined Louis Stark, the venerable labor reporter for *The New York Times*.[32] "Once embarked on this road, complete state control is inevitable." Such views won acquiescence within most of the judiciary who endorsed regulatory minimalism and pluralist self-government. "The collective bargaining agreement," argued William O. Douglas, one of the Supreme Court's most steadfast liberals, "calls into being a new common law—the common law of a particular industry or of a particular plant . . . a system of industrial self-government."[33]

Liberals like Douglas and Harvard law professor Archibald Cox were determined to shape the law to strengthen the union's capacity to uphold its side of the collective-bargaining relationship. Their commitment to grievance arbitration as a key element in this system of industrial self-governance therefore put them at odds both with those who advocated judicial review or new government supervision on the one hand, and with wildcat strikers and other advocates of workplace "self-help," on the other.[34] The Supreme Court even justified the Taft-Hartley purge of the Communists in such pluralist terms. When the CIO sought a judicial overthrow of that section of the law requiring union officers to sign anti-Communist affidavits, Chief Justice Vinson's majority opinion had a decidedly familiar ring. "Because of the necessity to have strong unions to bargain on equal terms with strong employers, individual employees are required by law to sacrifice rights which, in some cases, are valuable to them."[35]

The Supreme Court therefore offered a narrow reading of Section 304 of the Taft-Hartley Act, which had prohibited the expenditure of union dues money on political activities. Likewise, it struck down conservative attempts to argue that union shop contracts violated the First Amendment rights of those workers coerced into payment of their dues. And despite the spread of right-to-work legislation in the South and Mountain West, the Court generally sustained the capacity of unions to discipline scabs during strikes and penalize those who refused to pay their dues.[36] In a series of "duty of fair representation" cases during the 1940s and 1950s, the courts intervened to make sure that racial minorities were given equal treatment. But most jurists, the liberals especially, refrained from second-guessing internal union decisions as to most other complaints, including administration of the grievance procedure.[37] Industrial relations scholars George Strauss and Don Willner summed up liberal-labor opinion this way in 1953, "Those who seek greater regulation . . . operate on the premise that the greatest threat to local union democracy is dictatorship. Actually the real enemy is not dictatorship but apathy. . . . in local unions, as in any other organization, democracy cannot be imposed; it must grow from within."[38]

Radical Disallusionment

Not everyone was a pluralist. America's left-wing intellectuals were not numerous in the 1950s, but their influence on liberal thought, academic scholarship, and judicial opinion was soon to become quite potent. During the two decades after the end of World War II they remained largely immune to the lures of industrial pluralism, developing instead a critique of the unions and of the entire "labor metaphysic" that would become remarkably pervasive in the 1960s when pluralism, in all its forms, entered an era of substantial decomposition. Then, their disillusionment would become the common coin of American liberalism.

In the United States, as in Europe, the Left had long maintained a heavy ideological investment in the trade-union movement, even when the actual leadership and program of organized labor proved hostile to their radical vision of a transformed society. During the 1930s left-wing students, intellectuals, and professors helped build the new industrial unions: the Brookwood Labor College was practically a cadre school for the new Congress of Industrial Organizations, as were the Marxist study circles sponsored by Communist or Socialist professors and students at City College, Berkeley, Brooklyn, and the University of Michigan.[39] The spirit of the CIO was not populist, but popular front. Thus Michael Denning's recent, enormously intriguing study, *The Cultural Front*, is predicated upon a "proletarianization" of American culture during the "Age of the CIO." In that era, those who worked within the "cultural apparatus" made a self-conscious turn toward the union movement and the working class. From Orson Welles, to Paul Robeson, to Marc Blitzstein, to the youthful cartoonists who waged a successful 1941 strike against the Walt Disney Studios, the centrality of labor and its organizations was never in dispute. After attending a 1943 UAW convention, Dwight Macdonald reported the proceedings creatively democratic, and the delegates "eager, alert, suspicious."[40]

C. Wright Mills captured this sensibility at the end of World War II. His *New Men of Power* (1948) was written during that creative, pre–Cold War moment, before the postwar industrial-relations regime had been put in place. Organized labor still had the will and power to wage strike battles that reflected the moral dichotomies of the depression decade; to Mills trade-union leaders were a "strategic elite," the unions the "only organization capable of stopping the main drift towards war and slump." He saw union leaders as thoroughly political animals, "managers of discontent" who were nevertheless in a constant state of "conflict with the powers of property." Mills was not a pluralist, industrial or otherwise. Trade-union leaders might quest for power, but they were not proponents of a pluralistic equilibrium. "Modern rebels," wrote Mills, "need not be romantic figures."[41]

The demise of this perspective was stunning and tragic. Even as the *New Men of Power* appeared, Mills was turning his back on the labor movement. By the time he published *White Collar* in 1951, he had lost any hope in a labor-based "strategic elite." Unions were at best a liberal "pressure-group" that simultaneously served as an agent of repression. "Trade unions," wrote Mills, "are the most reliable instruments to date for taming and channeling lower-class aspirations, for lining up the workers without internal violence during time of war, and for controlling their insurgency during times of peace and depression."[42] As for the new class of semiproletarianized white-collar workers, they were hardly the kind of material that could lay the basis for a new round of union growth. Instead, Mills saw them as the raw material needed by a mass, coercive society, perhaps flavored by the scent of fascism. Indeed, the entire labor metaphysic had come under a cloud, if not a sustained attack.[43]

Dwight Macdonald traveled a similar path. During World War II this quintessential New York intellectual (OK, he was not Jewish, nor did he attend City College) had celebrated the vibrancy of the union movement, but his larger disillusionment at the end of World War II, during what Macdonald called the summer of Auschwitz and Hiroshima, colored his whole political universe. World War II had ended not in a liberal democratic victory over fascism, but with the triumph in the West of all those statist, bureaucratic, dehumanizing tendencies inherent in capitalist mass society. In a pivotal 1946 essay, "The Root Is Man," Macdonald identified Weber's concept of "rationalization"—"the organization from the top of human life"—as the fundamental problem of the twentieth century. Hiroshima and the death camps were therefore the amoral, but logical fruits of the war.[44]

Such a perspective made the unions and their leadership little more than functionaries within a sealed system. The war and labor's cooperation therein soured Macdonald on mass democracy and the institutions necessary to give it expression. Labor was but another "collaborationist" bloc, wrote Macdonald. "Such international working-class solidarity as once existed has vanished," he polemicized even before the Cold War froze all politics, "and the workers of the world . . . are as brutally and rabidly nationalistic as their own ruling classes are." Writing in the *New Yorker* during the 1950s, Macdonald made a decade-long assault upon what he called the "masscult and midcult," that had corrupted or co-opted all that was radical and oppositional in working-class culture. Macdonald's heroes were those ethically and aesthetically sensitive individuals whose virtue lay largely in their very marginality. These were the conscientious objectors, beatniks, the invisible poor, and the draft-card burners who would come to occupy such a large slice of our political imagination.[45]

How can we explain this abrupt shift in outlook? Many will point to McCarthyism, but the anti-Communist purges that destroyed the CIO left wing proved but a small part of the answer. For those intellectuals and writers oriented toward the Communist Party, the wrong unionists won office and the progressives were purged from labor's ranks, thus opening the door to a social and foreign-policy bargain that emasculated the unions, ensured the dominance of capital, and advanced the interests of the Cold War state. Despite their ostensible class analysis, commentators in or close to the Communist Party tended to see trade-union leadership as almost entirely a question of an individual's ideology and career development. A representative text was Clancy Sigal's *Going Away: A Report, a Memoir* (1961). In Sigal's fictional account, the eclipse of the labor movement was a product of a struggle for power in which "the rivalry of Victor Hauser [Walter Reuther] and K. T. Tolliver [R. J. Thomas] for presidency of the union was the expressed essence of all the conflicting drives in the American working class immediately after the war." Sociologist David Milton, who had been active in the Communist-led National Maritime Union during the 1940s, made the same point in academic language. As a result of a "right-wing" victory in the unions, "[t]he CIO was now fully incorporated into a reconstructed political economy on terms dictated by the state. . . . An era of labor revolt ended as it had begun, with the jailing and blacklisting of labor militants.[46]

Mills, Macdonald, and other anti-Stalinist radicals generally endorsed the growth of anti-Communist sentiment within the labor movement. But their disdain for the victors was almost as great as it was for those who saw themselves as defeated by the Murray-Reuther bloc inside the CIO. The labor metaphysic lost its allure because their disenchantment was a product not so much of a rightward-drifting politics within the labor movement as it was of the transformation in the expectations of so many left-wing American intellectuals in the years just after the end of World War II. It was a shift that expressed their difficulty in coming to terms with a world defined by the kind of incremental, social-democratic aspirations that industrial pluralism and interest-group unionism embodied. Many intellectuals saw this as enormously repressive, ethically and morally claustrophobic. The "iron cage" of Max Weber and Robert Michels had replaced the liberating visions of Marx and Trotsky as the most reliable guide to the inner structures of American society.

Harvey Swados and Michael Harrington exemplified how a new generation of radical intellectuals came to terms with this world. Like Bell and Macdonald, they were both products of the anti-Communist left, but both were somewhat younger, and if truth be told, far more familiar with the actual flavor of postwar urban poverty or the nit and grit of manual work. When in 1956 Swados ran out of money to write the great American novel, he returned to the factory and soon published *On the Line*, a bleak series of interconnected short stories in which the workers are crushed and dehumanized by a never-ending assembly line.[47] Swados was not interested in measuring either workers or their unions by the yardstick of Bell or Mills. It was not their relationship to socialism that provoked Harvey Swados, or the collaboration of the trade unions in the Cold War, or even the persistence of economic inequality. Rather, Swados took the dignity and meaning of work as his touchstone, and with it the continuing reality of class in American life. "The plain truth is that factory work is degrading," wrote Swados in a key essay, "The Myth of the Happy Worker," "and it is about time we faced the fact."[48]

Michael Harrington always defined himself as a pro-labor socialist, but *The Other America*, his influential 1962 rediscovery of the nation's forgotten poor, avoided any mention of socialism and kept the author's Marxism well hidden. Instead Harrington advertised his youthful links to the Catholic worker movement in order to appeal to the guilt of middle-class liberals and their Kennedyesque leaders. Although he praised the labor movement, unionization was not a solution, nor did pluralist democracy offer much of a way out. "[T]he dispossessed at the bottom of society are unable to speak for themselves," wrote Harrington. "The people of the other America do not, by far and large, belong to unions, to fraternal organizations, or to political parties. They are without lobbies of their own; they put forward no legislative program." Since they had no voice, nor interest representation, the government could not be a passive referee, but would have to step forward itself.[48]

Here was a new way—or rather a renewed way—of thinking about the old labor question. Swados and Harrington were putting in place the moral dichotomies that so powerfully framed the discourse of the Sixties. Unfortunately, the trade union that loomed largest in the consciousness of American intellectuals failed them at this moment of heightened social expectations. By the late 1950s the UAW's inability to tame the monotony of the assembly line, prevent the deindustrialization of Detroit, or keep pace with the civil rights movement came under sustained scrutiny. Old radicals like B. J. Widick and Sidney Lens won a new hearing and a more youthful audience when they criticized the UAW. In the 1962 Port Huron Statement, Students for a Democratic Society leader Tom Hayden, who had grown up in a working-class suburb of Detroit, indicted the unions not for a failure to build socialism, but for their incapacity to confront the problems of automation, joblessness, world peace, and the Negro revolution. Hayden was actually far more hopeful about the unions than Mills, Macdonald, or Swados. At the very least, a "revitalization of the labor movement" was on his agenda, but in the 1962 SDS document, Hayden's laborite hopes are hard to take seriously, given his indictment of a "labor bureaucracy . . . cynical . . . and afraid of rank-and-file involvement in the work of the union."[50]

Indeed, by the time Harvey Swados published his famous 1963 essay "The UAW—Over the Top or Over the Hill?" the critique of the nation's most progressive and powerful union had turned acerbic. Here, the alienation, humiliation, and speed-up experienced by automobile workers were seen less as the product of industrial life itself than as a consequence of the UAW's failure to fulfill the aspirations of its founding generation. In a critique of the Reuther circle that a generation of new leftists would later make of other labor-liberals, Swados declared that manipulation had replaced mobilization of the membership, bureaucracy had triumphed over locally initiated activism. "One cannot complain, as one might with almost any other union, of an absence of intellect," wrote Swados in *Dissent*. "What one can say, I think with justification, is that the UAW leadership no longer takes its own demands seriously."[51]

The McClellan Committee

This kind of left-wing disillusionment with the unions and with the whole structure of collective bargaining became pervasive throughout liberal political culture in the years after 1958. Pluralism's ideological architecture, in social thought, judicial opinion, and popular sentiment, became increasingly attenuated. Many liberals adopted views once held by those on the Left, while the hard, anti-union right, making good use of this critique, became increasingly vocal and aggressive. Of course, some industrial pluralists still advanced the old faith, but their audience was now largely confined to the band of technocratic scholars and practitioners huddling within the embattled domain called "industrial relations."[52]

Three important developments made for this ideological sea change. First, the recession of 1957–58, the deepest in two decades, demonstrated that postwar capitalism was hardly on automatic pilot. A self-governing equilibrium between capital and labor was not sufficient to make the economy function with fairness or efficiency. Second, the civil rights movement had begun to stir, which set a new and higher standard for those who claimed to speak for the underdog. Pluralism, industrial or otherwise, no longer seemed to describe social reality in the United States, especially when it justified oligarchic rule. And finally, the McClellan Committee hearings of 1957 and 1958 had a devastating impact on the moral standing of the entire trade-union world, belying labor's claim that it constituted the most important and efficacious movement for democracy and social progress.[53]

Opening the door to liberal defection and right-wing attack, the sensational set of corruption hearings chaired by Senator John McClellan marked a true shift in the public perception of American trade unionism and of the collective-bargaining system within which it was embedded. During the 1950s high-profile hearings, trials and investigations uncovered corruption, autocracy, and nepotism among the leaders of numerous trade-union locals, especially those on the New York docks, throughout the short-haul trucking industry, in some construction trades, and among unions that had organized bakeries, restaurants, and bars. Such union criminality was largely concentrated in highly decentralized, multi-employer industries, which gave individual union leaders, or their mob-connected surrogates, the opportunity to skim the pension fund, cut sweetheart deals, or simply run the local as a family business. Elia Kazan's 1954 film, *On the Waterfront*, became a controversial classic because of the justification it offered to those who broke with the solidarity of the waterfront and informed on their mates. Then two years later, when a union hoodlum blinded labor columnist Victor Riesel on a Manhattan street, the public outcry and political fallout proved enormous, laying the basis for the formation of the celebrated Senate investigating committee named after John McClellan of Arkansas.[54]

Most of the distinctions between mob-connected criminality, autocratic leadership, hard bargaining, and industrywide negotiating strength were purposefully lost on those who saw these labor corruption scandals as an opportunity to reopen the assault on the union movement. Echoing the attack on monopoly unionism long offered by the National Association of Manufacturers, a 1956 editorial in the *Wall Street Journal* thought the "connection between crime and the wide-ranging power of unions" hardly coincidental. "When one man can determine whether a million or more men all over the country are to eat or starve, there has been set up a situation ripe for every kind of corruption all down the line."[55] Barry Goldwater agreed wholeheartedly. "Graft and corruption are symptoms of the illness that besets the labor movement, not the cause of it. *The cause is the enormous economic and political power now concentrated in the hands of union leaders.*"[56]

Such were some of the atmospherics that accompanied the establishment of the McClellan Committee in 1957. Five of its eight members hailed from right-to-work states, but it did not take anti-union animus to reveal a pattern of crime and corruption in a number of unions, most of which had been AFL affiliates before the merger of the AFL and CIO in 1955. The Teamsters union served as the McClellan Committee's key target. Spurred on by chief counsel Robert Kennedy, whose initial ignorance about all things working-class was increasingly characteristic of liberalism in this period, the Committee forced union president Dave Beck into an abrupt retirement. Thereafter, Kennedy's celebrated feud with his successor, Jimmy Hoffa, transformed the new Teamster president into a larger-than-life icon whose combative persona soon made him the nation's most famous union leader. Politically, Hoffa stood in near-perfect agreement with his GOP interrogators—he would have no truck with liberal social-movement unionism—but as a symbolic target the combative Teamster "boss" proved a perfect foil for a new effort to discredit union power.[57] Indeed, the McClellan Committee deliberations proved a turning point in the moral history of American unionism. In a Gallup poll, pro-union sentiment had reached 76 percent, an all-time high, in February 1957 just before the hearings began. Thereafter it dropped steadily, reaching 50 percent in the mid-1960s, and even lower in subsequent decades.[58]

The McClellan Committee's legislative fruit was a 1959 law bearing the names of Robert Griffin, a Republican from Michigan, and Philip Landrum, a Democrat from Georgia. Its very name therefore embodied the anti-unionism of the coalition of Northern Republicans and Southern Democrats who had enacted Taft-Hartley and then campaigned against monopoly unionism in the 1950s. Landrum-Griffin tightened restrictions against secondary boycotts and gave the Labor Department greater power to regulate union financial affairs. But the most ideologically significant section of the law was a union member "bill of rights," whose meaning encapsulated an essentially right-wing understanding of union dynamics.

Historian Melvyn Dubofsky reminds us that the very first thing to know about this "bill of rights" is that it had nothing to do with the rising tide of civil rights activism that was then sweeping out of Montgomery, Little Rock, and the NAACP Legal Defense Fund. Southern Democrats were the chief proponents of this union bill of

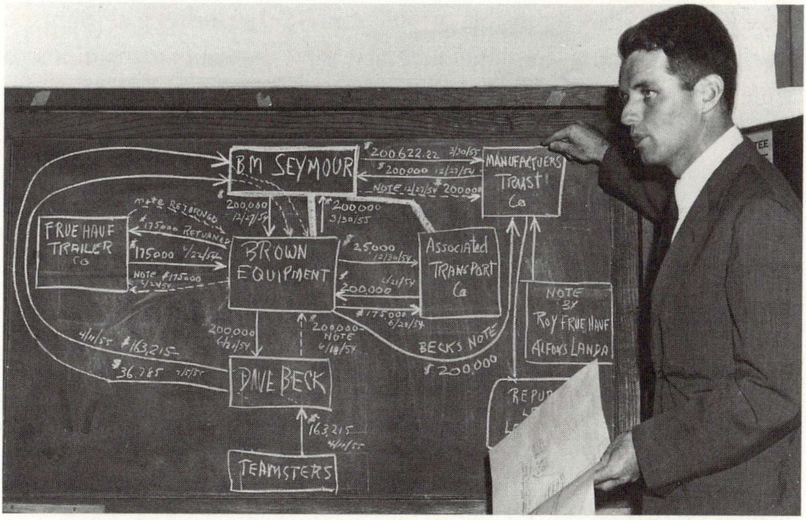

Robert Kennedy, counsel to the McClellan Committee, explains Teamster union corruption in 1957. (Credit: George Meany Memorial Archives)

rights along with the Goldwater wing of the Republican Party. When a potential link between the rights of union members and the rights of nonwhite workers became public, Northern Republicans assured their Southern allies that the legislation's provision for jury trials in cases brought under the law would preserve the "Southern way of life." In this telling instance, Republican anti-unionism trumped the party's still credible claim as an honest upholder of African American civil rights. A GOP "Southern strategy" was clearly in the making.[59]

The conservative proponents of Landrum-Griffin were not unaware of the power of the new rights discourse. During the Taft-Hartley debates anti-union conservatives had declared that limitations on union power were necessary to rebalance the scales between capital and labor. With the exception of Section 14b, which facilitated state "right-to-work" laws, the legal thrust of Taft-Hartley was designed to strengthen the hand of capital, either by limiting what unions could do, or by giving management new weapons, such as "employer free speech," to halt the spread of unionism. But in the 1960s and later, employer anti-unionism became increasingly oriented toward the ostensible protection of the individual rights of workers as against the undemocratic and bureaucratic unions in which they now found themselves enrolled. A national Right-to-Work Committee, funded by NAM and Southern textile interests, specialized in making use of the new rights discourse, civil libertarian if not actually that of the civil rights movement, in order to perforate the solidarity upon which trade unionism depended, both as a social ideology and as an organization of political and economic combat. Thus did Right-to-Work Committee official Reed Larson declare the NAACP "prostituted" when the organization aligned itself with the AFL-CIO legislative agenda. Because of its "marriage of convenience to monopolistic labor unions," the NAACP's "first priority goes not to restricting union racial discrimination, but to striking down all state laws against compulsory unionism."[60]

The Decay of Pluralism

The sordid atmospherics generated by these union corruption hearings were soon reflected throughout mainstream journalism and scholarship. There was first of all the same great sense of disappointment and disillusionment. Sumner Slichter, who a decade before had declared the United States a "laboristic society," now (1958) wrote that "in spite of their brilliant success, trade unions are suffering a great loss of prestige and moral influence."[61] Paul Jacobs, who had once helped purge the unions of their Communist element, won a hearing in *Commentary* for a critique that bemoaned, rather than celebrated, the "inevitable current moving the trade unions toward bureaucratization and oligarchy." The culprit here was the governmental effort "to maintain the kind of stable, responsible labor leadership which promotes harmony in labor-management relations."[62] When he was asked to write an assessment of unionism for the Center for the Study of Democratic Institutions five years later, Jacobs dolefully entitled it: "Old before Its Time: Collective Bargaining at Twenty-eight."[63]

A. H. Raskin of the *New York Times* turned this critique into the common wisdom of the late 1950s in one article after another. Their titles tell the tale: "The Moral Issue That Confronts Labor," "New Issue: Labor As Big Business," and "Labor's Time of Troubles: The Failure of Bread-and-Butter Unionism." In "The Obsolescent Unions," published in 1963, he declared that automation, government incomes policy, and a transformation in the class structure made for an "inevitable withering of union strength." Forces beyond its control hurled labor "inexorably into obsolescence."[64] The following year a similarly despondent cry came from Herbert Harris in *Harper's Weekly*. Labor has "lost the intellectuals" because "the American labor movement is sleepwalking along the corridors of history."[65]

Meanwhile, the idea of an industrial pluralism came under direct ideological assault, even from those who had been its most influential proponents. Daniel Bell was no fan of C. Wright Mills: in 1956 he had denounced the latter's *The Power Elite*, which was, of course, a radical assault upon the democratic presumption inherent in pluralist polyarchial theory. But within just a few years, Bell's labor journalism began to sound a lot like that of the Columbia University sociologist. Bell saw the great 1959 steel strike as a sham, largely useful to the corporations as a mechanism whereby the steel industry could "administer" a higher price schedule. "The desiccated language of collective bargaining is a trap," wrote Bell early in 1960, "its syntax too constricting, its images too mechanical." It was no longer "an instrumentality for economic and social justice." Instead collective bargaining had been subverted by both the corporation and the union, whose "interest in getting higher wages makes it become a partner in a collusive enterprise which strong-arms the rest of the community."[66]

John Kenneth Galbraith, whose influence among American liberals was now reaching its apogee, advanced much of the same functional cynicism in the 1960s. When Galbraith published *American Capitalism: The Theory of Countervailing Power* in 1952, his views lay entirely within a pluralist framework. Galbraith then held that "the operation of countervailing power is to be seen with the greatest clarity in the labor market where it is also most fully developed."[67] But fifteen years later, when *The New Industrial State* appeared, Galbraith had shifted toward the neo-Weberianism of Daniel Bell, if not that of C. Wright Mills himself. "The union belongs to a particular stage in the development of the industrial system," wrote Galbraith in his most ideologically ambitious book. "When that stage passes so does the union in anything like its original position of power." Obviously, that time had come, because Galbraith argued that in the modern "industrial system," a term he now preferred to "capitalism," the labor movement had lost many of its most important functions. Indeed, it now served the "technostructure" largely as a price-setting and industrywide planning mechanism. The interests of unions and corporations were concordant. "Since World War II," wrote Galbraith, "the acceptance of the union by the industrial firm and the emergence thereafter of an era of comparatively peaceful industrial relations have been hailed as the final triumph of trade unionism. On closer examination it is seen to reveal many of the features of Jonah's triumph over the whale."[68]

All this soon became part of the general discourse. A revealing, and perhaps consequential, case in point came on an April evening in 1967 when George Meany appeared at Georgetown University to take part in a panel discussion on the subject "Is Collective Bargaining Dead?" Meany acquitted himself well, insisting that the corporations were still hard bargainers, that millions of workers needed a collective institution to defend their interests, and that the right to strike was vital to the preservation of American democracy. But the students were skeptical, if not hostile: to these young men the unions were an antiquated institution; they condoned featherbedding and racial discrimination, while union workers were often overpaid and under worked.

Among the student panelists on the stage with the president of the AFL-CIO was one William Jefferson Clinton, then in his junior year at Georgetown. Clinton avoided the attack mode of the other student panelists, all of whom were from the School of Business, but his query to Mr. Meany had its own sharp, New Left flavor. "Many times institutions prove to be inflexible, restrictive and out of date," asserted Clinton, "and an individual must consequently assert himself with conformity to these institutions. Now, Mr. Meany, do you think that collective bargaining as an institutional arrangement may regiment men too far, and has become merely another institution against which man must assert himself?" Meany's answer was long and logi-

By 1967 the face of labor was increasingly at odds with the times. (Credit: Alexander Negative Collection, George Meany Memorial Archives)

cal, but in the spring of 1967, and for many years thereafter, few unionists could offer a satisfactory rejoinder.[69]

Soon the Vietnam generation made its own powerful contribution to the devaluation of the trade-union idea. Since mentors like Swados, Mills, and Herbert Marcuse, not to mention Bell and Galbraith, had declared that the working class and its institutions were unlikely to constitute late capitalism's prime agent of social change, New Left radicals began a furious search for an effective substitute. Among the candidates were an interracial movement of the poor, which had emerged from the civil rights experience, a harder-edged black nationalism that some linked to an ascendant Third World revolutionism, and finally the idea of a "new working class" of radicalized technocrats, engineers, and knowledge workers. The ideological half-life for these substitute proletariats proved remarkably short, even as they cast a long shadow forward over the political and academic landscape.[70]

This became clear in the early 1970s when the New Left made a massive "turn toward the working class." A new generation of critical intellectuals linked a systemic, neo-Weberian critique of the sort first offered by Mills and Macdonald, with the kind of rank-and-file issues that Swados and other critics of working-class alienation had once again put in the spotlight. But New Leftists infused their critique of corporate power, routinized work, union bureaucracy, and the racism and sexism endemic to working-class culture with a sense of the agency and insurgency they had earlier glimpsed in the civil rights and anti-war movements. There was plenty of cooperation between the New Left and unions like Hospital Workers Local 1199, the United Electrical Workers, the United Farm Workers, and the American Federation of State, County, and Municipal Employees. Many veterans of the student movement found themselves as activists in the unions, and not always in opposition to the leadership.[71]

But this process of generational interpenetration—as great as any since the Great Depression—did little to temper the critique offered by the young intellectuals and academics whose New Left voice was now becoming so influential. Thus we have Stanley Aronowitz and Alice and Staughton Lynd on the collaborationist character of the trade unions. Aronowitz held that the modern labor agreement is the essence of "class collaboration," while the union is "chiefly a force for integrating the workers into the corporate capitalist system."[72] The Lynds, meanwhile, felt it quite necessary to deny any anti-union views. Their caution was justified because *Rank and File*, published in 1973, stands as a sustained attack on institutional unionism. Contemporary labor organizations, they wrote, "have become a new kind of company union, financially independent of the rank and file because the company deducts union dues from the worker's pay check, and politically all-powerful because the contract takes away from rank and filers the right to strike."[73]

In *Strike!*, a book that came right out of the SDS rediscovery of the class struggle, Jeremy Brecher celebrated a labor history in which "the main actors in the story are ordinary working people," whose struggles against capital and the state were stymied by "unions and labor leaders (who) have most often striven to prevent or contain them."[74] Finally, it was left to Mike Davis to circle backward to a position not entirely different from that of Daniel Bell himself. By the late 1970s and early 1980s, when he published in the *New Left Review* the essays that would find their way into *Prisoners of the American Dream*, Davis had abandoned even a workerist perspective on American labor, largely because of what he saw as the Reaganite success in institutionalizing a set of debilitating racial polarities within the working class. "The unions have closed in around the laager of the seniority system, abandoning the unemployed, betraying the trust of working-class communities, and treating young workers as expendable pawns," wrote Davis. This "blinkered, Maginot-like defense of existing employment privileges risks the creation of a reactive anti-solidarity, as the unemployed become strike-breakers." U.S. unions, concluded Davis, were "abandoning the majority of the American working class."[75]

Judicial Liberalism versus Labor

The declining reputation of the unions, the decay of industrial pluralism, and the rise of a new discourse of individual rights soon had its impact on the legal status and meaning of the trade-union idea. Labor's reliance upon the procedural mechanisms adjudicated by the NLRB, designed to generate a pluralistic industrial democracy at the work site, came to seem far less potent and universal than the rights discourse generated by the state's conception of substantive justice and equal protection under the law. Rights claims, moreover, arose out of the moral fervor of the African American freedom struggle, and they were soon associated with a new politics of multicultural diversity, feminism, and gay liberation. By advocating state protection as opposed to collective action, American liberals implicitly endorsed the idea, long associated with anti-union conservatism, that the labor movement could not be trusted to protect the individual rights of its members or of workers in general. Only the state and its regulatory apparatus could safeguard the individual from social ills: not only racial and gender discrimination, but also unresponsive bureaucracies in the factory and office.[76]

A review of the Warren Court's industrial jurisprudence makes this turn of the ideological wheel all too clear. Indeed, the same species of liberalism that handed down *Brown vs. Board of Education*, ended judicial McCarthyism, and legalized abortion rights, also undermined the legal basis of union power and solidarity. Court rulings were not always consistent, but as we shall see, this very confusion demonstrated the waning power of the old laborite ideology.

In an effort to maintain the integrity of the collective bargaining system, the postwar Supreme Court turned labor-management arbitration into an exclusionary principle that exempted unionized workers from many of the statutory rights that those same courts and legislatures had begun to create or enforce. This was because the still dominant industrial pluralist paradigm privileged the private system of arbitration as a keystone of workplace jurisprudence. But in the 1960s and 1970s this established a rigid barrier between the world of work and the external sources of law, thus sealing arbitration and the collective-bargaining process from the rebirth of the rights-conscious constitutionalism that had been such an otherwise notable feature of post-1960s American jurisprudence. Ironically, this segregation was a product of the Court's most liberal justices—William O. Douglas among them—whose impulse was to defend both collective bargaining and the autonomy of the arbitration system from conservative legislators who deployed their own discourse of "rights," including "right to work," in the aftermath of the McClellan Committee hearings and the revival of a more militant brand of corporate anti-unionism.[77]

Thus when statutory employment rights have come in conflict with collectively bargained work rules, the former have been routinely "preempted" by the latter, under an expansive definition of Section 301 of the Taft-Hartley Act. Liberal jurists of the early postwar era thus kept state employment law out of the unionized workplace, but they also cut workers off from the potential benefits of the rights-conscious employment laws that the federal government promulgated after 1964. When unions were strong and statutory employment rights undeveloped, this system worked to enhance the attractive power of organized labor. But in the years after 1980 when union power collapsed, unorganized workers often had much greater access to a still-vibrant, rights-conscious employment law than did workers covered by a union contract. For example, when it comes to wrongful discharge claims, unionized workers, relying upon a cumbersome and expensive system of internal arbitration, are often at a disadvantage when disputes involve drug testing, sexual or racial harassment, defamation by their supervisor, unlawful searches, and mishandling of health insurance. Thus it is common practice for an arbitrator to award reinstatement but no back pay at all to a worker fired without just cause, but prevailing parties in unjust dismissal litigation cases receive jury awards well into six figures.[78]

A similar counterposition between the "rights" of workers and the potency of the union idea has arisen out of a series of judicial decisions that devalue union solidarity and privilege a more individualistic conception of worker rights. In the 1940s CIO attorneys had argued that unionism was not a commercial transaction, but an "exchange of ideas" in which constitutional rights were protected, but only insofar as the collective strength of the union was maintained.[79] But the distinction between the economic and political rights of an individual worker became more attractive with the demise of the group pluralist idea. As early as 1961 in a case involving the International Association of Machinists, William O. Douglas and Hugo Black, the two justices most sensitive to civil liberties, successfully led the Court to argue for this dichotomy. Felix Frankfurter still thought that "the notion that economic and political concerns are separable is pre-Victorian."

But Douglas held that a union could not compel the same degree of political allegiance: "Some forced associations are inevitable in an industrial society. One who of necessity rides busses and street cars does not have the freedom that John Muir and Walt Whitman extolled. . . . [But] if an association is compelled, the individual . . . should be allowed to enter the group with his own flag flying. . . ." Hugo Black put it even more strongly. Any attempt to make a dissenting unionist contribute to the political funds of his organization was "extortion" that the government had "no . . . power to enforce."[80]

Given such an outlook, it was not long before the courts began to question even the moral and organizational meaning of union solidarity itself. In the 1972 *Granite State* decision the Supreme Court asserted the right of workers to resign their membership in the midst of a strike and then scab on their workmates free from the disciplinary penalties sought by their former union associates. The Court argued, "When there is a lawful dissolution of a union-member relation, the union has no more control over the former member than it has over the man in the street." According to David Abraham's remarkably penetrating reading of this "right to resign" doctrine, the Court—once again led by Justice Douglas—subverted the legal and ethical basis of collective solidarity in favor of an "abstract and atomistic conception of our society." Douglas and other liberals have been sensitive to the "rights" of dissident workers because of the often well-grounded assumption that unions have been less than democratic. But liberal sensitivity on this score transformed the meaning of union solidarity into a coercive set of legal/administrative pressures that merely trampled on the work rights of the individual ex-unionist, which was not far distant from the views promulgated by the antiunion right. To Abraham, this line of argument "thwarted the function and jettisoned virtually the entire raison d'etre of labor law."[81]

When it came to racial justice, the clash between laborite solidarity and rights consciousness became even more contentious. This became clear in 1974 when the Supreme Court was asked to reinstate black activists fired from their jobs after staging a wildcat job action at the Emporium Capwell department store in San Francisco. Arguing that the store was a "20th century colonial plantation" and that the labor organization holding a collective bargaining contract there was insufficiently responsive to their interests, a group of African Americans sought to bypass the union and negotiate directly with Emporium Capwell executives. The grievance procedure was undoubtedly slow, perhaps ineffective, but the court ruled against the black militants, holding that the union has "a legitimate interest in presenting a united front on this as on other issues and in not seeing its strength dissipated and its stature denigrated by subgroups within the unit separately pursuing what they see as separate interests." Significantly, Thurgood Marshall wrote the Court's 8-1 majority opinion. He was enough of an old-fashioned labor-liberal to recognize the power of collective action, of exclusive jurisdiction, even if that required a degree of internal union coercion. "An employer confronted with bargaining demands from each of several minority groups would not necessarily, or even probably, be able to agree to remedial steps satisfactory to all at once," held Marshall. "Having divided themselves, the minority employees will not be in a position to advance their cause." Marshall thought the black workers should make their fight inside the union, so as to present a united front.[82]

Emporium Capwell remains the law of the land, but Marshall's forthright opinion may well have been a Pyrrhic victory for the solidarity principle. William O. Douglas, still a liberal, civil-libertarian icon, offered a blistering dissent that charged Marshall with making the black workers "prisoners of the union." His views were endorsed by Staughton Lynd, then at the height of his New Left influence, who believed that contemporary labor law merely sought to "get the workers off the streets, or the shop, and into the chambers of some purportedly neutral umpire." Instead, Lynd argued that both the letter and spirit of early New Deal jurisprudence protected the right of rank-and-file workers "to engage in concerted activity without the union's approval." But neither side really won this argument. To most observers, especially those of a younger, civil rights–oriented generation, the stolid ineffectuality of the union was taken for granted. *Emporium Capwell* was but another example of the incapacity of the unions and the labor law upon which they relied to defend the rights of individual workers, whatever their color, gender, or politics.[83]

This rights-based undermining of the solidarity principle was accompanied by a perverse calcification of the industrial pluralist idea so as to drastically narrow the strike power of unions and their workers. In the 1960s the Supreme Court severely restricted the right of a union or of its workers to take part in unofficial job actions or in wildcat strikes. Indeed, the courts now ruled "self-help" illegal when undertaken outside the scope of the union's grievance procedure or its system of industrial arbitration. A series of decisions, almost all written by the most liberal Supreme Court justices, institutionalized collective bargaining, but only under conditions that narrowly channeled and utterly bureaucratized the functions trade unions could perform for their members. In the 1960 *Lucas Flower* case, for example, the Supreme Court insisted that the mere presence of an arbitration clause in a collective-bargaining contract meant that the union had waived its otherwise statutorily protected right to strike over grievances. In the *Boys Market* decision of 1970, the high court made virtually all work stoppages illegal during the term of a contract, in the process again legitimizing labor injunctions of the sort that had once so crippled the union movement during the nineteenth century.[84]

At the same time, a sweepingly restrictive reinterpretation of the entire scope and meaning of collective bargaining further undercut the potency and appeal of American trade unionism itself. During the very same season in which Congress passed the 1964 Civil Rights Act, the Supreme Court questioned, in its ostensibly pro-union *Fibreboard* decision, whether or not trade unions had the right to bargain over what the courts defined as issues—such as production planning, price schedules, and investment decisions—that lay "at the core of entrepreneurial control." By 1980, in *First National Maintenance Corporation*, the Supreme Court had made up its mind, ruling that companies have no obligation to bargain over—or even to provide advance notice of—the closure of part of their operations. The Court's position was that "the harm likely to be done to an employer's need to operate freely in deciding whether to shut down part of his business for purely economic reasons outweighs the incremental benefit that might be gained through the union's participation in making the decision."[85]

And to take another set of transmutations: The courts have also ruled, in a series of decisions all through the 1950s and 1960s, that huge numbers of workers—professionals, supervisors, technicians, security personnel, and so forth—were, for the purposes of the labor law, not workers at all. In 1974 the Supreme Court held that the National Labor Relations Act did not cover anyone who had the authority to "formulate and effectuate management policies by expressing and making operative the decisions of the employer." Had this vast exclusion actually been applied, tens of millions of workers—indeed all those whose jobs had not been reduced to mindless routine—would have been deprived of the Wagner Act's framework of representation. And this proved precisely the case for many college teachers when the Supreme Court handed down a 1980 ruling curbing faculty unionism at Yeshiva University. The judges held that faculty members at a private university were ipso facto "managers" because they operated in a collegial manner, and could make effective recommendations to the administration regarding hiring, budgets, teaching load and content, and other policy matters. In a world of work in which complicated jobs required the exercise of much independent judgment, the *Yeshiva* decision proscribed collective bargaining in virtually any work setting not characterized by simple drudgery. Moreover, *Yeshiva* generated a Catch-22 conundrum: the more workers win control and participation at work, the less likely is it that the labor law will still protect them as workers.[86]

Thus the union idea has been devalued in two dramatic ways. To the extent that the courts continued to honor an outmoded set of pluralist assumptions governing the presumptively equal bargaining power of unions and their corporate adversaries, they generated a false equality between labor and capital. Because of corporate mobility, and the insulation of so many management prerogatives from the union's bargaining reach, such an equation is inherently biased against the unions. The liberal effort to shoehorn labor's interests into this untenable system put the union impulse in an increasingly unworkable legal structure, while at the same time offering capital new weapons with which to contain union power and narrow the scope of collective bargaining.

But at the same time, as both the courts and popular opinion have privileged a rights-based model of industrial justice, these collective institutions have lost their capacity to command the loyalty of their membership, upon which their strength depends. Individualistic, rights-based assumptions therefore replaced group pluralist ones and devalued the very idea of union solidarity. Labor was therefore stuck with the worst of both worlds, or as the legal scholar Reuel Schiller put it, "Industrial pluralism is an iron fist inside a velvet glove, an appealing vision . . . that undermined labor's strength."[87]

CHAPTER 5

Rights Consciousness in the Workplace

WE LIVE IN A WORLD in which the model of collective work rights embodied in the Wagner Act has been eclipsed, if not actually replaced, by a different set of work rights based on race, gender, or other attribute of the individual involved. As we saw in the previous chapter, rights consciousness can undermine the idea of class solidarity, not to mention the integrity of workaday trade unionism. In the courts and within the broad body of liberal opinion, individual rights and unionism were counterposed in the 1960s and 1970s, to the detriment of both. Just as the rights revolution expanded the idea of social citizenship, the labor movement, identified with a claustrophobic system of industrial pluralism, fell into disrepute. It stood on the wrong side of American political culture.

Two well-publicized working rights controversies make clear the practical impact of this reconceptualization, in which rights have an individual, racially coded character, but not a collective meaning. Low-wage, service-economy workers stood at the center of each conflict. Most were Hispanic or African American, and both groups of workers endured the kind of arduous, inequitable work lives that had earlier given moral urgency to the movements for both trade unionism and racial justice. But in the last decades of the twentieth century, these impulses no longer resonated in tandem.

In the 1980s Shoney's Inc., which operated 1,800 restaurants in thirty-six states, still did business in the Jim Crow spirit that had shaped the racial mentality of founder Ray Danner when he opened his first Nashville Big Boy decades before. More than two-thirds of all African American workers were confined to the kitchen, where they performed the most menial jobs. When Danner found a restaurant in which the dining room staff was too "dark," he ordered the managers there to dismiss the blacks and "lighten" it up. Danner used the "N" word with abandon and probably contributed money to the KKK.

This could not last, for his employment policies met resistance even from Southern white managers and workers. Despite Equal Employment Opportunity Commission (EEOC) hostility to class-action suits (Clarence Thomas was then chairman), the NAACP Legal Defense Fund won a smashing victory in 1992, a $132 million settlement that was the largest ever for racial job discrimination. Danner was forced to pay nearly half out of his own pocket, and when Wall Street got wind that he might still control the company, its stock plunged and the Shoney's board forced him out. Thousands of black workers took home sizable compensation claims, while Shoney's instituted de facto hiring and promotion quotas designed to rectify the situation. "Our goal is to set human resource standards to which other companies aspire," boasted a company spokeswomen.[1]

At virtually the same moment when the Shoney's case was reaching its successful climax, the Spanish-speaking women who worked for Sprint Corporation's La Conexion Familiar in San Francisco were getting restless. In the low-wage world of telecommunications Taylorism, their dignity was under constant assault. Supervisors there set tight production quotas, monitored toilet breaks and access to drinking water, and threatened to terminate union supporters. By 1994 most of the women had joined the Communications Workers of America (CWA), but just before the NLRB certification election, expected to be an easy win for the union, Sprint shut down La Conexion and laid off all 235 of its employees. The CWA charged that Sprint's layoff violated the labor law, because it sought to avoid unionization at La Conexion and intimidate thousands of the other company employees the CWA hoped to organize. Three years later the NLRB agreed, citing the company for more than fifty different labor law violations, including interrogation, bribes, threats, fabricating evidence, and firing workers in direct response to the union campaign. The government agency ordered Sprint to post throughout the company a detailed notice that it would cease and desist from illegal anti-union activity, rehire the La Conexion workers, and pay them back wages, perhaps as much as $12 million.[2]

But nothing happened. In contrast to the shaming and redemption through which Shoney's passed, Sprint executives felt no cause for alarm. They successfully lobbied the Clinton administration for various favors, reiterated their hard-line opposition to trade unions, and got a federal appeals court to throw out the adverse NLRB order. In its "Union-free Management Guide," the company declared that of the "myriad of challenges" faced by Sprint, paramount "is the threat of union intervention in our business." Like other companies facing the prospect of an organizing campaign, Sprint had its pick of anti-union consultants and law firms that specialized in helping corporations maintain a union-free workplace. Since neither Wall Street jitters, public approbation, nor government pressure held much of a threat, such firms were quite happy to advise a close skirting of the law. Getting rid of union activists is the best weapon to intimidate workers, declared a union avoidance lawyer of long experience. You don't have to get "nasty and illegal. You can get nasty all you want, you just don't have to get illegal."[3]

Not unexpectedly, penalties for proven violations of the labor law are trivial when compared to those involving discrimination because of race, gender, creed, or age. Under 1991 amendments to the Civil Rights Act, women and people of color can sue not only for back pay but also for compensatory and punitive damages up to $300,000. Workers illegally fired or demoted for trying to organize a union are merely compensated for lost wages, minus anything they have earned in the meantime. And plaintiffs under the civil rights law have access to a jury trial, whereas under the labor law, the NLRB and the civil trial judge are the final arbitrators.[4]

This chapter seeks to evaluate how and why a rights-conscious strategy became the most efficacious way to approach the labor question during the 1960s and 1970s. It tries to measure the success and failure of this approach, and suggests why the labor movement reaped so few dividends from what would otherwise have been a most nurturing social-cultural environment. This disjuncture between the rights revolution and the unionizing impulse is a remarkable one, and uniquely American. In Western Europe, in Canada (Quebec especially), and even in Poland, Spain, South Africa, and South Korea, the rights revolution of "the Sixties" (which was sometimes a decade or more delayed) strengthened social-democratic movements and increased trade-union numbers and power.[5] But in the United States this was an era of relative union stagnation, from which the democratizing rights consciousness of the era seemed surprisingly divorced. Indeed it was at odds with the whole discourse of labor and collective bargaining, not to mention the idea of an industrial democracy in the workplace.

Public Employee Unionism

Exceptions prove the rule. In public employment, American trade unions did ride a wave of rights consciousness to build collective organizations of considerable size and power. Teachers, hospital staff, and workers in municipal and state government had been largely unorganized in the 1950s and expected to remain so. Their employment security, white-collar status, and legal standing outside the labor law seemed to make them immune to collective action. Unlike the blue-collar working class, public employees often sat behind a desk, took a regular paid vacation, and kept their fingernails clean.

But two things happened after World War II to transform the status and expectations of public employees. First, all of a sudden, many blue-collar workers received more pay, equal job security, and some of the same perks as white-collar public employees. Corporate managers made certain that their white-collar staffs kept a half step ahead of their unionized blue-collar employees, but most levels of government let wages and benefits lag. Thus by the early 1960s truck drivers earned more than schoolteachers, and auto workers more than post-office clerks.[6]

Second, the ranks of these workers exploded after World War II. The permanent federal workforce doubled in size, but state and municipal payrolls tripled, or even quadrupled in the quarter century after the end of the war. Such labor, writes Stanley Aronowitz, has neither power nor aura, "only a kind of grudging indispensability." Thus teachers, social workers, hospital and mailroom clerks, garbage men and street maintenance workers were in chronically short supply. Public employment became increasingly black and brown, not only because administrators sought out a low-wage workforce, but because racial minorities, still excluded from so many private-sector service jobs, valued the steady work and the ostensible protections embedded within even the most pro-management set of civil-service work rules. But state and municipal workers still saw themselves as second-class citizens. Pay was low, the benefits few, and in many workplaces ethnic hierarchies froze new urban immigrants out of a chance for advancement.[7]

The offices, classrooms, and hospital hallways of New York City proved the birthplace of modern public-employee unionism. Here was the Akron and Flint of a new labor movement. Despite their exclusion from Wagner Act coverage, indeed despite state laws that severely penalized public employee work stoppages, the teachers, social workers, and sanitation men of the city pushed forward the frontiers of collective action all during the late 1950s and early 1960s. City employees in heavily Jewish and Italian occupations were soon joined by the increasingly large number of African Americans and Puerto Ricans who worked in blue-collar city services and on hospital, food, and cleaning staffs.

These organizing efforts won support and leadership from a creative cohort of not-so-old radicals who sparked the new labor movement in hospital employment and municipal service. These unionists included Jerry Wurf of the American Federation of State, County, and Municipal Employees (AFSCME); Albert Shanker and David Selden of the American Federation of Teachers (AFT); and the former Communists Leon Davis, Moe Foner, and Elliott Godoff, who led Hospital Workers Local 1199. Happily, the city remained a bastion of New Deal liberalism, where a strong private-sector union movement exerted considerable clout. Indeed, the mayor was none other than Robert Wagner, Jr., son of the late New Deal senator. Mayor Wagner's 1958 municipal order recognizing city workers for collective bargaining purposes inaugurated a series of competitive organizing drives, hard-fought elections, and in the 1960s, high-profile public employee strikes.[8]

On January 17, 1962, President Kennedy signed Executive Order 10988, which legalized collective bargaining between the federal government and its clerical and technical workforce. After the breakthrough in New York City, such an order was on the labor-liberal agenda, and from labor's point of view, it partly compensated for Kennedy's failure to make progress on more pressing issues: an economic stimulus package to finally pull the nation out of the recession that had lingered since the late 1950s, national civil rights legislation, and manpower training. The order facilitated the growth of public-sector unions whose power and autonomy were clearly inferior to those of the Wagner Act model: they could not strike, bargain for wages, or negotiate over the organization and assignment of personnel.

But the law governing public-sector unions—many Northern and Western states would soon follow the federal government—avoided many of the conceptual pitfalls inherent in private-sector labor law. The expectation that a self-contained, pluralist equilibrium might structure labor relations clearly did not apply in the public sector. There management was itself the agent of larger political forces, and so too were the unions who understood that political mobilization of the membership and community were of central import to their bargaining effectiveness. Moreover, a kind of due-process rights culture offered much protection, even legitimacy, to outspoken unionists. Few state agencies operated according to employment-at-will doctrines; individuals had to be dismissed for "just cause." Because company unions had never been so poisonous a threat in the public sector, and because of the civil-service protections that were kept in place, union recognition, jurisdiction, and security issues were therefore of far less import. Indeed, the federal law provided that a union could emerge in at least three forms: as the representative for its members only, as the exclusive voice representing all workers in a unit when it had attained a stable membership of more than 10 percent, and as the signatory to an actual bargaining contract in a unit where it had majority support from the employees.[9]

Public-sector unionism grew rapidly during the next two decades,

In 1967 you could get yourself arrested if you were a striking school teacher in Baltimore. Sixty-five year old Henry Waskow taught history there. (Credit: *Baltimore News American*)

not because of the militancy or potency of the workers there—although public school teachers would prove a major exception—but because even relatively ineffectual unions had considerable appeal to white-collar workers. Given the rights culture of that era, and an environment in which management was relatively neutral, public-employee unionism served as an effective lobbyist, educator, grievance facilitator, and interpreter of the civil-service rules. Over time such government unions tended to take on the characteristics of private-sector institutions, especially in the post office, public schools, prisons, hospitals, and in blue-collar municipal employment. Wages, seniority, and fringe benefits were all put on the bargaining table. Among school teachers, union density reached an extraordinary 80 percent, which was more than in coal mining and auto production. Indeed, by the end of the century public-sector unionism, over 4 million strong, represented about 40 percent of all organized workers.[10]

The Liberal Hour, but Not for Organized Labor

But the dramatic organizational effervescence in the public sector did not herald a revitalization of the larger trade-union movement. From the union perspective, the most remarkable thing about the 1960s and early 1970s was the extent to which organized labor proved so impotent, not only in terms of membership growth, but of policy-making clout, not to mention any capacity to make an impact on the rapid transformation of American political culture. The liberal hour had struck, Keynesian policy making reigned supreme, and union leaders were welcomed inside the White House as never before. Between 1962 and 1969 unemployment dropped by more than 50 percent, real wages continued their steady advance, and American workers exercised the strike weapon, especially during the years 1966 to 1973, to a degree not seen since the mid-1940s. And even during the administration of Richard Nixon, staunch AFL-CIO support for American foreign policy, in Vietnam and elsewhere, might well have been expected to generate a domestic dividend favorable to specific union interests.

Organized labor stood on the winning side when Congress passed landmark social legislation in this era, including the civil rights bills, Medicare and Medicaid, and the Occupational Safety and Health Act (OSHA). But the 1960s and 1970s were barren of virtually any legislative or ideological payoff for organized labor as an institution, or with notable exceptions, as a social movement with the kind of aura necessary to set the social and political agenda. It was a lost opportunity. Trade-union ranks grew by about 2 million during the boom years of the 1960s, but the proportion of all American workers in the unions continued its slow decline, from 30.4 percent in 1962 to 28.5 percent in 1973. Union political influence weakened even at the federal level, where long-sought labor-law reforms were defeated in 1965 and 1978, years during which both the White House and the Congress were controlled by the Democrats. In the mid-1970s, American trade unionism was far weaker—from a political, moral, and economic viewpoint—than it had been even a decade before.[11]

Why was this the case? During the 1960s the unions could not translate their economic power into policy influence. In all three administrations, economic policy makers believed that a macroregulation of the economy could spur growth and limit inflation, but efforts to reform the structure of the labor market, to strengthen the collective-bargaining power of labor, or to win some larger political control of investment and spending went nowhere. The Kennedy-Johnson tax cut that was passed in 1964 was predicated on principles of the most conservative, "commercial" Keynesianism, requiring of business no quid pro quo for the generous tax incentives offered by the government. Likewise, both Democratic administrations "jawboned" a set of wage-price guideposts during these years of growing inflationary worry, but this program of economic regulation was also divorced from any effort to strengthen or recast the tattered labor-management accord of the early postwar era.[12] In 1971 Richard Nixon did institute a formal set of wage-price ceilings, but they carried with them none of the political authority that gave to the World War II controls their progressive, social-patriotic quality. Indeed, Nixon, who had despised his brief wartime tenure as a young OPA attorney, deployed these controls in largely opportunistic fashion. He merely sought to forestall the inevitable Vietnam-era inflationary surge until his party could safely win the 1972 elections.[13]

Most labor leaders were Kennedy-Johnson liberals, but in the 1960s that was just the problem. They stood in an increasingly stolid and unresponsive center, not on the dynamic frontier where they had once defined, and stretched, the limits of conventional politics. Several individual unions, including the UAW, the Packinghouse Workers, and the Amalgamated Clothing Workers, sent money and manpower to bolster the civil rights drives and antipoverty efforts of those years. And the unions were almost uniform in their formal support for all the landmark legislation of the 1960s: the 1964 and 1965 civil rights laws, immigration reform, health insurance, and the Great Society antipoverty initiatives.

But most top leaders of the AFL-CIO remained entirely out of tune with the multiple insurgencies that began to animate left-liberal politics in the 1960s. The generation of trade unionists then in command was the same one that had battled the Communists in the 1940s and accommodated themselves to the constraints of the Cold War and the narrow compass of the Taft-Hartley labor relations regime. The AFL-CIO, including the affiliates in its industrial-union wing, had great internal difficulty when it came to confronting embedded patterns of racial discrimination. Almost all of the construction trade unions remained white ethnic job trusts that cracked open their doors to African American and Latino workers only after the most strenuous legal assault. The ILGWU, the USW, and the Textile Workers Union of America, representing workers in the garment trades, in steel, and in textiles, came under NAACP attack for a failure to end de facto segregation in many locals and departments. The UAW sustained a series of internal insurgencies led by African Americans who in the 1960s sought to win representation on the union's executive board and transform power relations inside an increasingly multicultural set of urban locals.[14]

Although the AFL-CIO lobbied for the 1964 Civil Rights Act, its top leadership feared a new era of mass mobilization: the AFL-CIO therefore declined to support either the 1963 March on Washington, the Delano marches and demonstrations led by Cesar Chavez in 1965, or the 1968 Poor People's March. George Meany, who presided over the merged organization for a quarter century, once told a group of European unionists: "Ideology is baloney. There can be no ideological differences among real trade-unionists."[15] Indeed, Meany was so hostile to the new liberalism emerging in the 1960s that he withheld AFL-CIO backing from the 1972 presidential bid of Democrat George McGovern, a Vietnam dove who had inaugurated his political career as a 1948 partisan of Progressive Party presidential candidate Henry Wallace. Meany and others in the AFL-CIO high command excoriated anti-war demonstrators, ignored the rise of a new feminist sensibility, and ridiculed gay demands for dignity and civil rights.[16]

Even Walter Reuther's UAW, which funded and patronized both the civil rights movement and the early New Left, failed to tap their energy on behalf of its institutional revitalization. Reuther hired scores of ex-socialists, ex-Trotskyists, ex-Communists, even some youthful veterans of the New Left, but they all had to conform to a regime that was liberal but also insular and autocratic. As Murray Kempton once put it, "The UAW, for the true believers in its midst, has the character of a full-scale religion."[17] Indeed, on two critical occasions, Reuther's link to the Democratic Party of Lyndon Johnson put the UAW apparat in opposition to the insurgent forces of the decade. In 1964 the autoworkers' chief conspired with LBJ and Democratic Party loyalists to deprive the insurgent, integrationist Mississippi Freedom Democratic Party of official recognition at the national party's Atlantic City convention that year. Then in 1967 and 1968 Reuther discredited himself with the more pro-labor elements of the anti-war movement by his steadfast refusal to repudiate the president and his war policy. His latter-day turn against the war was too little and too late.[18]

But leadership ideology alone does not explain the eclipse of unionism during the 1960s. The fate of a long and tempestuous automobile strike in the fall of 1964 demonstrates the extent to which union economic power had become divorced from labor's capacity to make working-class interests resonate with both public sentiment and elite politics. Although the phrase "industrial democracy" had long since become antique, the shop-floor tensions that had sparked this aspiration were still very much alive—especially to those automobile workers who confronted a harsh and unrelenting work pace and the supervisory authority that stood behind it. In more than a hundred

Protest signs from individual unions were plentiful at the 1963 March on Washington, but the AFL-CIO did not endorse the historic event. (Credit: Black Star)

General Motors factories, issues of democracy, dignity, and self-expression still motivated union workers. This part of the labor question had not been resolved by almost thirty years of collective bargaining. As in so many workplaces, the 1964 strike issues came right out of the 1930s. Like the steelworkers, who had shut down their entire industry in 1959, GM workers fought to determine who would control the pace of production, the number of workers on each job, and how much authority union shop stewards might command. They fought to "humanize" working conditions in what Walter Reuther called GM's "gold-plated sweatshop." A Buick local-union president told a *Wall Street Journal* reporter, "Work Standards—this is the high point—what we get from the company here is what makes or breaks you on the job." Late in September 1964 300,000 GM workers walked out in agreement with him.[19]

The GM strike was a militant and popular affair, forced on Reuther and other top UAW leaders by an impatient, self-confident workforce. It took place at the very height of the 1964 presidential campaign, during which the 1.3 million member UAW served as a linchpin of the Democratic victory. The significance of this now-forgotten strike lay not in its ostensible victory or defeat. As it turned out, the UAW failed to make a breakthrough on GM working conditions. But like the steel strike of 1959, which was the largest single stoppage in American history, the UAW's larger failure came through its incapacity to capture the imagination of the public or put the character of the factory work regime on the nation's legislative or political agenda.[20]

The strike was politically invisible during a campaign season otherwise significant for its renewal of ideological combat. Unlike the great GM strike of 1945–46, when the success or failure of UAW wage demands seemed central to the fate of the entire postwar standard of living, the strike battle nineteen years later caused few ripples outside of the auto industry itself. This was "free collective bargaining": indeed it was so "free" that it seemed to float above and beyond any larger political universe. Despite their own liberalism and much commitment and fury from the UAW rank and file, Reuther and other top union officials contributed to this depoliticization. In keeping with the Johnson administration strategy, they sought to defuse the conflict before it damaged liberal democratic aspirations in the November elections.[21] The postwar effort to defuse the labor question, advanced by both liberal pluralists and anti-labor conservatives, had successfully severed the link between labor's economic strength and its political influence.

Given such a dynamic, it is not surprising that the unions won no reform of the nation's increasingly dysfunctional labor law. In 1965 the repeal of Section 14b of the Taft-Hartley Act, which many Southern and Western states had used to proscribe the union shop, seemed well within grasp. By then Section 14b was a kind of scarlet letter, denoting the institutional illegitimacy that union officials sought to rip from their collective breast. Organized labor had been a powerhouse during President Johnson's 1964 campaign, and in the new Congress, liberal Democrats enjoyed their largest congressional influence since 1938. Repeal actually passed in the House of Representatives, but neither the president nor the most important Senate Democrats were willing to spend the political capital sufficient to suppress the inevitable Republican filibuster. Union chiefs had to realize "that labor's political power is not what they thought or hoped it was," reported Gardner Ackley, a key economic advisor to LBJ, "[a]nd they don't like to contemplate their apparent weakness." Thus highway beautification, immigration reform, and aid to education came higher on the presidential agenda. These were winnable, while repeal of 14b would have cost Johnson and the liberals dearly.[22]

Rights Consciousness

As we saw in the previous chapter, the eclipse of American trade unionism was not just a question of politics, but of ideas as well. In the two decades after the end of World War II, American liberalism had undergone a profound transformation. The value of social solidarity and the democratization of the corporate work regime had moved well to the margins. Labor-liberals remained concerned with economic inequality, but few connected this to an agenda that sought to restructure American capitalism or mobilize their constituency on anything approaching a class basis. During the early Cold War years most American liberals interpreted the twentieth-century advance of fascism and communism as indicative of the danger posed by such mass/class politics. As Gary Gerstle has shown, liberals saw class cleavages, or the appearance of such, as dangerous and irrational, while racial divisions were both more significant and also more easily solvable by good will and good statecraft. Thus did Reinhold Niebuhr, the Protestant theologian who would have such a large influence on post–World War II liberalism, excoriate his fellow progressives for thinking that the distribution of property was a more fundamental cause of social division and conflict than were racial and ethnic differences.[23]

The rise of a dynamic, morally incisive civil rights movement ratified this shift in liberal consciousness. In the months between the Birmingham demonstrations of May 1963 and the March on Washington twelve weeks later, a new social agenda rose to national prominence. Indeed, the summer of 1963 may well be taken as the moment when the discourse of American liberalism shifted decisively out of the New Deal–labor orbit and into a world in which the racial divide colored all politics. But the effort to inject a racial (and later a gender-based) egalitarianism into the world of work modeled itself, not on the struggles of the labor movement, but on the strategic vision and legal innovations of the movement for African American civil rights. From the early 1960s onward, the most legitimate, thought not necessarily the most potent, defense of American job rights would be found not through collective initiative, as codified in the Wagner Act and advanced by the trade unions, but through an individual's claim to his or her civil rights based on race, gender, age, or other attribute. If a new set of work rights was to be won, the decisive battle would take place, not in the union hall or across the bargaining table, but in the courts and the legislative chambers.

From a lawmaking point of view the decisive moment in this transformation came when, during the great political opening that followed the 1963 Birmingham demonstrations, a legal/administrative template derived from the World War II–era Fair Employment Practice Commission was rolled into the 1964 civil rights law as Title VII. The AFL-CIO strongly supported this then radical inclusion, and its lobbyists played a key role in persuading both the Kennedy administration and Congress on behalf of the larger civil rights community. George Meany wanted the aid of a federal club to help him end the most overt and embarrassing kinds of segregation within literally thousands of local unions. The 1964 Civil Rights Act ended segregation in all public accommodations, including theaters, restaurants, and swimming pools. Under Title VII, an Equal Employment Opportunity Commission championed demands for equitable hiring and promotion practices both in private employment and government service, and under conditions negotiated in thousands of union contracts. Thus the EEOC abolished the long-prevailing practice of listing jobs for "white" and "colored," as well as for "men" and "women," in newspaper help-wanted ads. And under Title VII many union work rules and seniority arrangements came under intense governmental review. Indeed, AFL-CIO officials had not foreseen the extent to which the application of Title VII would call into question a whole range of union traditions and de facto discriminatory prac-

Lyndon Johnson signs the 1964 Civil Rights Act. Martin Luther King, Jr., stands behind the president. AFL-CIO president George Meany is just to his left, in shadow. (Credit: Lyndon Baines Johnson Presidential Library)

tices, which is why so many union officials became so hostile to Title VII in just a few years.[24]

This was a great victory for American democracy and a signal effort to grapple with a newly discovered dimension to the old labor question. But this new set of legal and administrative remedies also had unforeseen consequences. Title VII separated the notion of discrimination in the workplace from the more powerful, pervasive causes of black unemployment and underachievement. The "fair employment" idea became thoroughly racialized, still later gendered, thereby moving out of a world in which employee rights were seen as part of the tradition guarded by the unions, the Labor Department, and the old New Dealers and into a realm in which work rights were defined, legislated, and litigated on an individual basis.

In a similar fashion, the reform of the labor market in the 1960s, long advocated by New Dealers and industrial unionists, came within a highly racialized context. The Johnson administration's "war on poverty" targeted the nation's African American population, who had been for so long excluded from the social citizenship embodied within the New Deal system. This racialization of American social policy was a product both of the administration's genuine liberalism and of its somewhat cynical efforts to accommodate, on the cheap, the costs of its new reformism. In this liberal era, poverty did decline; as measured by the Department of Labor, the number of poor people decreased from 23 percent in 1962 to 11 percent in 1973. There was a 30 percent reduction in infant mortality, a three-year increase in life expectancy, and a leap in school attendance for African Americans, Hispanics, and low-income whites. But this salutary result was less a product of targeted poverty programs, which were always underfunded, than of low levels of unemployment and the deployment or enrichment of New Deal–style social programs. The minimum wage reached its historic purchasing power peak in 1968, Medicare and Medicaid raised the health-care floor for the poor and elderly, while Social Security now covered more people and disbursed higher benefits. Thus the social wage did rise, but in a bifurcated fashion. African American unemployment remained at double the level of that for whites, and among inner-city youths, who were the presumed beneficiaries of so much attention, crime, poverty, and unemployment increased to three times the rate of that of their white suburban counterparts. All such comparative social indexes would worsen in the late 1970s, when economic growth dropped sharply.

The problem was that liberals of the 1960s believed that the overall economy worked rather well: economic policy makers in the presidential administrations of both Kennedy and Johnson believed that persistent poverty was a function of tepid economic growth combined with inadequate levels of education, training, and motivation among many poor and minority Americans. In 1964, an $11 billion tax cut, much of it directed toward business investment, provided the stimulus that Walter Heller, the influential chairman of the Council of Economic Advisors, predicted would spur annual growth rates and lower unemployment to 4 percent. By the late 1960s it did so, aided by an increase in military spending that supercharged the economy.[25]

The successful turnaround reinforced the belief that persistent poverty was a product of the failure of the poor to take advantage of the opportunities generated by a booming American capitalism. Most new funding therefore went to programs designed to help the poor get an education and secure a job. Unemployed adults took a back seat to youngsters, whose presumptive lack of motivation became the object of near obsessive inquiry. Head Start, the most popular and long-lived of these programs, provided nutritious food and intellectual stimulation to preschoolers. Upward Bound sought to aid disadvantaged teenagers. The Job Corps retrained unskilled adults and those who had dropped out of school. Such educational programs were far cheaper than the relief and public-works projects of the New Deal. Indeed, expenditures in what LBJ declared "a total commitment to pursue victory over the most ancient of mankind's enemies" amounted to less than 1 percent of the federal budget. As a New Jersey antipoverty official later remarked, "The antipoverty program was premised on the assumption that poverty existed primarily in the heads of the poor."[26]

Johnson administration officials therefore ignored the most important cause of postwar poverty: structural changes in the economy that made it increasingly difficult for poor people to earn a decent living. The decline of the Appalachian coal industry had thrown more than half a million miners out of work. The mechanization of Southern cotton production had pushed millions of African Americans off the land. Economic change in both Puerto Rico and Mexico had crippled labor-intensive agriculture, forcing millions of Latinos with few economic resources into northern cities. These massive population movements took place at precisely the time that industry was fleeing to the exurbs and rural regions, stripping central cities of more than a million blue-collar jobs. Minority workers would become trash collectors, janitors, dishwashers, hospital orderlies, and office clerks, but these insecure service-sector jobs were just a step above outright poverty.[27]

Leon Keyserling spoke for a generation of old labor-liberals when he argued that it was "not the personal characteristics of the poor," but "the high volume of idle manpower and plant" that generated poverty. And a union leader quipped, "If you train on a loose labor market you are just raising the educational level of the unemployed."[28]

Labor-liberal initiatives of a more structural sort designed to alter the urban-industrial balance of power, such as repeal of Section 14b, a large-scale urban jobs program, or efforts to channel the deployment of capital, barely made it onto the reform agenda before the liberal tide of the 1960s had run its course.

Title VII in the Field

This conceptual divide would become poisonously acute in just a few years, but in the mid-1960s the unions, the civil rights movement, and the Democratic liberals all seemed to advance much the same legislative agenda. A. Philip Randolph's program for the 1963 March on Washington included a dramatic, pro-union reform of the labor law and a doubling of the minimum wage. A popular placard at the August 1963 march pithily asserted "Civil Rights + Full Employment = Freedom."[29] Indeed, the 1964 civil rights law was a genuinely radical piece of social legislation, fully comparable to the Wagner Act in its intrusive, democratizing impact. Like the Wagner Act it brought the power of the central government to bear upon recalcitrant employers, as well as other managers of property, in order to make real the citizenship rights of those heretofore excluded and subordinate.

The law had a huge impact in the South, where patterns of segregation and discrimination had structured the world of African American labor for more than three New South generations. In Southern textiles, still the nation's largest manufacturing industry, black employment jumped from about 6 percent to more than 25 percent in little more than a decade. In South Carolina the black proportion of all mill workers soared from one in twenty to one in three. Segregated water fountains, time clocks, and eating rooms were abolished. African Americans won new and better jobs throughout much of the factory hierarchy. They called their supervisors by their first names now, just like their white coworkers. Economist Gavin Wright declared the impact of Title VII a "genuine revolution" within the textile industry, that century-old mainstay of the Southern economy.[30]

Like the Wagner Act, Title VII generated a wave of working-class empowerment and self-organization. Before passage of the law, "we had no leg to stand on," reported a black worker. "[I]t was difficult to do anything. . . . you were scared to talk." But as workers became alive to the impact of the law, they clamored for redress. The NAACP filed numerous-class action lawsuits, demanding nondiscriminatory hiring, promotion into heretofore "white" jobs, equal pay, and better pay. These suits generated a tangible social/political fission, not all that different from a CIO unionizing campaign in depression-era America. As in the 1930s, once-deferential workers organized themselves to bring their grievances and complaints to the attention of those "organizers" whose knowledge of law, politics, and corporate personnel policy was essential to make effective use of the new legislation. In the late 1930s these had been radical CIO staffers, in the late 1960s they were often movement-oriented lawyers.[31]

Civil rights attorneys filed lawsuits against almost every major textile company. Such legal action represented the apex of civil rights activism in those remote Southern mill towns bypassed by the marches and demonstrations held earlier in the decade. Indeed, EEOC investigators and lawyers still encountered the same kind of resentment and resistance in the late 1960s that had been faced by NLRB attorneys thirty years before when that agency sought to extend the labor law into the remote mill villages of the South. Susan Foshee, an EEOC staffer, recalled that, "Sometimes, when we would drive off the main highway onto the industrial road, we would notice that we were being followed by an automobile, usually there would be three or four white men in the auto. Sometimes you might see the barrel of a shotgun in an open window."[32] In a class-action suit whose outcome was reminiscent of a 1941 CIO legal victory over the non-union Little Steel companies, Cannon Mills was forced to pay $1,650,000 in back wages to 3,700 black workers in 1972. As in 1941, this mobilization of a powerful legal/administrative state empowered thousands of workers far from the nation's capital: "It gave people courage and encouragement to apply for positions, and to seek positions and promotions, jobs that they had never sought before," concluded the attorney who argued the case.[33]

This rights consciousness generated a newly powerful sense of legitimacy for the union struggle in the South, especially among African Americans. In the 1940s when Southern Bourbons wanted to discredit the labor movement in their region, they denounced it as a racially, politically subversive institution that strayed well beyond its presumptive role as a well-constrained collective-bargaining organization. Southern unions, especially African American unions, were illegitimate because they sought to transform the social structure of the South. As Mississippi Senator James Eastland put it in 1949, when denouncing a largely black union of Memphis cotton press workers, "[T]his is a Communist organization. . . . [I]nstead of being a labor organization . . . it is, in reality, a Communist organization and . . . the Negroes who belong to it are dupes." In defense, black unionists emphasized that their organization was a bona fide trade union first, an organization concerned with civil rights and political action to but a secondary degree.[34]

But twenty years later the rights revolution had thoroughly transformed the ideological landscape. When Hospital Workers Local 1199B sought to build a union organization in Charleston, South Carolina, they cast their struggle almost entirely in terms of the civil rights movement of that era. They were the "soul power" union, proudly reminding both members and adversaries alike that Martin Luther King himself had once called Local 1199 (in actuality a national organization) his favorite union. This self-definition proved a powerful motivator for black hospital workers, especially after Andrew Young, Ralph Abernathy, and others from the Southern Christian Leadership Conference poured into Charleston during the spring of 1969. Then the tactics, values, and demands of the civil rights movement were put on full, disruptive display. Union organizers knew, in Charleston and New York, that only by linking their fight to the civil rights movement could they prevail in this Deep South city. Conversely, South Carolina's conservative elite insisted that the conflict in the Charleston hospitals was a question of old-fashioned trade unionism, not civil rights. State officials avoided the brutal Bull Connor tactics deployed half a decade earlier in Birmingham; nor did they red-bait or race-bait the civil rights activists. Instead they insisted that the absence of a state collective-bargaining law made the effort to unionize illegal and futile. Thus we find the South Carolina governing class capitalizing on the eclipse into which the union idea had fallen, while at the same time paying a backhanded tribute to the power of a rights-conscious social movement.

Despite this elite disparagement, African American workers were sophisticated in their understanding of trade unionism, even when institutions like the TWUA or the UAW failed to adequately defend their interests. As historian Timothy Minchin makes clear, black workers in the textile industry attacked union patterns of discrimination and nonrepresentation, while at the same time supporting the principle of unionism for all workers, African American as well as white. Johnnie Archie, a black worker who had sued his own local, nevertheless continued to pay his union dues: "We wanted job security. If the supervisor didn't like the way I looked . . . he'd say, 'Don't you come back tomorrow,' but with a union, although we didn't get the representation that we thought we should have, we had job security. He couldn't run me off because he didn't like my looks."[35]

Thus the civil rights movement and its many heirs replicated the social and political dynamics that had helped the union movement of the 1930s succeed: linking ethnic consciousness and social citizenship, advancing federal power against that of entrenched local elites, and creating a new cadre of ideologically motivated organizers. "Back in the late 1960s," remembered one union organizer, "whenever you went into one plant the first thing you looked to was how many blacks were there working. . . . And if there were forty blacks you could count on forty votes." Doris Turner, a leader of the hospital workers, came to see the linkage between civil rights and union rights: "Really and truthfully, they were one struggle, just being waged in different places."[36] Cesar Chavez won support on this basis for his farmworker union from thousands of students, clergy, and liberals in California and elsewhere. The issues that animated the Memphis sanitation strike of April 1968 were quickly eclipsed by King's assassination in that strike-torn city, but a third of a century later, the "I Am a Man" picket signs carried by thousands of strikers and their supporters still resonate in the nation's political imagination.[37]

Rights consciousness transcended most of the usual demographic and occupational barriers. It spread to almost every segment of society, to just about every interest group and faction. A wildcat strike wave in the postal service raised wages and institutionalized collective bargaining even in that once authoritarian bureaucracy. "The

The Memphis sanitation strike of 1968 advanced the meaning of African-American citizenship. (Credit: AFSCME)

worker wants the same rights he has on the street after he walks in the plant door," asserted Jim Babbs, a twenty-four-year-old white worker at a Ford plant outside Detroit. "This is the general feeling of this generation, whether it's a guy in a plant or a student on campus, not wanting to be an IBM number." For a brief moment even the U.S. government acknowledged the desire for change in the structure of American work life. "All authority in our society is being challenged," announced a 1973 Department of Health, Education, and Welfare Report, *Work in America.* "Professional athletes challenge owners, journalists challenge editors, consumers challenge manufacturers . . . and young blue collar workers, who have grown up in an environment in which equality is called for in all institutions, are demanding the same rights and expressing the same values as university students."[38]

The Discourse of Rights

During the decades following the civil rights revolution, the legislative promulgation or judicial affirmation of workplace rights encompassing the gender, sexual orientation, age, disability, and parenthood of employees have put a new and expanded conception of social citizenship on the employment agenda. Title VII of the 1964 Civil Rights Act therefore stands with the Wagner Act itself as a pillar upon which the world of work has been reshaped. Within just a few years the Equal Employment Opportunity Commission achieved an even higher profile than the NLRB, and the judicial interpretation of Title VII became every bit as important and controversial as any Supreme Court labor law ruling. Unlike the Wagner Act, whose power would be restricted by subsequent laws and judicial rulings, Title VII opened the floodgates to a series of new laws, labeled "civil rights," though actually central to the expansion of work rights within the realm of factory, office, school, and salesroom.

The list of such legislation is quite remarkable. In 1968 came the Age Discrimination in Employment Act, in 1969 the Mine Safety Act, in 1970 the Occupational Safety and Health Act, in 1973 the Rehabilitation Act, in 1974 the Employee Retirement Income Security Act, and in 1978 the Pregnancy Discrimination Act (PDA). More recently the two most important pieces of "labor legislation" in the United States have been the Americans with Disabilities Act of 1990 and the Family and Medical Leave Act of 1993. Meanwhile the EEOC actually expanded its authority and jurisdiction during the period in which Republican presidents held the White House. Although highly contested, issues that encompass the hiring, pay, promotion, and layoff of employees became subject to governmental review and private litigation to an extent the union movement could hardly match, even in the heyday of the Wagner Act. Indeed, the unfolding of a feminist consciousness in the workplace generated laws covering areas of interpersonal relations and employer-employee contact once considered exclusively private.[39]

For example, what are the rights of pregnant women in the workplace? Can they receive "special" consideration? Progressive Era feminists and labor reformers had believed that the law must "protect" women workers, in some cases excluding them from whole occupations, in order "to preserve the strength and vigor of the race."[40] In effect, this was the view taken by Johnson Controls, which used large quantities of lead in its Vermont battery-production facility. Women workers had been excluded from high-paying, unionized, blue-collar work there until the impact of Title VII transformed the hiring process in the 1970s. But the new Occupational Safety and Health Administration also made everyone acutely aware that lead was particularly injurious to a fetus, and to a lesser extent, to the health of adult men and women.

In response Johnson Controls imposed a mandatory exclusion of all fertile women from jobs in which lead exposure was present. Women who chose to work on such jobs could do so only if they were surgically sterilized. The corporation deployed the new sense of health and safety consciousness at work, combined with an equally new concern with fetal rights, to build widespread support for their policy. In response an alliance of feminists and unionists (the UAW represented workers at Johnson Controls) argued that fertile women and their potential offspring were neither the only people at risk, nor the only ones to whom lead poisoning was dangerous. Johnson Controls used a doctrine of fetal protectionism both to discriminate against women and to avoid cleaning up the entire plant, for both adult men and adult women were at risk. The Supreme Court affirmed the UAW's position in a unanimous 1991 decision. Justice Harry Blackmun asserted that "Concern for a woman's existing or potential offspring historically has been the excuse for denying women equal employment opportunity. . . . [I]t is no more appropriate for the courts than it is for individual employers to decide whether a women's reproductive role is more important to herself and her family than her economic role."[41]

But if Title VII and the Pregnancy Discrimination Act made unequal treatment of pregnant women illegal, then pregnancy must be entirely irrelevant to a woman's employment standard and prospects. This was the view of many employers who argued that they could legally fire pregnant women whose absenteeism exceeded the corporate norm, as it applied to men and women beyond the age of childbearing. The issue came to a head in California when a large bank, California Federal Savings and Loan, fired a pregnant receptionist on the grounds that the new PDA nullified older protective labor statutes, which, like *Muller vs. Oregon* in 1908, saw women workers as uniquely different in their social role and biological makeup.

All feminists agreed that women needed liberal pregnancy leave, but they defined the meaning of women's rights in very different ways. The National Organization for Women and the American Civil Liberties Union argued that protective legislation was inherently dangerous to women's equal standing before the law and the employer. Pregnancy was therefore akin to a workplace disability that any worker might "suffer." But many other feminists made the argument that there was no getting around the fact that women were "different." Pregnancy was unique to women, thus equal treatment had a "disparate impact" on the capacity of women to both bear children and succeed in the workplace. The Supreme Court tilted toward this argument when it ruled that pregnancy protection laws did not violate the spirit or letter of Title VII. Writing for the majority, Justice Thurgood Marshall held that different standards for pregnant workers did not inevitably lead to inequitable treatment.[42]

Litigation over the meaning of the new work rights was not confined to fertile women. It soon moved smartly up the corporate hierarchy, where white, middle-aged managers, caught in the job-threatening profit squeeze of the mid-1970s, challenged the nineteenth-century "employment at will" doctrine. For more than a century U.S. courts had held that employers "may dismiss their employees at will . . . for good cause, for no cause, or even for cause morally wrong." But in the 1980s, state courts in Nebraska, Minnesota, Michigan and elsewhere came to see the "at-will" employment doctrine as increasingly idiosyncratic, given the rights-conscious "public-policy exceptions" inherent in the proliferation of laws that protected employees from dismissal for discriminatory reasons based on race, sex, age, disability, or "whistle blowing." Although far from the dominant opinion, some jurists held that the promises of fair treatment that were a common feature of corporate employee handbooks actually constituted an implied contract detailing the enforceable rights enjoyed by employees, regardless of their status.[43] Trade unionists welcomed such an expansion of American work rights, if only because it might offer a bit more protection to those who spoke up or sought to resolve their problems in a collective fashion.

Affirmative Action

In contrast some unionists found the idea of "affirmative action" far more problematic. The phrase, and the ever-shifting legal/administrative guidelines that stood behind it, undoubtedly encapsulate one of the most contentious transformations of the American work regime to come out of the rights-conscious 1960s. Ironically, affirmative action was but a minor administrative remedy during that decade because most policy makers and activists assumed that in an absence of outright discrimination, racial integration and equality would naturally become the norm. In this sense Title VII of the 1964 Civil Rights Act was "color blind." But it soon became clear that racism was not just a question of prejudice or personal bias. Racism could have an institutional structure, absolving individuals of any discriminatory intent, but generating unequal and inequitable racial outcomes in any event. Among workers, both black and white, their educational background, seniority standing, skill level, and social connections reflected a discriminatory legacy that was woven into the very fabric of American society. Racism was embedded in the labor market, in the educational system, in corporate recruitment practices, and in the routine activities of virtually all social and economic institutions. Of course, such a judgment is itself a highly controversial one: in recent years much of the debate over "affirmative action" has actually become a proxy for a larger argument over the meaning of racism itself and the social responsibility for its elimination.[44]

Institutional racism within the world of work, and within the unions themselves, became a burning issue from the late 1960s onward. By this time, the race riots—or "rebellions," depending upon one's political choice of language—had engulfed scores of cities and left thousands dead, injured, or in jail. Many had begun as a result of altercations with the police, but most observers interpreted these upheavals in economic terms, as a cry for jobs, income, and housing. These violent insurrections were quickly followed by more pointed black protests: at urban construction sites where unionized craft work remained lily white, and inside a dozen of the largest auto factories, where African American radicals used wild-cat strikes and incendiary rhetoric to attack both union and management as complicit in maintenance of a racially repressive regime. The work rules, seniority structures, and union power that had once seemed to liberate African Americans from management caprice and favoritism now entrapped them in an embedded racial hierarchy. This was most obvious in the craft unions, whose leaders often saw black demands for jobs and power as but another assault upon the insular, job-hoarding functionality of their organizations. But it was also the case in the politically liberal industrial unions, like the UAW and the Steelworkers, where the character and distribution of the good jobs had been so codified, by contract, seniority, and shop-floor politics, that African Americans, Hispanics, and white women found themselves clearly disadvantaged.[45]

Prodded by the EEOC and the NAACP, the courts soon brought under judicial review virtually the entire world of corporate personnel policy. In its famous *Griggs vs. Duke Power* decision of 1971, the Supreme Court ruled that even if employment tests, hiring methods, and promotion policies were administered in a nondiscriminatory fashion, they could still have an adversely "disparate" impact on blacks and other minorities. In such instances, affirmative steps must be taken to increase minority employment in order for a company or union to remain in compliance with Title VII. The legality of such affirmative-action hiring and promotion policies was the issue in *Weber vs. Kaiser Aluminum* (1978), when a white worker, Brian Weber, argued that Kaiser had discriminated against him because of the preferential treatment the employer gave black workers who sought to become skilled trades apprentices. In both *Griggs* and *Weber* the industrial unions endorsed such affirmative-action schemes. Hiring, and in some instances promotion, had always been a management prerogative.[46]

Indeed by the 1980s the quest for employment "diversity" had become a routinized feature of corporate personnel policy. A 1985 study of *Fortune* 500 companies found that more than 95 percent intended to "continue to use numerical objectives to track the progress of women and minorities . . . regardless of government requirements." The motivation was part public relations, part litigation avoidance, and part recognition that in a multiracial society, corporate policies that generated a diverse workforce were "an essential management tool which reinforces accountability and maximizes the utilization of the talents of [the firm's] entire work force." Indeed, there is much evidence that affirmative action/diversity programs, with their hiring goals, formal job postings, and interview rules, generated the same kind of rationalizing shock to the corporate labor market for professionals and executives as had the early industrial unions when they deployed New Deal labor law to reorder the blue-collar world of work a half century before.[47]

But union principles and diversity goals sometimes clashed. When employers—or civil rights litigators—sought to apply affirmative action principles to existing seniority systems, even the most liberal elements of the union movement objected. During the debates over passage of the 1964 civil rights law, the unions had been assured that under Title VII they would not be held responsible for discrimination arising under old seniority schemes. Seniority was part of the moral economy of the work regime; it represented the most important "property" interest a worker held in his job. Unions like the Steelworkers were willing to broaden and extend it so as to more equitably include African Americans and white women, but the courts agreed that if a "disparate impact" analysis were applied to existing seniority schemes, the raison d'être of the union itself would be called into question.

This dichotomy generated much tension between labor and civil rights organizations, because affirmative action rose to prominence during an era of economic stagnation and growing blue-collar unemployment. Indeed, it was something of a shell game, which is precisely the way it was deployed by Nixon administration officials in the celebrated Philadelphia Plan of 1969 and 1970, which established job quotas for minority workers in the construction trades and on the building sites of that city. Nixon was undoubtedly responding to craft-union racism and the African American protest against it. But his administration also had other fish to fry. Faced with the early symptoms of 1970s style stagflation, Nixon had already cut the federal construction budget and vetoed a Democratic jobs program. Black unemployment was rising rapidly. Thus the Philadelphia Plan generated few African American jobs: its chief purpose was to curb craft-union power, reduce construction industry wages, and drive a wedge between the unions and the civil rights community.[48]

For nearly a third of a century the politics of affirmative action has carried on its shoulders enormous moral freight. It has been particularly contentious and effective within higher education and among the upper reaches of the corporate hierarchy where the talk is of "glass ceilings" and executive role models. But in the working class, white collar as well as blue, affirmative action has rectified but a slice of the social and economic conditions that have made work and life less than satisfactory for so many minority Americans. Affirmative action has hardly been a substitute for traditional labor-liberal goals, including union power, full employment, and a set of genuine occupational opportunities available at all reaches of the job hierarchy. The legal victories won by its partisans have sustained a broad sense of gender and racial justice in this society. But as a practical matter the impact of successful affirmative action suits has often been Pyrrhic, as layoffs and downsizings slashed the good jobs that opened up after years of litigation. Thus in the years after a landmark consent decree in the basic steel industry, the number of black steelworkers plunged, from more than 38,000 in 1974 to less than 10,000 in 1988. Even as the proportion of blacks in some key trades increased, their actual numbers shrank. Given such devastating statistics, historian Judith Stein labels the conflict over affirmative action, the "narcissism of small differences." Indeed, the weakness of 1960s liberalism was not its ambitious social goals, argues Stein, who made an exhaustive study of race relations in the steel industry: "It was that liberalism lacked an economic blueprint to match its social agenda."[49]

Consequences

One might respond to this eclipse of the American trade unions and to the devolution of collective bargaining, by arguing that the protective functions these institutions once embodied are being taken over by an elaborate set of new agencies, new laws, and new advocates. If workers are protected against sexual harassment by a lawyer rather than their union shop steward, the employee's rights are protected nonetheless; and if the laws governing occupational safety and health regulate the work environment rather than a union contract clause, the factory air will smell just as sweet.

Affirmative action, in the world of work and education, has become an ideological battleground. (Credit: David Bacon)

The corporations have certainly come to understand that a union grievance and a federal regulation both limit managerial prerogatives in the workplace. Both are designed to reconfigure the labor question. Peruse for a moment the topics considered at a series of 1995 workshops sponsored by the Virginia Manufactures Association.

Among the issues were those of a traditionally Southern, anti-union sort, focusing on "changes at the National Labor Relations Board, and about what your company should do to remain union-free." But such labor law problems were embedded within another set of issues equally vexing to the factory supervisors and personnel managers in attendance. An "OSHA Update" and a workshop entitled "Employee Absences and Leaves: How to Navigate the Laws and Still Run Your Business" considered the impact of the Americans with Disabilities Act, the Family and Medical Leave Act, as well as older health and safety laws, on management's ability to "enforce performance standards." Other workshops told employers how to make use of changes in affirmative action, employment-at-will, and workers' compensation laws, as well as the complex web of litigation surrounding privacy issues, in areas such as drug testing, medical screening, e-mail, and surveillance. From the point of view of a factory manager, the era of declining union power had hardly been one of liberation from the regulatory state.[50]

But four problems arise with the complete substitution of a rights-based model of social regulation for one based on the collective advancement of mutual interests. The first is that of enforcement. The legal-regulatory system itself is simply not capable of enforcing by court order the inner life of millions of workplaces. Minimum wage laws are almost self-enforcing, but statutes that seek a more qualitative transformation of the work regime require something more. For example, at the Imperial Foods chicken processing plant in Hamlet, North Carolina, twenty-five workers died in 1991 when their low-wage, non-union factory burst into flames. In the wake of the fire, there were many calls for more money and personnel to put teeth into enforcement of Occupational Safety and Health Administration regulations. But no consistent regulation is really possible without hearing from the workers themselves, and their voice will remain silent unless they have some institution—such as a union—that protects them from the consequences of speaking up. Indeed the whole history of the OSHA has shown that no army of government inspectors can ensure management compliance with safety standards without the help of systematic, organized pressure at the work site itself.[51]

Second, the spread of employee rights has suffered through its necessary dependence upon professional, governmental expertise. No matter how well constructed, such regulation takes disputes out of the hands of those directly involved, furthers the influence of administrative professionals, sets up these experts as the target of everyone's resentment, and ends by increasing litigiousness and undermining government legitimacy. Taken to its logical conclusion, rights consciousness absolves individuals of the consequences of their own grievances. It makes difficult participatory, democratic problem-solving by the individuals directly involved because this way of thinking about workplace justice leaves it to another body—a court, a panel, a government agency—to sort out the various claims and reach a just approximation of the appropriate balance. Thus in the EEOC's unsuccessful suit against Sears, Roebuck, where women managers and sales personnel earned substantially less than men occupying similar jobs, the government case relied entirely upon corporate employment data as analyzed by statisticians, sociologists, and historians. Such argumentation was necessary, but without the voices and the textured lives, offered by a set of aggrieved workers, the EEOC brief lost some of its moral, political punch. Meanwhile Sears, arguing that women did not seek or want higher-paying jobs, offered flesh-and-blood workers and managers to substantiate company claims.[52]

Third, a discourse of rights has proven increasingly incapable of grappling with the structural crisis, both economic and social, that confronts American society. Individual workers—especially those from the professions and the ranks of management—have won a measure of protection, but a rights-based approach to the democratization of the workplace fails to confront capital with demands that cannot be defined as a judicially protected mandate. In too many cases, workers have used the new work rights that emerged out of the civil rights movement to democratize gender and racial hierarchies, only to see their real security and opportunities undermined by the dramatic transformation of their working environment, over which they have had virtually no control. Thus in the 1970s women workers won a large employment discrimination settlement against AT&T, but the downsizing of the corporation in the 1980s and the failure to win substantial compensation for those most effected, rendered their victory a limited one.

And finally, the rights revolution has not generated conditions that produced strong unions, or tempered managerial production prerogatives, despite the hopeful linkage between these worlds. In the textile industry, the rights revolution did little to alter the character of managerial authority. African American foremen were just as harsh as white, while many blacks found themselves subject to a speed-up in the previously all-white jobs they took over during the 1970s and 1980s. African Americans were more pro-union than most whites, but the balance of power in the industry still remained decisively in management hands. Thus the TWUA held 25 percent fewer collective-bargaining contracts in 1976 than it had a quarter century earlier. The situation was much the same in Charleston, where Local 1199's deployment of civil rights tactics and ideologies had had such an impact. Voting registration shot up and numerous blacks were elected to state and local office, but once the civil rights organizers had departed, union loyalists inside the hospital were eviscerated by an intransigent set of anti-union administrators.[53]

These complaints are not designed to add yet another voice to contemporary assaults on the American welfare state and its civil rights laws. The emergence of a vibrant sense of rights consciousness—whether it be held by second-generation Slavic workers in the 1930s, by African Americans in the 1960s, by middle-class women in the 1970s, or middle managers in the 1980s—remains crucial to the construction of a democratic polity. It's a good thing that Burger King and so many other companies have put that EEOC nondiscrimination declaration at the top of their employment applications. But collective action, institution building, and rights consciousness are not mutually exclusive, and we need to quickly redress the balance if the American system of work rights is not to devolve into an ineffectual formalism. The best way to make sure that does not happen is to return an autonomous, democratic unionism to the workplace.

CHAPTER 6

A Time of Troubles

LIKE HIS FATHER BEFORE HIM, Steve Szumilyas worked at Wisconsin Steel on Chicago's Southeast Side. At 4 P.M. on Friday, March 28, 1980, he was checking steel slabs before they went into the reheating furnace when his foreman came by with news that would shatter his world. The gates were being locked at the end of the shift; the mill was going down; 3,400 union steelworkers were out of a job. Szumilyas was on the street. Had it not been for his wife's new job, his family would have lost their suburban home. Steve Szumilyas would work again, but at wages only half those in basic steel.[1]

The Szumilyas layoff proved symptomatic of an era. "Nobody," wrote *Time* magazine, "is apt to look back on the 1970s as the good old days."[2] In the steel industry a competitive hurricane toppled giant blast furnaces as if they were made of straw. In 1975 twenty integrated companies operated forty-seven plants in the United States; by the end of the 1980s domestic capacity had dropped by 25 percent and there were only fourteen companies operating twenty-three plants left. The United Steelworkers of America, once a million strong, now represented but 200,000 workers in basic steel and an equal number in light manufacturing and the services. By the 1990s the United States was the only major industrial nation that was not self-sufficient in steel.[3]

Throughout this era, recessions became more severe and more frequent in the United States, unemployment rose to above 7 percent, and the growth in the efficiency of the economy—what economists call productivity—dropped like a stone. At the bottom line, profits of U.S. firms peaked in the mid-1960s and then proceeded to decline and stagnate for the next fifteen years. By the early 1980s they were approximately one-third less than a generation before; in the manufacturing sector only about one-half. Productivity growth fell to less than half of the postwar pace and dropped well behind that of most U.S. trading partners.[4]

U.S. economic growth would continue over the next two decades, but at an annual rate of about 2 percent—far lower than during the twenty-five years after World War II. Indeed, for two full decades, from the early 1970s to the early 1990s, real wages stagnated for most Americans, and for young males they actually dropped by 25 percent. Family income increased during these decades of slow growth, but this was largely because Americans were working longer hours and because women and teenagers were more likely to hold paying jobs. Meanwhile, income inequalities widened dramatically. Top corporate executives had earned about forty times as much as an ordinary worker in the 1960s; thirty years later, the multiplier was an astounding 157 times.[5]

For much of the union movement, the 1970s and 1980s were a disaster. Organized labor lost members and power in a downward spiral reminiscent of the 1920s. As a proportion of the entire workforce, union membership declined from 29 percent in 1973 to just above 16 percent in 1991. The losses were concentrated in the old, unionized core of the economy—what used to be called "basic" industry—where factory shutdowns devastated several of the nation's most famous industrial unions. Union membership fell by half a million in the auto industry, by 300,000 in companies where workers were represented by the Machinists, and by nearly 400,000 in the needle trades. Membership in the venerable International Ladies' Garment Workers' Union dropped by two-thirds in the two decades after 1973. Wages and union organization in the packinghouse industry collapsed just as rapidly when global grain-marketing firms like Cargill and Conagra entered meatpacking in the 1970s and 1980s. But the losses were not limited to unions whose members made products subject to a new wave of international competition. The venerable construction trades dropped nearly a million dues payers, while the Teamsters,

Steel workers and other unionists appealed to the government for aid early in the 1980s, but without success. (Credit: Jim West)

whose truck drivers, warehousemen, and food-processing workers were largely immune to pressure from foreign producers, lost almost as many members.[6]

Beyond Industrialism and Fordism

What accounts for this stunning new era of union decline and economic difficulty? Explaining labor's decline has become something of a cottage industry over the last quarter century, with a full line of custom-made products. But the output can be divided, roughly, into two kinds of explanations, though not necessarily on a Left-Right axis. The first prioritizes sociological and technological transformations in the mode of production as the key to understanding union decline; the second emphasizes the extent to which such sociotechnical changes have merely offered capital a more advantageous terrain upon which to carry out offensive operations. Or to be even more blunt about it: one school looks to the technics of production and the character of the market, the other to the politics of society and the labor movement itself to explain American unionism's late-twentieth-century failures.

"Post-industrialism" and "Post-Fordism" have become social science clichés of late, but these "big ideas" once packed a large explanatory punch. Both arose out of left-wing thought and experience, but as both have filtered up the policy food chain, they have been deployed with increasing intellectual vigor by those hostile or indifferent to contemporary trade unionism. The idea that the United States was becoming a post-industrial society first entered social-science discourse in the early 1960s when a set of theorists, including Daniel Bell, David Reisman, Peter Drucker, and others once schooled in Marxist teleology, began to deploy the term to explain the decline in U.S. class politics. Bell saw post-industrialism as but the latest stage in the evolution of society: just as manufacturing had replaced agriculture as the central mode of production, so too would information processing and the service economy displace the factory, mill, and mine. This perspective was seemingly sustained by the U.S. Census itself, which had begun to report, after 1956, that more workers labored in the service sector than in manufacturing. Moreover, the occupational growth rate of professionals, teachers, and other information-processing workers far outstripped that of the men and women who wore a blue collar.[7]

Initially, post-industrial theory had a social-democratic flavor because its proponents counterposed the professional and scientific expertise of the new society with the economics and culture of private ownership and the market. This was the perspective put forward by John Kenneth Galbraith in his progressive, optimistic *New Industrial State* (1967). "The mature corporation," he wrote at the high noon of the postwar boom, is "part of a comprehensive structure of planning" that "identifies itself with social goals" generated by an ever growing public sector. Likewise, Daniel Bell foresaw something close to a socialized economy as almost inevitable. "[W]e in America are moving away from a society based on a private-enterprise market system toward one in which the most important economic decisions will be made at the political level," wrote Bell in his enormously influential *The Coming of Post-Industrial Society* (1973). "In the post-industrial society, production and business decisions will be subordinated to, or will derive from, other forces in society."[8] And even further to the left, Alain Touraine and other proponents of a "new working class" saw the New Left upsurge as but an early stage in the emergence of a strategically located class of knowledge workers whose institutions would be as powerful in a post-industrial society as were the mass unions of the industrial age.[9]

Of course, the idea of a post-industrial world devalued all that was or is characteristic of the old order, including the production of things in actual factories, various forms of routine service work, and the existence of trade unions, either as defenders of a dying class of manual laborers or as an institution necessary to defend the interests of the knowledge workers themselves. Indeed, failure of the trade unions to organize white collar and professional workers, which was becoming well noted as the 1950s turned into the 1960s, seemed to confirm that these workers had an interest and outlook inherently hostile to the union idea. Elements of this perspective have been clearly present in the viewpoint of Robert Reich, Bill Clinton's first secretary of labor, whose celebration of a powerful new class of "symbolic analysts" left little place for unionism or class politics. "Symbolic analysis involves processes of thought and communication," wrote Reich, "rather than tangible production." In this schema, "post-industrialism" resolves the gritty conflicts of the old industrial order by simply leaving them behind: Steve Szumilyas should have been happy just to walk away from Wisconsin Steel and enter one of the government-funded, high-tech retraining programs advocated by Reich and other influential neoliberals.[10]

Post-Fordism, a first cousin to the post-industrial idea, flourished about a decade later, in the 1970s and 1980s. Emma Rothschild offered an early critique of the mass production idea in her *Paradise Lost: The Decline of the Auto-Industrial Age*, which decried the "pattern of industrial inertia" that had come to characterize an industry faced with "social obsolescence."[11] Her attack on Fordism as an increasingly inefficient production system was sustained a few years later by the MIT political scientists Charles Sabel and Michael Piore, who became the most influential proponents of the idea that the difficulties faced by unions and the working class were the function of a new, post-Fordist industrial revolution. During the first half of the twentieth century, mass production had made mass consumption possible, mass consumption had made mass production viable, and the two were made to work in harmonious tandem by the Keynesian politics and policies adopted by economically activist nation-states in the years just after World War II.

But postwar Fordism did not last for long. In what they called a "second industrial divide," Sabel and Piore held that cyberworld high technology, greater international competition, and a cultural differentiation of product markets had undermined the Fordist production regime and the consumption patterns on which it rested. Capital-intensive mass production, which both Henry Ford and Walter Reuther once thought the key to a general abundance, has now become an economic albatross whose very rigidities have exacerbated periodic recessions and rendered U.S. products less competitive. The nineteenth-century victory of mass production over a supple, creative craftism was hardly inevitable; it was in fact a "blind decision" whose technosocial debilities are only now becoming clear. Who wants to buy another Chevy when craftsmen at the Bavarian Motor Works can build a dozen different models that all feel custom made?[12]

To prosper, workers and corporations must therefore accommodate themselves to a new world of "flexible specialization" that requires a more highly educated workforce, rapid shifts in production technology, smaller firms serving specialized markets, and the creative deployment of skilled labor. In the 1970s and 1980s Germany, Austria, and Northern Italy were held the exemplars of this kind of production system, while Japan's capacity to penetrate U.S. markets seemed to demonstrate the virtues of a nonadversarial, highly flexible work regime. Thus for unionized workers in the United States, whose detailed seniority rules and precedent-laden grievance-arbitration procedures had defined the meaning of shop democracy on the assembly line, the new world of post-Fordist labor required a radical shift in ideology and institutions.[13] Once again Robert Reich proved an enthusiastic popularizer: In his 1983 bestseller, *The Next American Frontier*, Reich prophesized:

> This new organization of work necessarily will be more collaborative, participatory, and egalitarian than is high-volume, standardized production, for the simple reason that initiative, responsibility, and discretion must be so much more widely exercised within it. Since its success depends on quickly identifying and responding to opportunities in its rapidly changing environment, the flexible-system enterprise cannot afford rigidly hierarchical chains of authority.[14]

Such technosocial forecasting seemed to open up a new era of democratic producerism. Indeed, in *The Second Industrial Divide*, Piore and Sabel argued that computerized craftsmanship would give birth to a new world of Jeffersonian democracy. Instead of acting as adjuncts to machines, post-Fordian skilled workers might become sturdy industrial yeomen. The computer, wrote Piore and Sabel, is "a machine that meets Marx's definition of an artisan's tool: it is an instrument that responds to and extends the productive capacities of the user."[15]

"Globalization": And Its Limits

If a certain technological determinism lay at the heart of the post-industrial, post-Fordist vision, proponents of this brave new world retained something of a laborite sensibility that sought to reconceptualize a political economy in which the working class and its institutions might still play an animating, democratizing role. But most analysts of globalization, both left and right, saw the growing power of raw market forces as decisive to the future of the trade unions and of all other institutions that stood in the path of a worldwide market in goods, money, and labor. (Some wags called this "globalony.") In support of this perspective, World Bank officials chose to quote a rather famous nineteenth-century political economist when they published in 1996 a new edition of their *World Development Report.* Capitalism was a dynamic, revolutionary movement, argued Karl Marx in the *Communist Manifesto*:

> The bourgeoisie cannot exist without constantly revolutionizing the instruments of production. . . . All fixed, fast-frozen relations, with their train of ancient and venerable prejudices and opinions, are swept away, all new-formed ones become antiquated before they can ossify. . . . The need of a constantly expanding market for its products chases the bourgeoisie over the whole surface of the globe. It must nestle everywhere, settle everywhere, establish connections everywhere.[16]

The World Bank had the chutzpa to quote Marx because in our time advocates of a world market have so thoroughly seized the banner of radical change from labor and the Left. William Greider calls international finance capital the "Robespierre" of this revolution, a new and terrifying Committee of Public Safety ready to discipline nations, companies, unions, and politicians who stand athwart the free flow of money, labor, and goods.[17] "Now capital has wings," says New York financier Robert A. Johnson, "capital can deal with twenty labor markets at once and pick and choose among them. Labor is fixed in one place. So power has shifted."[18] Thus is the spatial mobility of capital pitted against the geographical solidarity of labor. In the United States, as well as abroad, ministers and managers defined the newly competitive world economy as a fait accompli to which workers, politicians, and public policy must necessarily accommodate.

Words like "reform" and "liberalization" now denote the process whereby an open market in labor and capital replaces the regulatory regimes that were erected earlier in the century. "For years socialists used to argue among themselves what kind of socialism they wanted," commented Denis MacShane, a former official of the International Metalworkers Federation, now a Labour MP. "But today, the choice of the left is no longer what kind of socialism it wants, but what kind of capitalism it can support."[19]

Indeed, from the point of view of the labor movement, the vision of a global, post-industrial, post-Fordist economic world stripped the unions of their functional rationale and social legitimacy. We have seen the extent to which a devolution of the union idea had been advanced by the collapse of pluralism in the 1960s and the emergence of a rights discourse shortly thereafter. But now the globalization of trade and the transformation of productive technology on a worldwide scale added yet more potency to the anti-union critique, undermining all the political and institutional structures that stood athwart the power and appeal of the world market.

The competitive challenge from Germany, Japan, and other masters of technologically advanced manufacturing undermined a key pillar of New Deal–era labor law and politics: trade unions are good for industrial society because they raise wages, not only for union members themselves but for the entire working population. Unions seek to take wages out of competition for individual firms, industries, and whole regions of the nation. Moreover, the labor movement has operated in the political sphere to raise the entire social wage, if only as a means to better defend its own wage standards. Thus even the most parochial unions seek universal health insurance, a higher minimum wage, more unemployment pay, and a well-funded welfare system.

But now such ideas seemed counterproductive, divisive, and vaguely unpatriotic. High wages made American manufacturing uncompetitive, and union work rules and formal grievance procedures stifled creativity and generated inflexibility. Keynesian programs of economic stimulation, whether through government tax policy or union wage advance, have worked best when the market coincided with a powerful, self-contained polity. In a more porous world of mobile capital, goods, and workers, such labor-liberal programs seemed more likely to generate inflation, trade deficits, and job losses.[20] In the United States the deregulation late in the 1970s of labor-intensive, highly competitive industries like trucking, airlines, and telephone cast aside the New Deal worry that "cutthroat" business practices would generate wage debasement. And since increases in compensation among unionized workers far outpaced income growth in the non-union sector—the union/non-union wage differential rose from 19 percent to 30 percent in the 1970s—American managers found themselves with a new incentive to put wages back into competitive play, especially in the growing list of industries where union and non-union firms coexisted.[21]

Moreover, the new international laissez-faire has challenged many of the social-democratic arrangements and regulations that were constructed during the mid-twentieth-century years as a safeguard, in Europe and the United States, against the recurrence of depression-era social Hobbesianism. The kind of social regulation once commonplace in the advanced industrial countries found no point of leverage in the increasingly globalized economy. Thus, at a 1998 meeting of the G-8 industrial nations in Cologne, a delegation of trade unionists, representing virtually all the big labor confederations in the developed world, found themselves completely stymied when they tried to put international labor standards, financial market regulation, and compensatory help to displaced workers on the agenda. In any national context, such initiatives would have been long-standing elements of mainstream politics, like minimum wage laws, banking regulations, and unemployment insurance. But in the global political economy, such ideas were considered anathema, either to the principles of free trade or to national sovereignty, and even to political parties—like those then running Great Britain, Germany, and the United States—that relied on the labor vote for their very survival.[22]

Now let's return to our original question. What has accounted for the stunning decline of the unions during the twenty-one years that began with the oil shock of 1973 and ended sometime after enactment of the North American Free Trade Agreement (NAFTA) of 1994? It is clear that a post-industrial, post-Fordist world is not, in fact, upon us. Manufacturing does employ less than 20 percent of all Americans, but as Stephen Cohen and John Zysman point out in *Manufacturing Matters*: "Services are complements to manufacturing, not potential substitutes or successors."[23] The computer revolution has actually blurred the line between the production of things and the production of ideas and services. A new program costs but pennies to actually manufacture, but tens of thousands of man- and woman-hours to create, de-bug, install, and market. Symbolic analysts, writing code for a new program, bear the same relationship to the productive process today, as did the skilled metal workers who turned out the tools and dies necessary to make the early twentieth-century assembly lines so efficient and productive.[24]

Trade and the interdependent globalization of production have had a tangible reality. In America's internationally competitive, labor-intensive industries, including textiles, clothing, auto parts, and light manufacturing of all sorts, imports from Mexico, South Korea, and both Chinas have slashed blue-collar jobs in many older industrial regions. When K-Mart sells some of the 225,000 corn brooms exported from Northern Mexico, where the workers earn $2.30 an hour, it buys far fewer brooms manufactured by $10-an-hour workers in Illinois. But defenders of the North American Free Trade Agreement point out that large job losses due to Ross Perot's "giant sucking sound" (U.S. jobs moving south) have not materialized during the 1990s. They are right, and the reason is simple: only about 15 percent of all low-skill U.S. workers are employed in manufacturing. Most are in retail trade and services. They aren't competing with Indonesian garment workers and Chinese toy makers. Trade, economists calculate, accounts for only 10 to 20 percent of the overall fall in demand for unskilled labor.[25]

But the impact of free trade has always been far more as an ideological construct than as a description of a single, integrated market leading to a new, unregulated "international division of labor." The world is not a seamless market in labor and goods. Nor do nations "compete" with each other in the same way that Coca-Cola steals market share from Pepsi. Although global trade increased fivefold during the 1970s and 1980s, capital flows, on a proportionate basis, reached only twice the level achieved in the years just before World War I. "The world is not as interdependent as you might think," wrote economist Paul Krugman in 1994. "The United States is still almost 90 percent an economy that produces goods and services for its own use." Therefore, national living standards are still overwhelmingly determined by domestic conditions rather than by competition for world markets.[26]

Equally important, the world economy is not a zero-sum game. Unlike the rivalry between cola companies, high production and consumption patterns in Europe or Japan have a symbiotically beneficial impact on the United States and Canada. Thus, the United States imports almost all its television sets, but employment in the production of programming content, from sappy soap operas to the talk-filled, twenty-four-hour news shows, exceeds by tenfold the jobs lost in manufacturing.[27] (Or to put it another way, a color TV costs about $250, but a domestic cable service bills each subscriber at least that amount, year after year!) Concludes Krugman, "the obsession with competitiveness is both wrong and dangerous," chiefly useful as "a political device [and] as an evasion."[28]

This becomes graphically and painfully clear when workers try to organize a union. Although the actual level of plant closings due to foreign competition has been relatively small, management use of the *threat* of closure has been pervasive and effective when deployed against the union movement. In potentially mobile industries, such as manufacturing, communications, and warehouse work, 70 percent of all employers make plant-closing threats during organization campaigns; in textiles and apparel manufacture, every employer faced with unionization asserts that production will decline or stop. The message is hardly subtle. During a 1995 UAW organizing campaign at ITT Automotive in Michigan, the company parked thirteen flat-bed tractor-trailers loaded with shrink-wrapped production equipment in front of the plant. Hot pink signs posted on the side read "Mexico Transfer Job." And during a campaign at Fruit of the Loom in the Rio Grande Valley, the company hung a banner across the plant that warned, "Wear the Union Label. Unemployed." Although employers rarely delivered on such threats, at least in the prosperous half of the 1990s, they remain effective, reports Cornell labor educator Kate Bronfenbrenner. In potentially mobile industries where managers used the tactic, unions lost more than two-thirds of all certification elections, a dismal record even when one discounts the vast number of campaigns that never even got off the ground.[29]

Of course, the geographic mobility of capital is not a new phenomenon. Textile mills have been moving from New England to the Piedmont South during most of the twentieth century; department stores and specialty shops have fled downtown business districts; while Texas and California built an aircraft industry based on low-wage labor and military contracts in the years just before World War II. In the 1950s the South used its low-wage advantage to lure hundreds of auto and electrical-products factories to the region. Thus, by the end of the 1970s North Carolina could claim both the highest proportion of blue-collar workers in the nation, as well as the lowest average hourly wage.[30]

Jefferson Cowie's recent history of the way in which RCA has shifted the locus of television production demonstrates that "globalization" is part of a complex dialectic that has certainly destroyed jobs and communities in the United States, but without offering capital the decisive managerial victory for which it continually struggles. When RCA, like other manufacturers of electrical products, began its search for labor early in the twentieth century, the corporation sought a simple package: low wages, a docile, quasi-rural workforce, and an abundance of young, unemployed women.

RCA first found such a labor poor among the Eastern European immigrant women of Camden, New Jersey, where the company turned out radio sets by the millions. But the United Electrical Workers' (UE) success in organizing these women in the 1930s sent RCA in search of a more exotic cultural mix, which it found among the Protestant farmgirls and small-town residents in and around Bloomington, Indiana. For almost a generation all was quiescent in central Indiana, but by the 1960s these Midwestern women had reproduced the union militancy that had so troubled RCA managers in Camden. Strikes, slowdowns, and an erosion in the sexual division of labor in Bloomington made life increasingly difficult for RCA managers.

Naturally, the corporation sought yet another spatial fix. But when RCA built a state-of-the-art factory just outside Memphis, history's locomotive was running in high gear. The civil rights revolution had begun to raise expectations all across the South, so RCA found that its Tennessee honeymoon was a stunningly short affair. The factory had been opened in 1966 and a heavily African American workforce recruited; not unexpectedly, the Memphis sanitation strike and the assassination of Martin Luther King transformed the consciousness of many of these workers. By late 1970, after contract rejections and a bitter set of strikes had soured the company on its mid-South sojourn, RCA simply shuttered the Memphis complex. The transformation in social consciousness that had taken a quarter century in Indiana had been compressed into less than five years in Tennessee.

So RCA was again on the run, this time to Ciudad Juarez where an inexhaustible supply of rural teenage women seemed on tap. Cowie's fine account of the maquiladora political economy and its shop-floor gender relations demystifies "the international division of labor" to demonstrate that almost all of the socially transformative impulses that were once at work in Camden, Memphis, and Bloomington have reappeared across the Rio Grande. Although RCA could now take advantage of currency fluctuations and a repressive, state-controlled labor movement to lower production costs, the proletarianization experience once again transformed docile girls into rebellious women. Cowie thus shows that globalization is a dialectical relationship, a product of labor solidarity in one nation or region, capital mobility, and the working-class capacity for its own remobilization. Indeed, he ends his tale on a hopeful note. The last chapter of *Capital Moves* reproduces a determined photo of Beatriz Lujan, an RCA union activist standing before an organizing poster, with the slogan "*Sindicalismo sin Fronteras*" boldly slashed beneath the logo of the still radical UE.[31]

Concession Bargaining

Throughout the industrial world the history of trade unionism during the past quarter century demonstrates that global competition and economic hard times are not a necessary predicate to labor's decline. Unions in the United States had achieved their greatest leap forward during the Great Depression itself; moreover the whole idea of unionism, from an economic perspective, is that of a working-class defense against the unfettered forces let loose by the market. In most northern European nations, as well as in Japan, real wages and union density held their own during the years after 1973. Labor relations in Margaret Thatcher's Britain did follow a trajectory similar to that in the United States, but in Germany, Nordic Europe, and Canada various forms of politicized bargaining stayed remarkably potent. And in Poland, Spain, Brazil, Indonesia, South Korea, and South Africa, the unions demonstrated a remarkable capacity to make the leap from an era of intense political and economic repression to one in which they had a role to play on the center stage of national politics.[32]

If the globalization of trade and the transformation of production technology does not preclude the maintenance of a strong union movement, then the search for the causes of U.S. labor's difficulties in the 1970s and 1980s must lie elsewhere. The best place to start is actually found in those sectors of the U.S. political economy relatively sheltered from the winds of international competition. Union labor's most significant difficulties first appeared not in manufacturing but in the construction industry and in municipal governance, two large, intrinsically domestic realms, quite different in demography and political economy, where unions and wages nevertheless came under fierce attack.

The construction industry was neither global, post-Fordist, nor subject to significant technological change. Unlike manufacturing, where employment fell in the thirty years after 1970, big commercial or governmental construction projects were frequently short of workers. Nor was the industry "deregulated." Despite much business agitation, the 1932 Davis-Bacon Act, which mandates that the federal government pay a "prevailing wage" (almost always the union wage) on all of its construction, remained intact. Thus, if you want to build a skyscraper in Chicago, the building cannot be assembled by robots in South Carolina or by low-wage workers in a Third World country. A contractor must still hire a set of local workers, some possessing skills of a remarkable sort, to build a product that is itself time sensitive and unique.[33]

Moreover, the industry was well organized, and to the extent that a labor-management accord governed industrial relations anywhere, it functioned most seamlessly in construction. There metropolitan-area associations of union-shop contractors recruited their workforce

Construction work was neither post-industrial nor post-Fordist, but unionism nevertheless came under devastating attack.
(Credit: Jim West)

almost entirely from the hiring halls maintained by the powerful, politically well-connected craft unions. Wages grew rapidly, both in actual purchasing power and in relation to that of other blue-collar occupations, especially in the superheated construction boom of the late 1960s. The building trades justified the big pay hikes as a function of the boom-and-bust nature of their industry; meanwhile, the union-shop contractors, predominant outside the South, knew they could shift high-wage costs onto the government and the big corporations who paid the bill.[34]

This system came under sharp attack late in the 1960s. Big corporations with heavy construction budgets, like DuPont, Dow Chemical, General Electric, and U.S. Steel, combined with some of the largest contractors, including Bechtel, Brown and Root, Fluor, and Dravo, to form the Construction Users Anti-Inflation Roundtable (CUAIR). "It's time for a showdown," asserted the Alabama contractor, Winton Blount, who would soon enter the cabinet of Richard Nixon. The CUAIR wanted a "hard crackdown on construction unions," to use the words of its chair, Roger Blough, the former CEO of U.S. Steel. Reflecting a spirit not dissimilar from that of the post–World War I contractors who decried the union shop as un-American, Stephen Bechtel demanded that the greedy "construction unions should be opened up."[35]

To accomplish all this the CUAIR sought to eviscerate the Davis-Bacon Act and its many state-level offspring, break the monopoly of the construction unions in their metropolitan strongholds, introduce Taylorist principles to the building-construction process, and anathematize the craft unions as insular, retrograde institutions out of step with technological innovations or racial progress. These corporate construction users encouraged the dramatic growth of the new, militantly anti-union Associated Builders and Contractors, which in turn asserted that "owners have begun to realize that in today's construction market the only flexible cost left is labor."[36]

The anti-union campaign was aided immeasurably by the disrepute into which so many of the construction unions had fallen, especially in liberal and even in some labor circles. By the early 1970s leaders of the construction trades were increasingly hostile to the cultural and racial changes sweeping the nation. They were bitter enemies of affirmative action, supporters of the Vietnam War, and visceral opponents of the New Left and the new feminism. All this became graphically manifest when hundreds of construction workers, many wearing blue or yellow hard hats, assaulted an anti-war demonstration on Wall Street on May 8, 1970. The altercation injured scores of students and "longhairs," and it forced Mayor John Lindsay, a liberal Republican, to hoist the American flag at city hall to full mast, despite official mourning for the four students recently killed by National Guard bullets at Kent State earlier that same week. Twelve days later the New York Building and Construction Trades Council (BCTC) put tens of thousands of workers on Lower Manhattan's crowded streets in a pro-war demonstration engineered with the behind-the-scenes backing of the Nixon administration. Class resentment toward Lindsay liberals, radical collegians, and white-collar Manhattanites fueled the anger of these construction workers even more than any difference of opinion over the war itself. Whatever the complex motivation of these rank-and-file unionists, "hardhat" became a universal symbol for blue-collar social conservatism, swaggering masculinity, and racial resentment.[37]

But the cultural and economic payoff proved insubstantial. Nixon had the hard hats to the White House, made Peter Brennan of the New York BCTC secretary of labor, and despite the Philadelphia Plan model, allowed the craft unions to drag their feet when it came to the integration and advancement of African American men, not to mention women of either race. But none of this stopped the business assault on craft wages and organization. The divorce between politics, not to mention cultural politics, and the industrial relations system was virtually complete. In 1972 the CUAIR transformed itself into the even more potent and active Business Roundtable, a vanguard formation in what one journalist called "the political rearmament of the business community."[38] Hundreds of heretofore "union shop" construction firms went "double-breasted," they set up subsidiaries that hired only non-union labor. And in 1976, over the objections of his own secretary of labor, President Ford vetoed a modest "common situs" labor law reform bill, designed to rationalize the labor market, limit strikes, and moderate wage growth, but all with the cooperation and participation of the craft unions.[39]

Thus when the big recessions of the mid-1970s and early 1980s sent building-trades unemployment soaring, the unions in that industry had few allies on the Left, the Right, or in the government. The net result was one of the most rapid cycles of deunionization since the triumph of the "American Plan" early in the 1920s. Since 1970 the percentage of union workers in construction has dropped by half, the dollar volume built by union labor from 80 to 30 percent. Almost every contract renegotiated by the craft unions in the 1980s included a set of substantial wage give-backs. Thus real wages declined by a quarter in the years since the mid-1970s, while average construction earnings actually fell below those in manufacturing. Although there are still pockets of well-paid tradesmen in New York, San Francisco, Chicago, and a few other big cities, the great exurban construction boom of the late 1980s and mid-1990s has been largely union free. "We're paying less than Wal-Mart" acknowledged the president of a non-union construction group in Alabama.[40]

Like construction, the problems faced by municipal labor were entirely homegrown. By the 1970s the cities faced a twofold difficulty. The first was structural, involving urban deindustrialization, a stagnant tax base, and the inflationary surge that drove upward expenditures on infrastructure, education, and welfare. In the late 1970s all of the old American cities, regardless of the quality or politics of their municipal leadership, faced a fiscal crisis to one degree or another. In Chicago, Detroit, New York, and Atlanta firemen, schoolteachers, policemen, and other municipal workers were fired. A *Business Week* critique of municipal governance in the mid-1970s might well have been lifted right out of a manufacturing handbook: "The big-city governments of the U.S. are overextended and over-manned. . . . They desperately need to increase productivity. They need to end once and for all the idea that the city is run primarily for the benefit of its employees."[41]

The cities were left to fend for themselves, however, because high levels of municipal services, and adequate public-employee wages, represented more than just another burdensome expense. The state and local fiscal crisis of the 1970s, embodied in both the near bankruptcy of New York City and the California Tax Revolt (Proposition 13), reflected a sharp debate over the extent to which universally accessible "public goods," like parks, schools, mass transit, and other social services would become part of a new and higher social wage. Those new social entitlements had been a product of the struggles fought and won by the civil rights movement and the public-employee unions during the 1960s.

However, that social wage did not come cheaply, and in the 1970s it left the newly militant public-employee unions exposed to the resentment and attack of those who sought to stigmatize the social entitlements newly legitimated during the previous decade. These unions were a convenient, vulnerable, and racially tinged scapegoat, resented both by that growing proportion of the urban working class whose incomes were stagnant and by the newly mobile bourgeoisie who now found monoclass "edge cities" like Tyson's Corner, Virginia, and Fairfield, Connecticut, an easy escape.[42] "Given competitive pressures, we just cannot afford the dreams of the 1960s," argued one of the nation's leading urban economists. The liberal journalist Nicholas von Hoffman agreed. After a long, difficult Philadelphia teacher strike in 1973, he pronounced that "the kids were the losers" and then defended a mayor once notorious for the politics of racial polarization: "Essentially, Mayor Rizzo is backing away from the urban pie-in-the-sky programs like Model Cities, in favor of holding the taxes steady and increasing government efficiency. . . . That can't happen with the modern government union's credo of less work, worse work and much more pay."[43]

The mass circulation *Daily News* perfectly captured this anti-tax, anti-urban disdain when in October 1975 President Gerald Ford denied New York City a desperately needed federal loan guarantee. "Ford to City: Drop Dead" ran the banner headline in the tabloid *News*.[44] In the quasi bankruptcy that followed, New York City's powerful municipal unions were forced to swallow a wage freeze, huge layoffs, and the emergence of an overt anti-unionism even within the Gotham Democratic Party, the same organization that had once sent Robert Wagner and Franklin Roosevelt to Washington.

Such municipal anti-unionism had an echo even within the ranks of those newly elected African American officials whose empowerment was a product of the civil rights movement itself. The American Federation of State, County, and Municipal Employees (AFSCME) had firmly linked the cause of black sanitation workers to the legacy of Martin Luther King when that union fought and won the world-famous Memphis strike of 1968. King's assassination in Memphis seemed to seal the linkage between public employee unionism and a new generation of black political leadership. Thereafter, AFSCME growth soared, reaching more than half a million workers in 1973. The union's success was propelled forward, not only by its linkage to the aspirations of so many African American public workers, but by the explosive growth in the services offered by state and local governments, as well as by the de facto alliance it had forged with so many big-city mayors.

But this virtuous conspiracy hit a brick wall in Atlanta when an AFSCME sanitation local there confronted Mayor Maynard Jackson, whose ties to the civil rights movement had as been deep and genuine as any African American politician of his generation. AFSCME workers wanted a raise, but as in New York, municipal finances were a mess and the business community was determined to halt the growth in union power and city taxes. So Jackson "took" a strike in March 1977 and then stunned AFSCME by firing hundreds of workers who did not immediately return to work. Jackson had the backing, not only of the white establishment, but of much of the old-line civil rights leadership. Martin Luther King, Sr., for example, advised Jackson, to "fire the hell out of them." The strike was quickly smashed and AFSCME humiliated. In Atlanta it would take a generation to recover. To Jackson the fiscal crisis had put labor and civil rights liberalism on opposite sides of the political divide. "I see myself as only the first domino in [labor's] Southern domino theory," he explained during the strike. "[I]f labor makes the move on black political leadership, it's going to have severe consequences for labor Southwide."[45]

Municipal labor's rout on these urban battlefields proved a stunning, precedent-setting setback because it took place within the very womb of the liberal polity. Given the fragility of the labor-management accord and the ideological eclipse of the New Deal's high-wage social policy, it was therefore inevitable that reversals of an even larger magnitude would come within the world of private-sector, blue-collar employment where competitive pressures from abroad and the profit squeeze of the 1970s had worked a radical shift in management thinking.

This became dramatically clear at the Chrysler Corporation in 1979 when the number-three automaker stood on the verge of bankruptcy. The story of the Chrysler bailout is like a piece of film—in this case it is the New Deal movie—run backward. The players were much the same as forty-five years before: an important corporation in economic difficulties, a politically sophisticated union, and an interventionist Democratic administration that saw the patterns set in the auto industry as the innovative template for many other firms and industries. But in this film version of the old New Deal drama the politics runs in reverse, deconstructing the institutional arrangements and social norms that had once sustained the Rooseveltian compact. Prodded by Chrysler's banking creditors, the Carter administration pushed for wage reductions, layoffs, and a squeeze on supplier plants, insisting that such concessions were the quid pro quo for a billion-dollar corporate loan guarantee. Chrysler CEO Lee Iacocca ratified this bit of regressive social engineering with the declaration: "It's freeze time, boys. I've got plenty of jobs at seventeen dollars an hour; I don't have any at twenty."[46]

The leadership of the UAW campaigned hard and long among its members both for wage reductions and an abandonment of its incremental efforts to win the four-day workweek and eliminate mandatory overtime. In the late 1930s, backed by the then new Fair Labor Standards Act, unionists like Sidney Hillman and John L. Lewis had placed wage standardization at the top of their social agenda, even when such a program put inefficient producers out of business. But now UAW president Douglas Fraser and other union officials legitimated the firm-centered logic of their corporate adversary. Recycling one of Walter Reuther's social-patriotic slogans, Fraser declared that his union now favored "an equality of sacrifice" between management, suppliers, workers, and banks. Executives did take less pay, the suppliers cut their prices, and the banks extended their loans, but this level of business sacrifice had little long-range social consequence.[47]

For American workers, on the other hand, the impact of the bailout was disastrous. The UAW did win a seat on the Chrysler board, but for the first time in forty years, autoworkers no longer earned the same wages in each of the Big Three auto firms. As the company slashed its payroll and closed many of its older, urban factories, Chrysler employment dropped by 50 percent. Deunionization swept the auto parts sector while pattern bargaining among the Big Three domestic producers was broken for a decade. Encouraged a year later by the Reagan administration's spectacular destruction of the Professional Air Traffic Controllers Organization (PATCO), opportunistic managers in other industries soon replicated elements of the Chrysler settlement, and not only in sectors subject to heightened competition from abroad. Inventive personnel managers now deployed a whole set of wage structures designed to embed new wage-and-benefit inequalities within the workforce: two-tier wage systems, the establishment of non-union subsidiaries ("double-breasting"), employee stock-ownership plans, profit sharing, outsourcing, and lump-sum wage bonuses.[48]

The Chrysler bailout therefore had a twofold consequence: the concessionary bargaining in what had once been a flagship firm of American industry offered a powerful model that quickly spread to other firms, where blue-collar wages fell; of equal import, the fragmentation of the collective-bargaining process implicit in the bailout gave to many union-management relationships a quality not far different from that of Japanese enterprise unionism, in which workers are given powerful incentives to identify their economic well-being with the fate of their own firm and its management.

Unions in the Reagan Era

The trade-union defeats that now came in rapid succession were also a consequence of the political isolation that had so marginalized the labor movement by the late 1970s. The unions had few allies and many critics. As Thomas Edsall, Walter Dean Burnham, and Richard Oestreicher have pointed out, the class content of American liberalism underwent a profound shift in the years after 1968. As a result of both racial polarization in the late 1960s and the enduring cultural and ideological legacy of the Vietnam War, the electorial base of the Democratic Party shifted toward the middle class, while traditional

The Reagan Administration's destruction of the Professional Air Traffic Controllers Organization in 1981 made union-busting just another management program to reduce labor costs. (Credit: Jim West)

working-class constituencies either defected to the Republicans or, with even more long-range consequence, simply dropped out of politics. In nearly every presidential election since 1968, class differentiation in voting between the major parties has narrowed, and public policy has become increasingly less egalitarian. The electoral lift the

Democratic Party received as a result of the Watergate scandal accentuated this recomposition, giving the Democratic legislative majorities of the late 1970s a "neoliberal" cast that owed little to either the organization or the ideas of traditional labor-liberalism.[49]

Labor's political weakness became graphically clear in the late 1970s despite Democratic control of the White House and both houses of Congress. A neoliberal marketization of labor relations and economic policy was now in the ascendancy. Pushed forward by Alfred Kahn in the Carter administration and Senator Edward Kennedy in Congress, the sweeping deregulation of the trucking, railroad, and airline industries soon destroyed labor-relations stability in the transport sector and cut unionization rates there by a third. The AFL-CIO's defeat in its 1978 effort to win a very modest reform of NLRB union certification procedures, designed to facilitate its organizing activities, proved even more decisive. The legislative politics of this battle demonstrated the fractious character of the Democratic Party, the intensity of opposition to virtually any liberalization of the labor law, and the seismic shift in sentiment among almost all of the large, unionized firms at the core of the manufacturing economy.[50]

As early as 1977 the AFL-CIO's Committee on Political Education asserted that "the 2-1 Democratic majority in the U.S. House is pure illusion." Labor complained that its opponents had picked up "a goodly number of Democratic votes outside the South." These Democratic defections were matched by unexpected and highly political opposition from those industrial firms that had long been advocates of pattern bargaining and stable labor relations. The AFL-CIO contended that any labor-law reform that led to unionization among low-wage competitor firms was actually in the immediate interests of those companies that had a substantial history of collective bargaining, but this argument carried little force in the late 1970s. Douglas Fraser captured the import of the shift in big-business sentiment when, in the aftermath of the 1978 defeat of the NLRB reform, he accused his bargaining adversaries of waging a "one-sided class war in this country," thus discarding "the fragile, unwritten compact previously existing during a period of growth and progress."[51]

Union efforts to secure legislative help proved equally ineffective when it came to the impact of low-wage competition on unionized U.S. jobs. During the 1970s and 1980s most unions abandoned "free trade" in favor of "protectionism." (I have put these phrases in quotes because the nomenclature cannot adequately capture the complex set of political ideas and economic prescriptions embodied within each concept.) During the early Cold War era, the AFL-CIO had stood for free trade in order to boost high-end manufacturing at home and give the struggling industries of Asia and Western Europe easy access to the vast U.S. market. U.S. unions sought to export—with covert funding from their own government—American-style contract unionism to societies where a more overt kind of class politics had long influenced the relationship between capital and labor.

The AFL-CIO remained a steadfast proponent of such politically inspired free trade almost until the very end of the Cold War. But key affiliates had begun to jump ship decades before. The International Ladies' Garment Workers' Union (ILGWU) sought restrictions on Asian apparel imports in the early 1970s, while a decade later the UAW pushed for domestic content legislation, mandating that foreign firms with high-volume imports establish U.S. assembly plants and manufacturing facilities. In the 1970s such union policies did not envision a simple "protectionist" quota wall around all U.S. production, but the jingoist appeal was clearly there. "BUY AMERICAN. THE JOB YOU SAVE MADE BE YOUR OWN" sprouted on bumper stickers and factory-gate parking lots. Rank-and-file auto workers picked up sledgehammers and ritualistically bashed Toyotas in protest against the import "invasion."[52]

But protectionism—and the barely concealed, anti-Asian racism that lurked just below it—saved few union jobs. This was because even the most American-sounding firms, like General Motors and Sunbeam, not to mention clothing manufacturers and retailers, had so globalized their production that the distinction between "import" and "American Made" had become thoroughly blurred. Hondas were built in Marysville, Ohio, Fords in Hermosillo, Mexico. Moreover, the Buy American strategy put several unions in league with low-wage, anti-union employers for whom the slogan was little more than a marketing ploy. In the 1980s both the ILGWU and the Amalgamated Clothing and Textile Workers Union (ACTWU) participated in the apparel industry campaign, "Crafted with Pride in U.S.A." As in the auto industry, the effort to actually determine which textile products were genuinely domestic was shot through with contradictions, but union collaboration with corporate leaders in the "Crafted" gambit was a political dead end. Roger Milliken proved the animating industry voice: as the autocrat of a union-free, South Carolina–based textile firm, his hatred of the ACTWU had few peers. Milliken, moreover, was a genuine right-winger whose search for a national politician that might represent his autarkic, authoritarian vision took him from Newt Gingrich, to Ross Perot, to Pat Buchanan, all of whom he financed with handsome contributions. "Consciously in bed with the enemy," is the phrase a union needle-trades official later used to describe this sorry episode.[53]

Industrial Democracy: Management Style

As it became clear that the maintenance of high and uniform wages no longer provided an effective rationale for collective bargaining in a post-Keynesian world, the union movement faced a threat even greater than that poised by the foreign imports, employer wage cuts, and mass layoffs. This was an ideological challenge, from within and without, that questioned the very meaning of trade unionism. In the early 1980s when unions faced such devastating layoffs and plant closures, many in organized labor themselves adopted the view that U.S. industry could save itself only by a radical reorganization that would enhance productive flexibility to make American workers competitive with their foreign rivals. Labor's "adversarial" relationship to management must cease, while "multiskilling" and team production would eliminate the old, seniority-based work rules and job classifications. Global competition had undermined the rationale for an autonomous, combative trade unionism, argued Ben Fischer, a steel union partisan who had cut his political teeth in the Depression-era socialist movement:

> Differences between labor and management in a firm pale when compared with differences between companies, industries, and national economies. . . . [T]he people who make steel . . . have little in common with foreign workers. Even conflict between plants is unavoidable. . . . Workers can be comrades and also competitors. The nostalgia associated with historical labor culture cannot overcome harsh reality.[54]

At a Labor Day rally in 1982. Union efforts to restrict Japanese cars and steel often turned xenophobic. (Credit: Jim West)

Economic adversity and international competition seemed also to have had an impact on management thinking. Echoing post-Fordist themes, a General Motors industrial-relations official explained: "For many years, we paid for hands and legs. We were under the Frederick Taylor method of management . . . [but] we need more than that today, we need a great deal more. . . . There is no doubt that the employee knows more about the job than any member of management can ever know, and so the employee must be enrolled in this battle to try and become more and more competitive."[55]

Given such an outlook it is not surprising that much of the U.S. trade-union movement welcomed the managerial effort to inaugurate a new era of labor-management cooperation denominated by a wide variety of names and schemes: "quality of work life," "jointness," "nonadversarial labor relations," "employee involvement," "team production," and "enterprise competitiveness." "Troubled times bring people together, and I think we can cooperate in ways that were unthinkable a few years ago," announced Donald Ephlin, a UAW vice president, early in 1981.[56]

All this represented a signal challenge to the industrial-relations orthodoxy of the New Deal system. The notion that labor and management had fundamentally different interests in the workplace had been central to the New Deal ethos, hardly limited to those who viewed class struggle as a motive force in world history. In the 1940s and 1950s managers had often analogized the workplace to a well-oiled machine, in which mass production demanded the construction of a quasi-military system of hierarchical control. The common nomenclature of that era described foremen as the factory's "noncommissioned officers" and the workers as the militarized "rank and file." Thus, discipline and hierarchy were built into the production process, generating grievances, conflict, and mass strikes.[57]

During the 1950s Clark Kerr spoke for an influential generation of industrial-relations intellectuals whose own careers were premised on the notion that adroit mediation and administration could resolve the resultant social tensions. Kerr did not see irrationality, ill will, or antiquated production technology at the core of labor-management disputes. Rather, "organized labor and management are primarily engaged in sharing between themselves what is, at any one moment of time, a largely given amount of income and power. . . . Conflict is essential to survival. The union which is in constant and complete agreement with management has ceased to be a union."[58]

But this perspective seemed increasingly dysfunctional after 1970. From a managerial perspective, the sharp productivity fall-off that began in 1969 looked particularly alarming when measured against the seemingly superior and more harmonious Japanese production system. Management's long espousal of a forthrightly hierarchical production model, its militant, peculiarly American attachment to "managerial prerogatives" had generated a hugely unproductive layer of lower-level supervisors, a bureaucratic stratum of far greater weight and cost than in Germany or Japan. In turn, unionists defended a set of work rules, seniority rights, and job classifications designed to generate some sense of order and predictability within a work site context that could be both arbitrary and authoritarian in its decision making. Such rigidities made it increasingly difficult for U.S. corporations to respond to rapid changes in productive technology and product markets. The willing consent of those in the office and shop was now even more vital than in the past. If high wages, job security, racial hierarchy, and Cold War patriotism could no longer sustain the cooperation essential to a highly productive workplace regime, then other incentives, ideas, social arrangements, and organizational structures would have to be found.[59]

One alternative was a return to welfare capitalism, the managerially driven effort to generate a union-free harmony within a single work site or company. For many years, sophisticated observers of the industrial-relations scene thought such corporate paternalism an anachronistic curiosity, a throwback to pre–New Deal patterns of workplace governance. But even during the heyday of industrial unionism, firms like DuPont, Thompson Products (now TRW), and IBM had kept the unions at bay by mimicking union grievance structures and offering union-competitive wages and benefits. They sought an industrial community, a "Gemeinschaft," to replace, or ameliorate, both Taylorized bureaucracy and market contractualism. In *Modern Manors*, his study of these paternalistic, anti-union firms, Sanford Jacoby labels an important element in their corporate philosophy, "authoritarian Mayoism," a reference not to Chairman Mao, but to the management consultant Elton Mayo, whose famous Hawthorne experiments in the 1920s taught a generation of managers that workers craved personal recognition and community even more than high wages or easy work.[60] Contemporary managers therefore sought to generate a "permanent Hawthorne effect," a social-psychological environment that motivates workers and links their aspirations to those of the company.

Jacoby calls such firms "modern manors" because they were not unlike the feudal baronies of old, offering security and identity in return for deference and fealty. As early as the 1950s, Sears Roebuck pioneered many of the Orwellian structures necessary to systemize such anti-union paternalism. Management there offered its employees a Janus-faced profile: generous profit-sharing forged a set of "golden handcuffs" for many full-time male employees, while a truly diabolical program of employee surveys and interviews provided management with much intelligence, as well as offering employees a catharsislike experience designed to relieve "emotional stress." Jacoby labeled this sophisticated Sears program, which successfully repulsed strong unionizing efforts in the early postwar years, "dirty science." By the 1970s, however, such union avoidance techniques became the industrial template guiding virtually every executive and human resource officer who sought to boost productivity and keep both the government and unions at bay.[61] General Foods, for example, at its "humanized factory," established work teams with the power to hire and fire, manage the daily production process, and rotate jobs. Critical to the success of this experiment was the careful psychological testing and selecting of work-team leaders, who were supposed to be particularly "flexible," "resourceful," and "cooperative."[62]

Despite its unwholesome pedigree, many trade unionists welcomed management's post-1970 interest in the reorganization of the work regime. During the 1930s and 1940s union strategy for ameliorating assembly-line tyranny had involved a dual thrust: strengthening the shop-steward movement and grievance-arbitration system at the base, while at the top, campaigning in Congress, among the federal government's regulatory bodies, and at the bargaining table to win for all workers health and safety reforms, apprenticeship standards, pension guarantees, and, during labor's more ambitious moments, some influence over corporate investment decisions and plant location. But both of these avenues toward workplace reform had been blocked by the mid-1970s, the former as a result of the more hostile legal environment and the union movement's own stolid, bureaucratic routinization of the grievance-handling apparatus, and the latter because of the decline of the New Deal labor-liberal political coalition.

Unions like the UAW therefore seized upon management's new interest in work-site cooperation and participation in order to advance labor's historic interest in democratizing the workplace. This was the influential perspective of UAW vice president Irving Bluestone, himself an old socialist, who hailed the new "quality of work life" programs that flourished in the late 1970s. Writing at a time when the UAW still saw the incorporation of the sixties generation of rights-conscious workers as vital, Bluestone was emphatic in insisting that such worker-management cooperation schemes were not simply designed with increased productivity in mind but rather would enable workers to "exercise the democratic right to participate in workplace decisions, including job structure and design, job layout, material flow. . . . In the broadest sense it means decision-making as to how the work place will be managed and how the worker will effectively have a voice in being master of the job rather than subservient to it." Some unionists really ran with this idea. In 1988 the UAW's West Coast regional director enthused: "The workers' revolution has finally come to the shop floor. The people who work on the assembly line have taken charge and have the power to make management do their jobs right."[63] Although a precise definition of what actually constitutes a cooperative work regime remains elusive, some scholars estimate that upward of 50 percent of all workplaces incorporate elements of the new system.[64]

The United States has now had more than twenty years of experience with the new-style industrial relations. What conclusions can be drawn? First, American workers welcomed the bundle of ideas that constitute worker/manager cooperation, participation, and job enrichment. The initial response of almost all workers to a participatory reorganization of the work environment is positive. Employees want challenging jobs and a voice in the enterprise regardless of the degree of unionization, level of technology, or demographic composition of the workforce. But this was as true in the 1930s when organization and collective bargaining offered a road toward these goals as in the 1980s and 1990s when the New Deal system reached such an advanced state of decay.[65]

Although the participatory impulse has been heartfelt among so many workers, the managerial effort to recapture this democratic sensibility holds little promise for the American trade-union movement.

All such managerial schemes are resolutely confined to a single firm, factory, or office. But long-term productivity and democratic participation require the reorganization of production, social provision, and finance on a far broader basis. Workers are keenly aware that penalties for failure to cooperate with management are all too often layoffs, work transfers, and plant closures. Without the protections offered by a solid welfare state, a broadly engaged union movement, and a relatively egalitarian wage structure, efforts to build industrial democracy in a single work site are largely doomed, for the imbalance of power between workers and managers cannot be ignored no matter how sincere the collaboration or elaborate the participatory scheme.[66]

But the bulk of the evidence demonstrates that most participation plans are antithetical to the union idea. Their spirit is that of the manipulative Hawthorne experiments. Since the 1970s quality of work life and team production consultants have happily sold their services to the most bitterly anti-union firms, touting them as a new form of industrial democracy and worker empowerment. Likewise, the elimination of costly supervisory strata, a notable feature of the team production idea, actually returns workers to the pre–Great Depression era of the working "straw boss" and incentive pay plans that embedded speed-up, labor discipline, and production quotas within the social organization of the work itself. Mike Parker, the nation's most knowledgeable observer of the team-production idea, has dubbed such productivity schemes "management by stress." Here flexibility is generated not by a true reskilling of each employee, as Sabel, Piore, and Reich once forecast, but by the willingness of the workers to undertake any one of a series of tightly defined and closely monitored jobs, regardless of formal training, seniority, or shop tradition. "Multiskilling," writes Parker, "thus becomes less an issue of training itself than of attitude and ideology; that is, of overcoming those institutional and psychological barriers that prevent workers from rapidly shifting their attention from one well-defined job to another."[67]

Not surprisingly, the managerial advocates of the new industrial relations have been almost uniformly hostile to suggestions that cooperation within the workplace take place in a context in which workers regain some elements of collective voice. Early in the Clinton administration, Secretary of Labor Robert Reich had been hopeful that a high-profile "Commission on the Future of Worker-Management Relations" could reach agreement on the kind of flexible, post-Fordist labor-relations advocated by those who sought to boost U.S. productivity and living standards. But even under the benign chairmanship of John Dunlop, who had long stood for the most conservative, cooperative kind of unionism, neither the plant-level works-council idea, advanced by unionists throughout continental Europe, nor a proposal for government-mandated health and safety committees won management support.

Nor did American managers prove willing to countenance any legislative innovations that might enable progressive employers and incrementalist unions, to say nothing of their more adversarial-minded counterparts, to reach agreement on the kind of labor-law reform needed to aid trade-union organization and advance even a minimal sort of "voice" for unorganized workers. Dunlop, AFL-CIO leaders, and many in the new Clinton administration had hoped to strike such a new social bargain. The unions would agree to a revision of Section 8(a)(2) of the National Labor Relations Act (the Wagner Act), banning company unions, after which firms would have a free hand to set up management-run employee-participation committees. In return the trade union movement would win long-overdue labor-law reforms—chiefly the "card check," which would allow unions to secure quick, formal certification when a majority of workers sign authorization cards—designed to make organizing easier. But such a deal collapsed even before the Republicans captured control of Congress in 1994. Labor remained suspicious that legally sanctioned employee participation schemes represented little more than a new form of union avoidance, while no significant segment of the business community was willing to countenance the renewed growth of trade unionism, whatever the quid pro quo. So despite the boom of the 1990s, the future did not look hopeful, either for American trade unions or for those workers who sought to join them.[68]

CHAPTER 7

What Is to Be Done?

"'ORGANIZED LABOR,' Say those words, and your heart sinks. I am a labor lawyer, and my heart sinks. Dumb, stupid, organized labor; this is my cause."[1]

Thus did Thomas Geoghegan assert the despair and the commitment that were the dual themes of his 1991 memoir, a battle-scarred account of the contemporary industrial scene during a Chicago decade that chilled union hearts like the winter wind off Lake Michigan. The title of his book said it all: *Which Side Are You On? Trying to Be for Labor When It's Flat on Its Back.*

Geoghegan's despair was a product not just of broken strikes, membership decline, and Republican control of the White House. All true, but the real problem arose out of a sense that union partisans could not construct a road forward out of the contemporary impasse. For all his hip radicalism, Geoghegan's perspective was not all that different from that of AFL-CIO president Lane Kirkland, who entitled a 1986 essay "It Has All Been Said Before." Academics and journalists have predicted the demise of the labor movement for a hundred years and more, averred a weary Kirkland. But American unions, having sensibly committed themselves "to work within the system," will endure, perhaps revive, though Kirkland could offer nothing more than a stoic approbation as a rally cry for his troops.[2]

Cold War Leadership

Kirkland ascended to the AFL-CIO presidency in 1979 when at the age of eighty-five, mentor George Meany finally retired. The transition was smooth, practically invisible, because Kirkland had been Meany's right-hand man for nearly two decades. Moreover, the AFL-CIO presidency is not a particularly powerful office. Meany and Kirkland presided over a very impressive "marble palace" with a fine view of Lafayette Park and the White House beyond. But in the American labor movement, more than 90 percent of all dues money and staff were controlled by powerful "affiliates" like AFSCME, the UAW, and the fast-growing Service Employees International Union (SEIU). When it comes to the collective bargaining and union-organizing responsibilities of an affiliate, the president of the AFL-CIO has less clout than a well-placed local union leader or business agent.

But the top leadership of the AFL-CIO does more than simply preside over a confederation of autonomous unions. An AFL-CIO president speaks for organized labor to Congress, the White House, and the public. His institutional authority is considerable when it comes to labor's "foreign policy" and almost as weighty when domestic politics and economic policy are under debate. Moreover, a certain charisma attaches to the leader of an institution that claims to speak for the 50 million family members whose livelihood is dependent on a unionized breadwinner. It mattered that the timid, colorless William Green led the AFL during the Great Depression, and not John L. Lewis. And in the 1960s George Meany's leadership of the AFL-CIO gave to organized labor a political profile quite different from that of Walter Reuther, his ambitious, socially conscious rival. In an infamous 1972 interview, Meany had declared: "Why should we worry about organizing groups of people who do not want to be organized? . . . Frankly, I used to worry about the membership, about the size of the membership. But quite a few years ago, I just stopped worrying about it.[3]

What did Lane Kirkland purport to stand for? In sum, he was the near-perfect embodiment of the Cold War labor bureaucracy. Unlike

Sam Gompers and George Meany, conservative unionists who had actually fought their way to power, Kirkland had practically no union experience beyond the insular headquarters of the AFL-CIO itself. He had spent most of the Second World War as a deck officer in the merchant marine, after which he took a degree at Georgetown University's School of Foreign Service. His liberalism was tough, calculating, constrained, forged during the era of Harry Truman, not Franklin Roosevelt. Inexplicably, Kirkland rejected a diplomatic career, but joined the AFL, where he did much work in research and congressional relations. And there he won the confidence of George Meany, whose hard-line anti-Communism he helped advance.

Meany and Kirkland shared a visceral hostility toward the American New Left, to the "New Politics" wing of the Democratic Party, and to the post-Vietnam, Communist-aligned insurgencies that challenged American power—and AFL-CIO-style unionism—in Nicaragua, South Africa, the Philippines, Brazil, and El Salvador. In 1972 George Meany had almost single-handedly forced the AFL-CIO to withhold an endorsement of George McGovern, the Democratic Party's presidential nominee.[4] Instead, the labor federation insisted upon an unworkable "guns and butter" liberalism, in the 1970s identified with the career of the Democratic senator "Scoop" Jackson of Washington. Had it not been for his attachment to the labor movement, Kirkland might well have drifted toward Reaganism, like so many other foreign-policy hawks in the Democratic Party. Certainly, as AFL-CIO president in the 1980s, Kirkland had no trouble aligning official labor's foreign policy with that of Republican presidents Reagan and Bush. AFL-CIO spending on international affairs, heavily subsidized by the government, actually exceeded its domestic budget during that decade. Leftists sourly labeled the federation, "AFL-CIA."[5]

Of course, Kirkland was not entirely oblivious to the parlous state of the American labor movement. For the first time in its history, the AFL-CIO actually sponsored a mass demonstration, "Solidarity Day," that brought hundreds of thousands of unionists to the Washington Mall in September 1981. (And Kirkland even called out the troops a second time, albeit a full decade later.) The AFL-CIO established a study commission whose report, "The Changing Situation of Workers and Their Unions," realistically assessed the failure of the nation's labor law, the potency of employer opposition, and the fragmentary nature of union power.[6]

This was a break from the absolute complacency of the Meany era, but the Kirkland leadership wasted many of its limited political resources on a legislative drive to outlaw employer use of permanent replacements during strikes. Such a goal naturally appealed to the leaders of the big industrial unions, who blamed their strike losses on hard-line employer tactics, but the campaign was conceptually flawed because a prohibition on permanent replacement workers would merely give union members the right to return to work under whatever terms and conditions management saw fit to impose. Such an antiscab law would have done little to resolve organized labor's more fundamental problem: the failure to organize new workers even in those sectors of the economy once heavily unionized. In heartland America—at Caterpillar, Greyhound, and Phelps Dodge—strikebreakers have been plentiful because employers can tap a huge reservoir of the underemployed and underpaid, who both covet and resent the high wages of the unionized minority.[7]

If Lane Kirkland could do nothing to stem the anti-labor tide, he did manage the union retreat with a certain organizational tidiness. By the end of his regime the AFL-CIO was once again an inclusive "House of Labor." Although the National Education Association (NEA) remained independent, the UAW rejoined the AFL-CIO in 1981 after a thirteen-year absence, the Mineworkers returned with a new reform leadership, and the Teamsters again began paying dues in the late 1980s, albeit in a vain effort to win some institutional shelter against the government's massive racketeering probe of the union's corrupt top leadership.[8]

Perhaps the most important AFL-CIO reform of the Kirkland era was that which encouraged union mergers designed to streamline the leadership apparat, avoid costly jurisdictional disputes, and generate a sufficient flow of dues to service the membership and organize new workers. Today, most national trade unions are organized on neither craft nor industrial principles. They are instead amalgamated unions that opportunistically enroll new workers regardless of occupation, employer, or region. Thus the UAW recruits health-insurance clerks, prison guards, and university teaching assistants; the Steelworkers organize Pittsburgh grocery workers; and the Communications Workers negotiate for state and municipal employees.

Although it is tempting to draw analogies between this organizing latitude and that of the pre–World War I Industrial Workers of the World, with their faith in "One Big Union," the implications for democratic governance are of questionable potency. Given the radically divergent interests of such workers and the resulting lack of unity and common purpose in the bargaining process, union democracy and organizational coherence often suffer. This was tragically apparent during the 1985–86 strike of United Food and Commercial Workers (UFCW) Local P-9, which fought a well-mobilized, CIO-style battle against wage concessions at Hormel in Austin, Minnesota. Unfortunately, the packinghouse locals—once among the most militant industrial unions in the CIO—represented less than 10 percent of all UFCW members. The UFCW's leadership came out of the old Retail Clerks International Union where regional wage disparities, exclusive craft traditions, and membership anomie had been the norm. UFCW officials, never enthusiastic over the P-9 strike, soon denounced it, after which it collapsed amid bitter and sustained recriminations.[9]

By the early 1990s Kirkland and many other top trade-union leaders wagered that any hope for a revival of the labor movement was dependent on forces that lay largely outside the union movement itself. As the Reagan era began to wane and the Cold War end, the AFL-CIO had mended its fences with even those Democrats whose political schooling had taken place in the 1960s. But until the Democrats actually recaptured the White House and strengthened their hand in Congress, efforts to make progress on national health insurance, labor law, trade legislation, collective bargaining, and a host of other long-shelved reforms were doomed. Indeed, Kirkland and many top unionists argued that additional money and effort devoted to organizing was pointless until the legal and political environment improved.[10]

The first two years of the Clinton administration seemed to offer the potential for such a legislative and political breakthrough. Although Bill Clinton had positioned himself as a neoliberal "New Democrat," his administration came to power with a New Dealish understanding that a progressive reform of American capitalism was still feasible if he could assemble an appropriately powerful political coalition. Clinton held the unions at arm's length, but his early efforts to raise the social wage and relegitimate government activism—through infrastructure construction, job training, and new employer mandates (like that requiring family and medical leave for employees in large firms)—were ideologically potent and socially useful efforts to give domestic politics a neo-Rooseveltian flavor.

The Health Insurance Debacle

Nothing was more central than the effort to win a system of universal health insurance. By the early 1990s the American health-care delivery system was a failure when compared with other Western nations. More than 20 percent of all people under the age of sixty-five had no insurance-paid access to a doctor. Moreover, health-care costs had risen at twice the level of inflation, and the United States devoted more of its total income to medical care than any other nation, 14 percent. Thus, the proportion of employees actually covered by corporate-sponsored health insurance peaked in the mid-1970s and headed south thereafter. For the unions, this chronic rise in health-care costs meant that the effort to build a private welfare state for their own members, which had once seemed so promising, now generated a nightmare at the bargaining table and on the picket line. During the 1980s management efforts to trim health-insurance costs precipitated more than 80 percent of all strikes that took place in the United States.[11]

The United Mine Workers of America fought the most spectacular of these struggles in 1989, an eleven-month siege of the Pittston Coal Company in defense of miners' health-care benefits and pension rights. The strike featured the arrest of some three thousand miners and UMW supporters during a campaign that resurrected the sit-down tactics and mass demonstrations characteristic of the union movement during the early twentieth-century era of industrial warfare. Such bitter bargaining conflicts demonstrated the symbiotic relationship between a high social wage and labor power at the point of production. In Canada and in most of Europe, where systems of universal health insurance were funded out of general tax revenue, labor fought its health-care battles at the ballot box and in the parliamentary committee chamber, thus reserving its picket-line clout for wage and workplace issues closer to the immediate interests of its working members.

President Clinton and his wife Hillary, who played a high-profile role during the health-care battle, rejected a Canadian-style, single-payer system. And so too did key labor strategists, including Kirkland and John Sweeney, the up-and-coming head of the SEIU, the nation's largest union in the hospital and health-care field. Most unions had long favored a single-payer system linked to Social Security, recognizing the economic efficiency of such a universal system and its political popularity among the American people. But now labor argued, with the Clintons, that political and economic realism demanded that any health-care reform had to be built upon the existing system of employer-paid benefits and private insurance. Chronic, Reaganite budget deficits had pushed new spending initiatives off the federal agenda, while the trillion-dollar growth of a privatized system of social provision had created a powerful, heterogeneous set of economic institutions whose accommodation most practical liberals thought essential to any health-care reform.[12]

The Clinton plan harked back to the era of Roosevelt corporatism early in the New Deal. Like the National Recovery Administration of 1933 and 1934, the health-insurance reform of the 1990s would have regulated and cartelized key sectors of the economy, "mandating" not wages and hours, but the provision of a minimal level of health insurance, purchased through a system of "managed competition" that contained free-market forces within a global budget set by a new federal authority. Like the NRA industry codes, the Clinton health plan was complex, requiring more than 1,350 pages of text to actually spell it out. Its Rube Goldberg flavor was a product of the bureaucratic micromanagement necessary to make equitable and universal the nation's sprawling, public-private system of health provision.

A Canadian-style, single-payer system would have simplified matters. But if the Clinton plan lacked coherence, it was nevertheless a social-democratic initiative of prime import. By guaranteeing health insurance to every worker regardless of wages or employer, the plan would have generated a substantial rise in the social wage and taken a large step to reverse the growth in social inequality. It would have empowered workers and unions by reducing the cost of losing or quitting a job, and it would have provided employers with a powerful financial incentive to transform part-time work into forty-hour-a-week jobs. Most important, the Clinton plan proposed to reinvigorate a sense of universal social citizenship, symbolized by the new Health Security Card that the President wanted all Americans to carry in their purse or pocket.[13]

In twentieth-century America, any scheme of substantial social reform must also contain a functional advance for a strategic sector of capitalist enterprise. Clinton, Kirkland, and other advocates of the new scheme therefore sought out a set of corporatist business partners whose interest in capping health-care costs matched that of liberal activists and union reformers. They thought they had found a powerful set of collaborators among those high-wage sectors of business that already provided health insurance: steel, auto, chemicals, telephone, and other large, unionized firms. To them the employer mandate held no additional cost, but instead spread the insurance burden equally among all employers. Old-line firms like Chrysler and Bethlehem stood to save hundreds of millions of dollars in health-insurance costs if the "free-loaders" like Wal-Mart, Marriott, and other low-wage, service-sector firms could no longer shift the health-care costs of their own employees to the state, to charity, or to the payroll of other firms. Thus Pizza Hut, a Pepisco subsidiary, employed 93,000 workers, but offered health insurance to but 3,000, mainly managerial personnel.

But the Clinton administration and the unions miscalculated, because American capitalism had transformed itself so dramatically since the last era of reform in the 1960s. Low-wage, low-benefit companies in the now swollen service sector of the American economy, especially restaurants, hotels, and mass retailers, bitterly resisted employer mandates, while almost all the smaller insurance companies, who sought to "cherry-pick" the youngest and least risky clients, assailed the plan. The National Federation of Independent Business, which represented many of these service-sector firms, and the Health Insurance Association of America, a cherry-picking coalition, proved fierce and effective lobbyists against the Clinton plan. In contrast, the old-line United States Chamber of Commerce initially endorsed the employer-mandate idea, but then, under intense pressure from numerous midsized businesses, reversed course in the very midst of the health-care debate.[14]

Moreover, the unions once again overestimated the extent to which American corporations could be enticed into making a corporatist bargain with labor and the state. In the absence of a system-shaking crisis reminiscent of the early 1930s, business executives remained hostile to any scheme that strengthened the capacity of the regulatory state. For example, most unionized phone companies would have benefited financially from the Clinton health plan, but the political and ideological costs were unacceptable. Telecommunication executives reasoned that if they advocated government-planning mandates when it came to health insurance, they would cripple their capacity to advance another round of deregulation in their industry. Thus, early in 1994 AT&T and all the Baby Bells pulled out of the big-business coalition that had endorsed the administration's health-care reform. Their apprehensions over escalating medical-insurance costs were trumped by a deeper resistance to an enhancement of the government's regulatory capacity.[15]

Indeed, by the time Congress rejected the Clinton plan, its fate had turned into an ideological referendum on the capacity of the state to ameliorate social problems and raise the social wage. If the Democrats succeeded in enacting health-care reform, argued William Kristol, a Republican Party strategist, they would "relegitimize middle-class dependence for 'security' on government spending and regulation" and "revive the reputation of . . . the Democrats . . . as the generous protector of middle-class interests."[16] Taking their cue from ideologues like Kristol, Congressional Republicans and other opponents of a new era of state activism effectively lobbied those corporations and large insurance companies that might well have found a version of the Clinton plan in their immediate financial interest.[17]

The collapse of the Clinton health-care plan generated a political vacuum that was immediately filled by a triumphant Republicanism that in the 1994 elections captured control of both the House and Senate for the first time in two generations. Newt Gingrich, installed as House Speaker, was a New South conservative whose ideological aversion to trade unionism and the welfare state came larded with a set of facile, technosocial imperatives derived from the most deterministic brand of post-Fordist industrial theory. He celebrated the writings of Alvin and Heidi Toffler, whose popular prognostications, including *Future Shock* (1970) and *The Third Wave* (1980), had much in common with the work of Daniel Bell and Peter Drucker.[18]

A New Labor Leadership

For the leadership of organized labor this crisis had a passing resemblance to that of early 1935 when the Supreme Court had declared the NRA unconstitutional. Since the capacity of the state to restructure the economy and ameliorate social problems had become problematic, the unions, argued CIO founder Sidney Hillman, would have to "go ahead on our own" to reforge their strength on the industrial battlefield.[19] Sixty years later, the near simultaneous collapse of the Dunlop Commission effort at labor law reform and the Clinton health-insurance plan finally discredited—even among some of the nation's most stand-pat unionists—the ineffectual corporatism and antique anti-Communism of the Meany-Kirkland lineage. To avoid a slow but certain death, the unions would have to organize workers once again, millions of them, and that required a new leadership, starting at the very top.

For a century no incumbent president of the AFL, the CIO, or the AFL-CIO had ever been ousted from power.[20] But in 1995 an insurgent faction led by SEIU president John Sweeney forced Kirkland to resign and then handily defeated his heir apparent, Tom Donahue. Like John L. Lewis, who had challenged the AFL hierarchs sixty years before, Sweeney was no radical. He was a middle-aged Irish-Catholic from the Bronx who sought to forge a social compact with the corporations and the state. Thus he had helped torpedo AFL-CIO adherence to single-payer health insurance and had backed the Clinton plan. Nor was the SEIU a model of internal union democracy: many of its older, urban affiliates like New York City's hotel and apartment house Local 32B-32J were classic fiefdoms ruled in an autocratic fashion.

But Sweeney represented a wing of the trade union leadership—

In 1995 John Sweeney, left, became AFL-CIO President, a post long held by Lane Kirkland. (Credit: Jim West)

largely composed of the old industrial unions and those institutions organizing service and government workers—whose most clear-sighted elements had come to understand that labor's capacity to actually make a social contract required that the unions once again demonstrate their willingness to play a disruptive, insurgent role in society.[21] Under the Sweeney regime that began in 1980, the SEIU had grown to more than a million members. While a set of clever mergers with independent employee groups and smaller unions accounted for some of this remarkable, Reagan-era growth, much of it was the fruit of a well-orchestrated militancy. Sweeney raised dues and poured a quarter of all SEIU income into organizing (5 percent is the union norm), which enabled his union to deploy hundreds of smart young organizers who used direct action and communitywide mobilizations to unionize janitors, health-care workers, and private-sector clericals.[22] The 1984 movie *Nine to Five* (starring Dolly Parton, Lily Tomlin, and Jane Fonda) took at least a bit of its inspiration from SEIU Local 925, which targeted women workers.

Such tactics became part of the debate over the strategic meaning of the leadership contest in the AFL-CIO. Early in 1995 the SEIU's

"Justice for Janitors" campaign had briefly deployed the tactics of the civil rights movement to block Washington's Potomac River bridges. When in convention debate Tom Donahue deplored the incident, urging Sweeney and his faction to "worry more about building bridges to the rest of society," the AFL-CIO challenger neatly turned the metaphor around. "I believe in building bridges, whenever the shelling lets up. . . . But I believe in blocking bridges whenever those employers and those communities turn a deaf ear to the working families that we represent."[23]

The Rank and File Dimension

Sweeney's victory was in part a palace coup, in part the culmination of a generation of internal struggle within the labor movement. Had Kirkland's neocorporatist, inside-the-beltway strategy not been such a disaster, neither Sweeney nor any other top union leader would have had the allies to push him aside. But Sweeney's success was not just the product of defeat and disillusionment at the top; the leadership switch represented the AFL-CIO's accommodation to an increasingly powerful, increasingly oppositional stratum within the union movement that searched for a way out of the Kirkland-Meany dead end.

The history of the post-Communist labor left falls into two phases. During the 1950s and 1960s union insurgents fought to reform, in some cases to overthrow, the entire system of industrial jurisprudence and contract unionism that was the essential legacy of the Wagner Act and the CIO. Compared to the 1980s this was an era of much strike militancy, frequent wildcat (unauthorized) stoppages, and periodic challenges to incumbent union officers. At the height of the postwar boom, slowdowns, boycotts, work-to-rule campaigns, and other forms of quasi-legal protest tested leadership authority and management power in a dozen industries.

Until the late 1960s the most militant workers were actually skilled white men: IAM airline mechanics, CWA telephone craftsmen, UAW tool and die makers, and Teamster steel and car haulers. They wanted more money and more power and security at work. To top unionists like Walter Reuther, Jimmy Hoffa and David J. Mac-

Donald of the United Steel Workers (USW) they were a constant headache. Indeed, MacDonald lost his USW presidency in 1965 to just such an internal union revolt.[24] It was not until 1969 that this insurgency was eclipsed by the more nationalist, African American militancy of groups like the Dodge Revolutionary Union Movement (DRUM), or the multiracial revolt of 1970 that finally raised wages and brought a semblance of collective bargaining to the post office. Because this version of the rank-and-file revolt framed its demands in the language of black militancy or New Left radicalism, it won a larger hearing in the corridors of media power, but the aspirations of these young workers actually echoed an older set of grievances. Nat Weinberg, a longtime UAW research aide, put it well in 1974: "The recent discovery of the job satisfaction problem is, in one sense, much like Columbus' discovery of America. The people most directly concerned—the Indians in one case and the workers in the other—knew all along that it was there."[25]

The recession of 1973–74 and the two decades of difficult economic conditions that followed, put an end to this sort of militancy. Although there was some continuity among the leading activists, oppositional politics within the unions took on a more tempered, reformist character during the years of union retreat and defeat. In an era of concession bargaining and union collaboration with management-initiated participation schemes, labor militants now found themselves the most steadfast defenders of contract unionism, industrywide bargaining, and the once much-maligned grievance procedure. Union militancy was no longer designed to overthrow the Wagner-era system of industrial relations, but rather to defend it against aggressive Reagan-era union busters and the labor movement's own shell-shocked leaders, who fearfully abandoned both the strike weapon and membership mobilization.[26] Therefore, it was not difficult to find local union officers and even international officials who linked themselves to the internal union left. This was the perspective of the "Steelworkers Fight Back" grouping, which ran Ed Sadlowski for USW president in 1977, of Richard Trumka's successful campaign for the UMW presidency five years later, of the "New Directions" caucus in the UAW, and of the remarkable insurgency within the International Brotherhood of Teamsters (IBT).[27]

The reform of the Teamsters union remains tentative at best, but the transformation that has taken place over more than a quarter century of agitation and organization represents the most significant victory of any rank-and-file grouping in the twentieth-century history of American unionism. It was integral to a considerable democratization of the Teamsters, to the Sweeney accession in 1995, and to the union victory in the United Parcel Service strike of 1997, which was the first nationwide strike won by a union in more than two decades. And because of Teamster union size, strategic leverage, and cultural aura, the transformation of this union has been and will be essential to the revival of the union idea.

Aside from the NEA, the Teamsters are the largest union in the United States. But the union is also a highly decentralized institution, in which real power lies at the level of the local or the metropolitan joint council. There are firmwide, or industrywide, bargaining structures inside the Teamsters covering companies like Northwest Airlines, United Parcel Service, and some sectors of the trucking industry, but decentralized, regional bargaining is characteristic of most of the big Teamster locals in short-hand carting, garbage picking, warehousing, food processing, and light manufacturing. Corruption, both political and financial, has run rampant in many of these locals, where a single extended family has often controlled an insular patronage machine for decades. Jimmy Hoffa tolerated and partook of much of this criminality, but he nevertheless clashed with these Teamster barons when he sought to nationalize union bargaining; his 1975 murder was at least in part a product of the conflicts his strategy had generated within the union.[28]

Cynical observers of American labor have often deployed the Teamster example to assert that if a union "brings home the bacon," then its membership can be relied on to ignore leadership malfeasance. This canard has always been problematic, but never more so than in the 1970s and 1980s when Teamster feudalism proved incapable of resisting a managerial onslaught that cut wages, gutted pension funds, and slashed union membership by almost a million.

This was the context in which the Teamsters for a Democratic Union (TDU) won a hearing from thousands of working IBT members. TDU's leading elements had come right out of the campus New

Left, but by the 1980s the ideology of this insurgency was not far different from that of the Reutherite UAW during its militant, democratic phase. TDU uncovered corruption and collusion, fought to defend wage and benefit standards, and by the late 1980s had become powerful enough to mobilize a successful opposition to a number of concessionary contracts negotiated by top union leaders. By 1989, when the government finally moved to root out Teamster criminality, TDU influence helped shape the settlement, especially those provisions that opened up the Teamster election process to make possible a genuinely democratic contest.[29]

Ron Carey's unexpected 1991 victory was the fruit of this strategy. Carey, a United Parcel Service local union leader from Queens, kept his distance from the TDU militants, but he adopted much of their strategy, especially after 1994 when he declared open war on the regional barons who still controlled the majority of the big Teamster locals. He discouraged "participation" schemes, fought erosion of existing contracts, and put more than sixty union locals in trusteeship. Sweeney's 1995 convention victory had many authors, but one of the most important certainly depended on the fact that Carey and the TDU had switched the Teamsters from the extreme right to the liberal left of the AFL-CIO internal politics. Tragically, Carey squandered much of the moral capital so arduously assembled by Teamster reformers when he laundered union dues money into his reelection campaign in 1996. Though this crime had little in common with older forms of Teamster corruption, it destroyed his credibility and opened the door to Jimmy Hoffa, Jr.'s election and the old guard recapture of many top Teamster posts.[30]

A New Agenda

The agenda of the Sweenyite leadership was not far different from that of those who revived the labor movement in the 1930s: open the door to the cadres of the Left, welcome the new immigrants, carve out a distinctive political presence somewhat independent of the Democrats, and, above all, "organize the unorganized." Some skeptics labeled the Sweenyite strategy "bureaucratic militancy," but whatever its limitations, it was a clear step to the left. For the first time in two generations America's top trade-union leadership stood, in fact and imagination, on the left-liberal side of the nation's political culture. The new AFL-CIO executive board was finally expanded to include a substantial number of women and people of color, and Sweeney's top officer slate was also politically balanced. The new secretary-treasurer was Richard Trumka, who became a symbol of militant union leadership after the Pittston strike; and Linda Chavez-Thompson, an AFSCME leader from Texas, became executive vice president. The AFL-CIO staff was now marbled with New Left veterans long frozen out of responsible posts by the Cold War culture that had lingered even beyond the fall of the Berlin Wall. Thus Sweeney appointed Barbara Shailor, for years a critic of AFL-CIO policy in Central America, head of the Federation's international affairs department, now appropriately renamed the Solidarity Center. And Bill Fletcher, a black intellectual with much organizing experience, served briefly as AFL-CIO education director.[31]

Although labor law reform had no chance in the Republican-dominated Congress, the Sweeney leadership concluded that a new commitment of union resources to organizing activity could not await a favorable revision of the law. "Labor must organize without the law," he asserted, "so that we can later organize under the law."[32] This perspective replicates that of the Progressive-era railroad and garment unions, which violated anti-union injunctions in order to build public support against the harsh judicial constraints of that era. And it is reminiscent of the CIO organizing strategy in 1936 and early 1937, when industrial action in Akron, Flint, Cleveland, Pittsburgh, and Detroit generated a social context that the Supreme Court could not ignore when it evaluated the constitutionality of the Wagner Act in April 1937. For the first time in two generations, men and women who cut their teeth as in-your-face organizers are ascending to the leadership of some of the big unions.[33]

The Sweenyite revival has energized key elements of the labor movement: probably five to ten thousand people nationwide who hold the key staff positions and local union offices. They have been aided by hundreds of others who teach, write, lecture, and preach on behalf of the unions. The "Iron Curtain" that once divided official labor and the American left—academic, feminist, cultural, and gay—is rusting away. Between 1996 and 1998 a series of university "teach-ins" put Sweeney, Trumka, and other unionists at the same podium with people like Betty Friedan, Julian Bond, Barbara Ehrenreich, Richard Rorty, and Cornel West. The symbolism was impressive: when at the flagship Columbia teach-in Sweeney declared, "We need your help," the audience of intellectuals, left-wing academics, and old-time radicals gave him the kind of lusty ovation unheard from this kind of crowd for almost half a century.[34] Thus the labor movement has returned to the campuses with living wage and anti-sweatshop campaigns. An AFL-CIO "union summer" project, which has put hundreds of youthful activists on the street each June and July, is proving a brilliant public relations idea. If much of this is atmospherics, so be it, for consciousness is often transformed in just such a subtle fashion. As in the 1930s and the 1960s, labor is building a new generation of union activists whose energy will power the movement for decades.

Organizing in a New World

The contemporary legal wilderness in which American unionists find themselves does have one important virtue: it makes necessary the creative rediscovery of organizing strategies that the Wagner-era labor law had made obsolete or illegal. When it comes to the "labor question" much of the U.S. political economy has returned to a pre–New Deal set of relationships, both legal and economic. The idea of collective bargaining between one union and one employer is clearly an antique notion. The proliferation in subcontracted and outsourced work, the increase in contingent employment, and the rise of the "virtual" corporation has begun to dissolve the once solid boundary between those inside and outside the firm. As a consequence, the Wagner-era legal framework stands as an obstacle to unionization. For more than sixty years the NLRA assumed that stable bargaining units could be defined and that union certification elections would involve a considerable proportion of the employees in a given business enterprise. But American capitalism has generated a bewildering array of institutions that hardly fit that structure. As a consequence, American unions need to explore new, more flexible organizing models.

Here are two ideas, both actually more characteristic of the Progressive era than of the decades that followed. The first is an updated version of the old craft-union structure, as found in the building trades, the Hollywood "talent" guilds, and to a lesser extent, in the garment trades and longshoring work. Craft or occupation unions exist independent of any one firm. Indeed, they thrive in an economy of rapidly shifting employment relationships. They seek to defend and advance the unique skills of a regional workforce independent of the internal labor market of a particular firm or institution. In unionized construction work, seniority has been unimportant; the key job security mechanism lies in the hiring hall, which distributes the work on an equitable basis. Nor are wages set according to the firm-centered model made so famous in the old mass-production industries. If the craft/occupational model could be stripped of its notorious racism and sexism, then the bargaining relationship might not be entirely dissimilar to that of the European works council: they handle the day-to-day grievances, while an overarching "joint board" or "trades council" bargains to establish the general wage and benefit level.[35]

Although firms in the information economy and in health care—which employ so many skilled, professional workers—fiercely resist such occupational unionism, physicians, nurses, teachers, computer programmers, and freelance writers have begun to generate union structures that resemble this organizational model. The Washington Alliance of Technical Workers, or WashTech, is far from setting up a "hiring hall" for programmers, but through a combination of unionization threat, adverse publicity, and legal action it did force Microsoft to upgrade and improve the wages, benefits, and career prospects for thousands of "permatempts" in the late 1990s. "We are professionals who are used to being treated professionally," asserted a software code writer active in WashTech, a Communications Workers of America affiliate. Microsoft has begun to either hire these contingent workers directly onto its payroll or insist that its subcontractors offer medical plans, paid vacations, and other benefits.[36]

The second laborite innovation stands at the opposite pole from that of a revival of the craft union. This is the idea of raising labor standards across the board, in either a municipality, a single large institution such as a university, or even for workers in a multinational industry, like apparel or athletic shoes. Given the complex, interdependent relationships that now govern the production of goods or the provision of services, unionists recognize that they must organize an entire labor market and not just the set of workers currently employed by any given firm. This has been the strategy developed by the SEIU's "Justice for Janitors" campaigns in Los Angles, Washington, D. C., and elsewhere. Harking back to the NRA era, when both the government and the unions sought to forestall cut-throat competition on labor costs, unions have put themselves at the center of a coalition designed to raise and stabilize wages and working conditions in an entire metropolitan industry. "If you organize shop by shop you pull workers into a vacuum," reflected one organizer, "where there are plenty of other workers out there who can replace them. . . . [T]he employer will always feel he can't afford a union wage because his competitors aren't paying one."[37]

Such an undertaking makes highly relevant the legacy of radical unions and the rich history of community mobilization. If a particular factory or office is no longer the sole focus of the unionizing effort, then organizers must put a greater premium on enlisting the influence and talents of the unemployed, of stay-at-home mothers, and of young people outside the wage-labor market. This was precisely the role played by the neighborhood-based unionism of the needle trades in the Progressive era, and by the CIO two decades later, when rent strikes, boycotts, demonstrations of the unemployed, ethnic mobilizations, and political insurgencies generated an organizing culture that permeated every activity and structure of the working-class community.[38]

The contemporary "living wage" movement is a natural product of this impulse, which was itself pioneered by left-wing unionists—by the Progressive-era Consumers League and by liberal Catholic clerics. Unlike the idea of a craft-union revival, this effort to raise wages and labor standards has made much ideological and political progress, even if its actual accomplishments have been scattered. The living-

A student and community based living-wage movement has filled the vacuum created by the federal government's failure to restore the purchasing power of the minimum wage and the union movement's incapacity to organize low-wage service workers. (Credit: Jim West)

wage movement targets the top of the enterprise food chain: the high-profile stores that sell brand products, the owners of office buildings that contract for janitorial services, and the state and city governments that subcontract so much of their work. As in earlier reform eras, this progressive reform of the labor-standards regime is pushed not only or primarily by the unions, but by a movement of citizen activists, some concerned with municipal jobs, others with Third World poverty and environmental conditions. The idea is not new, but its contemporary revival reflects two recent developments: the mandated work requirements inherent in the 1996 reform of the federal welfare law and perhaps even more important, the erosion of an older set of New Deal–era labor standards. Federal minimum wages no longer pretend to lift a worker and two dependents out of poverty. The twenty-first century minimum wage stands at but 70 percent of its purchasing power in 1968, and this despite the fact that the entire economy is about 50 percent more productive than in the

1960s.[39] The living-wage idea therefore harks back to the program of social amelioration pushed forward before enactment of the Fair Labor Standards Act of 1938, to the idea of an American standard of living, which proved such a potent rally cry in the years before 1940.

To see how some of these new ways of thinking about the labor question are being put into practice, take a look at Los Angeles. America's second-largest city is not yet a "union town," but a remarkable local labor movement has put such a specter close to the top of the municipal agenda. For decades, the city's fundamental raison d'être was that it was the anti-union alternative to San Francisco. But no more, for at the dawn of the twenty-first century more new workers are being organized there than anyplace else in the nation. And they are being organized through a creative amalgamation of political action, community mobilization, and militant unionism that recalls the CIO of the 1930s and the public sector union impulse of the 1960s. Politicized bargaining is being reborn in Los Angeles. Worker rights, minimum wages, affordable housing and health insurance—all traditionally areas of federal responsibility, though all largely neglected by Washington in recent decades—are becoming the responsibility of the city, the employers, and the unions. Indeed, everything is once again on the table: the investment program of the hotel and commercial real estate industry, the immigration policies of the federal government, budget politics in Sacramento, technological change in the entertainment industry, the shape of public transport, and the prospects for a majoritarian, multiracial coalition in the nation's most dynamic region.[40]

The labor movement in Los Angeles is a complex amalgam of the old and the new. At one pole of the spectrum, craft unionism is staking a claim to the new technologies of the twenty-first century. Hollywood sells image, ideas, and celebrity, but these are nonetheless fungible commodities in a world economy where entertainment is the fifth largest revenue producer (after cars, computers, travel, and agriculture). During the last decade, the Hollywood talent guilds, including the Screen Actors Guild, the Screen Writers Guild, and the American Federation of Television and Radio Artists conducted a series of strikes and tough negotiations in order to make sure that their members got a share of the "residual" payments generated when movies or advertisements were played on cable TV and the World Wide Web, or in DVD format and other new media. As in the 1930s and 1940s, the activism and solidarity of high-profile stars, including Susan Sarandon and Harrison Ford, has again demonstrated that the union idea has an appeal outside its wage-worker ghetto.[41]

At the other end of the income and ethnicity divide, Los Angeles has become the most exciting laboratory for the organization of low-wage workers in the country. Like New York and Chicago at the turn of the last century, the L.A. working class is overwhelming immigrant and largely Latino. This ethnic group represents 17 percent of California's total workforce, but Latinos constitute 36 percent of its service workers, 42 percent of its factory operatives, and fully half of all laborers. In Los Angeles the membership of the most dynamic unions, including the Service Employees, the Hotel and Restaurant Employees, the Teamsters, and UNITE are increasingly Latino. Key militants have often been Central American refugees, whose conception of unionism has held a radical, even a revolutionary edge. Because of their newly awakened sense of citizenship—in part a product of conservative Anglo efforts to demonize California's "illegal aliens" and limit Latin American immigration—Latinos have become an increasingly mobilized and politicized group. Thus in 1996, the 800,000-member Los Angeles Federation of Labor (LA FED) elected as its first Latino president Miguel Contreras, whose administration links voter registration, political mobilization, and union organizing as never before. The LA FED has successfully backed union-oriented Latino Democrats against candidates of the more nationalist, Latino political establishment. In 2001 the LA FED provided essential support to Antonio Villaraigosa, once a union organizer, in his unsuccessful but well-organized campaign for mayor.[42]

At the work site, in the community, and at the ballot box, the Latino working class has begun to make its rights-conscious voice heard in and through the union movement. In 1998, for example, Latino voters soundly rejected a state-ballot proposition designed to cripple union political strength. Prop 226, the so-called "paycheck protection act," would have forced unions to win the written approval of any individual member before a portion of their dues money could be used for political education or other issue-oriented union propaganda. Sponsored by right-wing Republicans, Prop 226 would have put into law a hyperindividualized conception of political agency. It was a referendum on the idea that unions should once again play a vigorous role in American politics. Californians narrowly turned back this assault on union power, but fully 75 percent of all Latino voters rejected it. That was six points more than the margin by which African Americans opposed it, and a dozen points more than the margin by which Latinos themselves opposed the banning of bilingual education, another measure on the 1998 ballot.[43]

The rise in Latino unionism has generated a far more favorable context for trade unionism in Southern California. In 1990 when SEIU sponsored a "Justice for Janitors" march down Wilshire Boulevard to the posh Century City office complex, the Los Angeles Police Department met the demonstrators with nightsticks and tear gas. A decade later, during SEIU's successful citywide janitorial strike, another march, along the very same route, was greeted with praise and support by virtually the entire city establishment, including the Republican mayor. In the battle for the political allegiance of Southern California's Latino immigrants, the labor movement has become the chief vehicle for engendering participation and citizenship. This is the kind of sea change in the political culture that once before made cities like Detroit, Akron, San Francisco, and Minneapolis the archetypical "union towns" of the CIO era.[44]

Such political mobilization produced the kind of legislation that has created the opportunity for organizing drives of a New Deal magnitude. For example, until 1992 California courts ruled that the state's 200,000 home health-care workers were "independent contractors," even though their minimum-wage salaries were paid by a combination of federal, state, and county funds. This army of workers, mainly middle-aged Latino and African American women, had no legally recognized employer who could be held responsible for their pay, supervision, and benefits. The SEIU mobilized to get the law changed, first in Sacramento, where the state passed a statute permitting each county to set up a consumer-controlled authority to oversee the home-care workers, and then in Los Angeles, where the SEIU prodded the county to establish its own home health-care supervisory council. Finally, in 1999 the SEIU won the right to represent all the

"Do you know what liberty and justice are? Give them to me now!"
(Credit: David Bacon)

74,000 Los Angeles County workers who feed, bathe, and clean for the elderly and disabled. In subsequent years tens of thousands of other California home health-care workers joined the unions and won significant wage increases.[45]

Ideas in Action

"When the union's inspiration through the workers' blood shall run," proclaims the first line of Ralph Chaplin's *Solidarity Forever*, "[t]here can be no power greater anywhere beneath the sun." The key word in that 1915 labor anthem is "inspiration": its meaning, character, and power. If questions involving the dignity and value of work are to return to the top of the national agenda, then the organizational shape of the American trade-union movement is actually of far less importance than the ideas and ideology, the inspiration, that sustains it. What ideas motivate American workers today, and what seem capable of generating the kind of mobilizations and alliances that will once again make a resolution of the labor question seem synonymous with the economic and civic health of the society as a whole?

It's important to make clear that some ideas, significant as they once were, no longer have much potency. The demand for a shorter workday, which motivated the labor movement for the century that ended in 1940, no longer seems to resonate among contemporary members, actual or potential. This is an extraordinary state of affairs, given the de facto extension of the U.S. working day and week, the domestic "speed-up" that envelops family relationships when all adults must bring home a paycheck, and the inadequate social wage (haphazard childcare, poor public transport) that makes parenting so difficult. Almost without exception, Europeans work fewer hours per year and have much longer vacations than their American counterparts. German workers put in about 1,640 hours per year, with five annual weeks of vacation, compared to 1,900 hours for U.S. workers, with less than half the vacation weeks.[46]

But compared to Europeans, U.S. workers are not interested in trading more leisure for less money, or even for taking their next pay hike in more vacation time rather than more cash income. This abandonment of one of the great ideas that unified the working class, and which had a particular appeal to women, represents a huge setback to the unions and to the fight for a humane society. But mourn as we might, it seems that in contemporary American culture, the return of the shorter workday to a central place on the political agenda is not now on offer.[47]

Likewise the idea of industrial pluralism is just about dead, and certainly with more justification. It no longer has explanatory meaning to many workers or managers, not to mention the general public, which hardly notices the collective-bargaining ritual. It has few advocates even within the old fraternity of industrial-relations practitioners. We have little by way of language to describe collective bargaining, and that which we do, such as "level playing field," or "union-management cooperation" obfuscates more than it describes.

The Keynesian idea—that unions are essential to boost mass purchasing power and thereby sustain economic growth—is more potent and still provides a rationale for strong unions that can police labor standards and sustain the welfare state through use of their political muscle. But at the dawn of the twenty-first century, Keynesianism has lost its luster, even among labor-liberals. During the boom of the 1990s prosperity seemed in no need of a Keynesian fiscal stimulus, and even if it now needs such a boost, the globalization of the world economy, accompanied by a leap forward in productivity, has reduced the impact that even the most potent unions once had on the overall health of the economy. Wage bargains in unionized industries, like auto, steel, and telephone, no longer establish the pattern that other employers feel it prudent to follow.

But other ideas still hold our imagination: industrial democracy is no longer a recognizable phrase, but the idea of workplace justice, of the interpenetrating character of the rights enjoyed by citizens in the community and within the private enterprise remains important, even explosive. Just as the CIO made the quest for industrial democracy a powerful theme that legitimized its strikes and organizing campaigns, so too can the contemporary labor movement capitalize on the nation's well-established rights culture of the last forty years.[48] At the University of Virginia, where I worked during the 1990s, there were no unions, no heritage of working-class rhetoric or action. But statues of Thomas Jefferson abound, and in recent years the civil rights movement and its achievements have become almost as iconic. Rights consciousness and rights rhetoric thus remain powerful weapons available to partisans of working people. When university administrators argued that the central Virginia labor market determined the wages of the predominantly African American house-cleaning staff, we silenced this particular mode of rationalization by pointing out that the legacy of Virginia's infamous, antebellum set of slave labor markets cast a shadow that could not be ignored even at the end of the twentieth century. Thus we made "Workers Rights Are Civil Rights" the theme for a notably successful labor teach-in early in 1997. Few knew the words to "Solidarity Forever" in Charlottesville, but clerical workers, housekeepers, and cafeteria workers may be coming to understand that the citizenship rights they are told they enjoy have no real potency without an organization that defends and advances them on a daily basis. As in so many other cities, the ideological task that lies before workplace democrats is to make union organizational rights as unassailable as are basic civil rights.[49]

Because they have become acutely aware and alarmed over this debilitating dichotomy, some pro-labor intellectuals, including Todd Gitlin, Michael Tomasky, and Richard Rorty, have argued that whatever its past legitimacy, "identity politics" (itself a pejorative term for rights consciousness) has reached a contemporary dead end—both in terms of its impact on the working-class movement as a whole and in its capacity to make a real impact on the polity. In contrast, those who defend a vigorous sense of rights consciousness, most notably Robin Kelley, Manning Marable, and Katha Pollitt, argue that the effort to reemphasize class politics represents an effort to devalue and delegitimize the agenda of feminists, gays, and those who still feel various forms of affirmative action are necessary to rectify past injustices.[50]

For labor partisans, the "identity" politics side of this debate cannot be dismissed, especially insofar as its advocates see the expression of such rights and identities coming in and through the unions themselves. The labor movement has always been ethnically and racially pluralistic; moreover, class itself is a gendered and racial construct. It might be advantageous if American workers, even those of a radical persuasion, expressed themselves largely through the language of class. But few see their primary identity, or their work rights, in this fashion. Thus the labor movement has surged forward not when it denied its heterogeneity, but when activists have capitalized on this particularistic diversity in order to conjoin these multiple identities. We have seen the potency of this orientation in contemporary Los Angeles. Likewise, this has certainly been the most efficacious strategy at a place like the University of Virginia, where racial hierarchies (and those of gender as well) are stark and contested, but where class issues, not to mention unionism itself, have an abstract and alien character.

An organized working class remains essential to the health of a democratic polity. Progressives like Henry Demarest Lloyd and Louis Brandeis were convinced that the nation's republican form of government would falter without an expansion of democratic norms to the world of work. The experience of the twentieth century sustains this view. When dictatorial regimes came to power in Europe during the interwar years, they immediately destroyed the independent labor movement in the territories where their police power commanded obedience. Conversely, the postwar democratization of Finland, Greece, Poland, South Korea, South Africa, Brazil, and Spain has been sparked by the reemergence of a powerful set of aggressive, independent unions. The United States remains a republic. But the problematic character of its democratic institutions, the decline in civic participation, and the overweening political influence of the corporations, has now become the common complaint, and not only on the Left. There are many reasons for this erosion of democratic norms, but the shrinking size and potency of the labor movement is unquestionably near the top of the list.[51]

Let's conclude with three strategic propositions for the union movement. Each is designed not so much to win a particular campaign or strike as to advance a laborite transformation of the political culture, to make organic the social and ideological linkages between our rights culture and the working-class movement.

The first is militancy. The union movement needs more of it, but even more important, American labor as a whole needs to stand behind those exemplary instances of class combat when and if they occur. The 1980s were a tragic decade for the unions, not because workers did not fight, but because when labor did take a stand—at International Paper in Jay, Maine; at Phelps Dodge in Arizona; at

Hormel in Austin, Minnesota; and at Continental and Greyhound—their struggles were both physically isolated and ideologically devalued.

We remember Pullman in 1894, Lawrence in 1912, Gastonia in 1929, and Memphis in 1968, not because the workers engaged in those strikes were any more militant or victorious than those of the 1980s, but because the labor movement as a whole, and liberal and left-wing intellectuals in particular, defended these struggles and gave them a transcendent meaning. This raising of the stakes contributed to success in the United Parcel Service strike in August 1997; to the great support won by Los Angeles janitors in the spring of 2000; and to the successful strike of telecommunications workers at Verizon later that same summer. All of these strikes have had an overt political character: gone are the days when collective bargaining represents a set-piece conflict, ghettoized from the rest of the polity.[52]

The second key is internal union democracy. This is not a luxury, an ethical imperative divorced from the hard work necessary to rebuild the unions and link them to a rights agenda. Instead it stands at the very center of that rebuilding process. Fighting for democracy in the workplace—not simply the right to form unions—is vital to restoring the social mission of labor and returning unions to their social-movement heritage. The unions need tens of thousands of new organizers; but the AFL-CIO cannot recruit, train, and deploy such an army, and even if it could, "organizers" who parachute into a campaign are far less effective than those who are part of the community and the workplace. Such a homegrown cadre cannot be recruited in the absence of a democratic, participatory union culture. Unfortunately, thousands of local unions, and not a few national or international organizations, are job trusts that exist to protect the incomes of an entrenched strata of long-service officials. The democratization of the union movement threatens the security and prerogatives of these men and women, but without that democratization the union movement will remain a shell.[53]

And finally there is politics. For two centuries, political parties have been a pillar of the democratic nation-state because they aggregate factions, crystalize ideologies, and generate a compelling vision of what they consider the good society. Thus labor-based political parties have been almost universal in the industrial West. They arise out of a logic that compels unionized labor to reach beyond its own ranks and forge alliances with those natural allies that are either unorganized or demobilized. In the United States, however, labor has never had its own party, not so much because of anything exceptional in the consciousness of American workers or their leaders, but because the distinctive federalism of the U.S. electoral system fatally penalizes those political/organizational gambits that stray too far beyond the two-party straightjacket. As the 2000 presidential election so graphically demonstrated, electoral federalism in the United States distorts and thwarts the popular will and marginalizes third-party alternatives. Absent a major crisis, labor is stuck with this winner-take-all system.[54]

But this does not mean that American unionism has not, and cannot have, a political dimension. From the era of Samuel Gompers and the Knights of Labor forward, American unionists have recognized that organization, bargaining, and political action are indissolubly linked. In 1908 Gompers first declared, "Reward your friends and punish your enemies"; five decades later Walter Reuther was fond of asserting that "labor's victories at the bargaining table are threatened every other year at the ballot box." Such hardnosed, pragmatic calculation has long been central to labor political action. In order to sustain trade-union organization and make progress in economic bargaining, the unions require a supportive political environment. Thus, even the most conservative trade-union leaders have not hesitated to throw money and manpower into the electoral effort. With few exceptions the unions have tilted Democratic since 1912; indeed, since the 1940s they have constituted a key element of the party in most urban industrial states. The AFL-CIO leadership's stepped-up political commitment in recent national campaigns lies squarely within this venerable tradition.[55]

But such a pragmatic calculus is not enough, for politics is not simply a question of who gets what in the American political economy. As this review of the labor question has tried to indicate, the fate of American labor is linked to the power of the ideas and values that sustain it. Although the Democratic Party once contained a strong social-democratic tendency that linked unionists to a broader liberal constituency, today it fulfills this function in but a pallid and self-contradictory fashion. A vigorous trade-union movement therefore needs a well-projected, clearly defined political posture in order to advance labor's legislative agenda and defend the very idea of workplace rights and collective action. Given the decay into which America's contemporary political-party system has fallen, labor must function as an independent, and sometimes as a disloyal, component of the Democratic Party coalition, at least until a reassessment of its political options can take place. This is the way the CIO helped recast the meaning of American liberalism in the 1930s, and how union Political Action Committees functioned in the 1940s. Such movement-building independence gave the civil rights impulse of the early 1960s a transformative impact on our political culture, and it may yet provide a template for the L.A. Federation of Labor as it seeks to transform millions of California's immigrant and minority workers into self-confident citizens. At stake is not just an effort to resolve America's labor question but the revitalization of democratic society itself.

NOTES

PREFACE AND ACKNOWLEDGMENTS

1. "American Trade Unions and the 'Labor Question:' Past and Present," in *What's Next for Organized Labor?: The Report of the Century Foundation Task Force on the Future of Unions* (New York: The Century Foundation Press, 1999), 59–117.

INTRODUCTION

1. Burger King employment applications, Charlottesville, 1998; Corvallis, 2000; in author's possession.

2. See for example, David Segal, "Denny's Serves Up a Sensitive Image: Restaurant Chain Goes on PR Offensive to Show Changed Ways with Minorities," *Washington Post* (April 7, 1999), E1; and Erin Kelly and Frank Dobbin, "How Affirmative Action Became Diversity Management," *American Behavioral Scientist* 41 (April 1998), 960–84. Big corporations have been lukewarm at best when the GOP Right has sought to revise Title VII employment law.

3. The Burger King application continues with the following: "Employment handbooks, manuals, personnel policies and procedures are not employment contracts and do not modify my status as an at-will employee." This is designed to forestall employment suits, increasingly popular since the early 1980s, which assert an implied employment guarantee that supersedes the at-will doctrine. See Richard Edwards, *Rights at Work: Employment Relations in the Post-Union Era* (Washington: The Brookings Institution, 1993), 163–87.

4. Karen Orren, *Belated Feudalism: Labor, the Law, and Liberal Development in the United States* (Cambridge: Cambridge University Press, 1991), 176–82.

5. As quoted in Walter K. Olson, *The Excuse Factory: How Employment Law Is Paralyzing the American Workplace* (New York: The Free Press, 1997), 237; Richard Kahlenberg, "Unionization As a Civil Right," *American Prospect* (September 11, 2000), 13; and see also Kent Greenfield, "Truth, or Consequenes: If a Company Lies, Employees Should Be Able to Sue," *Washington Post* (June 28, 1998), C1. Greenfield, a law professor, here denounces the failure of corporations to tell their employees the truth about future investment and plant closings. But Greenfield's solution is more litigation, not stronger unions, even though his essay appeared during a strike at General Motors that was designed to force management there to reinvest in and modernize existing facilities.

6. As quoted in Arthur S. Link, ed., *The Papers of Woodrow Wilson*, Volume 59, May 10–31, 1919 (Princeton: Princeton University Press, 1988), 290–91. President Wilson's message of May 20 was first brought to my attention by Steve Fraser, "The Labor Question," in Steve Fraser and Gary Gerstle, *The Rise and Fall of the New Deal Order, 1930–1980* (Princeton: Princeton University Press, 1989), 55.

7. N. Gordon Levin, *Woodrow Wilson and World Politics: America's Answer to War and Revolution* (New York: Oxford University Press, 1968), 1–10. And for a more contemporary restatement of the problem see Walter LaFeber, "The Tension between Democracy and Capitalism during the American Century," in Michael Hogan, *The Ambiguous Legacy: U.S. Foreign Relations in the "American Century."* (New York: Cambridge University Press, 1999), 152–82.

8. Lawrence Glickman, *A Living Wage: American Workers and the Making of Consumer Society* (Ithica: Cornell University Press, 1997), 17–24; Dana Frank, *Purchasing Power: Consumer Organizing, Gender, and the Seattle Labor Movement, 1919–1929* (New York: Cambridge University Press, 1994), 1–12; David Roediger, *The Wages of Whiteness: Race and the Making of the American Working Class* (London: Verso, 1991); and Alexander Saxton, *The Rise and Fall of the White Republic: Class Politics and Mass Culture in Nineteenth-Century America* (London: Verso, 1990) are most closely identified with the idea that "wage slavery" represents an effort by Irish and German immigrant workers to assert their "whiteness" over and against that of colored proletarians. And see also Matthew Frye Jacobson, *Whiteness of a Different Color: European Immigrants and the Alchemy of Race* (Cambridge: Harvard University Press, 1998).

9. Steward, Mitchell, and the Anthracite Commission quoted in Glickman, *A Living Wage*, 34, 83, 33. The import of the coal commission is discussed in Clarence Wunderlin, Jr., *Visions of a New Industrial Order: Social Science and Labor Theory in America's Progressive Era* (New York: Columbia University Press, 1992), 72–94.

10. Lloyd quoted in David Montgomery, "Industrial Democracy in Industry?: The Theory and Practice of the Labor Movement, 1870–1925," in Nelson Lichtenstein and Howell John Harris, *Industrial Democracy in America: the Ambiguous Promise* (New York; Cambridge University Press, 1993), 22.

11. For an elaboration of some of these themes, see Gary Gerstle, "Ideas of the American Labor Movement, 1880–1950," in Stuart Bruchey and Peter Coclanis, eds., *Ideas, Ideologies, and Social Movements: The U.S. Experience Since 1800* (Columbia: University of South Carolina Press, 1998). And see also Sean Wilentz, *Chants Democratic: New York City and the Rise of the American Working Class, 1788–1950* (New York: Oxford University Press, 1984), 61–103; and David Montgomery, *The Fall of the House of Labor* (New York: Cambridge University Press, 1987), 22–44.

12. William Forbath, "Caste, Class, and Equal Citizenship," *Michigan Law Review* 98 (October 1999), 57.

13. William Leiserson, "Constitutional Government in American Industries," *American Economic Review* 12 (March 1922), 56, 77; Forbath, "Caste, Class, and Equal Citizenship," 88.

14. As quoted in Joseph A. McCartin, *Labor's Great War: The Struggle for Industrial Democracy and the Origins of Modern American Labor Relatons, 1912–1921* (Chapel Hill: University of North Carolina Press, 1997), 8.

15. Joseph McCartin, "An American Feeling: Workers, Managers, and the Struggle over Industrial Democracy in the World War I Era," in Lichtenstein and Harris, *Industrial Democracy*, 73, 76.

16. I've taken the "dress rehearsal" phrase from Steve Fraser, "Dress Rehearsal for the New Deal: Shop Floor Insurgents, Political Elites, and Industrial Democracy in the Amalgamated Clothing Workers," in Michael Frisch and Daniel Walkowitz, *Working-Class America: Essays on Labor, Community and American Society* (Urbana: University of Illinois Press, 1983), 212–55; and see also, Melvyn Dubofsky, *The State and Labor in Modern America* (Chapel Hill: University of North Carolina Press, 1994), which emphasizes the extent to which virtually all the New Deal concepts were in ideological and institutional play during the World War I era.

17. Alan Dawley, *Struggles for Justice: Social Responsibility and the Liberal State* (Cambridge: Harvard University Press, 1991), 99. Along parallel lines, see Mary O. Furner, "Knowing Capitalism: Public Investigation and the Labor Question in the Long Progressive Era," in Mary O. Furner and Barry Supple, *The State and Economic Knowledge: The American and British Experiences* (New York: Cambridge University Press, 1990), 241–68; and Daniel Rodgers, *Atlantic Crossings: Social Politics in a Progressive Age* (Cambridge: Harvard University Press, 1998), 8–32.

18. Kathryn Kish Sklar, *Florence Kelley and the Nation's Work* (New Haven: Yale University Press, 1995), 155.

19. Justice Brewer quoted in Eileen Boris and Nelson Lichtenstein, *Major Problems in the History of American Workers* (Lexington: D. C. Heath, 1991), 413.

20. Gosta Esping-Anderson, *The Three Worlds of Welfare Capitalism* (Princeton: Princeton University Press, 1990), 35–54 passim; and Peter Swenson, *Capitalists Against Markets: The Making of Labor Markets and Welfare States in the United States and Sweden* (New York: Oxford University Press, forthcoming).

21. The literature is enormous. See for example, Seth Koven and Sonya Michel, *Mothers of a New World: Maternalist Politics and the Origins of Welfare States* (New York: Routledge, 1993), 1–42; and Theda Skocpol, *Protecting Mothers and Soldiers: Maternalist Origins of the American Welfare State* (Cambridge: Harvard University Press, 1993).

22. Nelson Lichtenstein, Susan Strasser, and Roy Rosenzweig, *Who Built America? Working People and the Nation's Economy, Politics, Culture, and Society* (New York: Worth Publishers, 2000), 222.

23. William Forbath, *Law and the Shaping of the American Labor* Movement (Cambridge: Harvard University Press, 1991), 98–127 passim.

24. Linda Gordon, *Pitied but Not Entitled: Single Mothers and the History of Welfare* (Cambridge: Harvard University Press, 1994), 214.

25. Fraser, "The 'Labor Question,'" 56.

26. Margo Anderson, "The Language of Class in Twentieth-Century America," *Social Science History* 12 (Winter 1988), 349–72.

27. Lawrence Mishel, Jared Bernstein, and John Shmitt, *The State of Working America* (Economic Policy Institute, 1996); David Moberg, "The U.S. Labor Movement Faces the Twenty-First Century," in Bruce Nissen, ed., *Which Direction for Organized Labor?* (Detroit: Wayne State University Press, 1999), 21–33.

28. Steven Greenhouse, "So Much work, So Little Time," *New York Times*, September 5, 1999; Geir Moulson, "Americans Work Longest Hours," September 5, 1999 (Associated Press Wire Story). The International Labor Organization report, "Key Indicators of the Labor Market," covered the years 1980–97. In France, Germany, and Japan workers seemed to capture more of the fruits of technological improvement. There productivity rose more than 50 percent faster than in the United

States while average working time actually declined. Higher unemployment in those nations can account for but a portion of this phenomenon. See also the now classic Juliet Schor, *The Overworked American: The Unexpected Decline of Leisure* (New York: Basic Books, 1992), 17–41.

29. Family income for 217 million people, 80 percent of the total population, now constitutes less than half of the total GDP, down from 56 percent in 1977. David Cay Johnson, "Gap Between Rich and Poor Found Substantially Wider," *New York Times* (September 5, 1999).

30. Lester Thurow, "The Boom That Wasn't," *New York Times* (January 18, 1999); Bob Ortega, *In Sam We Trust: The Untold Story of Sam Walton and How Wal-Mart Is Devouring America* (New York: Times Books, 1998), 346–67; Gene Koretz, "A New Economy but No New Deal," *Business Week* (July 10, 2000), 34; Aaron Bernstein, "Down and Out in Silicon Valley, *Business Week* (March 27, 2000).

31. Theda Skocpol, *Boomerang: Clinton's Health Security Effort and the Turn Against Government in U.S. Politics* (New York: W. W. Norton and Co., 1996); Marie Gottschalk, *The Shadow Welfare State: Labor, Business, and the Politics of Health Care in the United States* (Ithaca: Cornell University Press, 2000), 137–76 passim. The health care debacle is discussed at greater length in chapter 7.

32. John Judis, "False Dawn," *New Republic* (July 29, 1996), 6, 41.

33. Steven Greenhouse, "Unions Hit Lowest Point in Six Decades," *New York Times* (January 21, 2001), 18; Kenneth Jost, "Labor Movement's Future," *CQ Researcher* 6 (June 28, 1996), 570; John Lippert, "Suppliers and Demands," *In These Times* (July 8, 1996), 26–27.

34. David Gordon, *Fat and Mean: The Corporate Squeeze of Working Americans and the Myth of Managerial "Downsizing"* (New York: Free Press, 1996), 23–32, 61–90; Richard Rothstein, "Toward a More Perfect Union: New Labor's Hard Road," *American Prospect* (May–June 1996), 42–53.

35. Theoreticians of civil society are willfully ignorant of the union movement. A fine exception is Thomas C. Kohler, "Civic Virtue at Work: Unions As Seedbeds of the Civic Virtues," *Boston College Law Review* 36 (March 1995), 279–304; and see also Michael Yates, *Why Unions Matter* (New York: Monthly Review Press, 1998).

Chapter 1

Reconstructing the 1930s

1. Jim Grossfeld, "Labor Pains: Can Unions Appeal to Software Engineers As Well As to Strawberry Pickers?" *The New Democrat* (May–June 1997), 26–28; and see the brief survey of such views in Elizabeth Faue, "'Amnesiacs in a Ward on Fire': Gender and the Crisis of Labor Viewed from the 1930s," *Proceedings of the Forty-Sixth Annual Meeting, Industrial Relations Research Association* (January 1994), 122–28.

2. The argument is most forcefully advanced by Michael Piore and Charles Sable in their 1984 classic, *The Next Industrial Divide: Possibilities for Prosperity* (New York: Basic Books, 1984); and see also Stephen P. Waring, *Taylorism Transformed: Scientific Management Theory since 1945* (Chapel Hill: University of North Carolina Press, 1991), 78–159 passim.

3. Colin Gordon, *New Deals: Business, Labor, and Politics in America, 1920–1935* (New York: Cambridge University Press, 1994), 39.

4. As quoted in Stanley Vittoz, *New Deal Labor Policy and the American Industrial Economy* (Chapel Hill: University of North Carolina Press, 1987), 132.

5. Ronald Edsforth, *The New Deal: America's Response to the Great Depression* (Oxford: Blackwell Publishers, 2000), 11–33; see also Michael Bernstein, *The Great Depression: Delayed Recovery and Economic Change in America, 1929–1939* (New York: Cambridge University Press, 1987), 7–20, for an incisive survey of theories explaining the onset and unexpected length of the Great Depression.

6. Allan Nevins, *Ford: Expansion and Challenge, 1915–1933* (New York: Charles Scribner's Sons, 1957), 455–56.

7. Vittoz, *New Deal Labor Policy*, 15–33, 47–69 passim; Ron Schatz, *The Electrical Workers: A History of Labor at General Electric and Westinghouse, 1923–1960* (Urbana: University of Illinois Press, 1983), 53–79.

8. Anthony Badger, *The New Deal: The Depression Years, 1933–1940* (London: MacMillan, 1989), 20–22.

9. Irving Bernstein, *The Lean Years: A History of the American Worker, 1920–1933* (Boston: Houghton Mifflin, 1960), 432–34; Filene quoted in Meg Jacobs, "'Democracy's Third Estate': New Deal Politics and the Construction of a 'Consuming Public,'" *International Labor and Working-Class History* 55 (Spring 1999), 34.

10. Theodore Rosenof, *Economics in the Long Run: New Deal Theorists and Their Legacies, 1933–1993* (Chapel Hill: University of North Carolina Press, 1997), 28–43; see also, Arthur M. Schlesinger, Jr., *The Crisis of the Old Order, 1919–1933* (Boston: Houghton Mifflin, 1957), 190–93.

11. "Presidential Statement on N.I.R.A.—To Put People Back to Work," June 16, 1933, in Samuel Rosenman, ed., *The Public Papers and Addresses of Franklin D. Roosevelt*, 2 (New York: Random House, 1938), 251, 255.

12. Filene quoted in Gordon, *New Deals*, 195.

13. Section 7a language quoted in Irving Bernstein, *Turbulent Years: A History of the American Worker, 1933–1941* (Boston: Houghton-Mifflin, 1971), 30.

14. Robert Wagner, "Proposal for Better Industrial Relations," in Melvyn Dubofsky, ed., *American Labor since the New Deal* (Chicago: Quadrangle Books, 1971), 59. This brief summary elides much of the controversy that accompanied enactment of Section 7a of the NIRA, as well as the increasing difficulties that came with its enforcement. Top leaders of the AFL, such as President William Green and the key strategist Matthew Woll, were suspicious of the new powers assumed by the government under the National Recovery Administration. They initially advocated, and won much Congressional support for, a law that promised to spread employment by mandating a thirty-hour work week. It was in response to this near-successful legislative gambit that "Keynesians" like Sidney Hillman, of the Amalgamated Clothing Workers, and Jett Lauck, an influential advisor to John L. Lewis, pushed forward Section 7a of the NIRA. Of course, corporate executives, led by those in textiles and steel, remained staunch foes of 7a and did all they could to subvert it. They wanted higher prices, even higher wages if all firms were required to pay them, but the emergence of independent unionism and the consequent erosion of their managerial prerogatives was too high a price to pay. See Bernstein, *Turbulent Years*, 31–35; Melvyn Dubofsky, *The State and Labor in Modern America* (Chapel Hill: University of

North Carolina Press, 1994), 111–13; and Steven Fraser, *Labor Will Rule: Sidney Hillman and the Rise of American Labor* (New York: Free Press, 1991), 282–88.

15. This radical "consumerist" interpretation of the New Deal is gaining much well-deserved attention. See Michael Kazin, *The Populist Persuasion: An American History* (New York: Basic Books, 1995),144–45; Lizabeth Cohen, "The New Deal State and the Making of Citizen Consumers," (paper in author's possession); and above all, Meg Jacobs, "The Politics of Purchasing Power: Political Economy, Consumption Politics, and American State-Building, 1909–1959," (Ph.D. diss., University of Virginia, 1998), 117–46.

16. As quoted in Bryant Simon, *A Fabric of Defeat: The Politics of South Carolina Millhands, 1910–1948* (Chapel Hill: University of North Carolina Press, 1998), 88.

17. Gerold Markowitz and David Rosner, *"Slaves of the Depression": Workers' Letters About Life on the Job* (Ithaca: Cornell University Press, 1987), 2–16; see also, Harvey Green, *The Uncertainty of Everyday Life* (New York: HarperCollins, 1992), 72–89.

18. As quoted in Simon, *A Fabric of Defeat*, 87.

19. Richard Lowitt and Maurine Beasley, eds., *One Third of a Nation: Lorena Hickok Reports on the Great Depression* (Urbana: University of Illinois Press, 1981), 193. And see especially, Linda Gordon, "Share-Holders in Relief: The Political Culture of the Public Sector," Working Paper #134, Russell Sage Foundation (June 1998).

20. Lizabeth Cohen, *Making a New Deal: Industrial Workers in Chicago, 1919–1939* (New York: Cambridge University Press, 1990), 261, 289; see also, David Kennedy, *Freedom from Fear: The American People in Depression and War, 1929–1945* (New York: Oxford University Press, 1999), 168.

21. Kennedy, *Freedom from Fear*, 134, 469–70.

22. Mary Heaton Vorse, *Labor's New Millions* (New York: Modern Age Books, 1938), 285–86.

23. Irving Bernstein, *A Caring Society: The New Deal, the Worker, and the Great Depression* (Boston: Houghton Mifflin, 1985), 50.

24. "State of the Union Address to Congress," January 11, 1944, in Samuel Rosenman, ed., *The Public Papers and Addresses of Franklin D. Roosevelt*, 13 (New York: Random House, 1948), 40–41.

25. As quoted in Jennifer Klein, "Managing Security: the Business of American Social Policy, 1910–1960" (Ph.D. diss., University of Virginia, 1999), 6, 246.

26. David Brody "Free Labor, Law, and American Trade Unionism," in Stanley L. Engerman, ed., *The Terms of Labor: Slavery, Serfdom, and Free Labor* (Stanford: Standord University Press, 1999), 232. In *Hitchman vs. Mitchell* (1917) the Supreme Court ratified the "yellow-dog contract," arguing that unions could be enjoined from organizing because they were inducing breach of contract by the workers they were seeking to recruit. See also, David Brody, "A Question of Rights," *New Labor Forum* (Fall/Winter 1998), 131.

27. Kenneth Casebeer, "Aliquippa: The Company Town and Contested Power in the Construction of Law," *Buffalo Law Review* 43 (Winter 1995), 618.

28. Kennedy, *Freedom from Fear*, 280.

29. John L. Lewis, "The Battle for Industrial Democracy," *Vital Speeches of the Day* (July 15, 1936), 678.

30. As quoted in Sidney Milkis, "Franklin D. Roosevelt and the New Politics of Presidential Leadership," in Sidney M. Milkis and Jerome M. Mileur, eds. *The New Deal and the Triumph of Liberalism* (Amherst: University of Massachusetts Press, 2002)

31. As quoted in William Forbath, "Caste, Class, and Equal Citizenship: An Essay for David Brian Davis," forthcoming in E. Haltennum, L. Perry, S. Wilentz, *Moral Problems in American Life* (Yale University Press).

32. The most spirited, panoramic account of this "upheaval" is still found in Irving Bernstein's *Turbulent Years*, 217–317. His hundred-page chapter is entitled "Eruption." See also, Janet Irons, "The Challenge of National Coordination: Southern Textile Workers and the General Textile Strike of 1934," in Staughton Lynd, *"We Are All Leaders": The Alternative Unionism of the Early 1930s* (Urbana: University of Illinois Press, 1996), 72–101; and Bruce Nelson, *Workers on the Waterfront: Seamen, Longshoremen, and Unionism in the 1930s* (Urbana: University of Illinois Press, 1988), 127–88.

33. William Preston, *Aliens and Dissenters: Federal Suppression of Radicals, 1903–1933* (New York: Harvard University Press, 1963), 238–76 passim; Michael Kazin, *The Populist Persuasion: An American History* (New York: Basic Books, 1995), 101–106.

34. Gary Gerstle, *Working-Class Americanism: The Politics of Labor in a Textile City, 1914–1960* (New York: Cambridge University Press, 1989), 153–95 passim.

35. Francis Perkins, *The Roosevelt I Knew* (New York: Harper and Row, 1946), 217–20.

36. Ibid., 220; for additional context to these sojourns by the labor secretary, see George Martin, *Madam Secretary: Frances Perkins* (Boston: Houghton Mifflin, 1976), 307–11.

37. William Leiserson, "Constitutional Government in American Industries," *American Economic Review* 12 (March 1922), 62; and see also Nelson Lichtenstein, "Great Expectations: The Promise of Industrial Jurisprudence and Its Demise, 1930–1960," in Lichtenstein and Harris, *Industrial Democracy in America*, 118.

38. Sumner H. Slichter, *Union Policies and Industrial Management* (Washington, D.C.: The Brookings Institution, 1941), 1; Wayne Morse, "Address to Photo-Engravers' Union," January 17, 1943, in National War Labor Board, *Termination Report*, vol. 1 (Washington: Government Printing Office, 1947), 514.

39. David Brody, The Breakdown of Labor's Social Contract," *Dissent* (Winter 1992), 36–41; and "Labor Elections: Good for Workers?" *Dissent* 44 (Summer 1997), 71–78; Bernstein, *Turbulent Years*, 318–39 passim. The National Labor Relation Act's Section 8(a)(2) now proscribes company-sponsored employee organizations.

40. Melvyn Dubofsky, *The State and Labor in Modern America*, 119–28; Sanford Jacoby, *Modern Manors: Welfare Capitalism since the New Deal* (Princeton: Princeton University Press, 1997), 57–94, 143–92. In later years several such company representation plans—at DuPont and Thompson Products (later TRW) for example—transmuted themselves into institutions that came to be considered real, if weak, unions.

41. Lary May, "Movie Star Politics: The Screen Actors' Guild, Cultural Conversion, and the Hollywood Red Scare," in Lary May, ed., *Recasting America: Cultural and Politics in the Age of Cold War* (Chicago: University of Chicago Press, 1989),

125–53; Richard O'Connor, *Heywood Broun: A Biography* (New York: G. P. Putnam's Sons, 1975), 166–90. Note: both the ANG and the SAG became affiliated with the new Congress of Industrial Organizations (CIO), but this did little to transform their craft character. Rather, it demonstrated that the differences between the AFL and the CIO were far more of culture and politics than of organization and jurisdiction.

42. Sidney Fine, *The Automobile under the Blue Eagle: Labor, Management, and the Automobile Manufacturing Code* (Ann Arbor: University of Michigan Press, 1963), 146–47.

43. Among the outstanding books that explore these issues are Alan Brinkley, *Voices of Protest: Huey Long, Father Coughlin, and the Great Depression* (New York: Oxford University Press, 1982); Steven Fraser, *Labor Will Rule: Sidney Hillman and the Rise of American Labor* (New York: Free Press, 1991); Joshua Freeman, *In Transit: The Transport Workers Union in New York City* (New York: Oxford University Press, 1989); Peter Friedlander, *The Making of a UAW Local: A Study in Class and Culture* (Pittsburgh: University of Pittsburgh Press, 1975).

44. Steve Babson, *Building the Union: Skilled Workers and Anglo-Gaelic Immigrants in the Rise of the UAW* (New Brunswick: Rutgers University Press, 1991); E. P. Thompson, *The Making of the English Working Class* (New York: Vintage, 1963), 10. For a contrary view that privileges cultural homogeneity see Lizabeth Cohen, *Making a New Deal*, 333–49.

45. As quoted in Edward Levinson, *Labor on the March* (New York: Harper and Brothers, 1938), 116; and see also, Melvyn Dubofsky and Warren Van Tine, *John L. Lewis: a Biography* (New York: Quadrangle, 1977), 211–21; Robert Zieger, *The CIO: 1935–1955* (Chapel Hill: University of North Carolina Press, 1995), 22–29.

46. As quoted in Robert Zieger, *John L. Lewis: Labor Leader* (Boston: Twayne Publishers, 1988), 81.

47. Zieger, *The CIO*, 25.

48. As quoted in Zieger, *John L. Lewis*, 101.

49. Scores of books have been written on radical labor and its leaders. Among the most politically informed are Schatz, *The Electrical Workers*, 80–101; Lynd, ed., "*We Are All Leaders*," 1–26; Freeman, *In Transit*, 128–61; and Friedlander, *The Emergence of a UAW Local*, 119–31.

50. Lewis quoted in Dubofsky and Van Tine, *John L. Lewis*, 252–53; Richard Oestreicher, "The Rules of the Game: Class Politics in Twentieth-Century America," in Kevin Boyle, ed., *Organized Labor and American Politics, 1894–1994* (Albany: State University of New York Press, 1998), 35–40.

51. Roosevelt quoted in Dubofsky, *The State and Labor in Modern America*, 135; Badger, *The New Deal*, 251.

52. Kristi Anderson, *The Creation of a Democratic Majority, 1928–1936* (Chicago: University of Chicago Press, 1981).

53. Samuel Lubell, *The Future of American Politics* (New York: Harper and Row, 1952), 44–60; Henry Kraus, *Heroes of Unwritten Story: The UAW, 1934–1939* (Urbana: University of Illinois Press, 1993), 204.

54. Badger, *The New Deal*, 248.

55. Eric Leif Davin, "Blue Collar Democracy: Class War and Political Revolution in Western Pennsylvania, 1932–1937," *Pennsylvania History* 67 (Spring 2000), 240–97, quote on page 259; Oestreicher, "The Rules of the Game," 39.

56. Steve Babson, *Turning Points: Labor in the Twentieth Century* (Lanham: Rowman and Littlefield, 1999), 95.

57. The best studies of General Motors in its heyday remain Peter Drucker, *The Concept of the Corporation* (New York: John Day Company, 1946); and Alfred Chandler, Jr., *Strategy and Structure: Chapters in the History of American Industrial Enterprise* (Garden City: Doubleday, 1962), 158–99 passim. *Fortune* quoted in "General Motors," *Fortune* (December 1938), 41; Sloan quoted in *Detroit News*, April 2, 1937 in Paul Sifton, "The Record," in UAW Pre-1945 file, box 29, Paul Sifton Papers, Library of Congress.

58. This description of working conditions at General Motors is taken largely from Sidney Fine, *Sit-Down: The General Motors Strike of 1936–1937* (Ann Arbor: University of Michigan Press, 1969), 199–265, 303–307, 329–41 passim; Ronald Edsforth, *Class Conflict and Cultural Consensus: The Making of a Mass Consumer Society in Flint, Michigan* (New Brunswick: Rutgers University Press, 1987), 157–89; Irving Bernstein, *Turbulent Years: A History of the American Worker, 1933–41* (Boston; Houghton-Mifflin, 1970), 551–634 passim; and Nelson Lichtenstein, *Walter Reuther: The Most Dangerous Man in Detroit* (Urbana: University of Illinois Press, 1997), 74–81, 104–109.

59. Robert Travis to Henry Kraus, March 17, 1937, box 10, Henry Kraus Collection, Archives of Labor and Urban History, Walter Reuther Library, Wayne State University; "Roy Reuther Remembers the Great Sit-Down Strike," *Detroit Free Press*, February 10, 1967; Doug Reynolds, "We Exploit Tools, Not Men: The Speed-up and Militance at General Motors, 1930–40," in *Work, Recreation and Culture: Selected Essays in U.S. Labor History*, Martin Blatt and Martha Norkunas, ed. (New York: Garland Publishers, 1996).

60. For a spirited encapsulation of CIO enthusiasm, see Ruth McKenney, *Industrial Valley* (New York: Harper and Row, 1939); Mary Heaton Vorse, *Labor's New Millions* (New York: Modern Age Books, 1938); Cohen, *Making a New Deal*, 293–321; and Freeman, *In Transit*, 113–27.

61. Steve Jefferys, *Management and Managed: Fifty Years of Crisis at Chrysler* (New York: Cambridge University Press, 1986), 71–77; Zieger, *The CIO, 1935–1955*, 54–89 passim; and Robert Kanter Oral Interview, August 31, 1961, 11, in Archives of Labor and Urban History.

62. Dubofsky and Van Tine, *John L. Lewis*, 275–79. A considerable debate now exists as to the motivation for the shift in Supreme Court sentiment. For a thorough review of the legal scholarship, see Laura Kalman, "Law, Politics, and the New Deal(s): Moments of Change: Transformation in American Constitutionalism," *Yale Law Journal* 108 (June 1999), 2165–2213.

Chapter 2

Citizenship at Work

1. Paul Sultan, *Labor Economics* (New York: Henry Holt, 1957), 144–45.

2. Nelson Lichtenstein, *Labor's War at Home: The CIO in World War II* (New York: Cambridge University Press, 1982), 8–25.

3. As quoted in American Social History Project, *Who Built America? Working People and the Nation's Economy, Politics, Culture, and Society* (New York: Worth, 2000), 521.

4. James B. Atleson, *Labor and the Wartime State: Labor Relations and Law During World War II* (Urbana: University of Illinois Press, 1998), 55–72; Sultan, *Labor Economics*, 123.

5. Russell Davenport, *The Permanent Revolution* (New York: Time-Life Books, 1951), 92.

6. Geoffrey Perrett, *Days of Sadness, Years of Triumph, the American People, 1939–1945* (Madison: University of Wisconsin Press, 1985), 335.

7. Union official quoted in "What's Itching Labor?" *Fortune* (November 1942), 228; see also Lichtenstein, *Labor's War at Home*, 110–17, for a discussion of War Labor Board wage policy.

8. After 1932 a "married persons clause" in each federal budget appropriation encouraged managers to fire the women if their husbands were on the federal payroll. See Lois Scharf, *To Work and to Wed: Female Employment, Feminism, and the Great Depression* (Westport: Greenwood Press, 1980), 46–53.

9. The phrase is Walter Reuther's. Significantly, the early UAW called its organizing department the "Competitive Shops Department," making clear the organic relationship between the economic structure of the industry and the organizing impulse. Walter Reuther "A Program to Organize Competitive Shops," May 1938, box 11, Henry Kraus Collection, Archives of Labor History, and Urban Affairs, Wayne State University.

10. Robert Macdonald, *Collective Bargaining in the Automobile Industry: A Study of Wage Structure and Competitive Relations* (New Haven: Yale University Press, 1963), 134–59 passim; and Fred H. Yoiner, "Developments in Union Agreements," in Colston E. Warne, ed., *Labor in Postwar America* (Brooklyn, N.Y., 1949), 25–34. And even where union organizing campaigns failed, as in the textile South, the union specter served to raise wages all across the industry. See Timothy J. Minchin, *What Do We Need a Union For? The TWUA in the South* (Chapel Hill: University of North Carolina Press, 1997), 48–118 passim.

11. Paul Blumberg, *Inequality in an Age of Decline* (New York: Oxford University Press, 1980), 65–107. In Scandinavia, such pay compression, often backed by social-democratic governments, goes by the name of a "solidarity wage program."

12. UAW, *How to Win for the Union* (Detroit: UAW Education Department, 1941), 3.

13. Ibid.

14. Steve Jefferys, *Management and Managed: Fifty Years of Crisis at Chrysler* (New York: Cambridge University Press, 1986), 3–24,68–97; Toni Gilpin, "Left by Themselves: A History of the United Farm Equipment and Metal Workers union, 1938–1955," (Ph.D. diss., Yale University, 1992), 216–52; Stephen Amberg, "Triumph of Industrial Orthodoxy: The Collapse of Studebaker-Packard Corporation," in Lichtenstein and Meyer, *On the Line: Essays in the History of Auto Work* (Urbana: University of Illinois Press, 1989), 195–96; Rick Halpern, *Down on the Killing Floor: Black and White Workers in Chicago's Packinghouses, 1904–54* (Urbana: University of Illinois Press, 1997), 143.

15. UAW, "How to Win for the Union," 4.

16. Brian Gratton, "The Poverty of Impoverishment Theory: The Economic Well-Being of the Elderly, 1890–1950," *Journal of Economic History* 56 (Winter 1996), 39–61; Sanford Jacoby, *Employing Bureaucracy: Managers, Unions, and the Transformation of Work in American Industry, 1900–1945* (New York: Columbia University Press, 1985), 116–78 passim; Klein, "Managing Security: The Business of American Social Policy," 129–42.

17. Carl Gersuny and Gladis Kaufman, "Seniority and the Moral Economy of U.S. Automobile Workers, 1934–1946," *Journal of Social History* 18 (Spring 1985), 463–73.

18. Chamberlain, quoted in David Brody, *Workers in Industrial America: Essays on the Twentieth-Century Struggle* (New York: Oxford University Press, 1981), 181; see also Howell Harris, *The Right to Manage*, 95–104; and Sanford Jacoby, "American Exceptionalism Revisited: The Importance of Management," in Jacoby, ed., *Masters to Managers: Historical and Comparative Perspectives on American Employers* (New York: Columbia University Press, 1991), 173–200.

19. For a good review of the literature on this question up to 1990 see Eric Arnesen, "Crusades against Crisis: A View from the United States on the 'Rank-and-File' Critique and other Catalogues of Labour History's Alleged Ills," *International Review of Social History* 35 (Winter 1990), 106–25; and see especially, Steven Fraser, "Dress Rehearsal for the New Deal: Shop-Floor Insurgents, Political Elites, and Industrial Democracy in the Amalgamated Clothing Workers," in Michael Frisch and Daniel Walkowitz, *Working Class America: Essays on Labor, Community, and American Society* (Urbana: University of Illinois Press, 1983), 212–55; and Nelson Lichtenstein, "Reutherism on the Shop Floor: Union Strategy and Shop-Floor Conflict in the USA, 1946–1970," in Steven Toliday and Jonathan Zeitlin, eds., *The Automobile Industry and Its Workers: Between Fordism and Flexibility* (London: Polity Press, 1986), 121–43.

20. Quotation taken from Atleson, *Labor and the Wartime State*, 66; for a great deal more, see Fraser, *Labor Will Rule*, 77–113; and Nelson Lichtenstein, "Great Expectations: The Promise of Industrial Jurisprudence and Its Demise, 1930–1960," in Lichtenstein and Harris, eds., *Industrial Democracy in America: The Ambiguous Promise* (New York: Cambridge University Press, 1993), 113–41.

21. As quoted in Lichtenstein, *Walter Reuther*, 136.

22. William Forbath, *Law and the Shaping of the American Labor Movement* (Cambridge: Harvard University Press, 1991), 59–127; Christopher Tomlins, *The State and the Unions: Labor Relations, Law, and the Organized Labor Movement in America, 1880–1960* (New York: Cambridge University Press, 1985), 60–118 passim.

23. Dubofsky, *The State and Labor in Modern America*, 152. For a fine analysis of how the CIO used the state, in fashion quite alien to the AFL, see Gilbert J. Gall, *Pursuing Justice: Lee Pressman, the New Deal, and the CIO* (Albany: State University of New York Press, 1999), 75–112. The relevant chapter is entitled "Mobilizing the Administrative State."

24. James A. Gross, *The Reshaping of the National Labor Relations Board: National Labor Policy in Transition, 1937–1947* (Albany: State University of New York Press, 1981), 24–84, 260–67 passim; James Atleson, *Values and Assumptions in American Labor Law* (Amherst: University of Massachusetts Press, 1983), 44–66; and see the classic Karl Klare, "Judicial Deradicalization of the Wagner Act and the Origins of Modern Legal Consciousness, 1937–1941," 62 *Minnesota Law Review* (1978).

25. Meany quoted in Joseph C. Goulden, *Meany: The Unchallenged Strong Man of American Labor* (New York: Atheneum, 1972), 20.

26. Tomlins, *The State and the Unions*, 181–96; Craig Becker, "Democracy in the Workplace: Union Representation Elections and Federal Labor Law," *Minnesota Law Review* 77 (February 1993), 495–603. AFL partisans were not the only unionists to object to the growth of an increasingly rigid set of NLRB election procedures. Left-wing syndicalists, such as those who revered the IWW tradition, always feared and opposed state certification, and so too did much of the CIO after passage of the Taft-Hartley Act in 1947.

27. Christopher Tomlins, "AFL Unions in the 1930s: Their Performance in Historical Perspective," *Journal of American History* 1979 65(4), 1021–42.

28. Ralph C. James and Estelle Dinerstein James, *Hoffa and the Teamsters: A Study of Union Power* (Princeton: Van Nostrand Company, 1965), 89–142; Thaddeus Russell, "Jimmy Hoffa and the Rise of Teamster Power," (Ph.D. diss., Columbia University, 2000). As with the airline pilots, Teamster success was materially advanced by the de facto cartelization of the industry, which made the standardization of wages and working conditions relatively painless for employers. For the success of airline unionism, the forty-year reign of the Civil Aeronautics Board cannot be underestimated. See Isaac Cohen, "David L. Behncke, the Airline Pilots, and the New Deal: The Struggle for Federal Labor Legislation," *Labor History* 41 (Winter 2000), 47–62.

29. Matt Smith, "Seniority Leads to Serfdom," April 18, 1939, in Accession 1813, box 30, William Harrington Papers, Hagley Museum and Library. Smith was the British-born secretary of the Mechanics Educational Society of America, a radical organization of skilled auto workers crucial to the organization of the early UAW.

30. Dorothy Sue Cobble, *Dishing It Out: Watresses and Their Unions in the Twentieth Century* (Urbana: University of Illinois Press, 1992), 137–48.

31. Bruce Nelson, *Workers on the Waterfront: Seamen, Longshoremen, and Unionism in the 1930s* (Urbana: University of Illinois Press, 1988), 156–88, 266–73 passim.

32. Bruce Nelson, *Divided We Stand: American Workers and the Struggle for Black Equality* (Princeton: Princeton University Press, 2000), 38–45; Steve Babson, *Building the Union: Skilled Workers and Anglo-Gaelic Immigrants in the Rise of the UAW* (New Brunswick: Rutgers University Press, 1991), 63–154 passim; Eric Arnesen, "'Like Banquo's Ghost, It Will Not Down': The Race Question and the American Railroad Brotherhoods, 1880–1920," *American Historical Review* 1994 99(5), 1601–33.

33. B. J. Widick, *Detroit: City of Race and Class Violence* (Detroit: Wayne State University Press, 1989), 151–59; Thomas Sugrue, *The Origins of the Urban Crisis: Race and Inequality in Postwar Detroit* (Princeton: Princeton University Press, 1996), 77–86; Nelson, *Divided We Stand*, 56–61.

34. J. David Greenstone, *Labor in American Politics* (New York: Alfred A. Knopf, 1969), 81–109 passim; Michael Honey, *Southern Labor and Black Civil Rights: Organizing Memphis Workers* (Urbana: University of Illinois Press, 1993), 72–78, 182, 208–209; Craig Haney, "Riding the Punishment Wave: On the Origins of Our Developing Standards of Decency," *Hastings Women's Law Journal*, 9 (Winter 1998), 70–74. Exceptions to this pattern can be found in San Francisco, St. Louis, and in many smaller towns. For a more positive evaluation see, Colin Gordon, "The Lost City of Solidarity: Metropolitan Unionism in Historical Perspective," Working Paper No. 8 (March 1999), Center for Labor Studies, University of Washington.

35. Melvyn Dubofsky, "Technological Change and American Worker Movements," in *Hard Work: The Making of Labor History* (Urbana: University of Illinois Press, 2000), 179–200; E. Emmett Murray, *The Lexicon of Labor* (New York: New Press, 1998), 66.

36. Michael Goldfield, *The Color of Politics: Race and the Mainsprings of American Politics* (New York: New Press, 1997), 190–215 passim; Harvard Sitkoff, "Harry Truman and the Election of 1948," *Journal of Southern History* 37 (November 1971), 597–616.

37. But under the leadership of Adam Clayton Powell, Jr., these protests took on a more interracial, pro-union character in the late 1930s. Cheryl Greenberg, *Or Does It Explode?: Black Harlem in the Great Depression* (New York: Oxford University Press, 1997).

38. Bruce Nelson, "Class, Race, and Democracy in the CIO: The 'New' Labor History Meets the 'Wages of Whitness,'" *International Review of Social History* 41 (Fall 1996), 351–74; David Roediger, *Toward the Abolition of Whiteness* (London: Verso, 1994), 37–45; Gary Gerstle, "The Working Class Goes to War," *Mid-America: An Historical Review* 75 (October 1993), 303–22.

39. Robert Norrell, "Caste in Steel: Jim Crow Careers in Birmingham, Alabama," *Journal of American History* 73 (December 1986), 669–701; Bruce Nelson, "Organized Labor and the Struggle for Black Equality in Mobile during World War II," *Journal of American History* 80 (July 1993), 952–88.

40. As quoted in St. Clair Drake and Horace Cayton, *Black Metropolis: A Study of Negro Life in a Northern City* (New York: Harcourt, Brace, 1945), 332.

41. Roger Horowitz, *"Negro and White, Unite and Fight!": A Social History of Industrial Unionism in Meatpacking, 1930–1990* (Urbana: University of Illinois Press, 1997), 63.

42. Sugrue, *The Origins of the Urban Crisis*, 33–88, 209–71 passim; John McGreevy, *Parish Boundaries: The Catholic Encounter with Race in the Twentieth-Century Urban North* (Chicago: University of Chicago Press, 1996), 55–110 passim; and Kenneth Durr, "When Southern Politics Came North: The Roots of White Working-Class Conservatism in Baltimore, 1940–1964," *Labor History* 37 (1996), 309–31.

43. Gwendolyn Mink, *Old Labor and New immigrants in American Political Development: Union, Party, and State, 1875–1920* (Ithaca: Cornell University Press, 1986); Alexander Saxton, *The Indispensable Enemy: Labor and the Anti-Chinese Movement in California* (Berkeley: University of California Press, 1971); Roediger, *Toward the Abolition of Whiteness*, 69–81.

44. As quoted in Nelson, *Divided We Stand*, 98.

45. This discussion is taken from Lichtenstein, *Walter Reuther*, 210, and Nelson, *Divided We Stand*, 185–218. In his history of the CIO, Robert Zieger calls this kind of CIO approach, "class essentialist." Zieger, *The CIO, 1935–55*, 158.

46. Patricia Sullivan, *Days of Hope: Race and Democracy in the New Deal Era* (Chapel Hill: University of North Carolina Press, 1996), 63–67.

47. Mark Solomon, *The Cry Was Unity: Communists and African-Americans, 1917–1936* (Jackson: University Press of Mississippi, 1998), 102–23; Robin Kelley, *Hammer and Hoe: Alabama Communists during the Great Depression* (Chapel Hill: University of North Carolina Press, 1990), 57–116.

48. Rick Halpern, *Down on the Killing Floor: Black and White Workers in Chicago's Packinghouses*, 1904–54 (Urbana: University of Illinois Press, 1997), 109.

49. Daniel Letwin, "The Specter of 'Social Equality'" (paper in author's possession); Nelson, *Divided We Stand*, 89–119 passim. Until the 1950s advocacy of "social equality" proved so subversive that the FBI routinely labeled those who advocated such racial mores as ipso facto Communists.

50. As quoted in Roediger, *Toward the Abolition of Whiteness*, 10.

51. Judith Stein, "History of an Idea," *The Nation* 267 (December 14, 1998), 12–14. NAACP legal strategy during these years attacked educational segregation by forcing Southern states to equalize teacher salaries and actually fund black schools on a *separate but equal* basis.

52. Rosenwald Fund report quoted in Richard M. Dalfiume, "The 'Forgotten Years' of the Negro Revolution," *Journal of American History* 56 (June 1968), 100; Harold Preece, "The South Stirs," *Crisis* 48 (October 1941), 318.

53. Robert Korstad and Nelson Lichtenstein, "Opportunities Found and Lost: Labor, Radicals, and the Early Civil Rights Movement," *Journal of American History* 75 (December 1988), 793–99.

54. Herbert Garfinkel, *When Negroes March: The March on Washington Movement in the Organizational Politics of FEPC* (Glencoe, Ill. Free Press 1959); Merl E. Reed, *Seedtime for the Civil Rights Movement: The President's Committee on Fair Employment Practice, 1941–1946* (Baton Rouge: Louisiana State University Press, 1991).

55. "20,000 Members in 1943," *Crisis* 50 (May 1943), 140–41; Dominic Capeci, Jr., *Race Relations in Wartime Detroit: The Sojourner Truth Housing Controversy of 1942* (Philadephia: Temple University Press, 1984), 75–99, 111–13; St. Clair Drake and Horace Cayton, *Black Metropolis*, 341.

56. Robert Korstad, "Democracy Denied: Winston-Salem Tobacco Unionism," (University of North Carolina Press, forthcoming), chapter 6; Barbara Griffith, *The Crisis of American Labor: Operation Dixie and the Defeat of the CIO* (Philadephia: Temple University Press, 1988). Both Korstad and Griffith show the way in which post–World War II liberal unionists felt they had to downplay the extent to which African Americans supported CIO unionism in the South in order to appeal to white workers in that region.

57. Gilbert J. Gall, "Thoughts on Defeating Right-to-Work: Reflections on Two Referendum Campaigns," in Kevin Boyle, *Organized Labor and American Politics: 1894–1994*, The Labor-Liberal Alliance (Albany: State University of New York Press, 1998), 195–207. Gall reports that one of the most dramatic moments in the Ohio campaign came when a black electrician, Theodore Pinkston, who for five years had been denied admission to the International Brotherhood of Electrical Workers, became a public spokesman for the unions in their effort to roll back the right-wing campaign.

58. Judith Stein, *Running Steel, Running America: Race, Economic Policy, and the Decline of Liberalism* (Chapel Hill: University of North Carolina Press, 1998), 43; Roger Horowitz, *"Negro and White: Unite and Fight!": A Social History of Industrial Unionism in Meatpacking, 1930–1990* (Urbana: University of Illinois Press, 1997), 96.

59. Honey, *Southern Labor and Black Civil Rights* 137–38.

60. Samuel Lubell, *The Future of American Politics* (Garden City: Doubleday, 1952), 57.

61. Lizabeth Cohen, *Making a New Deal*, 279–81; Nancy Weiss, *Fairwell to the*

Party of Lincoln: Black Politics in the Age of FDR (Princeton: Princeton University Press, 1983); Nan Elizabeth Woodruff, "Mississippi Delta Planters and Debates over Mechanization, Labor, and Civil Rights in the 1940s," *Journal of Southern History* 60 (May 1994), 263–84; Sumner Rosen, "The CIO Era, 1935–1955," in Julius Jacobsen, ed., *The Negro and the American Labor Movement* (Garden City, N.Y.: Anchor Books, 1968), 188–208.

62. Horowitz, *"Negro and White, Unite and Fight!"*, 150.

63. Gunnar Myrdal, *An American Dilemma* (New York: McGraw-Hill, 1944), 1962), 416.

64. Granger, quoted in Eileen Boris, "'The Right to Work Is the Right to Live!: The Rights Discourse of Fair Employment," in Manifred Berg and Martin Geyser *The Culture of Rights* (New York: Cambridge University Press, 2001); Rosenman, "State of the Union Address" (January 1944), *Papers and Addresses of Franklin Roosevelt*, vol. 13, 42.

65. Allan Winkler, "The Philadelphia Transit Strike of 1944," *Journal of American History* 59 (July 1972), 73–79; William Harris, "Federal Intervention in Union Discrimination: FEPC and West Coast Shipywards during World War II," *Labor History* 22 (Summer 1981), 325–47.

66. Thomas Sugrue, "The Tangled Roots of Affirmative Action," *American Behavioral Scientist* 41 (April 1998), 889; Eileen Boris, "Fair Employment and the Origins of Affirmative Action in the 1940s," *National Women's Studies Association Journal* (Fall 1998), 144–46.

67. August Meier and Elliott Rudwick, *Black Detroit and the Rise of the UAW* (New York: Oxford University Press, 1979), 114–17; Maurice Zeitlin and Frank Weyher, "Black and White, Unite and Fight": Interracial Working-Class Solidarity and Interracial Inequality in America," Working Paper Series (Los Angeles: Institute of Industrial Relations, UCLA, 1998), 14; Eileen Boris, "'You Wouldn't Want One of 'Em Dancing with Your Wife': Racialized Bodies on the Job in World War II," *American Quarterly* 50 (March 1998); Daniel Kryder, *Divided Arsenal: Race and the American State during World War II* (New York: Cambridge University Press, 2000), 88–132.

68. Dominic Capeci, Jr., and Martha Wilkerson, *Layered Violence: The Detroit Rioters of 1943* (Jackson: University Press of Mississippi, 1991); Nelson, "Organized Labor and the Struggle for Black Equality in Mobile during World War II," 952–1029.

69. As quote in Alice Kessler-Harris, *A Woman's Wage: Historical Meanings and Social Consequences* (Lexington: University of Kentucky Press, 1990), 74; Gallup quoted in Irving Bernstein, *A Caring Society: The New Deal, the Worker, and the Great Depression* (Boston: Houghton Mifflin, 1985), 291.

70. Linda Gordon, *Pitied but Not Entitled: Single Mothers and the History of Welfare* (Cambridge: Harvard University Press, 1994), 193–95.

71. Elizabeth Faue, *Community of Suffering and Struggle: Women, Men, and the Labor Movement in Minneapolis, 1915–1945* (Chapel Hill: University of North Carolina Press, 1991), 69–99 passim; Robert Zieger, *The CIO, 1935–1955* (Chapel Hill: University of North Carolina Press, 1995), 86–88.

72. Faue, *Community of Suffering and Struggle*, 100–25 passim; Joshua Freeman, *In Transit*, 123–26.

73. Faue, *Community of Suffering and Struggle*, 126–46; This process took place

even in the Communist-oriented unions. For the travail of one female labor partisan, see Daniel Horowitz, *Betty Friedan and the Making of* The Feminine Mystique: *The American Left, the Cold War, and Modern Feminism* (Amherst: University of Massachusetts Press, 1998), 121–79.

74. Nancy Gabin, *Feminism in the Labor Movement: Women and the United Auto Workers, 1935–1975* (Ithaca, N.Y.: Cornell University Press, 1990), 50–51.

75. As quoted in Karen Anderson, *Wartime Women: Sex Roles, Family Relations, and the Status of Women during World War II* (Westport: Greenwood Press, 1981).

76. Kessler-Harris, *A Women's Wage*, 108.

77. Margaret C. Rung, "Paternalism and Pink Collars: Gender and Federal Employee Relations, 1941–1950," *Business History Review* 71(3) (1997), 381–416.

78. Ruth Milkman, *Gender at Work: The Dynamics of Job Segregation by Sex during World War II* (Urbana: University of Illinois Press, 1987), 77–83, 99–152; Kessler-Harris, *A Women's Wage*, 111–12. A somewhat more sanguine reading of postwar progress for women workers is offered in Dennis Deslippe, *"Rights, Not Roses": Unions and the Rise of Working-Class Feminism, 1945–1980* (Urbana: University of Illinois Press, 2000).

79. Judith Sealander, "Feminist against Feminist: The First Phase of the Equal Rights Amendment Debate, 1923–1963," *South Atlantic Quarterly* 81 (1982), 147–61; Eric Foner, *The Story of American Freedom* (New York: Norton, 1998), 157–59; Gwendolyn Mink, *The Wages of Motherhood: Inequality in the Welfare State, 1917–42* (Ithaca; Cornell University Press, 1995), 31–51.

80. K. R. Willoughby, "Mothering Labor: Difference As a Device toward Protective Labor Legislation for Men, 1930–1938," *Journal of Law and Politics* 10 (Fall 1994), 445–89; Skocpol, *Protecting Soldiers and Mothers*, 379–423.

81. Alice Kessler-Harris, *In Pursuit of Equity: Women, Men and the Quest for Economic Citizenship in Twentieth-Century America* (New York: Oxford University Press, 2001), 17–18, 141–43.

82. Ibid, 100–111, 171–77.

83. Jill Quadagno, "Women's Access to Pensions and the Structure of Eligibility Rules: Systems of Production and Reproduction," *Sociological Quarterly* 29 (1988), 541–58; Bruce Fehn, "'Chickens Come Home to Roost': Industrial Reorganization, Seniority, and Gender Conflict in the United Packinghouse Workers of America, 1956–1966," *Labor History* 34 (Spring 1993), 324–41.

Chapter 3

A Labor-Management Accord?

1. Bruce Nissen, "A Post–World War II "Social Accord?" in Nissen, ed., *U.S. Labor Relations, 1945–1989: Accommodation and Conflict* (New York: Garland Publishing, 1990), 174–79; Samuel Bowles, David Gordon, and Thomas Weisskopf, *Beyond the Waste Land: A Democratic Alternative to Economic Decline* (Garden City: Anchor Press, 1983), 70–75; John Sweeney, "America Needs a Raise," in Steven Fraser and Joshua Freeman, eds., *Audacious Democracy: Labor, Intellectuals, and the Social Reconstruction of America* (Boston: Houghton Mifflin, 1997), 13; Reich was a

prolific advocate after he left office as well. See, for example, Robert Reich, "Broken Faith: Why We Need to Renew the Social Compact," *The Nation* 266 (February 16, 1998), 11–17.

2. C. Wright Mills, *The New Men of Power: America's Labor Leaders* (New York: Harcourt, Brace and Company, 1948), 146–47; Russell Davenport, *The Permanent Revolution* (New York: Time-Life Books, 1951), 92; Elizabeth Fones-Wolf, *Selling Free Enterprise: The Business Assault on Labor and Liberalism, 1945–1960* (Urbana: University of Illinois Press, 1994), 108–34.

3. Jack Metzgar, *Striking Steel: Solidarity Remembered* (Philadelphia: Temple University Press, 2000), 58–83, 94–117.

4. Nissen, "A Post–World II "Social Accord?" in *U.S Labor Relatons*, 193–200. Radicals like Kim Moody and Mike Davis have also accepted the existence of such an accord, even if they have argued that it was designed to serve the interests of elites in both labor and capital. See Kim Moody, *An Injury to All: The Decline of American Unionism* (London: Verso, 1988), 24–40; Mike Davis, *Prisoners of the American Dream* (London: Verso, 1986), 102–27.

5. Among the key texts are Clark Kerr, John Dunlop, Frederick Harbison, and Charles Myers, *Industrialism and Industrial Man* (Cambridge: Harvard University Press, 1960); and Derek Bok and John Dunlop, *Labor and the American Community* (New York: Simon and Schuster, 1970).

6. Among recent labor histories that explicate this experience, see Dubofsky, *The State and Labor in Modern America*, 107–95 passim; Zieger, *The CIO, 1935–1955*, 177–90,212–27; Lichtenstein, *Walter Reuther*, 154–84; 220–47.

7. Fraser, *Labor Will Rule*, 503–505.

8. Leo Troy, "The Rise and Fall of American Trade Unions: The Labor Movement from FDR to RR," in Seymour Martin Lipset, ed., *Unions in Transition* (San Francisco: ICS Press, 1986), 75–89.

9. *Proceedings of the Seventh Constitutional Convention of the CIO*, Chicago (November 20–24, 1944), 313; Sumner Slichter, *The Challenge of Industrial Relations* (Ithaca: Cornell University Press, 1947), 4.

10. This perspective is advanced most forcefully in Theda Skocpol and Kenneth Finegold, "State Capacity and Economic Intervention in the Early New Deal," *Political Science Quarterly* 97 (Summer 1982), 255–78; a useful critique is found in Peter Swenson, "Arranged Alliance: Business Interests in the New Deal," *Politics and Society* 25 (March 1997), 66–116.

11. Philippe Schmitter, "Still the Century of Corporatism?" in *Trends toward Corporatist Intermediation*, Philippe Schmitter and Gerhard Lehmbruh, eds. (Beverly Hills: Sage Publications, 1982); Wyn Grant, ed., *The Political Economy of Corporatism* (New York: Cambridge University Press, 1983); Leo Panitch, *Working-Class Politics in Crisis: Essays on Labor and the State* (London: Verso, 1980), 132–86; and Ronald Schatz, "From Commons to Dunlop: Rethinking the Field and Theory of Industrial Relations," in Lichtenstein and Harris, eds., *Industrial Democracy in America*, 87–112.

12. Nelson Lichtenstein, "From Corporatism to Collective Bargaining: Organized Labor and the Eclipse of Social Democracy in the Postwar Era," in Fraser and Gerstle, *The Rise and Fall of the New Deal Order*, 122–34; Zieger, *The CIO, 1935–1955*, 141–252 passim; George Lipsitz, *Rainbow at Midnight: Labor and Culture in the 1940s* (Urbana: University of Illinois Press, 1994), 45–68, 99–119; Andrew Workman,

"Manufacturing Power: The Organizational Revival of the National Association of Manufacturers, 1941–1945," *Business History Review* 78 (Summer 1998), 279–301.

13. U.S. Department of Labor, *Termination Report of the National War Labor Board* (Washington: Government Printing Office, 1947), 150–55, 211–91, 338–402; Sultan, *Labor Economics*, 71.

14. Meg Jacobs, "How about Some Meat?": The Office of Price Administration, Consumption Politics, and State Building from the Bottom Up, 1941–1946," *Journal of American History* 84 (December 1997), 910–41; National Association of Manufacturers, "Would You Like Some Butter or a Roast of Beef" (newspaper advertisement), reproduced in Jacobs, "How about Some Meat?" 935; Horowitz, *Beyond Left and Right: Insurgency and the Establishment* (Urbana: University of Illinois Press, 1997), 112.

15. This was certainly Walter Reuther's perspective as well as that of labor-liberal policy makers like Leon Keyserling. See Lichtenstein, *Walter Reuther*, 220–47; Jacobs, "The Politics of Purchasing Power," 255–320; and even Alan Brinkley, *The End of Reform*, 157–61, who argues that while a "reform" in the structure of capitalism was indeed off the agenda, the Keynesian redistribution of income was still a viable liberal project.

16. Daniel Fox, *Health Policies, Health Politics: The British and American Experience, 1911–1965* (Princeton: Princeton University Press, 1986); Alan Derickson, "Health Security for All? Social Unionism and Universal Health Insurance, 1935–1958," *Journal of American History* 81 (March 1994), 1333–56.

17. Lichtenstein, *Walter Reuther*, 270.

18. Zieger, *The CIO*, 227–41; Barbara S. Griffith, *The Crisis of American Labor: Operation Dixie and the Defeat of the CIO* (Philadelphia: Temple University Press, 1989); Robert Korstad, *Daybreak of Freedom* (University of North Carolina Press, forthcoming), chapters 4–7.

19. "Unionized South Will Oust Reaction, Murray Declares," *Wage Earner* April 12, 1946.

20. Gilbert Gall, *The Politics of Right to Work: The Labor Federation As Special Interest, 1943–1979* (New York: Greenwood Press, 1988), 55–93; David Brody, "The Uses of Power II," *Workers in Industrial America: Essays on the Twentieth-Century Struggle* (New York: Oxford University Press, 1981), 215–21; David Plotke, *Building a Democratic Political Order: Reshaping American Liberalism in the 1930s and 1940s* (New York: Cambridge University Press, 1996), 190–226; Kevin Boyle, *The UAW and the Heyday of American Liberalism, 1945–1968* (Ithaca: Cornell University Press, 1995), 35–82; and Joshua Freeman, *Working-Class New York: Life and Labor since World War II* (New York: The New Press, 2000).

21. See generally Sanford Jacoby, "American Exceptionalism Revisited: the Importance of Management,' in Jacoby, ed. *Masters to Managers: Historical and Comparative Perspectives on American Employers* (New York: Columbia University Press, 1991), 173–200; David Vogel, "Why Businessmen Distrust Their State: The Political Consciousness of American Corporate Executives," in *British Journal of Political Science* 8 (January 1978), 45–78; Gordon, *New Deals*, 5–34.

22. Mills, *The New Men of Power*, 223–50; Howell John Harris, *The Right to Manage: Industrial Relations Policies of American Business in the 1940s* (Madison: University of Wisconsin Press, 1982), 23–40; Thomas Ferguson, "Industrial Conflict and the

Coming of the New Deal: The Triumph of Multinational Liberalism in America," in Gerstle and Fraser, eds., *The Rise and Fall of the New Deal Order*, 3–31.

23. This paragraph relies heavily on Vogel, "Why Businessmen Distrust Their State," 45–78; see also Jacoby, "American Exceptionalism Revisited," 173–200.

24. Sloan quoted in Joshua Freeman et al., *American Social History Project, Who Built America? Working People and the Nation's Economy, Politics, Culture and Society* (New York: Pantheon, 1991), 472.

25. Gordon, *New Deals*, 35–86; and Vogel, "Why Businessmen Distrust Their State," 62–71.

26. Catherine McNicol Stock, *Main Street in Crisis: The Great Depression and the Old Middle Class on the Northern Plains* (Chapel Hill: University of North Carolina Press, 1992); Peter Irons, *The New Deal Lawyers* (Princeton: Princeton University Press, 1982).

27. Kazin, *The Populist Persuasion*, 78–133 passim; for the argument that the Court's "four horsemen" were accommodating themselves to a more expansive interpretation of the commerce clause well before 1937, see Barry Cushman, *Rethinking the New Deal Court: The Structure of a Constitutional Revolution* (New York: Oxford University Press, 1998)

28. All histories of the New Deal contain an account of FDR's "Court-packing" debacle. A fine one is found in David Kennedy's *Freedom from Fear: The American People in Depression and War, 1929–1945* (New York: Oxford University Press, 1999), 331–40.

29. See especially, David Horowitz, *Beyond Left and Right: Insurgency and the Establishment* (Urbana: University of Illinois Press, 1997), 159, 203; and also Leo Ribuffo, "Why Is There So Much Conservatism in the United States and Why Do So Few Historians Know Anything about It?" *American Historical Review* 99 (April 1994), 409–49.

30. Charles S. Maier, "The Two Postwar Eras and the Conditions for Stability in Twentieth-Century Western Europe," in Maier, *In Search of Stability: Explorations in Historical Political Economy* (New York: Cambridge University Press, 1987), 153–84; Anthony Carew, *Labor Under the Marshall Plan: the Politics of Productivity and the Marketing of Management Science* (Detroit: Wayne State University Press, 1987); Guido Baglioni and Colin Crouch, eds., *European Industrial Relations: The Challenge of Flexibility* (London: Sage Publications, 1990), 127–53.

31. As quoted in Fones-Wolf, *Selling Free Enterprise*, 22.

32. As quoted in Lichtenstein, *Walter Reuther*, 230.

33. As quoted in Lawrence Richards, "The Culture of Anti-Unionism, 1943–1963," (seminar paper in author's possession, 1998).

34. For a discussion of the impact of Hayek and *The Road to Serfdom*, see Brinkley, *The End of Reform*, 157–61.

35. V. O. Key, *Southern Politics in State and Nation* (New York: Knopf, 1949); Steven Lawson, *Black Ballots: Voting Rights in the South, 1944–1969* (New York: Columbia University Press, 1976), 23–115 passim.

36. Ira Katznelson and Bruce Pietrykowski, "Rebuilding the American State: Evidence from the 1940s," in *Studies in American Political Development* 5 (Fall 1991), 301–39.

37. Ira Katznelson, Kim Geiger, and Daniel Kryder, "Limiting Liberalism: The

Southern Veto in Congress, 1933–1950," *Political Science Quarterly* (Vol. 108, No. 2, Summer 1993), 283–306.

38. Michael Brown, *Race, Money, and the American Welfare State* (Ithaca: Cornell University Press, 1999), 99–134.

39. Daniel Clark, *Like Night and Day: Unionization in a Southern Mill Town* (Chapel Hill: University of North Carolina Press, 1997), 168–98; Timothy Minchin, *What Do We Need a Union For?: The TWUA in the South, 1945–1955* (Chapel Hill: University of North Carolina Press, 1997) 69–98; Daniel Kryder, *Divided Arsenal: Race and the American State during World War II* (New York: Cambridge University Press, 2000), 168–206.

40. F. Ray Marshall, *Labor in the South* (Cambridge: Harvard University Press, 1967), 229–66, 276; Griffith, *Operation Dixie*, 22–45, 161–76.

41. James C. Foster, *The Union Politic: The CIO Political Action Committee* (Columbia: University of Missouri Press, 1975), 108–75, 196–207 (quote on p. 199); Boyle, *The UAW and the Heyday of American Liberalism*, 83–106.

42. Gavin Wright, *Old South, New South: Revolutions in the Southern Economy since the Civil War* (New York: Basic Books, 1986), 226–69 passim; Margaret Weir and Theda Skocpol, "State Structures and the Possibilities for a 'Keynesian' Response to the Great Depression in Sweden, Britain, and the United States," in Peter B. Evans et al., *Bringing the State Back In* (New York: Norton, 1984), 143–45.

43. Quotation taken from Joseph Huthmacher, ed., *The Truman Years* (Hillsdale: Franklin Watts, 1972), 111.

44. Tom Sugrue, *Origins of the Urban Crisis*, 125–77; Jefferson Cowie, *Capital Moves: RCA's Seventy-Year Quest for Cheap Labor* (Ithaca; Cornell University Press, 1999), 41–99; Bruce Schulman, *From Cotton Belt to Sun Belt* (New York: Oxford University Press, 1991), 127–66; and Tami Friedman, "Communities in Competition: Capital Migration across the North-South Divide, 1935–1995" (paper delivered at the Organization of American Historians, April 1998).

45. James Boylan, *The New Deal Coalition and the Election of 1946* (New York, 1981), 151–67; Joel Seidman *American Labor from Defense to Reconversion* (Chicago: University of Chicago Press, 1953), 233–44; Jacobs, "How about Some Meat?" 940–41. Even unionists like Walter Reuther, who had been among the most outspoken corporatists and planning advocates, made a rhetorical about-face. After the Republican congressional sweep, he adopted much of the language of the anti–New Deal right, now urging "free labor" and "free management" to join in solving their problems, or a "superstate will arise to do it for us." Still later, after the Taft-Hartley restrictions were in place, Reuther put the issue even more bluntly: "I'd rather bargain with General Motors than with the government. . . . General Motors has no army," as quoted in Lichtenstein, *Walter Reuther*, 261.

46. Ellen Schrecker, *Many Are the Crimes: McCarthyism in America* (Boston: Little, Brown, 1998), 182–200, 309–58.

47. Zieger, *John L. Lewis*, 163–67; Louis Stark "CIO to Follow AFL on Anti-Red Order" *New York Times* (September 11, 1947), 9.

48. The Cold War literature is huge. An excellent survey that avoids the usual bipolar focus is James E. Cronin, *The World the Cold War Made: Order, Chaos, and the Return of History* (New York: Routledge, 1996), 33–61.

49. Sidney Lens, *The Counterfeit Revolution* (New York: Beacon Press, 1952), 1–12. The abrupt Communist shift from shrill anti-interventionism to militant pro-war enthusiasm after the German invasion of the Soviet Union was long Exhibit A in the liberal brief against the party. For anti-Stalinist left-wing laborites, the party's unconditional defense of the World War II no-strike pledge was an equally potent Exhibit B.

50. Stuart Ball, "A Balance of Power: The Prerequisite to True Collective Bargaining," *Vital Speeches of the Day* 13 (March 1, 1947), 303.

51. Fones-Wolf, *Selling Free Enterprise*, 53–55; Minchin, *What Do We Need a Union For?*, 32–47; and throughout, Griffith, *Operation Dixie*.

52. See Mary Sperling McAuliffe, *Crisis on the Left: Cold War Politics and American Liberals, 1947–1954* (Amherst: University of Massachusetts Press, 1978), 33–47; Harvey A. Levenstein, *Communism, Anticommunism, and the CIO* (Westport: Greenwood Press, 1981), 208–29; Ellen Schrecker, "McCarthyism and the Labor Movement: The Role of the State," in Steve Rosswurm, ed., *The CIO's Left-Led Unions* (New Brunswick: Rutgers University Press, 1992), 139–57.

53. Studies that see U.S. Communism largely as the Stalinist product of Soviet foreign policy include Theodore Draper, *American Communism and Soviet Russia* (New York: Viking, 1960); Irving Howe and Lewis Coser, *The American Communist Party: A Critical History* (New York: Praeger, 1957); and Harvey Klehr et al., *The Secret World of American Communism* (New Haven: Yale University Press, 1995). Social and labor historians of the current generation recognize the weight of Moscow's heavy hand, but most also assert the complex, indigenous sources of Communist influence within the United States during the 1930s and 1940s. See for example, Michael Honey, *Southern Labor and Black Civil Rights: Organizing Memphis Workers* (Chapel Hill: University of North Carolina Press, 1993); Maurice Isserman, *Which Side Were You On?: The American Communist Party during the Second World War* (Middletown: Wesleyan University Press, 1982); and Robin Kelley, *Hammer and Hoe: Alabama Communists during the Great Depression* (Chapel Hill: University of North Carolina Press, 1990). And for an exhaustive, balanced survey, see Schrecker, *Many Are the Crimes*, 1–33.

54. Sanford Jacoby, *Modern Manors: Welfare Capitalism since the New Deal* (Princeton: Princeton University Press, 1997), 172–78, for an account of how Fred Crawford of Thompson Products used employer "free speech" to defeat the UAW.

55. Among the classic essays on this subject are F. J. Roethlisberger, "The Foreman: Master and Victim of Double Talk," *Harvard Business Review* 23 (1945), 283–98; and Donald E. Wray, "Marginal Men of Industry: The Foreman," *American Journal of Sociology* 54 (1949), 298–301; and see Lichtenstein, "'The Man in the Middle': A Social History of Automobile Industry Foremen," in Lichtenstein and Stephen Meyer, *On the Line: Essays in the History of Autowork* (Urbana: University of Illinois Press, 1989), 153–89.

56. Charles P. Larrowe, "A Meteor on the Industrial Relations Horizon," *Labor History* 2 (Fall 1961), 259–87; Virginia A. Seitz, "Legal, Legislative and Managerial Responses to the Organization of Supervisory Employees in the 1940s." *American Journal of Legal History* 28 (January 1984), 218–35.

57. Lichtenstein, "'The Man in the Middle': A Social History of Automobile

Industry Foremen," 177–78; "Testimony of George Kennedy," *Hearings before the Committee on Education and Labor, House of Representatives*, 80th Congress, 1st Sess., "Amendments to the NLRA," February 20, 1947, 1074.

58. "The Foreman Abdicates," *Fortune* 32 (September 1945), 38.

59. As quoted in Seitz, "Legal, Legislative, and Managerial Responses to the Organization of Supervisory Employees in the 1940s," 240.

60. Peter DeChiara, "Rethinking the Managerial-Professional Exemption of the Fair Labor Standards Act," *The American University Law Review* 43 (Fall 1993), 139–89. The classic discussion of white-collar status and mentality is found in C. Wright Mills, *White Collar: The American Middle Classes* (New York: Oxford University Press, 1951), especially 289–323, where Mills examines and then rejects the possibility that a union white-collar breakthrough could transform American politics.

61. Howell Harris, *The Right to Manage*, 159–75; Lichtenstein, "The Man in the Middle," 167–90; Charles T. Joyce, "Union Busters and Front-Line Supervisors: Restricting and Regulating the Use of Supervisory Employees by Management Consultants during Union Representation Election Campaigns," *University of Pennsylvania Law Review* 135 (1987), 493.

62. Joyce, "Union Busters and Front-Line Supervisors," 453–93.

63. Alonzo Hamby, *Beyond the New Deal: Harry S. Truman and American Liberalism* (New York: Oxford University Press, 1973), 293–310; Robert Griffith, "Forging America's Postwar Order: Domestic Politics and Political Economy in the Age of Truman," in Michael Lacey, ed., *The Truman Presidency* (New York: Cambridge University Press, 1989), 72–78.

64. "UAW Press Release on GM Contract," May 25, 1948, file 5, box 72, UAW-Donald Montgomery Collection, Archives of Labor History, Wayne State University; and see also W. S. Woytinsky, *Labor and Management Look at Collective Bargaining: A Canvas of Leaders' Views* (New York: Twentieth Century Fund, 1949), 105–109.

65. Lichtenstein, *Walter Reuther*, 279–80. See also two excellent books that put the domestic political economy firmly within Cold War debates over the specter of a looming "garrison state": Michael Hogan, *A Cross of Iron: Harry S. Truman and the Origins of the National Security State, 1945–1954* (New York: Cambridge University Press, 1998), 265–314; and Aaron Friedberg, *In the Shadow of the Garrison State: America's Anti-Statism and Its Cold War Grand Strategy* (Princeton: Princeton University Press, 2000), 40–61, 98–115.

66. Daniel Bell, "The Treaty of Detroit," *Fortune* (July 1950), 53.

67. George Ruben, "Major Collective Bargaining Developments—A Quarter Century Review," reprinted from Bureau of Labor Statistics, *Current Wage Developments* (Washington: Government Printing Office, 1974), 46–47.

68. Katherine Van Wezel Stone, "The Post-War Paradigm in American Labor Law," *Yale Law Journal* 90 (June 1981), 1509–80; Tomlins, *The State and the Unions*, 258–81 passim. A longer discussion of "industrial pluralism" and its difficulties is found in chapter 4.

69. James Atleson, *Labor and the Wartime State: Labor Relations and Law during World War II* (Urbana: University of Illinois Press, 1998), 221–71 passim; and Tomlins, *The State and the Unions*, 317–28.

70. Staughton Lynd, "The Right to Engage in Concerted Activity after Union Recognition: A Study of Legislative History," *Indiana Law Journal* 50 (1975), 720–

56. Shulman quoted in Neil Chamberlain, ed., *Sourcebook on Labor* (New York: McGraw-Hill, 1958), 641. Some of these disruptive stewards were Socialists or Trotskyists, so Shulman drove home his argrument with a bit of cynical sociology: "Any enterprise—whether it be a privately owned plant, a governmentally operated unit, a consumer's cooperative, a social club, or a trade union—any enterprise in a capitalist or a socialist economy, requires persons with authority and responsibility to keep the enterprise running. . . . In any industrial plant, whatever may be the form of the poltical or economic organization in which it exists, problems are bound to arise. . . . These are not incidents peculiar to private entreprise. They are incidents of human organization in any form of society."

71. B. J. Widick, "A Shop Steward on the Frustrations of the Contract System, 1954," in Eileen Boris and Nelson Lichtenstein, *Major Problems in the History of American Workers* (Lexington: D.C. Heath and Co., 1991), 506.

72. Katherine Van Wezel Stone, "The Legacy of Industrial Pluralism: The Tension between Individual Employment Rights and the New Deal Collective Bargaining System," *University of Chicago Law Review* 59 (1992), 575–644.

73. Thomas Geoghegan, *Which Side Are You On? Trying to Be for Labor When It's Flat on Its Back* (New York: Farrar, Straus and Giroux, 1991), 164.

74. Klein, "Managing Security: The Business of American Social Policy," 409. And see also, Joel Rogers, "In the Shadow of the Law: Institutional Aspects of Postwar U.S. Union Decline," in Christopher Tomlins and Andrew King, eds. *Labor Law in America* (Baltimore: Johns Hopkins University Press, 1992), 283–302.

75. As quoted in Klein, "Managing Security," 410, 426; see also Jacoby, *Modern Manors: Welfare Capitalism since the New Deal*, especially his chapter on Kodak, 57–94.

76. Brown, *Race, Money, and the American Welfare State*, 135–64; Jennifer Klein, "The Business of Health Security: Employee Health Benefits, Commercial Insurers and the Reconstruction of Welfare Capitalism, 1945–1960," *International Labor and Working Class History* 58 (Fall 2000), 293–313. Brown argues that the political threat posed by Taft-Hartley pushed unionists and their Democratic Party allies toward a collectively bargained welfare state, as a new source of union legitimacy and institutional support.

77. Statistics taken from Klein, "Managing Security," 473.

78. David Stebenne, *Arthur Goldberg, New Deal Liberal* (New York: Oxford University Press, 1996), 120–53; Jack Stieber et al., eds, *U.S. Industrial Relations 1950–1980*: A Critical Assessment (Madison: Industrial Relations Research Association, 1981), 1–46; Robert Sobel, *IBM: Colossus in Transition* (New York: Times Books, 1981), 138–84.

79. Klein, "Managing Security," 506.

80. Minchin, *What Do We Need a Union For?* 119–68; Barry Bluestone and Bennett Harrison, *The Deindustrialization of America: Plant Closings, Community Abandonment, and the Dismantling of Basic Industry* (New York: Basic Books, 1982), 6–8, 25–27, 118–29.

81. See articles by Joel Rogers, "In the Shadow of the Law"; "Divide and Conquer: Further Reflections on the Distinctive Character of American Labor Laws," *Wisconsin Law Review* 1 (1990), 11–147; and "A Strategy for Labor," *Industrial Relations* 34 (July 1995), 367–81.

82. U.S. Department of Labor, *Handbook of Labor Statistics*, Bulletin 2217, Washington, D.C. 1984, 201–203; Harold Levinson, "Pattern Bargaining: A Case Study of the Automobile Workers," *Quarterly Journal of Economics* (Spring 1959), 299.

83. Thomas Byrne Edsall with Mary D. Edsall, *Chain Reaction: The Impact of Race, Rights, and Taxes on American Politics* (New York: W. W. Norton, 1991), 116–53; Beth Stevens, "Blurring the Boundaries: How the Federal Government Has Influenced Welfare Benefits in the Private Sector," *The Politics of Social Policy in the United States*, 123–48.

84. Sanford Jacoby, "Current Prospects for Employee Representation in the U.S.: Old Wine in New Bottles?" *Journal of Labor Research* 16, (Summer 1995); David Brody, "The Breakdown of Labor's Social Contract," *Dissent* (Winter 1992); Sanford Jacoby and Anil Verma, "Enterprise Unions in the United States," *Industrial Relations* 31 (Winter 1992), 137–58. To understand how the works-council system functions, consider the case of Ford in Germany. The corporation has no recognition agreement with IG Metall, the big metal union. Instead Ford deals directly with its works council on plant problems and only indirectly with IG Metall on pay matters via the employers federation of which it is a leading member. The works council members all happen to be IG Metall members, but there is nevertheless a creative tension between the council, the national union, and the company.

85. Stebenne, *Arthur Goldberg*, 316–51; Brody, *In Labor's Cause: Main Themes on the History of the American Worker* (New York: Oxford University Press, 1993), 221–45; Glenn Perusek and Kent Worcester, *Trade Union Politics: American Unions and Economic Change, 1960s–1990s* (New York: Humanities Press, 1995), 3–56; James D. Rose, "The Struggle over Management Rights at U.S. Steel, 1946–1960: A Reassessment of Section 2-B of the Collective-Bargaining Contract," *Business History Review* (Autumn 1998), 446–77.

86. W. W. Rostow, *The Diffusion of Power* (New York: MacMillian, 1972), 138–43; Stebenne, *Arthur Goldberg*, 279–315; James Cochrane, "The Johnson Administration: Moral Suasion Goes to War," in Crauford Goodwin, ed., *Exhortation and Controls: The Search for a Wage-Price Policy, 1945–1971* (Washington: The Brookings Institution, 1975), 199–214.

87. In his recent *Fat and Mean*, the late David Gordon argues that from the early postwar years onward managerial ranks and salary costs swelled rapidly, not because of any turn toward an economy of "symbolic analysts"—the Robert Reich description—but because managers needed a thick layer of supervision to maintain their prerogatives and because the proliferation of the managerial strata was one effective way to push income distribution in a more inequitable direction. Historian David Stebenne arrives at similar conclusions using archival, not econometric, data. See Stebenne, *Arthur Goldberg*, 188–232; and Gordon, *Fat and Mean*, 33–60.

88. Julius Rezler, *Automation and Industrial Labor* (New York: Random House, 1969), 64–79, 197–212; Charles P. Larrowe, *Harry Bridges: the Rise and Fall of Radical Labor in the United States* (New York: Lawrence Hill, 1972), 345–58.

89. Robert Zieger, "George Meany: Labor's Organization Man," in Melvyn Dubofsky and Warren Van Tine, *Labor Leaders in America* (Urbana: University of Illinois Press, 1987), 324–49; John Berry, "The Pressure Builds for Shorter Workweeks," *AFL-CIO News* (November 1961).

90. Margaret Weir, *Politics and Jobs: the Boundaries of Employment Policy in the*

United States (Princeton: Princeton University Press, 1992), 62–83; Gary Mucciaroni, *The Political Failure of Employment Policy*, 1945–82 (Pittsburgh: University of Pittsburgh Press, 1990); Jonas Pontusson, "Labor, Corporatism, and Industrial Policy: The Swedish Case in Comparative Perspective," *Comparative Politics* 6 (January 1991); Gosta Esping-Anderson, *Politics Against Markets: The Social Democratic Road to Power* (Princeton: Princeton University Press, 1985).

91. Benjamin Hunnicutt, *Work without End: Abandoning Shorter Hours for the Right to Work* (Philadelphia: Temple University Press, 1988), 320–40; Juliet Schor, *The Overworked American: The Unexpected Decline of Leisure* (New York: Basic Books, 1991), 122–38; Reuther quoted in Lichtenstein, *Walter Reuther*, 291.

92. Boyle, *The UAW and the Heyday of American Liberalism*, 1945–1968, 132–60; Steven Amberg, *Labor and the Postwar Political Economy* (Philadelphia: Temple University Press, 1992), 228–74.

93. Stebenne, *Arthur Goldberg*, 291–300; Kennedy quoted in Bernstein, *Promises Kept: John F. Kennedy's New Frontier* (New York: Oxford University Press, 1991), 143. Later Kennedy said he had meant to say steel executives, not "all businessmen."

94. Irving Bernstein, *Promises Kept: John F. Kennedy's New Frontier*, (New York: Oxford University Press, 1991), 145–46; and see Grant McConnell, *Steel and the Presidency* (New York: Norton, 1963).

95. Metzgar, *Striking Steel: Solidarity Remembered*, 207. Metzgar offers an insightful guide to the way in which the post-1950 labor movement and its accomplishments have been systematically devalued by liberals and the left in the postwar years. See, especially, the chapter "The Contest for Official Memory," 202–29.

96. Jacoby, *Modern Manors*, 236–62.

97. Exceptions prove the rule. See Walter Uphoff, *Kohler on Strike: Thirty Years of Conflict* (Boston: Beacon Press, 1966).

98. Lipsitz, *A Rainbow at Midnight*, 160; Plotke, *Building a Democratic Political Order*, 233–36.

99. Clark Kerr, *Industrialism and Industrial Man: The Problem of Labor and Management in Economic Growth* (Cambridge: Harvard University Press, 1960); Reed Larson, *Stranglehold: How Union Bosses Have Hijacked Our Government* (Ottowa, Ill.: Jameson Books, 1999), 101–107; Gilbert Gall, "Forming Electoral Coalitions; Lessons from Right-to-Work Campaigns" (paper in author's possession).

100. "Testimony of Ira Mosher," hearings before the Committee on Education and Labor, House of Representatives, 80th Congress, 1st Sess., *Amendments to the NLRA* (March 7, 1947), 2685.

101. Donald Richberg, "How Shall We Deal with Labor Union Monopolies?" *Vital Speeches of the Day* 22 (December 1, 1955), 125.

102. Meg Jacobs, "The American Middle-Classes and the Fear of Inflation in the 1950s" (paper presented at Harvard Business School, November 1999).

103. Ibid.; Rose, "The Struggle over Management Rights at U.S. Steel, 1946–1960," 446–77; and see Metzgar, *Striking Steel*, 94–117.

104. Barry Goldwater, *The Conscience of a Conservative* (Shepherdsville, Ky.: Victor Publishing Co., 1960), 56; Lichtenstein, *Walter Reuther*, 347; Robert Alan Goldberg, *Barry Goldwater* (New Haven: Yale University Press, 1995), 67–76; Gilbert Gall, *The Politics of Right to Work: The Labor Federations As Special Interests, 1943–1979* (New York: Greenwood Press, 1988), 93–128. And see in particular Rick Perl-

stein, *Before the Storm: Barry Goldwater and the Unmaking of the American Consensus* (New York: Hill and Wang, 2001), 3–67.

CHAPTER 4

Erosion of the Union Idea

1. Paul Jacobs, "Old Before Its Time: Collective Bargaining at Twenty-eight," in Jacobs, *The State of the Unions* (New York: Atheneum, 1963), 257–93; Richard Lester, *As Unions Mature: An Analysis of the Evolution of American Unionism* (Princeton: Princeton University Press, 1958), 29–34.

2. Joel Rogers, "Divide and Conquer: Further 'Reflections on the Distinctive Character of American Labor Laws,'" *Wisconsin Law Review* 1 (1990), 57–59.

3. Seymour Martin Lipset, *The First New Nation: The United States in Historical and Comparative Perspective* (New York: W. W. Norton, 1979), 191–96.

4. Kim Moody, *An Injury to All: The Decline of American Unionism* (New York: Verso, 1988), 41–69, 147–64; John Hutchinson, *The Imperfect Union: A History of Corruption in American Trade Unions* (New York: Dutton, 1970). On the American labor scene, rotation in office has been most often characteristic of those unions representing high-prestige, well-paid trades and occupations: film and theater, airlines (pilots, not mechanics), professional sports, and the university professorate.

5. Solomon Barkin, *The Decline of the Labor Movement* (Santa Barbara: Fund for the Republic, 1961), 55.

6. Aaron Brenner, "Rank-and-File Teamster Movements in Comparative Perspective," in Glenn Perusek and Kent Worcester, eds., *Trade Union Politics: American Unions and Economic Change, 1960s–1990s* (Atlantic Highlands: Humanities Press, 1995), 111–39.

7. Teamster scholarship tilts toward the sensational. Two studies that examine Hoffa as a union strategist are Ralph and Estelle James, *Hoffa and the Teamsters: A Study of Union Power* (Princeton: Van Nostrand, 1965); and Arthur Sloane, *Hoffa* (Cambridge: MIT Press, 1991).

8. Galenson quoted in Brenner, "Rank and File Teamster Movements," 119; and see also Samuel Friedman, *Teamster Rank and File: Power, Bureaucracy, and Rebellion at Work in a Union* (New York: Columbia University Press, 1982), 116–18; and Dan Moldea, *The Hoffa Wars: Teamster Rebels, Politicians, and the Mob* (New York: Paddington Press, 1978).

9. Frederick Harbison, "The UAW-General Motors Agreement of 1950," *Journal of Political Economy* 58 (October 1950), 408; and see Lichtenstein, "UAW Bargaining Strategy and Shop-Floor Conflict, 1946–1970," *Industrial Relations* 24 (Fall 1985), 369–79.

10. Arthur Kornhauser, *When Labor Votes: A Study of the Auto Workers* (New York: University Books, 1956), 19; Samuel Lubell, *The Future of American Politics* (Garden City: Doubleday, 1956), 229.

11. Key quoted in Joel Rogers, "Divide and Conquer," 2.

12. Robert Zieger, "George Meany: Labor's Organization Man," in *Labor Leaders in America*, Melvyn Dubofsky and Warren Van Tine, eds. (Urbana: University of Illi-

nois Press, 1987), 328–29; Joseph Goulden, *Meany: The Unchallenged Strong Man of American Labor* (New York: Atheneum, 1972), 271–83,

13. Henry Fleisher, interview with Don Kennedy, Washington, D.C. (May 4, 1979), 21–28, AFL-CIO Oral History Project, George Meany Memorial Archives, Silver Spring, Md.

14. As quoted in Reuel Schiller, "From Group Rights to Individual Liberties: Post-War Labor Law, Liberalism, and the Waning of Union Strength," *Berkeley Journal of Employment and Labor Law* 20 (1999), 6; this chapter relies heavily on Schiller's understanding of the relationship between postwar pluralism and the labor law.

15. Robert Dublin, "Constructive Aspects of Industrial Conflict"; and Arthur Ross, "Conclusion"; both in Arthur Kornhauser, Robert Dublin, Arthur Ross, eds., *Industrial Conflict* (New York: McGraw-Hill, 1954), 44, 532.

16. Michael Kazin, "Introduction: Daniel Bell and the Agony and Romance of the American Left," in Daniel Bell, *Marxian Socialism in the United States* (Ithaca: Cornell University Press, 1995), ix–xxxvii; Robert Dahl, "Workers' Control of Industry and the British Labor Party," *American Political Science Review* 41 (October 1947), 875–900.

17. Robert Booth Fowler, *Believing Skeptics: American Political Intellectuals, 1945–1964* (Westport: Greenwood Press, 1978), 176–86; Lipset quoted in Richard Pells, *The Liberal Mind in a Conservative Age: American Intellectuals in the 1940s and 1950s* (New York: Harper and Row, 1985), 141.

18. Peter Drucker, *The Practice of Management* (New York: Harper and Brothers, 1954), 3, 381–82; Drucker, *The Concept of the Corporation* (New York: John Day Company, 1946, 1972), 8, 12; Stephen Waring, *Taylorism Transformed: Scientific Management Theory since 1945* (Chapel Hill: University of North Carolina Press, 1991), 79–88. Of course, the executives and spokesmen for big business did not share Drucker's sanguine narrative. Alfred Sloan and other GM executives repudiated Drucker's study as "hostile" and "anti-business." See Drucker's "Epilogue," in the 1972 reprint of *The Concept of the Corporation*, 291–310.

19. Arthur Schlesinger, Jr., *The Vital Center* (Boston: Houghton Mifflin, 1949), 173.

20. Howard Brick, "Talcott Parson's 'Shift Away from Economics,' 1937–1946," *Journal of American History* 87 (September 2000), 490–515.

21. Schlesinger, Jr., *The Vital Center*, 154, 174.

22. Jeffery Halprin, "Getting Back to Work: The Revaluation of Work in American Literature and Social Theory, 1950–1985," (Ph.D. diss., Boston University, 1987), 42–89, 114–67 passim, Dublin quoted at 57; Clark Kerr, "The Prospect for Wages and Hours in 1975," (1958) in Kerr, *Labor and Management in Industrial Society* (Garden City: Doubleday, 1964), 203–31.

23. Earl Latham, "The Group Basis of Politics: Notes for a Theory," *The American Political Science Review* 46 (June 1952), 376–97; David Truman, "The American System in Crisis," *Political Science Quarterly* 74 (December 1959), 488.

24. As quoted in Schiller, "From Group Rights to Individual Liberties," 11. These immediate postwar years were also the moment at which the cult of Alexis de Tocqueville first arose. His *Democracy in America*, which celebrated a diverse world of voluntary associations, was republished at the end of World War II. Pells, *Liberal Mind in a Conservative Age*, 149.

25. Daniel Bell, "Taft-Hartley, Five Years Later," *Fortune* (July 1952), 69; and see Daniel Bell, *The End of Ideology: On the Exhaustion of Political Ideas in the Fifties* (Glencoe: The Free Press, 1960), 208, 213. The title of Bell's book is extraordinarily ironic. Socialist ideas were indeed exhausted, but on the Right, an ideological offensive of the first magnitude was in birth. Had Bell noted the remarkable ideological fervor that accompanied the right-to-work campaigns of the 1958 campaign season, as well as the "movement" that coalesced around Barry Goldwater, he might have recast his notion of an "end of ideology."

26. Reinhold Niebuhr, "'End of an Era' for Organized Labor," *New Leader*, (January 4, 1960), 18.

27. Will Herberg, "Bureaucracy and Democracy in Labor Unions," *Antioch Review* 3 (1943), 405; Kerr, "Unions and Union Leaders of Their Own Choosing," (1958), reprinted in Kerr, *Labor and Management in Industrial Society*, 34. In 1955 Herberg would publish the pluralist classic *Protestant, Catholic, Jew*, which devalued the theological and cultural divide between the major denominations.

28. Kerr, *Labor and Management in Industrial Society*, 27.

29. Seymour Martin Lipset, *Political Man: The Social Basis of Politics* (Garden City: Doubleday, 1960), 389, 431, 433. It is a wonder, therefore, that among these ex-radicals, the two most respected guides to the nation's ideological/political life were James Madison, whose *Federalist Paper No. 10* warned of an unfettered majoritarianism, and Robert Michels, the German sociologist who posited an "iron law of oligarchy" even within the ostensibly democratic unions, parties, and voluntary organizations of the industrial West. "Who says organization says oligarchy," he wrote in his 1911 book, *Political Parties: A Sociological Study of the Oligarchical Tendencies of Modern Democracy* (New York: Collier Books, 1962). And see Seymour Martin Lipset, Martin Trow, James Coleman, *Union Democracy: The Internal Politics of the International Typographical Union* (Garden City: Doubleday and Company, 1956), 2.

30. Osar Ornati, "Union Discipline, Minority Rights, and Public Policy," *Labor Law Journal* 5 (July 1954), 473–77; "The Text of General Eisenhower's Speech at A.F.L. Convention," *New York Times* (September 18, 1952), 12.

31. As quoted in Stebenne, *Arthur Goldberg*, 169.

32. Louis Stark, "Democracy—and Responsibility—in Unions," *New York Times Magazine* (May 25, 1947), 58.

33. As quoted in Dubofsky, *The State and Labor in Modern America*, 213. This was the famous *Steelworkers Trilogy* ruling of 1960.

34. Staughton Lynd, "Government without Rights: The Labor Law Vision of Archibald Cox," *Industrial Relations Law Journal* 4, 483–95; Ronald Schatz, "From Commons to Dunlop: Rethinking the Field and Theory of Industrial Relations," in Lichtenstein and Harris, *Industrial Democracy in America*, 87–112.

35. As quoted in Schiller, "From Group Rights to Individual Liberties," 48.

36. David J. Sousa, "'No Balance in the Equities': Union Power in the Making and Unmaking of the Campaign Finance Regime," *Studies in American Political Development* 13 (Fall 1999), 374–401.

37. Schiller, "From Group Rights to Individual Liberties," 18–29; and see Clyde Summers, "Individual Rights in Collective Agreements—A Preliminary Analysis," *New York University Twelfth Annual Conference on Labor* (1959).

38. George Strauss and Don Willner, "Government Regulation of Local Union Democracy," *Labor Law Journal* 4 (August 1953), 533.

39. Fraser, *Sidney Hillman*, 332.

40. Michael Denning, *The Cultural Front: The Laboring of American Culture in the Twentieth Century* (London: Verso, 1996), xiii–xx, 3–50; Dwight Macdonald, "The World's Biggest Union: How Are the Auto Workers Facing the Future?" *Common Sense* (November 1943), 411.

41. C. Wright Mills, *The New Men of Power: America's Labor Leaders* (New York: Harcourt, Brace and Co., 1948), 6–7.

42. C. Wright Mills, *White Collar: The American Middle Classes* (New York: Oxford University Press, 1951), 318.

43. Ibid., 350–54.

44. Gregory D. Sumner, *Dwight Macdonald and the Politics Circle* (Ithaca: Cornell University Press, 1996), 115; see also Michael Wreszin, *A Rebel in Defense of Tradition* (New York: Basic Books, 1994), 160–90.

45. Dwight Macdonald, *The Responsibility of Peoples (And Other Essays in Political Criticism)* (Westport: Greenwood Press, 1957), 45; Sumner, *Dwight Macdonald*, 85–109.

47. Clancy Sigal, *Going Away: A Report, a Memoir* (New York: Viking, 1961); David Milton, *The Politics of U.S. Labor: From the Great Depression to the New Deal* (New York: Monthly Review Press, 1982), 162. A recent heir to this perspective is Michael Goldfield, *The Politics of Color: Race and the Mainsprings of American Politics* (New York: New Press, 1997), 188–261.

47. Harvey Swados, "The Myth of the Happy Worker," reprinted in Swados, *On the Line* (Urbana: University of Illinois Press, 1990), 241–42.

48. Ibid., 243.

49. Michael Harrington, *The Other America: Poverty in the United States* (New York: Macmillian, 1962), 6; Maurice Isserman, *The Other American: The Life of Michael Harrington* (New York: Public Affairs Press, 2000), 195–98.

50. Paul Jacobs, *The State of the Unions* (New York: Atheneum, 1963), 257–93; B. J. Widick, *Labor Today: The Triumphs and Failures of Unionism in the United States* (Boston: Houghton Mifflin, 1964); Port Huron Statement quoted in James Miller, *"Democracy Is in the Streets": From Port Huron to the Siege of Chicago* (New York: Simon and Schuster, 1987), 370.

51. Harvey Swados, "The UAW—Over the Top or Over the Hill?" *Dissent* (Fall 1963), 321–43.

52. Schatz, "From Commons to Dunlop," 105–12; Bruce E. Kaufman, *The Origins and Evolution of the Field of Industrial Relations in the United States* (Ithaca: ILR Press, 1993), 103–55. In December 1968 when Clark Kerr delivered a talk at the Chicago meeting of the Industrial Relations Research Association, his audience was naturally interested in how this IR scholar/practitioner and former president of the University of California proposed to solve the crisis generated by the recent wave of student radicalism. Kerr proposed to calm the campus by deploying several of the well-worn mechanisms of the industrial pluralist trade: grievance procedures, recognition of student groups and interests; power sharing on various committees and at the Board of Trustee level, etc. He compared the year 1968 with other eras of violence and

conflict, including 1886 and 1919, and concluded, "It is no more possible to produce B.A.'s with billy clubs than coal with bayonets." But Kerr was wrong, as Ronald Reagan and Richard Nixon would demonstrate. Clark Kerr, "Industrial Relations and University Relations," Proceedings of the Industrial Relations Research Association (December 29–30, 1968), 15–25.

53. Thaddeus Russell, "Cleaning the House of Labor: The McClellan Committee and the AFL-CIO, 1956–1959" (Master's thesis, Columbia University, 1992).

54. A remarkably good account of the McClellan Committee investigation is found in Arthur Schlesinger, Jr., *Robert F. Kennedy and His Times* (Boston: Houghton Mifflin, 1978), 120–90; for studies of union corruption see Burton Hall, ed. *Autocracy and Insurgency in Organized Labor* (New Brunswick: Transaction Books, 1972); Hutcheson, *The Imperfect Union*, especially 142–45; and see the relevant essays in Daniel Bell's *End of Ideology* collection.

55. As quoted in Russell, "Cleaning the House of Labor," 17.

56. Barry Goldwater, *The Conscience of a Conservative* (Shepherdsville, Ky.: Victor Publishing, 1960), 45.

57. I discuss this political and ideological shift in *Walter Reuther*, 346–50; see also David Reinhard, *The Republican Right since 1945* (Lexington: University Press of Kentucky, 1983), 138–45; and Mike Davis, *Prisoners of the American Dream* (London: Verso, 1986), 166–70.

58. Russell, "Cleaning the House of Labor," 4; and see generally, Jean-Claude Andre, "Congress, Business, and the Postwar Decline of Labor: Rethinking the McClellan Committee, Its Origins, and Its Consequences," (Master's Thesis, University of Virginia, 2000); and Anthony Baltakis, "Agendas of Investigation: The McClellan Committee, 1957–1958," (Ph.D. diss., University of Akron, 1997.)

59. Dubofsky, *The State and Labor in Modern America*, 220–221. Northern Democrats had also won a huge victory in the 1958 elections, but their liberalism was far less attuned to labor issues than in earlier years. Aside from beating back "right-to-work" legislation, the unions reaped few rewards from the election of so many "friends" to Congress.

60. Gall, *The Politics of Right to Work*, 92–128; Fones-Wolf, *Selling Free Enterprise*, 257–84; Reed Larson, "Is Monopoly in the American Tradition?" *Vital Speeches of the Day* 39 (June 15, 1973), 527–28.

61. Sumner Slichter, "Are We Becoming a 'Laboristic' State?" *New York Times Magazine* (May 16, 1948), 11, 61–66; Slichter, "New Goals for the Unions," *Atlantic Monthly* (December 1958), 54.

62. Paul Jacobs, "Union Democracy and the Public Good," *Commentary* (January 1958), 74

63. Paul Jacobs, "Old before Its Time: Collective Bargaining at Twenty-eight," in Jacobs, *The State of the Unions* (New York: Atheneum, 1963), 257–93.

64. A. H. Raskin, "The Moral Issue That Confronts Labor," *New York Times Magazine* (March 31, 1957), 17–23; "New Issue: Labor As Big Business," *New York Times Magazine* (February 22, 1959), 9, 69–72; "Labor's Time of Troubles: The Failure of Bread-and-Butter Unionism," *Commentary* (August 1959), 93–99; "The Obsolescent Unions," *Commentary* (July 1963), 18.

65. Herbert Harris, "Why Labor Lost the Intellectuals," *Harper's Weekly* (June 1964), 79.

66. Daniel Bell, "The Subversion of Collective Bargaining," *Commentary* (March 1960), 185, 195.

67. John Kenneth Galbraith, *American Capitalism: The Theory of Countervailing Power* (Boston: Houghton Mifflin, 1952), 114.

68. John Kenneth Galbraith, *The New Industrial State* (Boston: Houghton Mifflin, 1967), 263–64, 274, 280–81.

69. "Is Collective Bargaining Dead?" FOCUS, Georgetown University, April 18, 1967 in *News From the AFL-CIO* (transcript), 2–4, AFL-CIO Press Releases, George Meany Archives, Silver Spring, MD.

70. Peter Levy, *The New Left and Labor in the 1960s* (Urbana: University of Illinois Press, 1994), 108–21. Mills was by now uncompromising in his rejection of the "labor metaphysic." In *The Marxists*, his last book, Mills declared, "wage workers in advanced capitalism have rarely become a 'proletariat vanguard,' they have not become the agency of any revolutionary change of epoch." Mills, *The Marxists* (New York: Delta Books, 1963), 128. Ironically, it was the neoconservative right, not the New Left, that made the most effective use of such a reordering of the class hierarchy. The idea that American culture, academia, and journalism is ruled by a "new class" of left knowledge workers traces its lineage back to this same mid-1960s disillusionment with the traditional proletariat. The critique was made by neoconservative ex-socialists who looked to the "new class" theories of Milovan Djilas, and to New Left efforts to account for the politics of students, professionals, and other intellectual workers. Isserman, *Michael Harrington*, 275–78; Barbara and John Ehrenreich, "The New Left: A Case Study in Professional-Managerial Class Radicalism," *Radical America* (May–June 1977), 7–24.

71. Levy, *The New Left and Labor*, 147–66.

72. Stanley Aronowitz "Trade Unionism in America" *Liberation* (December 1971), 22–27.

73. Alice and Staughton Lynd, *Rank and File: Personal Histories by Working-Class Organizers* (Boston: Beacon, 1973), 3–4.

74. Jeremy Brecher, *Strike!* (New York: Fawcett, 1972), 10. Even Burton Hall, the veteran union democracy watchdog, who should have understood something of the dialectical relationship between union organization and rank-and-file insurgency, edited a 1972 collection entitled *Autocracy and Insurgency in Organized Labor*. His main theme was that which Sylvia Kopaid first described in 1924 as "this amazing separation that exists between union leaders and union rank and file," an actual "class struggle" between leaders and those they presume to lead. See Burton Hall, ed. *Autocracy and Insurgency in Organized Labor* (New York: New Politics, 1972), 2.

75. Davis, *Prisoners of the American Dream*, 153.

76. Ruth O'Brien, "Duality and Division: The Development of American Labour Policy from the Wagner Act to the Civil Rights Act," *International Contributions to Labour Studies* 4 (1994), 21–51.

77. Katherine Van Wezel Stone, "The Legacy of Industrial Pluralism: The Tension between Individual Employment Rights and the New Deal Collective Bargaining System," *The University of Chicago Law Review* 59 (1992), 575–644.

78. Ibid., 624–30. This discrepancy is noted and bemoaned by some conservatives. See the chapter "Why Business Will Miss Unions," in Olson, *The Excuse Factory*, 234–41.

79. Gilbert Gall, "'Rights Which Have Meaning': Reconceiving Labor Liberty in the 1940s." *Labor History* 39 (August 1998), 273–89.

80. As quoted in Schiller, "Policy Ideals and Judicial Action," 328–30.

81. David Abraham, "Individual Autonomy and Collective Empowerment in Labor Law: Union Membership Resignations and Strikebreaking in the New Economy," *New York University Law Review* 63 (December 1988), 1281, 1314, 1316–23; see also Kevin C. Marcoux, "COMMENT: Section 8(b)(1)(A) from *Allis-Chalmers* to *Pattern Makers' League*: A Case Study in Judicial Legislation," *California Law Review* 74 (1986), 1442–43.

82. *Emporium Capwell Co. vs. Western Addition Community Org.*, 420 U.S. 50 (1975), 56, 68–70.

83. Staughton Lynd, "The Right to Engage in Concerted Activity after Union Recognition: A Study of Legislative History," *Indiana Law Journal* 50 (1974–75), 720, 752; E-mail, Reuel Schiller to Lichtenstein (December 5, 2000); E-mail, David Abraham to Lichtenstein (December 22, 2000).

84. Stone, "The Post-War Paradigm in American Labor Law," 1533–34; Tomlins, *The State and the Unions*, 314–28; Lynd, "The Right to Engage in Concerted Activity after Union Recognition: A Study of Legislative History," 720–56.

85. Atleson, *Values and Assumptions in American Labor Law*, 124–30, 130–32; Paul C. Weiler, *Governing the Workplace: The Future of Labor and Employment Law* (Cambridge: Harvard University Press, 1990), 1–48 passim.

86. Karl E. Klare, "The Bitter and the Sweet: Reflections on the Supreme Court's *Yeshiva* Decision," *Socialist Review* 99 (September–October 1983); James P. Begin and Barbara A. Lee, "NLRA Exclusion Criteria and Professional Work," *Industrial Relations* 26 (Winter 1987) 83–95; George Feldman, "Workplace Power and Collective Activity: The Supervisory and Managerial Exclusions in Labor Law," *Arizona Law Review* 37 (Summer 1995), 525–62.

87. Schiller, "Policy Ideas and Judicial Action," 179.

CHAPTER 5

Rights Consciousness in the Workplace

1. Steve Watkins, "Racism Du Jour at Shoney's,' *The Nation* 257 (October 18, 1993), 424–26; "Shoney's Co-Founder Quits Board, Sells Stock after Multimillion Bias Decision," *Jet* 83 (March 29, 1993), 4; Jeff Seinstein, "Shoney's 'Workforce 2000' Courts Minority Employees," *Restaurants and Institutions* 101 (March 6, 1991), 26.

2. Kate Bronfenbrenner, "We'll Close! Plant Closings, Plant-Closing Threats, Union Organizing and NAFTA," *Multinational Monitor* 18 (March 1997), 10–12.

3. Bill Mesler, "Hotline to the White House: Sprint, Blatantly Anti-Union, Has Drawn N.L.R.B. Censure but Bill Clinton's Praise," *The Nation* 264 (June 30, 1997), 20–24; Kim Phillips-Fein, "A More Perfect Union Buster," *Mother Jones* 23 (September–October 1998), 62–66.

4. Richard Kahlenberg, "Unionization As a Civil Right," *American Prospect* (September 11, 2000), 13. In 1997 the median jury award in employment bias and sexual harassment cases was $250,000.

5. Ronald Fraser, ed., *1968: A Student Generation in Revolt* (New York: Pantheon Books, 1988), 181–84, 350–60; David Caute, *The Year of the Barricades: A Journey through 1968* (New York: Harper and Row, 1988), 71–114, 211–58; Charles Sabel, *Work and Politics: The Division of Labor in Industry* (New York: Cambridge University Press, 1982), 145–67.

6. Paul Blumberg, *Inequality in an Age of Decline* (New York: Oxford University Press, 1980), 65–87; and see also C. Wright Mills, *White Collar: The American Middle Classes* (New York: Oxford University Press, 1951), 239–86 for an early, union-conscious reading of "status" anxiety among the lower middle class; as well as Mark McColloch, *White-Collar Workers in Transition: The Boom Years, 1940–1970* (Westport: Greenwood Press, 1983).

7. Stanley Aronowitz, *From the Ashes of the Old: American Labor and America's Future* (Boston: Houghton Mifflin Company, 1998), 140; Joshua Freeman, *Working-Class New York: Life and Labor since World War II* (New York: The New Press, 2000), 179–200.

8. Aronowitz, *From the Ashes of the Old*, 71; Leon Fink and Brian Greenberg, *Upheaval in the Quiet Zone: A History of Hospital Workers Union, Local 1199* (Urbana: University of Illinois Press, 1989), 91–111; Marjorie Murphy, *Blackboard Unions: The AFT and the NEA, 1900–1980* (Ithaca: Cornell University Press, 1990), 196–226 passim; Freeman, *Working-Class New York*, 201–214.

9. Irving Bernstein, *Promises Kept: John F. Kennedy's New Frontier* (New York: Oxford University Press, 1991), 215–16.

10. Aronowitz, *From the Ashes of the Old*, 78–79.

11. Kevin Boyle, *The UAW and the Heyday of American Liberalism* (Ithaca: Cornell University Press, 1995), 206–56. Excellent statistical data is found in Leo Troy, "The Rise and Fall of American Trade Unions: The Labor Movement from FDR to RR," in Seymour Martin Lipset, ed., *Unions in Transition: Entering the Second Century* (San Francisco: ICS Press, 1986), 75–93. For a contrary view, see Taylor Dark, *The Unions and the Democrats: An Enduring Alliance* (Ithaca: Cornell University Press, 1999), 1–31, 47–98. Dark argues that the AFL-CIO actually maintained its political power even during an era when the size of the union movement declined. To make this case Dark redefines the meaning of effective political influence. His argument rests heavily on a rather circumscribed political universe, that of Congressional Democrats, White House aides, and the union officials who seek to influence their programs and policies.

12. Stebenne, *Arthur Goldberg*, 253–304; Bernstein, *Promises Kept*, 133–57.

13. Hobart Rowen, *Self-Inflicted Wounds: From LBJ's Guns and Butter to Reagan's Voodoo Economics* (New York: Random House, 1994), 49–84; Allen Matusow, *Nixon's Economy: Booms, Busts, Dollars, and Votes* (Lawrence: University of Kansas, 1998), 84–116.

14. The literature is extensive and frequently polemical. See William Gould, *Black Workers in White Unions: Job Discrimination in the United States* (Ithaca: Cornell University Press, 1977), an excellent survey by a former UAW attorney who later served as Clinton's first chairman of the NLRB. Kevin Boyle, "'There Are No Union Sorrows That the Union Can't Heal': The Struggle for Racial Equality in the United Automobile Workers, 1940–1960," *Labor History* 35 (1995), 5–23; Sugrue, *Origins of the Urban Crisis*, 91–123; Timothy Minchin, *Hiring the Black Worker: The Racial Integration of the Southern Textile Industry, 1960–1980* (Chapel Hill: University of

North Carolina Press, 1999), 234–41; Alan Draper, *Conflict of Interests: Organized Labor and the Civil Rights Movement in the South, 1954–1968* (Ithaca: ILR Press, 1994); Herbert Hill, "Black Workers, Organized Labor, and Title VII of the 1964 Civil Rights Act: Legislative History and Litigation Record," in Herbert Hill and James E. Jones, Jr., *Race in America: The Struggle for Equality* (Madison: University of Wisconsin Press, 1993), 263–341; Lichtenstein, *Walter Reuther*, 370–95.

15. As quoted in Lichtenstein, *Walter Reuther*, 334.

16. Dark, *The Unions and the Democrats*, 76–98; for an eye-popping account of the growing rigidity in AFL-CIO foreign policy, see Ted Morgan, *A Covert Life: Jay Lovestone, Communist, Anti-Communist, and Spymaster* (New York: Random House, 1999), 326–52; and Maurice Isserman, *The Other American: The Life of Michael Harrington* (New York: Public Affairs, 2000), 256–302, which demonstrates the extent to which militant hostility to the New Left and retrograde Stalinophobia infected the highest circles of the AFL-CIO under George Meany.

17. This paragraph is taken largely from chapter 14, "An American Social Democracy," in Lichtenstein, *Walter Reuther*, 299–326.

18. I discuss these developments in *Walter Reuther*, but accounts can also be found in Boyle, *Heyday of American Liberalism*, 161–232 passim; and Todd Gitlin, *The Sixties: Years of Hope, Days of Rage* (New York: Bantam Books, 1987), 151–62.

19. Norman Miller, "Auto Union Ferment," *Wall Street Journal* (September 24, 1964); Lichtenstein, *Walter Reuther*, 398–99.

20. This point is very well made in Metzgar, *Striking Steel*, 1–16.

21. Lichtenstein, *Walter Reuther*, 399–401.

22. Gilbert Gall, *The Politics of Right to Work: The Labor Federations As Special Interests, 1943–1979* (Westport: Greenwood Press, 1988), 172–83.

23. Gary Gerstle, "The Protean Character of American Liberalism," *American Historical Review* 99 (October 1994), 1070; Alan Brinkley, *The End of Reform* (New York: Knopf, 1995), 201–64.

24. An excellent discussion of this sea change is found in Judith Stein, *Running Steel, Running America: Race, Economic Policy, and the Decline of Liberalism* (Chapel Hill: University of North Carolina Press, 1998), 69–88; see also, Paula F. Pfeffer, *A. Philip Randolph, Pioneer of the Civil Rights Movement* (Baton Rouge: Louisiana State University Press, 1990), 190–95; and Hugh Davis Graham, *The Civil Rights Era: Origins and Development of National Policy* (New York: Oxford University Press, 1990), 139–41. For a set of polemics on the extent to which organized labor supported Title VII, see Herbert Hill, "Meany, Reuther and the 1964 Civil Rights Act," *New Politics* 7 (Summer 1998), 82–107; Nelson Lichtenstein, "Walter Reuther in Black and White: A Rejoinder to Herbert Hill;" and Herbert Hill, "Lichtenstein's Fictions Revisited: Race and the New Labor History," both in *New Politics* 7 (Winter 1999), 133–63.

25. Gary Mucciaroni, *The Political Failure of Employment Policy, 1945–1982* (Pittsburgh: University of Pittsburgh Press, 1990), 224–54; Walter Heller, *New Dimensions of Political Economy* (Cambridge: Harvard University Press, 1966), 42–47; Bernstein, *Promises Kept*, 118–59 passim.

26. James Patterson, *America's Struggle against Poverty, 1900–1994* (Cambridge: Harvard University Press, 1994), 133–54 passim; Gary Burtless, "Public Spending on the Poor: Historical Trends and Economic Limits," and Hugh Heclo, "Poverty Politics," both in Sheldon Danziger, Gary Sandefur, Daniel Weinberg, eds., *Confronting*

Poverty: Prescriptions for Change (Cambridge: Harvard University Press, 1994), 51–84, 396–437; Community Action Program official Charles Morris quoted in his, *A Time of Passion, America 1960–1980* (New York: Harper and Row, 1984), 95; see also Daryl Scott, *Contempt and Pity: Social Policy and the Image of the Damaged Black Psyche, 1880–1996* (Chapel Hill: University of North Carolina Press, 1997), 141–59.

27. Margaret Weir, *Politics and Jobs: The Boundaries of Employment Policy in the United States* (Princeton: Princeton University Press, 1992), 83—110; Ira Katznelson, "Was the Great Society a Lost Opportunity?" in Fraser and Gerstle, *Rise and Fall of the New Deal Order*, 185–211.

28. As quoted in Stein, *Running Steel, Running America*, 28, 75.

29. As quoted in William E. Forbath, "Why Is This Rights Talk Different from All Other Rights Talk? Demoting the Court and Reimagining the Constitution." *Stanford Law Review* 46 (July 1994), 1804.

30. Minchin, *Hiring the Black Worker*, 3

31. Ibid., 57.

32. EEOC, *Making a Right a Reality: An Oral History of the Early Years of the EEOC, 1965–1972* (Washington: Government Printing Office, 1990) (Foshee interview excerpt taken from www.eeoc.gov/35th/voices/making.html).

33. Minchin, *Hiring the Black Worker*, 61; for the steelworker lawsuit, see Gilbert Gall, *Pursuing Justice: Lee Pressman, the New Deal, and the CIO* (Albany: State University of New York Press, 1999),78–93.

34. Michael Honey, *Black Workers Remember: An Oral History of Segregation, Unionism, and the Freedom Struggle* (Berkeley: University of California Press, 1999), 213–36, Eastland quoted on page 230.

35. Minchin, *Hiring the Black Worker*, 243.

36. Nelson Lichtenstein, Susan Strasser, Roy Rosenzweig, *Who Built America? Working People and the Nation's Economy, Politics, Culture, and Society*, vol. 2 (New York: Worth Publishers, 2000), 631; Minchin offers an almost identical quote, re. black union consciousness, in *Hiring the Black Worker*, 249; Fink and Greenberg, *Upheaval in the Quiet Zone*, 113; Moody, *An Injury to All*, 249–70.

37. Honey, *Southern Labor and Black Civil Rights*, 287–91.

38. Department of Health, Education, and Welfare, *Work in America* (Cambridge, Mass.: MIT Press, 1971), 49; see also, Robert Ellis Smith, *Workrights* (New York: E. P. Dutton, 1983). Smith, a privacy specialist and ACLU attorney, in effect rediscovered the denial and struggle for an entire set of rights long associated with organized labor. But Smith was largely uninterested in unions or in collective action to secure such human rights on the job.

39. Sally Kenney, *For Whose Protection? Reproductive Hazards and Exclusionary Policies in the United States and Britain* (Ann Arbor: University of Michigan Press, 1992), 139–84; Vicki Schultz, "Reconceptualizing Sexual Harassment," *Yale Law Journal* 107 (1998), 1683–1805; and Gwendolyn Mink, *Hostile Environment: The Political Betrayal of Sexually Harassed Women* (Ithaca: Cornell University Press, 2000).

40. As quoted in Cynthia Daniels, *At Women's Expense: State Power and the Politics of Fetal Rights* (Cambridge: Harvard University Press, 1993), 60.

41. Ibid., 90.

42. Lise Vogel, *Mothers on the Job: Maternity Policy in the U.S. Workplace* (New Brunswick: Rutgers University Press, 1993), 69–90.

43. Richard Edwards, *Rights at Work: Employment Relations in the Post-Union Era*

(Washington, D. C.: The Brookings Institution, 1993), 168–69; Charles Heckscher, "Crisis and Opportunity for Labor," *Labor Law Journal* 38 (August 1987); and see also Heckscher, *The New Unionism: Employee Involvement in the Changing Corporation* (New York: Basic Books, 1988), 158–76.

44. John David Skrentny, *The Ironies of Affirmative Action: Politics, Culture, and Justice in America* (Chicago: University of Chicago Press, 1996), 1–35.

45. The literature is large. For starters see, Gould, *Black Workers in White Unions*, 99–135; James E. Jones, Jr., "The Rise and Fall of Affirmative Action," in Herbert Hill and James E. Jones, Jr., *Race in America: The Struggle for Equality* (Madison: University of Wisconsin Press, 1993), 345–69; and Paul Moreno, *From Direct Action to Affirmative Action: Fair Employment Law and Policy in America, 1933–72* (Baton Rouge: Louisiana State University Press, 1997).

46. Paul Weiler, *Governing the Workplace: the Future of Labor and Employment Law* (Cambridge: Harvard University Press, 1990), 23–24; and Moreno, *From Direct Action to Affirmative Action*, 267–82.

47. Erin Kelly and Frank Dobbin, "How Affirmative Action Became Diversity Management," *American Behavioral Scientist* 41 (April 1998), 969–70; and see most recently, David Segal, "Denny's Serves Up a Sensitive Image: Restaurant Chain Goes on PR Offensive to Show Changed Ways with Minorities," *Washington Post* (April 7, 1999), E1. Only the ideological right still rails against this abandonment of the employment "at-will" doctrine. See the Manhattan Institute's Walter S. Olsen, "How Government Has Created a Hiring Hell for Employers," *The American Enterprise* 8 (July–August 1997), 50–52.

48. Stein, *Running Steel, Running America*, 150–52.

49. Ibid., 195.

50. Brochure, Virginia Manufactures Association, "Employment and the Law," (November 8 and 9, 1995), Richmond Marriott Hotel in Frank Ix and Company (unprocessed box and collection), Alderman Library Special Collections, University of Virginia.

51. This and the following paragraphs rely heavily on Heckscher, *The New Unionism*, 200–30; Weiler, *Governing the Workplace*, 48–104; and Richard Edwards, *Rights at Work: Employee Relations in the Post-Union Era* (Washington, D.C.: The Brookings Institution, 1993), 102–33.

52. Robert Nelson and William Bridges, *Legalizing Gender Inequality: Courts, Markets, and Unequal Pay for Women in America* (New York: Cambridge University Press, 1999), 205–42. The EEOC case was not aided by the switch in administrations, from that of the Democratic Jimmy Carter, during which the case was filed, to the more unsympathetic Ronald Reagan.

53. Minchin, *Hiring the Black Worker*, 255–62; Fink and Greenberg, *Upheaval in the Quiet Zone*, 155–57.

Chapter 6

A Time of Troubles

1. David Bensman and Roberta Lynch, *Rusted Dreams: Hard Times in a Steel Community* (New York: McGraw-Hill, 1987), 1–2.

2. As quoted in Peter Carroll, *It Seemed Like Nothing Happened: The Tragedy and Promise of America in the 1970s* (New York: Holt, Rinehart and Winston, 1982), ix.

3. Stein, *Running Steel, Running America*, 295.

4. Richard K. Lester, *The Productive Edge: How U.S. Industries Are Pointing the Way to a New Era of Economic Growth* (New York: W. W. Norton, 1998), 34–37; David M. Gordon, "Chickens Home to Roost: From Prosperity to Stagnation in the Postwar U.S. Economy," in Michael A. Bernstein and David E. Adler, *Understanding American Economic Decline* (New York: Cambridge University Press, 1994), 34–76; an extensive, even alarmist, early survey is found in Ira C. Magaziner and Robert B. Reich, *Minding America's Business: The Decline and Rise of the American Economy* (New York: Harcourt Brace, 1982), 11–59.

5. Jeffrey Madrick, *The End of Affluence: The Causes and Consequences of America's Economic Dilemma* (New York: Random House, 1995), 134–46; and see more generally, Edward Wolff, *Top Heavy: The Incrasing Inequality of Wealth in American and What Can Be Done about It* (New York: New Press, 1995); and Thomas Palley, *Plenty of Nothing: The Downsizing of the American Dream and the Case for Structural Keynesianism* (Princeton; Princeton University Press, 1998), 58–59.

6. Taylor Dark, *The Unions and the Democrats: An Enduring Alliance* (Ithaca: Cornell University Press, 1999), 15–16; Pelley, *Plenty of Nothing*, 31–38.

7. Howard Brick, "Optimism of the Mind: Imagining Postindustrial Society in the 1960s and 1970s," *American Quarterly* 44 (September 1992), 348–80; Daniel Bell, *The Coming of Post-Industrial Society: A Venture in Social Forecasting* (New York: Basic Books, 1973, 1999); a fine discussion of the debate that emerged over the meaning of the rise in white collar and professional work is found in Paul Blumberg, *Inequality in an Age of Decline* (New York: Oxford University Press, 1980), 9–64.

8. John Kenneth Galbraith, *The New Industrial State* (New York: Alfred Knopf, 1967); Bell, *The Coming of Post-Industrial Society*, 344.

9. Alain Touraine, *The Post Industrial Society; Tomorrow's Social History: Classes, Conflicts and Culture in the Programmed Society* (New York: Random House, 1971); Andre Gorz, *Farewell to the Working Class* (Boston: South End Press, 1982); and Barbara and John Ehrenreich, "The New Left: A Case Study in Professional-Managerial Class Radicalism," *Radical America* (May–June 1977), 7–22.

10. Robert Reich, *The Work of Nations: Preparing Ourselves for Twenty-first Century Capitalism* (New York: Random House, 1991), 182; and see also Chris Toulouse, "Political Economy after Reagan," in Glenn Perusek and Kent Worcester, *Trade Union Politics: American Unions and Economic Change, 1960s–1990s* (Atlantic Highlands: Humanities Press, 1995), 22–56.

11. Emma Rothschild, *Paradise Lost: The Decline of the Auto-Industrial Age* (New York: Random House, 1973), 21–23, 245–46; Rothschild's attack on Fordism as an increasingly inefficient production system was soon sustained from within the halls of the Harvard Business School. See William Abernathy, *The Productivity Dilemma: Roadblok to Innovation in the Automobile Industry* (Baltimore: Johns Hopkins University Press, 1978).

12. Charles Sabel and Jonathan Zeitlin, "Alternatives to Mass Production," *Past and Present*, revised and updated in Zeitlin and Sabel, *Worlds of Possibilities: Flexibility and Mass Production* (New York: Cambridge University Press, 1994); Michael Piore and Charles Sabel, *The Second Industrial Divide: Possibilities for Prosperity* (New York: Basic Books, 1984), 19–48.

13. Piore and Sabel, *The Second Industrial Divide*, 133–64.

14. Robert Reich, *The Next American Frontier* (New York: Penguine Books, 1983), 246.

15. Piore and Sabel, *Second Industrial Divide*, 261, 305–306. And see also Shoshana Zuboff, *In the Age of the Smart Machine: The Future of Work and Power* (New York: Basic Books, 1984). Piore, Sabel, and Zuboff stood on the left but their faith in a technocratic progressivism fed rather easily into the Reaganite optimism of such technomarket futurists as George Gilder and Ben Wattenberg.

16. As quoted in Kim Moody, *Workers in a Lean World: Unions in the International Economy* (New York: Verso, 1997), 44.

17. William Greider, *One World, Ready or Not: The Manic Logic of Global Capitalism* (New York: Simon & Schuster, 1997), 25.

18. As quoted in ibid., 24.

19. Ibid., 36.

20. Vincent Cable, "The Diminished Nation-State: A Study in the Loss of Economic Power," *Daedalus* 124 (Spring 1995), 23–54.

21. David Gordon, *Fat and Mean: The Corporate Squeeze of Working Americans and the Myth of Managerial "Downsizing"* (New York: Free Press, 1996), 221; Joel Rogers, "In the Shadow of the Law: Institutional Aspects of Postwar U.S. Union Decline," in Christopher Tomlins and Andrew King, *Labor Law in America: Historical and Critical Essays* (Baltimore: Johns Hopkins University Press, 1992), 283–302.

22. Steve Fraser and Nelson Lichtenstein, "Teamsters and Turtles," *New Labor Forum* 6 (Spring/Summer 2000), 23–29.

23. Stephen Cohen and John Zysman, *Manufacturing Matters: The Myth of the Post-Industrial Economy* (New York: Basic Books, 1987), 7.

24. A very fine account of the excitement, skill, and productive potential inherent in tool and die work is found in Steve Babson, *Skilled Workers and Anglo-Gaelic Immigrants in the Rise of the UAW* (New Brunswick: Rutgers University Press, 1991), 15–62 passim.

25. Richard Freeman, "Are Your Wages Set in Beijing?" *Journal of Economic Perspectives* 9 (Summer 1995), 15–33; "Does Trade Hurt Workers?" *The Wilson Quarterly* 20 (Winter 1996), 12; Dan McGraw, "Happily Ever NAFTA? So Far the Trade Pact's Impacts Have Been Limited," *U.S. News and World Report* 121 (October 28, 1996), 46–49.

26. Paul Krugman, "Competitiveness: A Dangerous Obsession," *Foreign Affairs* 73 (March–April, 1994), 31–33.

27. Cohen and Zysman, *Manufacturing Matters*, 4, 178–93; Moody, *Workers in a Lean World*, 6–14.

28. Krugman, "Competitiveness: A Dangerous Obsession," 43.

29. Kate Bronfenbrenner, "We'll Close! Plant Closings, Plant-Closing Threats, Union Organizing and NAFTA," *Multinational Monitor* 18 (March 1997), 8–14; Bronfenbrenner, "Raw Power: Plant-Closing Threats and the Threat to Union Organizing," *Multinational Monitor* 21 (December 2000), 24–30.

30. James C. Cobb, *The Selling of the South: The Southern Crusade for Industrial Development, 1936–1990* (Urbana: University of Illinois Press, 1993), 35–63, 209–28; Thomas Hanchett, "U.S. Tax Policy and the Shopping-Center Boom of the 1950s and 1960s," *American Historical Review* 101 (October 1996), 1082–1110.

31. Jefferson Cowie, *Capital Moves: RCA's Seventy-Year Quest for Cheap Labor* (Ithaca: Cornell University Press, 1999), 195; and see also Lichtenstein, "Vanishing Jobs in a Racialized America," *Radical History Review* 78 (Fall 2000), 178–88.

32. Moody, *Workers in a Lean World*, 201–26; Peter Lange, Michael Wallerstein, and Miriam Golden, "The End of Corporatism? Wage Setting in the Nordic and Germanic Countries," in Sanford Jacoby, ed., *The Workers of Nations: Industrial Relations in a Global Economy* (New York: Oxford University Press, 1995) 76–100.

33. Jeff Grabelsky and Mark Erlich, "Recent Innovations in the Building Trades," in Bruce Nissen, ed., *Which Direction for Organized Labor?* (Detroit: Wayne State University Press, 1999), 168; Marc Linder, *Wars of Attrition: Vietnam, the Business Roundtable, and the Decline of Construction Unions* (Iowa City: Fanpihua Press, 1999), 95–144.

34. Linder, *Wars of Attrition*, 59–94

35. Ibid., 182, 202

36. Ibid., 173.

37. Joshua Freeman, *Working-Class New York*, 237–46.

38. Ibid., 243.

39. An excellent account of corporate political remobilization during the 1970s is found in David Vogel, *Fluctuating Fortunes: The Political Power of Business in America* (New York: Basic Books, 1989), 113–239 passim.

40. Grabelsky and Erlich, "Recent Innovations in the Building Trades," 169–77; quote on page 175. Given the cyclical character of the industry and its relative danger, even non-union contractors have admitted that they face a skill shortage. In the absence of union apprenticeship programs, which constituted a kind of training tax upon the entire industry, non-union contractors have solved their shortage in key crafts, either by allowing skills to erode or pirating labor from each other.

41. As quoted in Roger Alcaly and David Mermelstein, eds., *The Fiscal Crisis of American Cities: Essays on the Political Economy of Urban America with Special Reference to New York* (New York: Random House, 1976), 126.

42. Studies of the 1970s urban fiscal crisis include Robert Kuttner, *Revolt of the Haves: Tax Rebellions and Hard Times* (New York: Simon and Schuster, 1980); William Tabb, *The Long Default: New York City and the Urban Fiscal Crisis* (New York: Monthly Review Press, 1982).

43. Tabb, *The Long Default*, 5; Nicholas von Hoffman "The Liberal Side," *Washington Post* (April 2, 1973).

44. Tabb, *The Long Default*, 27.

45. Joseph McCartin, "Rethinking Liberalism's Decline: What Labor History Can Teach Us," (preliminary notes on book project), 14–18.

46. Robert Reich and John Donahue, *New Deals: The Chrysler Revival and the American System* (New York: Times Books, 1985), 126.

47. Kim Moody, *An Injury to All: The Decline of American Unionism* (New York: Verso, 1988), 165–91; Harry Katz, *Shifting Gears: Changing Labor Relations in the U.S. Automobile Industry* (Cambridge: MIT Press, 1985), 51–58.

48. Bennett Harrison and Barry Bluestone, *The Great U-Turn: Corporate Restructuring and the Polarizing of America* (New York: Basic Books, 1988), 38–52.

49. Thomas Byrne Edsall, *The New Politics of Inequality* (New York: W. W. Norton, 1984), 23–66; Kevin Phillips, *The Politics of Rich and Poor: Wealth and the Ameri-*

can Electorate in the Reagan Aftermath (New York: Random House, 1990), 32–53; Robert Kuttner, *The Life of the Party: Democratic Prospects in 1988 and Beyond* (New York: Penguin Books, 1987), 1–33, 72–109; Thomas Ferguson and Joel Rogers, *Right Turn: The Decline of the Democrats and the Future of American Politics* (New York: Hill and Wang, 1986), 78–161.

50. Vogel, *Fluctuating Fortunes*, 169–74.

51. Kim Moody, *An Injury to All*, 146–48; Gary Fink, "Labor Law Revision and the End of the Postwar Labor Accord," in Kevin Boyle, ed., *Organized Labor and American Politics, 1894–1994*: The Labor-Liberal Alliance (Albany: State University of New York Press, 1998), 239–57.

52. Dana Frank, *Buy American: The Untold Story of Economic Nationalism* (Boston: Beacon Press, 1999), 160.

53. Ibid., 192–99. The "Crafted with Pride" campaign collapsed in the early 1990s when many textile and apparel manufacturers decided to move production offshore and endorse NAFTA. Milliken remained one of the few major firms to oppose the treaty, but by 1994 he owned eight European plants.

54. As quoted in Christoph Scherrer, "Surprising Resilience: The Steelworkers' Struggle to Hang On to the Fordist Bargain," in Persuek and Worcester, *Trade Union Politics*, 153.

55. As quoted in Mike Parker, "Industrial Relations Myth and Shop-Floor Reality," in Nelson Lichtenstein and Howell Harris, *Industrial Democracy in America: The Ambiguous Promise*, p. 255.

56. Ephlin quoted in Frank, *Buy American: The Untold Story of Economic Nationalism*, 173.

57. Howell Harris, *The Right to Manage: Industrial Relations Policies of American Business in the 1940s* (Madison: University of Wisconsin Press, 1982), 99–123; see also Stephen Waring, *Taylorism Transformed: Scientific Management Theory since 1945* (Chapel Hill: University of North Carolina Press, 1991).

58. Clark Kerr, "Industrial Conflict and Its Mediation," in *Labor and Management in Industrial Society* (New York: Anchor Books, 1964), 169–70.

59. Stephen Waring, *Taylorism Transformed*, 132–59; Sabel and Piore, *The Second Industrial Divide*, 251–308.

60. Sanford Jacoby, *Modern Manors: Welfare Capitalism since the New Deal* (Princeton: Princeton University Press, 1997), 40, 156.

61. Ibid., 110, 118, 134.

62. Steve Fraser, "Industrial Democracy in the 1980s," *Socialist Review* 72 (November–December 1983), 108.

63. Irving Bluestone, quoted in "Human Dignity Is What It's All About," *Viewpoint*, AFL-CIO Industrial Union Department, 8 (1978); Barry Bluestone and Irving Bluestone, *Negotiating the Future: A Labor Perspective on American Business* (New York: Basic Books, 1992), 189–246; Bruce Lee, "Worker Harmony Makes NUMMI Work," *New York Times* (December 25, 1988).

64. Thomas Kochan and Paul Osterman, *The Mutual Gains Enterprise: Forging a Winning Partnership among Labor, Management, and Government* (Boston: Harvard Business School Press, 1994), 79–109.

65. Richard Freeman and Joel Rogers, *What Workers Want* (Ithaca: Cornell University Press, 1999), 101–16.

66. Jonas Pontusson, "Unions, New Technology, and Job Redesign at Volvo and British Leyland," in Miriam Golden and Jonas Pontusson, *Bargaining for Change: Union Politics in North America and Europe* (Ithaca: Cornell University Press, 1992), 277–306; Parker, "Industrial Relations Myth and Shop-Floor Reality," in Lichtenstein and Harris, *Industrial Democracy in America*, 249–74; Ruth Milkman, "Labor and Management in Uncertain Times," in Alan Wolfe, ed., *America at Century's End* (Berkeley: University of California Press, 1991), 131–51.

67. Richard Gillespie, *Manufacturing Knowledge: A History of the Hawthorne Experiments* (New York: Cambridge University Press, 1991); Nelson Lichtenstein, "The Union's Early Days: Shop Stewards and Seniority Rights," in Mike Parker and Jane Slaughter, *Choosing Sides: Unions and the Team Concept* (Boston: South End Press, 1988), 65–73; Parker, "Industrial Relations Myth and Shop-Floor Reality," 271–72.

68. A. B. Cochran, III, "We Participate, They Decide: The Real Stakes in Revising Section 8(a)(2) of the National Labor Relations Act," *Berkeley Journal of Employment and Labor Law* 16 (1995), 458–519; Jane Slaughter and Ellis Boal, "Unions Slam Dunlop Commission Proposals," *Labor Notes*, February 1995, 1, 14; and see also, Richard Freeman, ed., *Working Under Different Rules* (New York: Russell Sage Foundation, 1994).

Chapter 7

What Is to Be Done?

1. Thomas Geoghegan, *Which Side Are You On? Trying to Be for Labor When It's Flat on Its Back* (New York: Farrar, Straus and Giroux, 1991), 1.

2. Lane Kirkland, "It Has All Been Said Before" in Seymour Martin Lipset, ed., *Unions in Transition: Entering the Second Century* (San Francisco: Institute for Contemporary Studies, 1986), 393, 404.

3. Bruce Nissen, ed., *Which Direction for Organized Labor?* (Detroit: Wayne State University Press, 1999), 14.

4. However, the Reutherite UAW, plus numerous AFL-CIO affiliates, worked hard for McGovern in 1972. Meany claimed that McGovern's record was insufficiently pro-labor, but the senator's real crime, from an AFL-CIO point of view, was his alignment with the reform forces inside the party that had marginalized the influence of organized labor. A McGovern operative is said to have remarked, "The one thing the AFL-CIO can't forgive McGovern for is the one thing he can't do anything about: if he's nominated, he won't owe them anything." Taylor Dark, *The Unions and the Democrats: An Enduring Alliance* (Ithaca: Cornell University Press, 1999), 89.

5. Paul Buhle, *Taking Care of Business: Samuel Gompers, George Meany, Lane Kirkland, and the Tragedy of American Labor* (New York: Monthly Review Press, 1999), 204–32. In his excellent account Buhle reports that, according to Kirkland friend and columnist George Will, the AFL-CIO leader's deepest aspiration was to serve in a Democratic cabinet—not as labor secretary, but as secretary of state. Meanwhile, Geoghegan captured something of the political, generational animosity that existed between labor's old guard and the laborite New Leftists who had begun to make their way onto the staff of reformed unions like the UMW. "They hated the staff, i.e. the

'kids,' the people like me, the VISTA volunteers, the grad students. To them, we were the real Jacobins. . . . To hear them talk, you would think we had set up guillotines in the streets." Geoghegan, *Which Side Are You On?*, 16.

6. AFL-CIO, *The Changing Situation of Workers and Their Unions* (Washington, D.C.: AFL-CIO, 1985).

7. Richard Rothstein, "Toward a More Perfect Union," *The American Prospect* (May–June 1996), 48; Moody, *An Injury to All*, 314.

8. The history of these union disaffiliations is complex. The NEA, which began as a professional association of teachers and administrators, evolved into a genuine trade union, but it never joined the AFL-CIO because a merger could not be worked out with the American Federation of Teachers. John L. Lewis had pulled the UMW out of the AFL in 1947 in a dispute over compliance with the Taft-Hartley Act, and Walter Reuther had broken with George Meany's AFL-CIO in 1968 in a vain effort to set up a new and more dynamic labor federation. Meanwhile the Teamsters had been expelled from the AFL-CIO in 1958 because Jimmy Hoffa and his associates had become such high-profile symbols of union corruption. Much of this is covered in Robert Zieger, *American Workers, American Unions* (Baltimore: Johns Hopkins University Press, 1995), 158–67.

9. Moody, *An Injury to All*, 196–98.

10. Dark, *Unions and the Democrats*, 133–57 passim.

11. Klein, "Managing Security," 514–23. Klein reports that from the 1930s to the 1970s corporate health and pension coverage rose in tandem with that of government provision and union power. After 1975 the onset of public austerity and union weakness generated a reversal of the whole process.

12. Marie Gottschalk, *The Shadow Welfare State: Labor, Business, and the Politics of Health Care in the United States* (Ithaca: ILR Press, 2000), 86–113.

13. Theda Skocpol, *Boomerang: Clinton's Health Security Effort and the Turn against Government in U.S. Politics* (New York: W. W. Norton, 1996), 48–73; and see Cathie Jo Martin, *Stuck in Neutral: Business and the Politics of Human Capital Investment Policy* (Princeton: Princeton University Press, 2000), 168–89.

14. Martin, *Stuck in Neutral*, 168–89; and see also John Judis, "Abandoned Surgery: Business and the Failure of Health Care Reform," *The American Prospect* (Spring 1995), 65–73.

15. Gottschalk, *The Shadow Welfare State*, 149–58; Skocpol, *Boomerang*, 133–88 passim.

16. Kristol quoted in Skocpol, *Boomerang*, 145. William Kristol was the son of neoconservatives, Irving Kristol and Gertrude Himmelfarb, and the former chief aide to Republican vice president Dan Quayle.

17. Martin, *Stuck in Neutral*, 185–89.

18. The Tofflers had been Communists, or close to the party, during the late 1940s. They were members of that youthful cohort who worked for Henry Wallace and then industrialized. By the time they came out of a Cleveland factory in the 1950s, they had repudiated Marxism, but not its sense that history moves by grand sociotechnical stages. Gingrich had been a fan since the early 1970s. See the excellent essay by John Judis, "Newt's Not-So-Weird Gurus: In Defense of the Tofflers," *New Republic* 213 (October 9, 1995), 16–24.

19. Fraser, *Sidney Hillman*, 324.

20. But there had been election contests. After the death of Philip Murray in 1952 Walter Reuther narrowly edged out Allen Haywood for CIO president. And in 1921 John L. Lewis himself had unsuccessfully challenged Samuel Gompers for AFL leadership. Indeed, a socialist actually defeated Gompers in 1894, but the AFL chieftain came back the next year.

21. The key pro-Sweeney unions were the UAW, the USW, AFSCME, SEIU, and the reformed Teamsters. Significantly, the historically "Jewish" unions, UNITE and especially the AFT, backed the old order, in part because of a continuing mistrust of Sweeney's New Leftish supporters, thought to be shaky on Israel.

22. Steve Babson, *The Unfinished Struggle: Turning Points in American Labor, 1877–Present* (New York: Roman and Littlefield, 1999), 168–69; Buhle, *Taking Care of Business*, 244–45; Harold Meyerson, "A Second Chance: The New AFL-CIO and the Prospective Revival of American Labor," in Jo-Ann Mort, *Not Your Father's Union Movement: Inside the AFL-CIO* (New York: Verso, 1998), 1–26.

23. Bruce Nissen, "Introduction," in Nissen, ed., *Which Direction for Organized Labor?* (Detroit: Wayne State University Press, 1999), 12.

24. John Herling, *Right to Challenge: People and Power in the Steelworkers Union* (New York: Harper and Row, 1972), 41–57; Burton Hall, ed., *Autocracy and Insurgency in Organized Labor* (New Brunswick: E. P. Dutton, 1972); Samuel Friedman, *Teamster Rank and File: Power, Bureaucracy, and Rebellion at Work and in a Union* (New York: Columbia University Press, 1982), 59–91.

25. As quoted in Mike Parker, "Industrial Relations Myth and Shop Floor Reality: The "Team" Concept in the Auto Industry," in Lichtenstein and Harris, *Industrial Democracy in America*, 252.

26. Detroit-based *Labor Notes*, founded in 1979 by a steadfast cohort of New Left veterans, best exemplifies this tendency. Many of their publications were, in effect, primers instructing a new generation on the virtues and methods of traditional unionism, albeit of a militant, democratic, and inclusive character. See, for example, Mike Parker and Jane Slaughter, *Choosing Sides: Unions and the Team Concept* (Boston: South End Press, 1988); and Dan La Botz, *A Troublemakers's Handbook: How to Fight Back Where You Work—and Win!* (Detroit: Labor Notes, 1991).

27. Kim Moody, *An Injury to All*, 221–47; Glenn Perusek, "Leadership and Opposition in the United Automobile Workers," in Glenn Perusek and Kent Worcester, *Trade Union Politics: American Unions and Economic Change, 1960s–1990s* (Atlantic Highlands: Humanities Press, 1995), 169–87. The Sadlowski campaign was transitional in that themes from the humanistic 1960s were combined with the grim defensiveness of the 1970s. Thomas Geoghegan reports that when Sadlowski offered the utopian, New Leftish comment that it would be a good thing if some dirty, brutal jobs, like coal mining and coke-oven work, were simply abolished, he was pounced on by the Steelworker old guard. Thereafter, it would be hard to find any union oppositionist who did not defend even the most routine of industrial jobs. Geoghegan, *Which Side Are You On?*, 79–81.

28. Thaddeus Russell, "Out of the Jungle: Jimmy Hoffa and the Remaking of the American Working Class," (Ph.D. diss., Columbia University, 2000), 211–65; Arthur A. Sloane, *Hoffa* (Cambridge: MIT Press, 1991), 351–409.

29. Aaron Brenner, "Rank and File Teamster Movements in Comparative Perspective," in Perusek and Worcester, *Trade Union Politics*, 111–39. The original TDU

campus activists actually derived their politics from the "third camp" Trotskyism of Max Schactman, although their spirit was that of the post 1970 New Left turn-to-the-working class.

30. Jim Larkin, "Teamster Tragedy: Carey is Dead, Long Live the Reformers," *Progressive* 62 (January 1998) 20–23; and see also Mike Parker and Martha Gruelle, *Democracy Is Power: Rebuilding Unions from the Bottom Up* (Detroit: Labor Notes, 1999). Instead of taking on TDU activists as the core of his administration, Carey relied on a group of Clintonite Democratic Party insiders adept at campaign fund-raising and telemarketing. When this inside-the-beltway cohort tried to deploy in the Carey reelection campaign the same tactics that worked in the 1996 Clinton-Gore effort, they found the legal guidelines far more stringent in the Teamsters, where elections were closely monitored by the federal courts.

31. Barbara Shailor, "A New Internationalism: Advancing Workers' Rights in the Global Economy," in Jo-Ann Mort, *Not Your Father's Union Movement: Inside the AFL-CIO* (New York: Verso, 1999), 145–55; Bill Fletcher, Jr., and Richard Hurd, "Political Will, Local Union Transformation, and the Organizing Imperative," in Bruce Nissen, ed., *Which Direction for Organized Labor?* (Detroit: Wayne State University Press, 1999), 191–216.

32. John Sweeney with David Kusnet, *America Needs a Raise: Fighting for Economic Security and Social Justice* (Boston: Houghton Mifflin, 1996), 87.

33. These include John Wilhelm of the Hotel Employees and Restaurant Employees (HERE), Andrew Stern of SEIU, and Bruce Raynor of UNITE. See Harold Meyerson, "John Sweeney's Movement Four Years Later," *Dissent* 47 (Winter 2000), 47–56.

34. When he published *The New Men of Power* in 1948 C. Wright Mills was counting on just this kind of alliance. "To have an American labor movement capable of carrying out the program of the left, making allies among the middle class, and moving upstream against the main drift, there must be a rank and file of vigorous workers, a brace of labor intellectuals, and a set of politically alert labor leaders. There must be the power and there must be the intellect." Mills, *The New Men of Power* (Urbana: University of Illinois Press, 2001), 291.

35. Stephen Herzenberg, John A. Alic, and Howard Wial, *New Rules for a New Economy: Employment and Opportunity in Postindustrial America* (Ithaca: Cornell University Press, 1998), 1–12; Steve Early, "Membership-Based Organizing vs. the Mobile Organizer Model: Worker Empowerment Is the Way to Win" (paper in author's possession); William Forbath, "Will Labor Rise Again? History in the Future Tense" (paper in author's possession); Dorothy Sue Cobble, "Organizing the Postindustrial Work Force: Lessons from the History of Waitress Unionism," *Industrial and Labor Relations Review* 44 (Summer 1991), 419–36.

36. Mark Fitzgerald, "Temps Step to WashTech," *Editor and Publisher* (August 28, 1999), 39.

37. Forbath, "Will Labor Rise Again?"

38. Ruth Needleman, "Building Relationships for the Long Haul: Unions and Community-Based Groups Working Together to Organize Low-Wage Workers"; Immanuel Ness, "Organizing Immigrant Communities: UNITE's Workers Center Strategy"; Waldinger et. al., "Helots No More: A Case Study of the Justice for Janitors Campaign in Los Angeles," all in Kate Bronfenbrenner et al., *Organizing To Win: New Research on Union Strategies* (Ithaca: ILR Press, 1998), 69–119.

39. Robert Pollin and Stephanie Luce, *The Living Wage: Building a Fair Economy* (New York: New Press, 1998), 1–36 passim.

40. Bernard Weinraub, "New Risks and Venues Emerge in a Multifaceted Business," *New York Times* (January 1, 2001), C6; Peter Bart, "Hollywood's Strike Zone," *Variety* (March 27, 2000), 2; "The Entertainment Industry—Cut!" *The Economist* (October 14, 2000), 79;

41. Harold Meyerson, "A Vision for the City: Introduction," *L.A. Weekly* (March 9–15, 2001).

42. Ruth Milkman, "Introduction," in Milkman, ed., *Organizing Immigrants: The Challenge for Unions in Contemporary California* (Ithaca: ILR Press, 2000) 11; Harold Meyerson, "Rolling the Union On," *The Nation* (June 17, 2000), 50–52; James Bates, Claudia Eller, "Behind the Scenes Events, Dictated Guild Settlement: In the End, Measured, Level-Headed Negotiations Delivered Writers Respectable Gains," *Los Angeles Times*, May 7, 2001; Robert Kuttner, "Out of Los Angeles, A Resurgence for Labor," *Boston Globe*, May 6, 2001.

43. Meyerson, "Rolling the Union On," 51.

44. Harold Meyerson, "Enter the Janitors, Transforming L.A.," *LA Weekly* (April 14–20), 2000.

45. Steven Greenhouse, "In Biggest Drive since 1937, Union Gains a Victory," *New York Times* (February 26, 1999), 1; Nelson Lichtenstein, "Union Gains Echo Old Triumphs and Hopes," *Los Angles Times* (March 7, 1999), M2.

46. Catherine Romano, "Lazy American Workers? No More," *Management Review* 83 (December 1994), 5; the popularity of Juliet Schor's *The Overworked American: The Unexpected Decline of Leisure* (New York: Basic Books, 1991) demonstrated that the work-time issue was a real one, but it has not achieved in the United States the political/cultural visibility that is manifest in France and Germany, where efforts to make shopping a weekend and nighttime activity are highly controversial.

47. For a well-told tale recounting the demise of the shorter-hours idea, see Benjamin Kline Hunnicutt, *Kellogg's Six-Hour Day* (Philadelphia: Temple University Press, 1996).

48. Elaine Bernard, "Workplace Democracy," *Boston Review* 21 (Summer 1996), 7.

49. For more on these teach-ins, see Nelson Lichtenstein, "Workers' Rights Are Civil Rights: How to Put the Labor Movement Back at the Center of American Political Culture," *WorkingUSA* (March/April 1998), 57–66.

50. Richard Rorty, "The People's Flag Is Deepest Red," Todd Gitlin, "Beyond Identity Politics: A Modest Precedent"; Michael Eric Dyson, "The Labor of Whiteness, the Whiteness of Labor, and the Perils of Whitewashing"; Manning Marable, "Black Leadership and the Labor Movement," all in Steven Fraser and Joshua Freeman, *Audacious Democracy: Labor, Intellectuals, and the Social Reconstruction of America* (Boston: Houghton Mifflin, 1997), 57–63, 152–72, 199–212; see also Robin Kelley, *Yo Mama's Dysfunctional!: Fighting the Culture Wars in Urban America* (Boston; Beacon Press, 1997); Richard Rorty, *Achieving Our Country: Leftist Thought in Twentieth-Century America* (Cambridge: Harvard University Press, 1998); and David Hollinger, *Postethnic America: Beyond Multiculturalism* (New York: Basic Books, 1995), 105–29.

51. Aaron Bernstein, "Too Much Corporate Power?" *Business Week* (September 11, 2000), 145–58; and see the debate over the health of American civic society, past and present. The key players are Robert Putnam, *Bowling Alone: The Collapse*

and Revival of American Democracy (New York: Simon and Schuster, 2000); and Theda Skocpol and Morris P. Fiorina, eds., *Civic Engagement in American Democracy* (Washington: The Brookings Institution Press, 2000). Putnam is not very interested in unions, but he does find that Americans who came of age during the New Deal and World War II constituted America's "long civic generation." They have been "exceptionally civic—voting more, joining more, reading more, trusting more, giving more." Putnam put the blame for the recent decline in civic participation on an improbable list of technosocial phenomenon, including too much TV watching and the entrance of women into the workforce. Putnam discounts the importance of translocal organizations, but Skocpol believes that in the twentieth century nationwide organizations, including the trade unions, have been the key focus of civic engagement.

52. "Unions Enjoy a Streak of Victories: Adaptation Has Keyed Resurgence," *Sacramento Bee* (September 6, 2000), 1.

53. Mike Parker and Martha Gruelle, *Democracy Is Power: Rebuilding Unions from the Bottom Up* (Detroit: Labor Notes, 1999), 25–30.

54. Richard Oestreicher, "The Rules of the Game: Class Politics in Twentieth-Century America," in Kevin Boyle, ed., *Organized Labor and American Politics, 1894–1994: The Labor-Liberal Alliance* (Albany: SUNY Press, 1998), 19–50.

55. Julie Greene, *Pure and Simple Politics: The American Federation of Labor and Political Activism, 1881–1917* (New York: Cambridge University Press, 1998), 142–214 passim; Lichtenstein, *Walter Reuther*, 350–53; Joseph Goulden, *Meany: The Unchallenged Strong Man of American Labor* (New York: Atheneum, 1972), 404–29.

Index

Page numbers in *italics* refer to illustrations.

POLITICS AND SOCIETY IN TWENTIETH-CENTURY AMERICA

Civil Defense Begins at Home: *Militarization Meets Everyday Life in the Fifties*
BY LAURA MCENANEY

Cold War Civil Rights: *Race and the Image of American Democracy*
BY MARY L. DUDZIAK

Divided We Stand: *American Workers and the Struggle for Black Equality*
BY BRUCE NELSON

Poverty Knowledge: *Social Science, Social Policy, and the Poor in Twentieth-Century U.S. History*
BY ALICE O'CONNOR

Suburban Warriors: *The Origins of the New American Right*
BY LISA MCGIRR

The Politics of Whiteness: *Race, Workers, and Culture in the Modern South*
BY MICHELLE BRATTAIN

State of the Union: *A Century of American Labor*
BY NELSON LICHTENSTEIN